The PR Professional's Handbook

To my clever and talented nieces and nephews Rupert, Emma, Sarah and Kris.

CIPR

The PR Professional's Handbook

Powerful, practical communications

PR in Practice

Caroline Black

KoganPage

Publisher's note

Every possible effort has been made to ensure that the information contained in this book is accurate at the time of going to press, and the publishers and author cannot accept responsibility for any errors or omissions, however caused. No responsibility for loss or damage occasioned to any person acting, or refraining from action, as a result of the material in this publication can be accepted by the editor, the publisher or the author.

First published in Great Britain and the United States in 2014 by Kogan Page Limited

2nd Floor, 45 Gee Street
London EC1V 3RS
United Kingdom
www.koganpage.com

1518 Walnut Street, Suite 1100
Philadelphia PA 19102
USA

4737/23 Ansari Road
Daryaganj
New Delhi 110002
India

ISBN   978 0 7494 6842 2
E-ISBN   978 0 7494 6843 9

British Library Cataloguing-in-Publication Data

A CIP record for this book is available from the British Library.

Library of Congress Cataloging-in-Publication Data

Black, Caroline, 1956–
    The PR professional's handbook : powerful, practical communications / Caroline Black.
        pages cm. — (PR in practice)
        ISBN 978-0-7494-6842-2 (pbk.) — ISBN 978-0-7494-6843-9 (ebook)
1. Public relations — Handbooks, manuals, etc.   2. Communication in organizations — Handbooks, manuals, etc.   3. Business communications — Handbooks, manuals, etc.   I. Title.
    HD59.B557 2014
    659.2—dc23
                                                                                        2014004437

Typeset by Amnet
Print production managed by Jellyfish
Printed and bound by CPI Group (UK) Ltd, Croydon, CR0 4YY

CONTENTS

PR in Practice Series

Published in association with the Chartered Institute of Public Relations
Series Editor: Anne Gregory

Kogan Page has joined forces with the Chartered Institute of Public Relations to publish this unique series, which is designed specifically to meet the needs of the increasing numbers of people seeking to enter the public relations profession and the large band of existing PR professionals. Taking a practical, action-oriented approach, the books in the series concentrate on the day-to-day issues of public relations practice and management rather than academic history. They provide ideal primers for all those on CIPR, CAM and CIM courses or those taking NVQs in PR. For PR practitioners, they provide useful refreshers and ensure that their knowledge and skills are kept up to date.

Professor Anne Gregory PhD is Director of the Centre for Public Relations Studies at Leeds Metropolitan University, UK. She has authored over 70 publications; as well as being editor of the Kogan Page/CIPR series of books which she initiated, she is Editor-in-Chief of the Journal of Communication Management. Anne also leads specialist commercial research and consultancy projects from the Centre working with prestigious public and private sector clients. She is a non-executive director of Airedale NHS Foundation Trust. Originally a broadcast journalist, Anne spent 12 years as a senior practitioner before moving on to academia. She was President of the Chartered Institute of Public Relations (CIPR) in 2004, leading it to Chartered status and was awarded the CIPR's Sir Stephen Tallents Medal for her outstanding contribution to public relations in 2010. In June 2012 she became Chair of the Global Alliance of Public Relations and Communications Management, the umbrella organization of over 60 public relations institutes from around the world.

Other titles in the series:

The above titles are available from all good bookshops. To obtain further information, please go to the CIPR website (**www.cipr.co.uk/books**) or contact the publishers at the address below:

Kogan Page Ltd
2nd Floor, 45 Gee Street
London EC1V 3RS
United Kingdom
Tel: 020 7278 0433

www.koganpage.com

FOREWORD

Trying to write a handbook on public relations which covers 'the ground' effectively is difficult. Attempts to do so normally end up several hundreds of pages long, or shorter books skate over the surface without giving any real detail about anything.

The key, in a relatively brief book, is selectivity. There is always far too much to capture to give a true and comprehensive overview of public relations, but too little space. So boiling it down to the important topics is crucial. The comfort is the knowledge that if you have inspired them, readers will then be prompted to find out more for themselves. In this task, Caroline Black has not disappointed. She has managed to squeeze into this tome a good variety of the theories underpinning the science and art of public relations, along with a thoughtful snapshot of the practice and the practitioner. The occasional deep-dive into aspects of the practice go to prove its depth, breadth and importance. What also comes across is the energy and excitement of the profession public relations is. Clearly it is a profession with a rosy future as organizations increasingly recognize the importance of communication. In an age where they are defined by what others say about them and where they are held to account by a host of stakeholders who are empowered by new technologies, public relations has moved centre stage.

Starting with a section on why public relations is important and a brief history, Caroline goes to the heart of the matter, the issue of trust: why it's important and the role of public relations in building it. She then moves on to describing some of the key theories, before covering the subject of what it means to be a public relations professional.

What follows is a choice of topics, including the links between public relations and marketing; planning campaigns; understanding audiences and channels, and the role of research. These more general themes are then enhanced by some particular areas of focus embracing creativity, visual communications, issues and crisis management and evaluation. To round off, Caroline returns to the practitioner and the specific skills they need to develop such as briefing, writing and presentation.

This book does not attempt to encompass all the public relations specialisms and areas of work, but it does give a very good grounding in and flavour to the more generic requirements of those seeking to pursue a career in the profession. Without these being grasped and honed, success will not be possible. It is for this reason that *The PR Professional's Handbook* should be on the bookshelf of every person aspiring to enter one of the most exciting, challenging and rewarding professions that is on offer today.

Professor Anne Gregory
Consultant Editor

Introduction

I am going to make a guess about who you are and why you have opened this book:

- You're interested in communications and in public relations. (The title probably attracted your attention... it's direct and straightforward, I hope.)
- You're curious because there are so many of these damned books. (Is this one any different? Any better? Any help?)
- You're busy and there are a million demands on your time. (This woman had better get to the point and get to it in a nanosecond.)
- Theory is fine – indeed sometimes helps explain things – but you need the practical stuff. (How do I write a decent communications plan? How do I tackle digital communications? How can I boost my creativity?)
- You're professional and capable. And so you are expected to know a great deal and tackle all sorts of challenges and make the most of all sorts of opportunities. Sometimes it would be good to get a sense check about what you are doing or what you are about to recommend. (If you had a mentor you'd pick up the phone.)

You are:

- an undergraduate studying for a degree in public relations or communications;
- starting a career in public relations or communications;
- an experienced PR practitioner responsible for coaching or mentoring less-experienced colleagues;
- an executive who is taking on public relations or communications having previously worked in another area (eg switching from marketing or HR) or who is expanding your management responsibilities and taking on public relations or communications;
- a marketing professional who works with public relations or communications consultancies and wants to talk the same language.

Am I right? If so, read on.

I work with people like you every day – as a Fellow of the Chartered Institute of Public Relations (CIPR) and as an accredited trainer running open and bespoke workshops for the public and private sectors and for not-for-profit organizations; as a lecturer on the Advanced Certificate in Public Relations with students from Barings, British Aerospace Engineering (BAE), Sky, AXA and hundreds of other private sector businesses; as a consultant and trainer to the Foreign and Commonwealth Office, Cancer Research UK, Roehampton University, National Association of Securities Dealers Automated Quotations (NASDAQ); and as a mentor and coach to communications professionals who want to do their jobs to the best of their abilities.

I hope that what I have included in this book helps you on a practical and pragmatic level from day one. There is much I have had to leave out – the rest of the Kogan Page *PR In Practice* series fills in the details for specific areas you might like subsequently to dig deeper into.

PR is a fascinating area and a great profession. It is a challenge and suits those with curious minds and the ability to adapt. There is always a new angle, always something to think about, a different problem to solve every day. I hope this gets you started on a great career.

01
The role and importance of public relations in organizations

At the outset, let's be clear: are we talking public relations or communications? And do we use the term 'communication' (singular) or 'communications' (plural)? (People who favour 'communication' say that 'communications' refers to telephone networks and networking protocols: ie information and communications technology.)

The answer is that all three terms apply to our work. In 2010, public relations leaders from 32 countries endorsed the Stockholm Accords, a set of principles on the *role* of public relations in organizational governance and management, and communication programmes for internal and external publics, and on the *value* of public relations in increasing the organization's sustainability. The Accords are a project of the Global Alliance for Public Relations and Communication Management, the confederation of the world's major professional associations.

In the Stockholm Accords, every mention of 'public relations' is followed by 'and communication management'. While all public relations roles involve communications, not all communications roles can be described as public relations. So communications can perhaps be seen to be a broader area and public relations is really an applied communications discipline. 'Communications' is a much broader concept than 'public relations'. PR is a sub-set, a form of professional communication. There is no public relations without communication. I have heard it said that teaching PR without teaching communication is like teaching surgery without teaching medicine.

We have used the term public relations for a long time and have invested in it. Graduates study for degrees in Public Relations, and PR degrees are a recognized route to employability, even if the eventual roles turn out to be in corporate communication, marketing communication or corporate affairs. Jobs are often advertised as PR roles. Public relations has professional bodies and trade associations. Our subsequent training and professional development is all about improving our skills as communicators.

We work in teams and departments called 'Communications' or 'Public Relations' or even 'Engagement and Communications'. So I am going to use both terms in this book because we use both terms when we talk about the work we do.

Every organization, regardless of whether it is a private sector company, a government department, a local council or a not-for-profit institution, needs to communicate if it is to achieve its business aims. The creation and maintenance of a positive reputation through targeted, well-planned communications can make a powerful contribution to an organization's success. Success that may be measured by improved profitability, the shifting of opinion, the raising of funds, the retention of staff or the changing of public behaviours.

Yet there is a huge variance in how the business of communications is positioned and perceived in organizations. The most enlightened organizations see communications as a crucial management function, right up there locked into business strategy, with the Director of Communications sitting on the board reporting to the Chief Executive, and respected as a vital member of – and advisor to – the senior team. In these organizations communications is both a science and an art; it's dynamic and creative. Communicators recognize the importance of audience research and engagement, they obtain and interpret information, they solve problems and they generate value. Communications builds, enhances and repairs reputation and the ability of an organization to succeed.

The *Financial Times* set out a clear definition of corporate communications:

Corporate communication is a management function or department, like marketing, finance, or operations, dedicated to the dissemination of information to key constituencies, the execution of corporate strategy and the development of messages for a variety of purposes for inside and outside the organization.

In today's global corporation, this function serves as the conscience of the corporation and is responsible for the organization's reputation. Previously called 'public relations' or 'public affairs,' corporate communication has taken on new importance in the 21st century as a result of corporate scandals or crises at companies like Enron and Toyota.

The department usually oversees communication strategy, media relations, crisis communications, internal communications, reputation management, corporate responsibility, investor relations, government affairs and sometimes marketing communication.

The person running the department is the chief communications officer of the firm, and reports directly to the chief executive officer in many of the top global organizations due to the critical importance of the function today.

(http://lexicon.ft.com/Term?term=corporate-communication)

But not all organizations approach the business of communications like this. You may have worked in places or for clients where communications is an afterthought, a bolt-on, something delegated at the end of the business process to anyone who is willing to do the task. The discipline of communications is no discipline at all. It is a tactical function, a task. There is little belief that it can contribute to business development at the highest level. At best it is seen as a sales aid, raising awareness and demand for a product. At worst it is seen as a fluffy 'nice to do' activity, but not something crucial. Communications that is understood as mere publicity, just coverage in traditional and social media, is limited and constrained because it is never understood or supported at the top table.

During my career, I have worked with thousands of communications professionals, many seasoned practitioners, many who are just starting out in the business. All of them have needed to demonstrate the benefits of communications to their senior people and to their businesses. Often the key is to educate colleagues, to set out clear, realistic expectations of what communications can – and cannot – do and to set crystal clear objectives. The reason communications is not respected or factored in to the business is often because it is poorly understood or because past experience has been less than positive. It is the communicator's job to champion communications. So this chapter is to give you ammunition so you can argue for communications in your organization. We'll look at the reasons why corporations want and need to communicate. I have included some case histories that demonstrate the power of communications. Some have won awards, others are humbler and less well-known examples. These offer lessons that will help you to develop your sense of what works and why so that you can present your recommendations confidently and professionally.

Why organizations communicate

There are many reasons why communications is such an important part of business strategy. For many organizations the starting point and purpose of communications is to create awareness – of a policy, a service, a product. How can people buy if they don't know what's available? How can they support a cause if they don't know there is an issue?

But while people may be aware, they may not understand – they might be aware of recycling but they don't know why it is important. A brand might achieve 80 per cent spontaneous awareness but consumers may not appreciate the care taken in its production – which may be vital in terms of purchasing decision. Or staff know there is a change coming but they aren't sure why that change is necessary or what their part is in making that change happen.

And while people may understand, they may then not favour an organization, its brand, its policy, its business ethics. Communications may need to bring people around so that they prefer – and even like – that particular brand, that particular organization's approach, that particular government policy.

Then when successful communications has managed to create awareness, educate people and won their support, the job of communications is to encourage people to act – to buy, to vote, to join, to donate, to stop a damaging or start a beneficial behaviour. And once they have bought, voted, joined, donated, the purpose of communications is to retain their interest and win their loyalty – perhaps over a lifetime.

Get organizational communications right and the benefits are enormous. For example:

- An increased self-belief of staff and volunteers.
- Shifting interest so that what seemed like a marginal issue is now mainstream.
- Influencers get behind you and are prepared to act as advocates.
- You can set the agenda, online and in the media – and punch above your weight.
- Support for a policy or approach increases so there is a consensus for action and you can take that action with reduced opposition.
- Your reputation and credibility are enhanced.
- You sell more goods and services.
- Your share price increases.

If you DON'T communicate, you can bet someone else will and they will gain momentum and seize the competitive advantage. Stakeholders won't know about you, your cause, your product. They won't understand what you stand for or why your product might be right for them. They will remain ignorant and will continue to think, feel, act the same way. And in the end they might even forget your brand name altogether.

A short history of communications

Arguably you can't NOT communicate. Even if your organization's strategy is to 'say nothing', doesn't that communicate something? When though did communications begin as a management function? Communications and technology have always been interlinked. Change in communications technology is happening as I sit here writing, and as you sit there reading. So let us look to the past for a moment. For the public relations practitioner, the roots of modern public relations illustrate clearly how public relations can be used to change perceptions, effect patterns of behaviour and accomplish far more than simply shifting products off shelves. So it's fascinating to start with a brief history of public relations as we can see a dynamic and changing communications practice, affected by political, social, economic and other factors.

The very earliest public relations and communications

The provision of information to precipitate change has been in evidence for thousands of years. Archaeological digs have unearthed shards of tablets written nearly 4,000 years ago which contain information for Mesopotamian farmers – handy hints and tips to help them improve productivity, including information on how to deal with field mice. In the ancient world, the concept of public will and the power of public opinion was widely acknowledged as vital to any politician's success. The Caesars knew the importance of effective communication when they addressed the citizens of Rome in order to gain support and approval – from the Latin comes the expression *vox populi, vox Dei* (the voice of the people is the voice of God).

The fight organizer at the Coliseum knew he had to reach his potential customers with information about his product, ie the dates and times of events. If he was smart, he would also be aware that word-of-mouth accounts and reports of remarkable shows and outstanding gladiators – in other words the positive reputation of the Coliseum – would be the ultimate persuasive pull, encouraging even greater numbers of eager Romans to attend those events. Here we see roots of showbiz publicity – armour-clad fighters as A-list celebrities – and it drew the crowds then just as positive film reviews do now.

The first organized groups of persecuted Christians used the symbol of the fish for internal communications purposes, as a secret sign that only other Christians would recognize. It could be argued that this is one of the earliest examples of the use of a badge – a logo or brand device – as corporate identity. Other examples are the use of crests in heraldry and of uniforms and regimental banners on the battlefield. Flags were the earliest corporate identity of a country, identifying one ship as friend and the other as foe.

There are many examples of early communication designed expressly for the purpose of creating understanding between an organization and its target audiences, ranging from stone tablets, with hieroglyphics describing new laws, and 'wanted' posters, seeking highwaymen and bandits, through to handbills, discussing new and challenging old political or social ideas.

Industrialization and communications

With the industrialization of society and the formation of many new organizations with political or commercial interests came the conscious understanding and widespread use of mass media. First there were manuscripts. Before the invention of printing all books and other written materials had to be written out by hand. This was a time-consuming and labour-intensive process, and could take months or years. The subject matter was sacred (Lindisfarne Gospels) or political (Magna Carta). While paper was available in parts of Europe from the 12th century, its use did not become widespread until the end of the Middle Ages. There was no paper mill in England until the 15th century. Before this, parchment (also known as vellum) was used – this was made from stretched, treated animal skins. A large manuscript might require one whole cow or sheepskin to make a folded sheet of two to four pages, and a thick book could require the hides of entire herds. Some manuscripts were made even more precious by 'illumination', where bright colours and gold were used to embellish initial letters or to portray entire scenes. As a result medieval books were hugely expensive and precious items for the rich and powerful.

The technology of moveable type and the ability to bind pages and print multiple copies changed all this and ultimately enabled the development of the newspaper. Many reference works (for example Ruth Towse's *A Textbook of Cultural Economics*, 2010) cite the *Courante uyt Italien, Duytslandt, &c.* as the world's first modern newspaper. A weekly publication, it was published in Amsterdam in June 1618. In the United States the first daily paper *The Courant* was published in 1703. In the UK *The Times* was established in 1785, acquiring a printing press capable of making 1,100 impressions per minute in 1814.

The development of audio-visual technology enabled even more sophisticated communications. The development of photography and then portable cameras enabled the lay person to see images of remote parts of the world, different nations and their people, battlefields and curiosities – this had a huge impact on communication. Even today those earliest photographs – of men in trenches, African tribesmen, New York under construction – have huge impact.

From print to broadcast

The flexible and cheap medium of radio got (and still gets) the message to even those who could not read. The first extended broadcast of the human voice was transmitted through the air on December 24, 1906 from Brant Rock, Massachusetts, by Canadian Reginald Fessenden. He was convinced that the 'wireless telegraph', which up until then carried just the Morse code, could carry the human voice. The most common use for wireless at that time was communication with merchant ships at sea, directing them to ports where the cargo would bring the best price. The shipboard wireless operators were called 'Sparks'. That night Sparks on ships across the Atlantic heard what they had dreamed about – and thought impossible:

> On December 24, 1906, at 9 pm eastern standard time, Reginald Fessenden transmitted human voices from Brant Rock near Boston, Massachusetts to several ships at sea owned by the United Fruit Company.
>
> The host of the broadcast was Fessenden. After giving a resume of the program, Fessenden played a recording of Handel's 'Largo' on an Ediphone thus establishing two records – the first recording of the first broadcast. Fessenden then dazzled his listeners with his talent as a violinist, playing appropriately

for the Christmas season, 'Oh Holy Night' and actually singing the last verse as he played. Mrs. Helen Fessenden and Fessenden's secretary Miss Bent, had promised to read seasonal passages from the Bible including 'Glory to God in the highest – and on earth peace to men of good will', but when the time came to perform they stood speechless, paralyzed with mike fright. Fessenden took over for them and concluded the broadcast by extending Christmas greetings to his listeners – as well as asking them to write and report to him on the broadcast wherever they were.

(Institute of Electrical and Electronics Engineers)

In 1926, John Logie Baird transmitted the very first television picture from one room to another. By 1927, he used telephone wires to successfully send a moving image from London to Glasgow and in 1928, he made the first trans-Atlantic television broadcast. The BBC first began television broadcasting in 1936. In 1954 the Television Act established commercial television and set up the Independent Television Authority (ITA). A year later independent television began, in the London area, with a live transmission from the Guildhall. The first TV commercial ever screened was in 1955 for Gibbs SR toothpaste. Television facilitated an enormous quantity and variety of output and its range and reach, combining visual with audio, made it the most powerful medium of all in the 20th century.

The emergence of communications as a management function

With these developments in media, media exposure to reach a specific listener/reader/viewer (ie a defined and measurable audience) has become the goal for the communications practitioner working in government, in companies and in charitable organizations. The goals are status, kudos and influential endorsement.

Aside from these developments in media, periods of political, economic or social crisis always precipitate faster developments in public relations practice and a more widespread use of public relations techniques. These factors have moved public relations forward and helped to define it as the management practice we know today.

Political roots

Successive governments have used public relations to effect changes in behaviour at home and abroad by running campaigns explaining new policies relating to public spending, taxation, the economy, foreign affairs, migration/immigration, social issues, public health, education, policing, law and order, agriculture, fisheries and food, business, trade and industry, environment, transport, redevelopment, culture, media and sport. Successful communications campaigns win votes – take any UK General or US Presidential election campaigns and look at the techniques and messaging used.

There are two main strands concerning the history of the development of communications as a management function. Uninterrupted by the Second World War with its attendant trading restrictions and rationing, the public relations industry in the United States developed quickly in the 1940s and 50s, alongside the advertising industry. Consequently public relations consultants and consultancies appeared in the United States long before they appeared in the UK – the United States has therefore claimed to be the originator of modern public relations and corporate communications practice.

In the UK advertising professionals who had been fully employed producing wartime propaganda, became the first professional public relations practitioners. They worked in-house for government and commercial organizations and as consultants in newly established public relations consultancies or branches of US consultancies that were beginning to expand as international networks.

Commercial applications

Posters and packaging had been the main advertising media up until the 1940s. After this, advances in technology, particularly in mass communications, gave advertisers new and incredibly powerful routes to customers, enabling them to project their products into the home, most importantly via the TV screen. Vast numbers of magazines – dependent on advertising for their growth and survival – were launched, designed to appeal to a society that was becoming ever more fragmented, with women emerging as a vital target audience with their own spending power and independence to make choices about the way they lived their lives and the way they spent their money. Manufacturers of fast moving consumer goods (FMCG) were among the first to use the new media to promote their products, from hairspray to cigarettes, chocolate bars to beer, toothpaste to toilet soap. As cars became more affordable, petrol and car advertising began to appear. It was the era of *Mad Men*. Public relations worked alongside advertising to create strong brands with perceived values and personalities, via consumer campaigns using media relations and editorial promotions, leaflets, exhibitions and demonstrations.

The last 20 years of the 20th century saw enormous changes in the way people lived and worked. Against a political backdrop which believed the state should sell off publicly owned utilities and industries and which encouraged entrepreneurialism, heavy industries were replaced by light industries, manufacturing declined and service industries boomed. Alongside this there was even greater need for business-to-business public relations to explain what was going on and to give companies a competitive edge. Deregulation was also a major driver for communications.

At the same time, more people were encouraged to become homeowners and to take responsibility for themselves, their families, their own health. Mortgage lenders, building societies and banks, insurance brokers, financial services providers and healthcare companies became the communications heavyweights. Privatization helped the general public to understand that they too could own stocks and shares. Corporate and financial public relations became a vital part of the communication strategy for most successful organizations. With the banking, stock market and financial system breakdown in 2007–08, communications became even more important, to explain to savers and borrowers what was happening and why, to engage with stakeholders and to get vital messages across to all stakeholders to try to calm nerves.

Digitization, fragmentation and targeting

Seismic changes in micro- and digital technology in the 20th and 21st centuries mean any human being can communicate with the rest of the world via a device that fits into the palm of a hand. Now with digital technologies, we see a complete revolution in the way we send and receive messages. Web-based communications have both private and public functions, are not as heavily regulated as other media, enable interconnection, have no boundaries and enable anyone who has access to a device to be a communicator. You or I can tweet, blog, make videos and audio recordings, take photographs and publish all of it in a matter of seconds from our phones and tablets; we can all communicate with anyone and everyone, someone who is in the room next door or on the other side of the planet, in seconds. Workers in multinational corporations communicate across cultures instantly.

The picture is changing all the time – websites like Internet World Stats (http://www.internetworldstats.com/stats.htm) are useful sources of information to see how the internet is growing in terms of penetration and usage in different regions globally. At the time of writing Africa was experiencing the fastest growth, most of which is coming from mobile phone penetration.

Alongside this are the anti-capitalists, pressure groups, environmentalists, those who speak for the underdog and the dispossessed. These groups can organize themselves professionally to protest against globalization, human rights abuses, animal exploitation and environmental damage caused by governments and corporations all over the world. The message of revolution, the call for democracy can be made digitally, galvanizing people to take action and take to the streets.

The media is fragmented. More magazines come and go every year, fewer as print publications, more online. Broadband and the huge choice of online, downloadable and on-demand viewing and listening, plus endless cable and satellite channels has steadily changed the way we use media for entertainment and information gathering. We are able – and prepared – to watch a feature film on a phone or tablet rather than a full-sized screen. Opportunities for media coverage via media relations have never been greater, while at the same time the world has become wise to the fact that public relations is a powerful tool. This includes people who work in the media who know organizations want coverage, airtime and column inches, and increasingly look for reciprocal deals through advertising, sponsorship and joint activities. The interdependence of media and advertiser remains as strong as ever.

Where are we now?

For the professional, communications/public relations is a mature discipline and is now a central feature of many successful companies' strategies. It is ranked alongside – and sometimes even in place of – advertising and has achieved professional status, with vocational training and recognized qualifications. Planning, research and evaluation mean that the positive contribution made by communications to the organization's business strategy can now be measured and more clearly appreciated.

Even if people are spending more time gazing at screens, they still need to buy groceries (even if they are delivered to the door). They still enjoy a glass of wine, going on holiday, furnishing their homes, planning for their families' futures. Businesses will always need to trade with each other, companies are always looking for investors, voluntary organizations are still seeking to raise funds and put their causes on the map, and government departments still need to get policy and educational messages across.

But while organizations can now communicate with their target audiences via an increasing number of sophisticated channels, the main purposes of corporate communications remain constant – to raise awareness, change hearts and minds, and perhaps ultimately to change behaviours.

The profession continues to have a problem of perception among the public and journalists too. I mentioned at the start that in June 2010, the Global Alliance for Public Relations and Communication Management, an association of national public relations associations, issued a set of principles, known in the business as the Stockholm Accords. These principles were set out for public relations professionals to:

> administer on a sustained basis and to affirm throughout the profession, as well as to management and other relevant stakeholder groups. The accords argued that contemporary society requires public relations professionals who can deal with global interactions, relationships, and responsibilities and who can manage relationships among organizations and stakeholders in a global, digitized world where issues and crises related to poor organizational governance have become commonplace.

More recently, at the World Public Relations Forum 2012 in Melbourne, almost 800 public relations academics and professionals from 29 countries endorsed the so-called 'Melbourne Mandate'. This is a strong call to action on areas of value for public relations and communication management in three particular spheres:

- the character of the organization and its values;
- the ability of the organization to listen – and its culture;

- the responsibility of practitioners to society, the organization, their profession and themselves.

The Global Alliance has recently developed a toolkit to help professionals find a practical application of the Melbourne Mandate in their daily work. The toolkit includes:

- the Melbourne Mandate Integrity Index, a tool developed to measure the perceptions of organizations' values in the minds of internal and external stakeholders;
- a series of case studies on ethical and responsible communication;
- examples of multinational companies that have adopted a number of characteristics of the Melbourne Mandate in their organizational life.

It's worth downloading this toolkit, which can be found at http://www.globalalliancepr.org/website/sites/default/files/nolie/Association%20Workshop/Melbourne-Mandate-Toolkit%200613.pdf

The issue is that, if people are asked if they believe the public relations profession delivers this sort of value to society, most people – journalists included – express surprise that such a description is what public relations is all about. Industry guru James Grunig said:

> ...if one were to monitor the typical discussions among public relations practitioners in trade media and online discussions, he or she would find much more talk about messaging, publicity, media relations, media monitoring, and marketing support than about the roles and responsibilities of public relations in organizational governance. In the minds of most people, public relations has become institutionalized as a messaging activity whose purpose is to make organizations look good in the media or to sell products, usually through devious means, rather than as a management activity that improves relationships among stakeholders and organizations...

> (Grunig, 2011)

We need to work hard to present ourselves positively as the real contributors we can be. That is a challenge for all of us each and every day.

The Edelman Trust Barometer

Edelman is the world's largest independent public relations consultancy. It has offices in 60 cities and employs 4,000 employees worldwide. Each year the consultancy conducts and publishes its *Trust Barometer*, measuring public trust in and the credibility of government, business and not-for-profit organizations.

Talking to 31,000 respondents via an online questionnaire across 26 countries, the publication of this study is now a recognized event in the PR calendar. At the time of writing, the most recent report (2013) announced that consumer trust in business had increased despite negative headlines about tax avoidance from many corporations. All sectors, excluding financial services, experienced an increase in trust compared with the previous year, with automotives, energy brands and pharmaceuticals seeing the most significant improvement. This increase in trust was attributed to businesses creating jobs and apprenticeships and also listening to customer needs.

Questionable motives behind business decisions and corruption or fraud were cited as the top reasons for a lack of trust in business where trust had diminished over the previous year. In 2012 Starbucks, Google and Amazon had all been accused of tax avoidance and Barclays had been fined for its part in the London Interbank Offered Rate (LIBOR) rate-rigging scandal.

The report also found a widening gap between the trust people have in business and the trust people have in the leaders of those institutions to tell the truth. CEOs and government officials remained the least credible spokespeople. Consumers continued to have more trust in ordinary employees, people they could relate to. Edelman believes this points to a 'democratization' trend that appears to have emerged in recent years.

Importantly in the UK, trust in media had decreased. The Jimmy Savile enquiry (2012) and the *News of the World* hacking scandal (2006), followed by the Leveson Inquiry (2012) would appear to have had a serious impact on the way the media is viewed and trusted.

Corruption and incompetence were cited as key reasons for a lack of trust in Government – half of the general public thought that the UK Government was incompetent. (http://trust.edelman.com/).

Conclusion

Whatever your job title, or whoever you manage whose responsibilities include public relations and communications, it is important and worthwhile to remember the profession's roots and development and how far it has come in a relatively short time. Public relations, as defined in the 21st century, is a much more considered profession, not just a sub-set of marketing, not just a way to get people to think well of an organization, and certainly not just a way to get press coverage. If this is the career you have chosen, welcome. The role you play in your organization's management and development is a crucial one. Keep up with industry developments, remind yourself every day that the work you do is valuable and important, and make sure you adhere to codes of practice that support us in our quest to act with integrity as fully-fledged, qualified and recognized professionals.

02
Key theories for public relations practitioners

While this book has been written to be more practical than academic, a few key models and theories won't go amiss. Most of us will benefit from understanding some of the key ideas about communication. Also all public relations courses demand some theoretical underpinning, so you need to study theory if you aim to gain an academic qualification.

Theory helps clarify our thinking and gives substance to our recommendations, giving us a concrete and rational foundation for decision-making. Theory is especially helpful when thinking about how to tackle an issue, how to work out a plan of action or what is going on in the communications process. Theory is useful when devising plans and writing communications strategies, explaining concepts to colleagues and clients or giving focus when we need direction. And theory is useful when working with apprentices and trainees to get them to think systematically. Theories help us remember important principles so that we can dive into them throughout our careers to support our ideas.

These are my 12 top theories, the ones I have found most useful in over 30 years as a practitioner, consultant and lecturer. With each I offer a brief critique so you can consider usefulness and application to your own practice.

Theory 1 – Shannon and Weaver – the 'transmission' model of communications

One of the oldest and simplest theories about communications came from Shannon and Weaver (1949). But Shannon and Weaver were not PR professionals; they worked for Bell Laboratories, Inc. in the United States.

FIGURE 2.1 Shannon and Weaver's 'transmission model' of communications

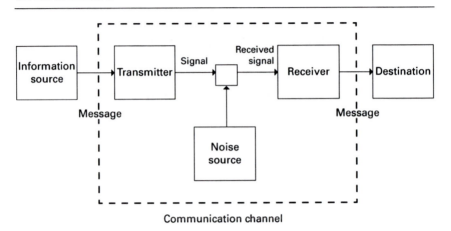

Shannon and Weaver were focused on issues about message accuracy and delivery efficiency in telephony. Their model is both simple to understand and generally applicable and this originally made it attractive to not only people working in PR and communications but also to academics who have since developed more sophisticated models and theories to explain the process of human and organizational communications.

Shannon and Weaver's original model – often called the transmission model – consisted of five sequential elements:

1 *an information source*, which produces a message;

2 *a transmitter*, which 'encodes' the message into signals;

3 *a channel*, which carries the signals that have been adapted to allow transmission;

4 *a receiver*, which 'decodes' the message from the signal;

5 *a destination*, where the message arrives.

They also included a sixth element – *noise*, defined as any interference with the message travelling along the channel that could change or impair the signal and so change the original message into something different from that intended.

This 'transmission' model, which has been around for a long time, is somewhat simplistic. But it does serve as a reminder to practitioners about the basic processes involved in communications and in PR. It is also the basis for social scientist and guru on propaganda Harold Lasswell's (1948) explanation of communications as being:

Who says **what** to **whom** in **what channel** with **what effect.**

Shannon and Weaver argued that there are three problems that arise when thinking about communications:

1   *The technical problem* – how accurately can the message be
    transmitted?

2   *The semantic problem* – how precisely is the meaning 'conveyed'?

3   *The effectiveness problem* – how effectively does the received
    meaning affect behaviour?

They assumed that sorting out the technical problems would largely solve
the semantic and effectiveness problems (and that really is simplistic).

A brief critique

You can see that there are a few problems with this model. It is linear and
one-way – there is no engagement with the receiver. The sender is called
the 'information source' – it is not a complex sender. The receiver appears
to be passive and accepting, a simple and willing absorber of information,
hardly a critical interpreter of what he or she is exposed to. There is no way
to assess whether the receiver has accurately picked up the message – and
then believed it or acted upon it. There is no consideration of the context
of meaning (is this teacher to parent, politician to floating voter?); nor to
when – in terms of time – the communication takes place. But then again this
theory was devised by and for telecommunications engineers. Consequently
this simple model cannot reflect the complex psychology of the human being
or the physiology of the human brain. Nor does it accommodate the existing
relationships between sender and receiver, or the infinite ways a message can
be encoded in terms of words and pictures. Also it does not allow for the
unique characteristics of the multiple channels that could be used to get the
message across and that affect how a message will be seen and interpreted.

However, Shannon and Weaver is a really useful starter theory; I use this
diagram (Figure 2.2) when I am discussing communications principles with
many people from diplomats, to palliative care nurses. It helps us start to
unpack the relationship between our organization and our stakeholders.

Theory 2 – James Carey – transportation/ communications links

Invention and technology have played a huge part in the development of
corporate communications. James Carey was an American academic and
journalism specialist. In his book *Communication As Culture* (1989) Carey
discussed the development of the telegraph and its understated role in developments in communication. The non-electric telegraph was invented by
Claude Chappe in 1794 and was a visual system using semaphore, a flag-
based alphabet, and depending on a line of sight for communication. The
optical telegraph was subsequently replaced by the electric telegraph, the
invention of Samuel Morse. Morse proved that signals could be transmitted

FIGURE 2.2 Multi-channel communication model

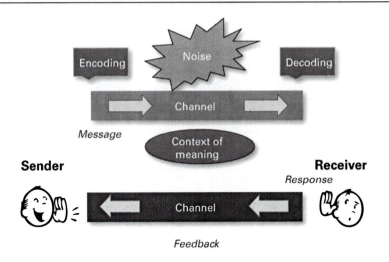

FIGURE 2.3 Diagram of a Morse code telegraph key

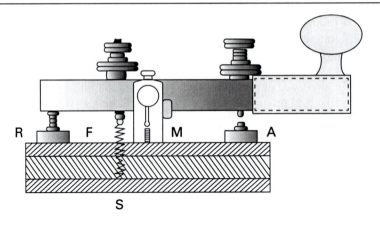

by wire and, to facilitate this, developed the Morse code. The first news dispatched by electric telegraph was in May 1844. The death knell for the electric telegraph came with the invention of the telephone in 1877.

So before the 19th century the movement of information was more or less the same as the transport of goods or people and both were described as 'communication'. Before the telegraph (and the telephone) most decisions – particularly business and political decisions – were made 'face to face'. Carey argued that the telegraph 'permitted for the first time the effective separation of communication from transportation'. After the telegraph, as soon as messages could travel faster than the people, horses or trains that delivered them, everything changed, in terms of how humans communicated across distances and over time. Geography became irrelevant, enabling communities to move away from the local, towards the national, and international or global. The telegraph allowed people from one side of the world to communicate almost instantaneously with someone on the other side of the world.

A brief critique

How quaint this seems in today's digital world but this helps us look at the origins of modern communication. Because this shows to some extent where plain English came from. The short brief telegraph demanded a prose style that Carey noted was more 'lean and unadorned'. Think of a tweet – all those years ago it was the simple telegraph that first called for the plainest of writing and, as a knock-on effect, changed the way news was written. At the same time style became more objective because those words would be read by individuals of many different beliefs and opinions, from many different communities, regions and countries.

Technological advances continue to have a huge impact on how we practise communications – what messages work; how we encode our message; what channels to use so that the receiver sees and hears it accurately and so on. The meaning of the message comes from the process listeners, readers and/or viewers go through when they make sense of what they see, hear and feel. Meaning is not 'extracted' from but 'constructed' by the message. It's clear that, while we don't need to be technicians, everyone working in the field of public relations and communications must keep abreast of developments in technology because you can bet your bottom dollar these developments will have an impact on professional practice.

I think this theory is useful in that it reminds us that messages need to be clear, meaningful and concise. Because then messages can be passed on – and the nirvana of communications in the 21st century is positive word of mouth. We risk losing or confusing meaning if we bang on too long or in a style that is overly complex. In the noisy world we live in, where so many organizations compete for attention, brevity and clarity remain vital.

Theory 3 – Grunig and Hunt's four models for public relations

Managing Public Relations written by Grunig and Hunt (1984) highlighted four models for how organizations can chose to practise public relations. The four models developed more or less chronologically through the 20th century. This is probably the most often-cited theory of public relations and these theories are still relevant, taught as part of graduate, postgraduate and vocational qualifications across the UK and overseas.

The four models:

1 *Press agent model* – one-way communication where an organization tells an audience what it wants it to believe. Little or no research to determine the audience's needs, interests or inclinations to agree with the organization's objectives. This is the simple, original, historic model for PR with the focus on getting favourable coverage (ie publicity) for your organization, cause, celebrity or brand via the media:

   – One-way transfer of information.

   – No feedback.

   – Little or no research.

   – Information is not always accurate.

   – 'All publicity is good publicity'.

2 *Public information model* – a journalist's approach to public relations, offers truthful, accurate information about an organization leaving out damaging or harmful information. This model developed pretty much as a reaction to attacks on large corporations and government agencies by investigative journalists. The leaders of these institutions needed more than simple propaganda peddled by press agents to counter the attacks on them in the media. So they hired their own journalists to act as public relations practitioners, and press handouts were written and distributed to give their point of view and explain actions. This is also the model where essential information is provided to the people and persuasion or attitude change is not essential. Examples might be letting people know about the weather, about road traffic, or internally about new appointments and so on. The approach is very much 'let's get the facts out':

   – one-way transfer of information;

   – some evaluation on effectiveness;

   – little or no research about the audience(s);

   – used most often by government;

   – truthful and accurate.

3 *Two-way asymmetrical model* – emphasizes a change in attitudes or behaviours in the audience only in accordance with the objectives and goals of the organization. Persuasive communication really has its origins here. In 1917 during the First World War US President Woodrow Wilson set up The Creel Committee – also called the Committee on Public Information (CPI). Committee members included the so-called founder of modern public relations practice, social scientist Edward Bernays (1891–1995). Communications took a more scientific approach that made the practice two-way with practitioners both seeking information from and giving information to

publics. Theories introduced by Bernays and Miller (1928) were those of propaganda, persuasion, and the 'engineering of consent'. This model is clearly at work when attempts are made to influence publics to adopt a preferred point of view or behaviour. Research provides input into the process (for example research into why people buy a new car helps manufacturers create motivating relevant messages):

- scientific persuasion;
- two-way transfer of information;
- research done to persuade audience(s);
- messages created to persuade;
- model slanted in favour of organization.

4 *The two-way symmetrical model* – uses research to better understand the audience and to resolve disputes. Each party – the sender and receiver – is willing to alter messages – and even behaviours – to accommodate the other's needs. The two-way symmetrical model makes use of research and other forms of two-way communication. Unlike the two-way asymmetrical model, however, it uses research to facilitate understanding and communication rather than to identify messages most likely to motivate or persuade publics. A good example might be management and workforce in a consultation process enabling a change of policies and practices resulting in higher productivity and better pay and conditions. This model includes ideas and principles like 'telling the truth', 'interpreting the client and public to one another' and 'management understanding the viewpoints of employees and neighbours as well as employees and neighbours understanding the viewpoints of management'. It is perhaps a communications ideal as many organizations are unwilling to 'go all the way' and engage so fully with audiences as they wish to retain the concept of control. It could be argued that modern technology and digital communications are forcing even the most reluctant organization to have to consider this model seriously to maintain a competitive or an ethical position that enhances reputation:

- Behaviour change on both sides.
- Research done to understand, not manipulate, the audience.
- Strategies include consultation, bargaining, negotiation, discussion, compromise.
- Best model of communication?

A brief critique

Thirty years on and we still often return to this model. It is such a well-trodden theory for the PR practitioner, but is it still relevant? I think it is and

I have worked with many people across the world who see this theory as the start point for the development of their organizations' public relations and communications strategies. For it compels us to consider our organization's belief systems and values – whether we wish to engage with others or preach to them, whether we believe that we need a symbiotic relationship with our audiences and stakeholders, whether we might not know everything about an issue and, in so doing, acknowledge that others may know a great deal more than us, and we should listen to them so we can formulate ideas, policies and products that are sound and right.

Now the ultimate in two-way communications must be the crowdsourcing. This is the practice of gathering intelligence from the public and using that information to complete organizational tasks. Crowdsourcing expands the available pool of skills and talents and also allows organizations to gain insight into their audiences and stakeholders. The term was first coined in 2006 by *Wired* magazine author Jeff Howe in an article titled 'The Rise of Crowdsourcing'. Howe suggested that crowdsourcing encouraged the best-qualified and most creative participants to join in on a project. Wikipedia was created this way, originally launched as a collaboratively written and edited online encyclopedia in January 2001. And after the earthquake in Haiti in 2010, an emergency service was created and established in response to a tweet sent out asking for help.

In 2011 Barack Obama tweeted to his millions of followers 'In order to reduce the deficit, what costs would you cut and what investments would you keep? BO'. Never before have political leaders been able to engage with the electorate so immediately and directly. In the political arena more and more people are using social media as a grassroots organizing tool to bring about political change. Twitter and Facebook have been used to plan protests and to spread revolutionary messages, eventually toppling regimes in Egypt, Yemen, and Libya.

And Iceland took crowdsourcing to its logical conclusion in 2011 when it drafted its new constitution using input from Twitter and Facebook users. In 2012, politicians in Finland began using a crowdsourcing platform called Open Ministry to draft new legislation. Social media is a way people get through to politicians and one way politicians communicate with the people, and this sort of two-way dialogue suggests that, one day, direct daily democracy may become a reality.

Theory 4 – Robert Cialdini and influence

Arguably one of the key tasks of corporate communications is to influence others to 'comply' with what you want; which may be to understand an issue, engage in debate, prefer or like or support your point of view, or behave a different way.

Robert Cialdini, Regents' Professor Emeritus of Psychology and Marketing at Arizona State University has made influence his life's work. Having observed extensively how influence works by studying 'compliance professionals' (people skilled in getting others to do what they want them to do – salespeople, fundraisers, recruiters, advertisers and so on) he published, in 1984, *Influence: The psychology of persuasion*. I was given this book when I first worked in the advertising industry and I go back to these ideas time and time again. I have seen all sorts of reconfigurations of these theories, including Nudge Theory, a concept found in behavioural science, political theory and economics (see the paragraph at the end of this section).

Cialdini arrived at what he called his six 'weapons' of influence and we can see these six principles at work in many successful PR and communications programmes. But do take care – influence in the wrong hands becomes manipulation. There are many examples when this thinking has been used for evil ends. Use these strategies for good, not to persuade people to do things that are wrong. Examine your conscience and apply this thinking ethically:

1 *Reciprocity*

   People generally aim to 'return a compliment'. They invite people to come to dinner having been invited themselves; they pay back debts; they treat others as they are treated. It's 'you... me... you... me...'. This leads us to feel obliged to offer concessions or discounts to others if they have offered them to us first because we feel uncomfortable if we feel indebted to them. For example, you may give money to a fundraiser who has given you a little badge or sticker; a free tasting of a new food product in-store may make you buy a pack; you might decide to buy more from a supplier if they have offered you preferential terms first. You can sometimes use this principle by simply reminding the other person of how you have helped them in the past. The key thing is to give – a service, information or a concession. Your target will then be primed to return the favour. To use reciprocity ethically to influence others, identify objectives, and consider what you want the target to do. You can then identify what you can give to them in return.

2 *Commitment and consistency*

   Once we've committed to something, we're then more inclined to go through with it because, says Cialdini, we human beings have an innate desire to be consistent. For example, people who sign a petition supporting a new community facility are more likely to donate money to that cause when asked later. Get people's commitment early on, either verbally or in writing. For example, if the communications programme is building support for the building of a new supermarket, communicate early on with stakeholders, and take their comments and views into account.

3 *Social proof*

   This principle relies on people's sense of 'safety in numbers' because people tend to follow the lead of others similar to themselves. For example, we're more likely put some money into a dish for staff tips if there's money already in that dish; we'll buy a product if lots of others have done so and provide testimonials that it's good; and we're more likely to support a policy if support seems high already. The assumption is that if lots of other people are doing something, then it must be OK, safe to do, good and right to do too. We're more likely to be influenced if we feel uncertain. Another key factor is whether those people already behaving a certain way are like us in terms of life stage and lifestyle. Internally you could use social proof when trying to get support for a new project by getting the support from influential people in your organization whose opinions others respect. And if you are selling a product, say how many people use it and get them to recommend it on social networking sites.

4 *Liking*

We're more likely to be influenced by people we like. And people are more likely to buy from people like themselves, from friends, and from people they know and respect. Likeability comes in many forms – people might be similar or familiar to us, they might give us compliments, or we may just simply trust them. Put in the time and effort needed to build trust and rapport with clients and people you work with, and behave with consistency. Develop your emotional intelligence together with active listening skills. But don't try too hard to be liked by others – people can always spot a phoney. Companies that use sales agents from within the community employ the 'liking' principle extensively and with huge success.

5 *Authority*

We feel a sense of duty or obligation to people in positions of authority. This is why advertisers of pharmaceutical products employ doctors to front their campaigns, and why most of us will do most things that our manager requests. Job titles, uniforms, and even accessories like cars or gadgets can lend an air of authority, and can persuade us to accept what these people say. To use authority, get support from influential and powerful people, and ask for their help in backing the idea. If you're marketing a product or service, use case histories of well-known and respected customers, use comments from industry experts, and talk about impressive research or statistics to build up authority.

Well-produced brochures, professional presentations, impressive offices, and smart clothing can also lend authority.

6 *Scarcity*

This principle says that things are more attractive when their availability is limited, or when we stand to lose the opportunity to

FIGURE 2.4 The spectrum of influencing strategies

Pulling styles

Use when the other party

- Has strong views or opinions
- Has a vested interest in the status quo
- Has difficulty in accepting your propsals
- Has not revealed what they will find acceptable
- Does not recognize your power

and/or when

- The relationship is new or trust is low
- Previous attempts to push have failed
- You want to build a lasting relationship

Pushing styles

Use when the other party

- Has little or no experience of the issue
- Recognizes the need for help
- Has no vested interest in the status quo
- Does not feel threatened by accepting your proposal
- Recognizes the legitimacy of your power
- Trusts your motives

Inspiration | Feel Good | Ask | Deal | Favour | Reason | Clubbing | Authority | Force

Energy

Bridging: elicit different views by drawing out, involving, sharing

Attracting: find common ground by appealing to shared aims and values, inspiring

Observable behaviours in influencing engagement

- Open questions
- Building
- Listening
- Clarifying
- Disclosing
- Encouraging
- Motivating

Energy

Persuading: using logic, reason and facts to propose one's own position

Asserting: demand, dictate or bargain to meet one's own needs, inspiring

Observable behaviours in influencing engagement

- Telling
- Reasoning
- Logic
- Disagreeing
- Leading questions
- Threats
- Arguments

acquire them on favourable terms. For instance, we might buy something immediately if we're told that it's the last one, or that a special offer will soon expire. With this principle, people need to know that they're missing out on if they don't act quickly.

If you're selling a product, limit the availability of stock, set a closing date for the offer, or create special editions of products. This principle can be trickier to apply within your organization if you're trying to influence others to support your ideas or projects. You can, however, use urgency to get support for your ideas. For example, you can highlight the possible urgent consequences of the problem that your idea helps to solve. From this has also come a great deal of thinking about influencing strategies and whether people are more influenced by a push or a pull towards a goal.

A note on Nudge Theory

We human beings are not always rational, logical creatures, acting in the most advantageous way for ourselves. We are suggestible, we are apathetic, we have preferences and prejudices. Our motivations and decision-making can be nudged towards a behaviour using positive reinforcements and indirect suggestions. Richard Thaler and legal scholar Cass Sunstein wrote *Nudge: Improving decisions about health, wealth and happiness,* in 2008 and defined a nudge as '... any aspect of the choice architecture that alters people's behaviour in a predictable way without forbidding any options or significantly changing their economic incentives. To count as a mere nudge, the intervention must be easy and cheap to avoid. Nudges are not mandates. Putting fruit at eye level counts as a nudge. Banning junk food does not.'

In the UK, the Nudge Unit – set up by the Government to find innovative ways of changing public behaviour and now owned and run by NESTA (National Endowment for Science, Technology and the Arts) – uses insights from behavioural psychology to look at how people make bad choices – from filling in their tax forms late to drinking too much alcohol – and then tests small changes to the way these choices are presented to improve lives and save taxpayers' money. The Unit has claimed to have saved the Government more than £300 million. Its insights are now in demand from governments and other organizations around the world.

A brief critique

Cialdini's theory and those that have developed since remain, as far as I am concerned, hugely important and practically useful in the development of any organization's public relations and communications strategies, because these theories are about human nature and what persuades us and affects us. It is essential that we are alert to the possibility of manipulation and so vital that we always think ethically about what we propose and why, and then what we actually do in terms of activities.

Theory 5 – Patrick Jackson and others – the 'people change ladder'

Patrick Jackson was a public relations practitioner working in the United States. In 1956 he founded Jackson & Wagner, a behavioural public relations and management consulting firm, and he was editor of US newsletter *PR Reporter* for over 25 years. He and others (Center, Jackson, Smith and Stansberry 2007) considered the steps communicators have to go though in order to effect behaviour change:

1 Build awareness – eg publicity, advertising, face-to-face communications.
2 Develop a latent readiness – an inclination to make change during which opinions begin to form.

FIGURE 2.5 Setting communications objectives

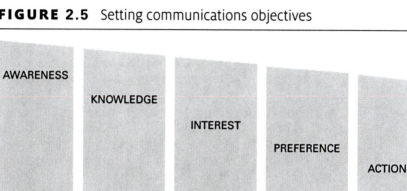

AWARENESS

KNOWLEDGE

INTEREST

PREFERENCE

ACTION

3 Trigger a desire to change – via a natural or planned event.

4 Utilize an intermediate behaviour during which an individual begins to investigate new behaviours.

5 Changing behaviours and adopting the new behaviour.

The International Association for the Measurement and Evaluation of Communications objectives 'funnel' owes much to this theory (Figure 2.5).

A brief critique

It's quite a straightforward and easy theory, this one, and makes complete sense in practical terms. How can you get people interested if they aren't aware? How can you get them to do something different if they aren't interested? All too often when setting public relations and communications objectives, people simply say their aim is 'to create awareness'. But ask yourself 'why'? Awareness alone rarely suffices. Awareness is merely a first step along the way to getting attitudinal and/or behavioural change, and by itself is rarely the end game.

Theory 6 – Mendelsohn's 'Three Assumptions' for success

In their book *Strategic Public Relations Management: Planning and managing effective communications programs* (2008), Erica Weintraub Austin and Bruce E. Pinkleton make reference to the PR practitioner Mendelsohn. Mendelsohn ran campaigns in the 1960s attempting to increase traffic safety. Mendelsohn (1973) believed campaigns often failed because campaign designers overpromised, assuming the public would automatically receive and enthusiastically accept their messages, and blasting the public with messages not properly targeted and likely to be ignored or misinterpreted. His 'Three Assumptions' are still a really good starting point for communications planning:

1 Target your messages.
2 Assume your target public is uninterested in your messages.
3 Set reasonable, midrange goals and objectives.

A brief critique

Do I need to say more? This simple triad of ideas for anyone planning public relations is elegant in its spareness. The idea of clear targeting and clear messages will always be important to the communicator because this ensures focus and hence a greater likelihood of success in terms of objectives. Some of us have such huge objectives they can never realistically be met in our tenure in the job. So the idea of the midrange goal makes our job more manageable and achievable, and ultimately more satisfying.

Theory 7 – hierarchy of effects theory of persuasion

This is a sequential representation of how advertising influences a consumer's decision to purchase – or not – a product or service. The hierarchy of effects theory is used to set up a structured series of message objectives with the aim of building on each successive step until the sale is achieved. Although this model is often used to plan advertising campaigns it is a useful one to look at in relation to PR programmes too as often these require a stepped approach depending on where the consumer is at the start of the process. This thinking informs the International Association for the Measurement and Evaluation of Communication's (AMEC) communications objectives funnel (see Chapter 4 on planning):

- Step 1 *Exposure* – some PR programmes get no further than this – just putting the message out. But just placing a message in an environment cannot guarantee it is seen or acknowledged.
- Step 2 *Attention* – even paid-for placed advertising will fail if the audience is not paying attention. A PR message must be capable of attracting attention and cutting through the noise of daily life. Complex messages have to capture even higher levels of attention, especially with attention spans diminishing as they are. Creativity, presentation and encoding are key elements at this stage. Carefully selected culturally specific and acceptable multi-sensory PR and

communications techniques, using symbols, colours and music, are used to grab people's attention and wake them up.

Some aspects of attention are controlled by the potential receiver and some are involuntary responses to sensory cues. A sudden noise, for example, can get someone's attention (essentially a human response mechanism to ensure quick responses to danger). Conversely something amusing will draw attention because the receiver enjoys seeing it. Advertising practitioners may use physiological triggers – like fast cut video – to get and retain attention. But this is an exhausting process requiring high levels of mental processing. So sometimes even though attention is gained, the desired message is lost in terms of being able to remember what it was all about.

- Step 3 *Involvement/engagement* – although research indicates people pay attention to sudden changes in sounds or visual effects, it is also true that they stop paying attention if a message seems irrelevant, uninteresting, or distasteful. Messages that are relevant keep people interested and prime them to absorb the information. This is saying essentially that communications needs to answer the question 'What's in it for me?' Once that is demonstrated, techniques like storytelling, examples and case histories and the use of novel content keep the receiver engaged and interested.

- Step 4 *Comprehension* – keeping the receiver's attention does not ensure he or she will understand the message.

- Step 5 *Knowledge and ability (learning how)* – however good people are feeling about a brand, an issue or a company they may be unable to follow through on an idea if they lack the skills or resources to do so. Examples include potential voters who can't get to a polling station, heavy drinkers intending to stop but who can't quit if they don't get social support; a parent who can't volunteer in the evenings if he or she can't get childcare. An effective campaign anticipates the target public's needs to provide the help they require.

- Step 6 *Persuasion (attitude change)* – following on from the earlier discussion about Cialdini's weapons of persuasion, a change of attitude often precedes behavioural change. People who lack the skills to follow through on an idea may tune out the details, figuring it is not relevant for them. Attitude change is another of the necessary steps in the persuasion process. But sometimes attitude change is all that is necessary. Often a campaign has an outcome, a changed behaviour in mind. And people often hold attitudes that are inconsistent with their behaviour. Overeaters believe that healthy eating is a good thing yet they still eat takeaways and fatty foods.

- Step 7 *Storing the new position in memory* – this is important because people receive so many messages from so many sources every day. To be able to act when the time comes people need to remember the message, so being able to lodge the message in the memory is vital. Encoding messages so they are memorable is essential.

- Step 8 *Information retrieval* – once the message is lodged and stored, you may need to jog the memory to enable access to trigger the changed behaviour when the time comes. Skilled, planned communication builds in reminders and memory access devices such as jingles, slogans and multi-channel message prompts.

- Step 9 *Motivation (decision)* – people need to be given solid reasons to act in the way you want them to. The benefits need to be seen to outweigh the effort/cost. Plus benefits must seem realistic and easy to obtain (because the greater the effort required by the target, the less likely it is that they will make that effort.) But if the audience believe a proposed behaviour change is easy, and will have major personal benefits, and is critically important, then they may more likely act as you wish them to. As communicators our challenge is to discover what will motivate our target audience to change.

- Step 10 *Behaviour change* – people need to be able to keep it up – giving up smoking for a day is a start – but long-term behaviour change needs constant reinforcement. Anticipating demand and handling unsuccessful attempts in a positive way can help cement behaviours in the long term.

- Step 11 *Reinforcement of behaviour/attitude* – most people are familiar with the phrase 'buyer's remorse'. This is what people feel if they have second thoughts about a decision they have made. 'Buyer's remorse' sometimes comes from a bad experience with an organization, such as a poor in-store experience (unrelated to the product or service originally the focus of the communication campaign). Follow-up communications help targeted audiences to continue to feel positive towards the organization, the product or idea.

- Step 12 *Post-behaviour consolidation* – this is the final step in a message-receiver's decision-making process. At this point, the receiver considers the campaign messages, the attitudes and behaviours involved, and the successes or failures encountered in implementing the targeted attitudes or behaviours. At this point too he/she incorporates this new information into a pre-existing worldview. People develop long-term connections with brands and organizations. For example, Cancer Research UK holds annual fundraising events that bring people together year after year, remembering their loved ones in a spirit of fundraising and support. This reinforces the corporate messages consistently. Affecting the targeted audience's worldview is the most long-term outcome for a communication campaign. And for programmes focused on building long-term, mutually beneficial relationships, this outcome is the nirvana.

A brief critique

Sounds like other theories? Of course it does, as many are linked and many are developments on earlier thinking. What is interesting here are the ideas of repetition and reinforcement. A single exposure to a message is rarely enough – we need to see and hear a message repeatedly and to have our memories jogged. So when we are constructing a public relations programme we need to build these steps into our action plan. Therefore, while this is a theory, it is also a process. Having worked in an advertising agency and as a client, these ideas ring true to me, particularly in the world of marketing communications, where repeated exposure to a brand is usually necessary to achieve the desired outcome, ie sales.

Theory 8 – Elaboration Likelihood Model (ELM)

The Elaboration Model of Persuasion is one of the leading theories describing how we process messages. In 1980 Richard E Petty and John T Cacioppo developed ELM. The theory is simple: in order to evaluate any message, a person must be motivated and able to assess its merit. Cacioppo and Petty (*Communication and Persuasion* (1986)) concluded that there is a big variation in the amount of elaboration (or 'thoughtful attention') people are willing to engage in when considering messages. Sometimes people put in a great deal of thought (high elaboration) and sometimes only very little thought (low elaboration). People just don't have the time, willingness or mental capacity to analyse every factor of every issue. So they rely on other cues to make decisions. When a lot of thought goes into the analysis of a persuasive message, the central route to persuasion is used. If little thought or effort goes into analysing a message the peripheral route to persuasion is used.

Deciding which route is used when forming or changing an attitude, based on a persuasive message, can be thought of as a series of steps (Shavitt and Brock, 1994):

- First, a person comes into contact with a persuasive message.
- Next, the motivation of the individual comes into play, and people are more or less motivated dependent on how much effort they have to make to engage with, understand and interpret a message. If the person is lacking motivation, the peripheral route is taken.
- If motivation exists, then the next question is ability. Ability is influenced most by factors such as gender, IQ and opportunity. Again, if the person is not able to engage, the peripheral cues are used.
- Then, if a person is both motivated and able to consider a persuasive message, the next step is how the thinking process goes. If the person

TABLE 2.1 Cacioppo and Petty's Elaboration Likelihood Model (ELM)

The central route	The peripheral route
• Requires lots of consideration of the messages	• Is defined by the reliance on simple cues and environmental characteristics of the message to make decisions and judgements
• Is all about relating information in a persuasive message to knowledge someone already has to arrive at a conclusion	• People rely on cues such as the attractiveness of the sender of the message, the perceived credibility of the sender, the length of the communication
• The thoughts and responses that a person has in response to a message are called cognitive responses	• If motivation or ability to assess a message is low, peripheral cues are relied upon to make a decision
• In generating cognitive responses, a person is able to analyse the merit of the position taken	• Cialdini's six weapons of influence are effectively peripheral cues that aid decision-making
• In essence, the central route produces much stronger, longer-lasting attitudes than those that come from the peripheral route	

feels neutral about the message, the peripheral cues are used. But if the person feels something other than neutral about the message (either a favourable or an unfavourable response) – the central route to persuasion is taken. This results in either a positive attitude change, in the event of a favourable response to a message, or a negative attitude change in the event of an unfavourable response to a message. The type of cognitive process (neutral, favourable or unfavourable) is influenced by the initial attitude held and the quality of the argument presented.

ELM theory is borne out by recent developments in cognitive neuropsychology. The brain's underlying structural operating systems match the ELM's central and peripheral processes. Some commentators have called this 'fast-' and 'slow-' learning systems – the fast-learning system is where new information is quickly taken in without much thought (likened to the peripheral route) and the slow-learning system is like the central route where information is slowly analysed before being stored.

The Heuristic-Systematic Model (HSM) shares much in common with the ELM. Together, these are the two main theories of processing that social psychologists look at to describe how attitudes are formed and changed in response to a persuasive message. HSM emphasizes that people use mental shortcuts (heuristics) in decision-making: thoughtful and attentive decision-making is called systematic processing and automatic processing is called heuristic processing.

In a nutshell we human beings are great at making sense of things quickly but sometimes we jump to conclusions before all the evidence is in. When faced with a new problem – and even before we have seen the whole picture – we are likely to make up our minds quickly based on past experience.

In *Thinking, Fast and Slow*, neurologist Daniel Kahneman (2011) presents us with a model of the brain, where we use two radically opposed modes of thought: 'System 1' and 'System 2'. System 1 is fast, intuitive, associative, metaphorical, automatic, impressionistic, and it can't be switched off. Its operations involve no sense of intentional control, but it's the 'secret author of many of the choices and judgements you make'. System 2 is slow, deliberate and effortful. Its operations require attention. System 2 takes over, rather unwillingly, when things get difficult. It's 'the conscious being you call "I"'. Kahneman says though that this is a mistake – you're wrong to identify with System 2, for you are also and equally and profoundly System 1. Kahneman compares System 2 to a supporting character who believes him- or herself to be the lead actor and often has little idea of what's going on.

A brief critique

Phew! For me this is quite a lot to take in but it's worth it. Because it's all about the audience – again – and what we put before them, how much time they have to process what is before them, and so what they are likely to do with it. For me it's important thinking because it reflects modern living and the pressures we are all under to do more with less time. Most people feel pressured and so short-cuts and assumptions are made all the time. As public relations practitioners and communicators, we need to appreciate these factors in designing communications interventions that people can handle and act upon.

Theory 9 – emotional intelligence (EI)

Most theories involving communications and behaviour become more powerful and meaningful when related to emotional intelligence. This theory gives us a way of understanding and assessing human behaviours, management styles, attitudes, interpersonal skills and potential. It can help us think about how we communicate personally and corporately and brings compassion and humanity to our work.

Early emotional intelligence theory was developed during the 1970s and 80s by psychologists Howard Gardner (Harvard), Peter Salovey (Yale) and John 'Jack' Mayer (New Hampshire). But it was Daniel Goleman's seminal work *Emotional Intelligence* (2006) that put emotional intelligence on the map. He also coined the term 'EQ' (EQ – emotional quotient, contrasting with intelligence quotient – IQ).

The theory is quite simple. To be successful we need more than just conventional intelligence (IQ). We've all worked with people who are brilliant but hopeless when it comes to people and relationships. EQ says that to be successful we need to be aware of and able to control and manage our own emotions, and those of other people. Goleman identified the five 'domains' of EQ as:

- knowing your emotions;
- managing your own emotions;
- motivating yourself;
- recognizing and understanding other people's emotions;
- managing relationships, ie managing the emotions of others.

Organizations that embrace EQ reduce stress for individuals, decrease conflict, improve relationships and understanding, and increase stability, continuity and harmony. Public relations professionals who understand EQ can bring a greater humanity and empathy to their work, especially important when considering stakeholders and target audiences. We'll consider audiences in Chapter 5.

A brief critique

Again this is all about people and their behaviour and this is an essential theory that can help us plan how we communicate with our audiences. I think emotional intelligence is still often either ignored in business or brushed aside as too messy to deal with. But we human beings are a complex mass of emotions, and organizations that ignore the emotional side of communications, concentrating on the rational and logical, will almost inevitably fail to truly connect and engage with their target audiences.

Theory 10 – public relations as diplomacy

Dr Jacquie L'Etang, who is currently Professor of Public Relations and Applied Communication at Queen Margaret University, Edinburgh, wrote a scholarly and influential paper for the journal *American Behavioral Scientist* in 2009. Entitled 'Public relations and diplomacy in a globalized world: an issue of public communication', Jacquie compares and contrasts public relations with diplomacy and looks at public relations' diplomatic work for nation states. She draws her ideas from a range of disciplines including public relations, international relations, strategic studies, media studies, peace studies, management studies, cultural studies and anthropology.

By linking public diplomacy to public relations she 'reconnects public relations to power'. She is therefore making the case for PR as a hugely powerful force on the global stage and concludes her paper by saying:

> ... of much greater importance than the self-images of PR is that PR and media practitioners, communities, and publics gain a critical self-awareness and reflexivity concerning the possible assumptions, motivations, and language practices of those practicing public communication. Any work that uncovers the processes of public communication in our complex postmodern world, and the role of PR in particular, is useful and beneficial to human understanding of this semi-profession and its potential influences in the pursuit of power. This points to the necessity for an empirical turn in the field not based on normative theory or idealistic stances that elaborate what PR ought to be and do. Untangling and making known the intricacies of PR's relationship to power and revealing the processes and social effects of its contribution to public communication, media shaping, and public understanding are the most valuable tasks that PR academics can now assume. The continued integration and scholastic exchanges among those in public diplomacy and PR can contribute to a nuanced understanding of these occupations and, most important, place the concept of power at the centre of PR practice and scholarship, where it properly belongs.

> (http://www.prconversations.com/wp-content/uploads/2009/12/
> public-relation-and-diplomacy-letaing.pdf)

A brief critique

This is such important thinking. It is truly big picture, and moves PR well away from the simplistic notion that public relations is another terms for media relations. L'Etang is saying that there is great power in effective public relations and communications, the power to shape society and to make the world a better place. For us as practitioners, this should make us feel proud and powerful too and give us greater confidence to present our case, to lead our organizations, to be a force for good.

Theory 11 – the rhetorical and ethical orientation of PR

More recent theories look at how organizations communicate externally, looking at their rhetoric, and how this impacts on how they are perceived in terms of reputation. In 'External organizational rhetoric: bridging management and sociopolitical discourse', *Management Communication Quarterly* (2011) Robert Heath of the University of Houston, explored how organizations 'engage constructively and destructively in the discourse that defines their legitimacy'.

Heath and others have also explored systems theory and the ethical aspects of public relations, the contention being that organizations that use legal, rather than ethical, standards to make business decisions when faced with a serious issue, risk their reputation. The Enron collapse is frequently cited as the clearest example of why legal standards should never be used as a substitute for ethical principles. Both systems theory and rhetoric support the argument that an organization must be good internally and make decisions from an outside-in perspective. Bowen and Heath (2005) conclude that moral autonomy and good intention should be the basis for ethical issues management.

Heath's work on the creation of meaning has been often cited as particularly influential. This is especially apposite for social media where meaning is *now*, with crowdsourcing and co-creation. Heath believes that the public relations process becomes enriched through the role co-created, shared meaning plays in society. He says that public relations can add value to society by assuring that choices become enlightened, risks are ethically managed, and relationships are mutually developed. His contention is that a thorough consideration of public relations helps organizations reflect on their meaning in and for society and so helps society to be more fully functioning.

A brief critique

Again, this is big picture thinking that should inspire us all. On a practical level, it is also thinking that should give us pause for thought and help us develop our consultancy skills so that we are able to give the best advice possible within our organizations or to our clients. We must be able to act as the conscience of our organizations, to be alert for any practice we see that would harm corporate reputation and be prepared to advise accordingly. No longer is this simply instinctively right, it is proven to be essential if an organization is to continue to have the right to operate and to be successful.

Theory 12 – postmodernist PR theory

Academics working in the field of public relations are now suggesting that public relations should be freed from its narrowly defined position within organizational communication management. Up until now, the theory and practice of public relations has been based on it being a strategic management function – the 'modernist' theory. 'Postmodernist' PR theory rejects the manager as a rational being who has the ability to determine organizational outcomes through strategies and instead suggests that postmodern public relations practitioners will be activists within organizations.

In her book *Public Relations As Activism: Postmodern approaches to theory and practice*, Derina Holtzhausen (2013) focuses on the postmodernization of society, and the possibilities postmodern theories offer to explain and understand public relations practice in today's changing society. She looks at these issues and their application to public relations theory and practice and suggests that public relations practice can be seen as a form of activism, where dissensus and dissymmetry offer more appropriate approaches to current public relations practices than seeking consensus and symmetry.

A brief critique

This is cutting-edge academic thinking and these latest ideas and theories demonstrate that the role of the public relations practitioner is evolving; it is more dynamic, harder to define, responsive to societal shifts, able to be more confident and assured. It is also appreciating that, particularly as a result of the explosion of the use of social media across the world by every sector of society, one-way communications is effectively dead as a concept. Given that the individual can express his or her views on any issue, that debate and discussion are the norm, and centralized power is a thing of the past, the message is clear – keep abreast of new ideas and new theories about our fascinating profession. They will help with your day-to-day practice, give you food for thought and enable you to be a competent and confident consultant.

03
The professional public relations practitioner

Communications is an attractive career choice for many, with PR ranking consistently among new graduates' top three career choices. Professional standards are improving all the time, with the introduction of vocational public relations and communications diplomas and degrees. But it is a highly competitive business, hard to break into and hard work when you get there.

Good communicators who approach the job with a sound ethical approach can make a very real and positive difference to society, sometimes in small ways and sometimes in very dramatic ways, sometimes for start-ups, sometimes for government departments, sometimes for major plcs and sometimes for marginalized and disenfranchised groups. You can give a technology blogger copy about a new mobile phone at 10 am and speak to a respected political commentator working for an elite media organization about a new government policy at 2 pm. You can write a press release about a new strain of meningitis one day and manage a corporate event for an energy company the next. You can work with the chief executive of a major charity on a crisis plan on a Thursday and advise an online retailer on a Friday. Or you might lead a trade press trip round a state-of-the-art frozen pea factory in York in January and present the versatility of the pistachio nut as a food ingredient in Rome in February.

I have worked with hundreds of PR professionals over the years – in-house practitioners, consultancy teams and freelance consultants – as a consultant, as a colleague and as a client. When I run training courses or speak at seminars, I am frequently asked, 'What does it take to be a good PR professional? Have I got "it"?' Here we look at the personal qualities you need, the skills you will have to acquire, the qualifications and routes into the profession and how to look after yourself when you're holding down what can be a very demanding role indeed.

A word of advice – always be scrupulously honest with yourself. If you suspect that you haven't got the right skills, or you don't know how to do something, or if you've lost the enthusiasm and verve having done the job for a while, don't beat yourself up. This is not failure, this is learning. Keep on reassessing where you are, talk to your line manager, try a different sort of PR job, perhaps in a specific sector or industry you love, get some training to refresh yourself or to learn new skills. Move on if you need to, to check that it's not just this job that's preventing you from realizing your potential. And change direction if you must. There is nothing sadder than someone who feels trapped because they don't feel they can do anything else or because they know deep down they don't want to go any further.

Working as a communications /PR professional

So often in my career I have been asked, 'So what do you actually *do*?' The easy answer is to list what don't I do! The job is infinitely varied and, particularly as you become more experienced, you will find that no day is the same as the next. But if you want to explain to a rookie what might be in store for them in terms of a list of tasks they might be expected to complete during the working week, it would probably include some – or even all – of the following:

- Daily monitoring – looking at all relevant channels to assess 'the conversation' about an organization and its sector – this includes online media covering blogs and social media, broadcast media and printed media. Coverage is analysed and key issues are communicated to those who need to know. The PR practitioner advises on what response and action to take.
- Updating the online press office pages on the organization's website.
- Managing social media feeds – Twitter, YouTube, Facebook, etc.
- Researching media contacts and updating contact details.
- Responding to bloggers and contributing to online discussions.
- Contacting writers (journalists and bloggers) proactively.
- Writing – tweeting, blog posts, news stories, feature material, background information, brochures and leaflets, letters, internal and external newsletters, reports.
- Managing creative work – photography, video, podcasts, design and print.
- Managing presentations and events – launches, lunches, conferences and meetings.
- Briefing spokespeople or acting as spokesperson.

- Communicating with and updating colleagues/clients.
- Planning future projects and programmes.

It's a tough job and there will be demands made of you that might not be made of others. In-house practitioners may be expected to take responsibility for tasks that do not fall into any other neat category and so are lumped under 'PR'. Consultants may have to juggle a number of clients, each of whom are making demands on you at the same time, while working on two new business pitches, updating the consultancy blog and website. Whether in-house or consultant, another frequent cause of tension is the naïve expectation that the PR practitioner's main or even sole responsibility is to deliver vast quantities of positive media coverage, whatever the story, whatever the day of the week. The management of issues and crises make particular demands on PR practitioners, in terms of time and tension levels. Just running a good press office might mean you are on call 24 hours a day, 7 days a week.

Personal qualities and professional/ business skills

As you can see effective public relations practitioners need a number of both personal qualities and professional/business skills. These are entirely different and separate from any consideration of academic achievement or formal qualifications. These qualities and skills might appear on a job description or people specification. Some people believe that personal qualities are innate while professional skills can be learnt. What is certainly true is that many of the professional skills build on personal qualities. I would contend that all of these are all relevant whether you are working in-house or as a consultant. There are one or two more business-orientated skills that are specific to the consultant.

While you don't necessarily have to have every one of these qualities or be accomplished in every skill, the more you have the more effective a practitioner you are likely to be. If you are responsible for recruiting or appraising people who will be working as public relations practitioners – including appointing consultants – these checklists will help by giving some ideas for creating or updating job descriptions and appraisal systems.

Getting started in communications

People get into the communications business in a variety of ways:

- Via an internship – standard internships have traditionally taken the form of unpaid periods (often three months), with no guarantee of

TABLE 3.1 Personal qualities and professional/business skills needed to succeed in PR

Personal qualities

Good interpersonal communication:
- You build rapport with people – clients, colleagues, journalists – and always seek a win–win outcome
- You are interested in and gain pleasure from expressing yourself verbally and in the written form
- You can communicate with a wide variety of people, from consumer or customer to senior colleague or client, so the ability to adapt both approach and language and to empathize is fundamental

Perspective/sense of humour:
- You can deal well with difficult people or difficult situations
- You put things into perspective and help others do the same
- You use appropriate humour to help the communication process, break the ice and defuse explosive situations

Calm under pressure:
- You deal well with pressure and meet deadlines
- If the unexpected happens you take it in your stride – and when the going is tough you remain centred and focused
- You can take a leadership role in the event of a crisis

Creative:
- You come up with lots of ideas
- You support other people's creative ideas
- You find solutions to problems by looking inwards and outwards and draw from a wide variety of sources

Organized:
- You can juggle effectively so everything gets done
- You know where everything is – and your team members can find things easily if they need to
- You can use schedules, critical paths and timing plans to help plan projects

Willing to learn:
- You seek out new experiences and have a go at something you have never done before – with the right coaching and support
- You reflect on what you have learnt on your own and with others
- If you make a mistake you learn from it

(Continued)

TABLE 3.1 (*Continued*)

Curiosity/enquiring mind:
- You are curious about people, your industry, your product, your issue, your organization, the media
- You ask great questions
- You do research and use all the resources available to you before arriving at any conclusion

Approachable:
- You can build relationships with a wide number of people, both inside and outside the organization
- People are willing and keen to communicate and work with you
- People respond to you and it's easy to build coalitions

Self-confident:
- Your verbal and non-verbal behaviour communicates confidence
- You build confidence in others by being positive and assertive
- You have a 'can do' attitude

Focus:
- You can focus on the task in hand even though you have a lot on
- You are not distracted by trivia
- You think clearly to arrive at quality solutions and ideas

Practical:
- You can translate creative ideas into workable and practical solutions
- You are not afraid to get your hands dirty
- You look for way to make things work

Energetic:
- You have lots of staying power
- You are prepared to 'go the extra mile' to get the result
- You encourage others to give their best

Enthusiastic:
- You are genuinely interested, even in a small project or unlikely issue
- You attack even small projects with energy
- You encourage others to see the positive side

TABLE 3.1 (*Continued*)

Assertive:
- You are assertive but never aggressive or passive
- You recognize when others are assertive and respect that
- You meet aggression with assertiveness to calm the situation

Tough/resilient:
- You take setbacks in your stride
- You learn lessons from mistakes
- You help others to see that setbacks and disappointments are temporary

Integrity:
- You adhere to the principles outlined in the CIPR professional code of conduct
- You alert people if there is something that will affect the organization's reputation
- You respect matters told to you in confidence

Professional/business skills

Public relations essentials:
- Sound understanding of the basics of the industry
- A grasp of definitions and purpose of communications
- Experience and/or appropriate qualifications

Business strategy:
- Understands the need for profitability and productivity
- Works within the organization's corporate/business strategy (in-house)
- Can set, run and/or contribute to a corporate/business strategy (consultancy)

Planning and evaluation:
- Understands principles of research and auditing
- Able to set SMART objectives for communications
- Can write a strategy paper, outlining channels and tactics and including a logical implementation
- Understands principles of ongoing measurement
- Can write an evaluation report at the end of a programme or campaign outlining results and making recommendations for the future

(Continued)

TABLE 3.1 (*Continued*)

Writing:
- Is reader/listener-orientated
- Good clear, concise writing-style appropriate for business
- Writes effective blogs, tweets, postings and comments
- Writes media material (releases, features, photo captions) following journalistic principles
- Can write to brief for other materials (reports, copy, speeches, letters, etc)

Channel management
Digital and social media:
- Understands how to create, manage and create content for interactive websites
- Uses and understands the principles of using social media and social networks eg Twitter, Facebook, YouTube and LinkedIn for corporate communications
- Targets and works with specific and targeted online media (eg bloggers/ online journalists)
- Keeps up with developments by readings and researching

Media relations:
- Understands how print, broadcast and online media work
- Knows how best to work with different media professionals
- Understands how to prioritize and target media
- Can run an effective press office operation

Event management:
- Understands event management as a discipline and can plan and manage simple events on time and to budget
- Capable of writing a brief and appointing and managing event management contractors when necessary

Consultancy:
- Can act as an effective consultant, whether in-house, working as an internal consultant to colleagues, or in consultancy, working for fee-paying clients
- Gives clear advice and recommendations
- When appropriate alerts client to issues and difficulties

(*Continued*)

TABLE 3.1 (*Continued*)

Presenting:
- Makes effective internal and external presentations
- Constructs effective pitches (consultants)
- Delivers effective briefings and debriefings

Project management:
- Can construct a project plan
- Delegates and/or manages every component of the project
- Brings projects in on time and to budget

Reputation management:
- Understands the principles of reputation management
- Audits and monitors clients' reputation effectively using appropriate insight tools (eg surveys, questionnaires, focus groups, etc)
- Recommends strategies to create, protect, enhance and repair reputation

Issues and crisis management:
- Conducts thorough risk audits
- Prepares policy statements and questions and answers for proactive issues management
- Creates contingency plans for communications management in the event of a crisis
- Conducts crisis management exercises regularly to test processes

Specialist sector skills:
- Gets a thorough grounding on the industry sector he or she works in (eg healthcare, public affairs, consumer, etc) including issues, legal frameworks and codes of conduct
- Seeks opportunities to expand knowledge and contact lists
- Is recognized as a communications expert in the specialist field

Budget management and profitability:
- Assesses budgetary requirements for the communications operation
- Manages budgets effectively including those of suppliers (eg for in-house practitioners PR consultancies, freelance support, etc)
- Manages time to control over-servicing and renegotiates fees if necessary (consultancy)

(*Continued*)

TABLE 3.1 (*Continued*)

Client management:
- Takes good briefs from clients and interrogates objectives carefully
- Provides insight and creative solutions to clients
- Aims to ensure win–win every time, in terms of the results and the relationship

Marketing communications:
- Understands other marketing disciplines – advertising, design, direct marketing, sales promotion, etc
- Seeks to work towards integrated campaigns with creative synergy and proposes solutions that can work for and enhance other disciplines
- Builds positive working relationships across disciplines

employment once completed. The benefits include gaining work experience (good for the CV), insight into the work itself and making good contacts. The CIPR publishes guidelines on using interns, so that exploitation is avoided. Internships can help graduates make the transition from academia and can be an important 'gateway' to the industry.

- Via graduate recruitment schemes – a graduate may be hired because he or she has a qualification in communications or marketing. In my own experience, a good (2:1) degree from a respected university is at least as desirable. A growing number of universities and colleges offer degrees in public relations and marketing, either as full-time or part-time courses. The CIPR regularly reviews the scope and standards of higher education communications/PR degrees and further education diplomas and certificates.

- Via secondment, when a temporary transfer to a communications role within an organization becomes a permanent switch.

- By migrating from one industry to another – for example, journalists and marketing consultants switching to public relations, nurses moving to healthcare public relations.

- By migrating from consultancy to in-house and vice versa.

- By taking on public relations as part of another role – for example, as part of the marketing role – or by switching departments in-house.

- By entering as a PA or secretary, gaining on-the-job experience and training and then being promoted.

Where will I work?

Once you've landed a job you'll work in one of three settings:

1 *In-house* – for one company, government department or organization exclusively, closely aligned to the management and providing a service to the whole organization.

   The in-house PR may also be subcontracting to and then managing consultancies, so he or she may be a client as well as a PR practitioner. The in-house practitioner may be working alone, be part of a small team, work in association with colleagues in other locations in the UK or abroad or be part of a huge department, servicing a large organization.

   In-house suits those who want to work in one organization or industry and who want to specialize in a subject. It is also a little more likely to suit people who want to be able to manage their lives in terms of what hours they might work or where they might be from one week to the next as most in-house jobs – though by no means all – are governed by the organization's employment terms and conditions which may include flexitime.

2 *Consultancy* – working for one or more clients in a consultancy, which may be generalist or may offer expertise in one particular sector, eg consumer PR. The consultant needs to be able to be something of an entrepreneur too as building business – by winning and keeping clients – is vital in consultancy.

   Consultancy teams are made up of board directors, account directors, account managers and account executives, with account teams constructed to reflect the needs of the client and the size of the budget. Because of the nature of consultancy, the life better suits people who are able to and ideally who want to move around from subject to subject, industry to industry, location to location. Hours vary, given that the consultant is offering a service to clients who may need support at unsocial times including evenings and weekends. Because consultants usually work for more than one client he or she will need to juggle time and may need to spend considerable time travelling from one location to another or away from home.

3 *Freelance/interim* – Growing numbers of in-house and consultancy practitioners decide to work on a freelance or interim basis. Having acquired good experience themselves, they set up on their own and offer a valuable service to in-house teams and consultancies to cope with additional work, extra projects, specialist support, maternity cover and so on. While income is not guaranteed and so not a great choice for some, freelance offers the ultimate in freedom in terms of being able to build the lifestyle and working pattern that suits you. It especially suits keen writers, those who need to or want to work from home and those who have parenting or caring responsibilities.

Training and qualifications in public relations

The Chartered Institute of Public Relations (CIPR) and the Public Relations Consultants Association (PRCA)

The CIPR

The CIPR is the professional body for PR practitioners in the UK. With 9,500 members involved in all aspects of PR, it is the largest body of its type in Europe. The CIPR advances the PR profession in the UK by making its members accountable through a code of conduct, developing policies, representing its members and raising standards through education and training.

The CIPR grants recognition to university courses at undergraduate and postgraduate level by assessing course content, teaching staff and monitoring annual performance. The Institute also offers the most established industry-recognized PR qualifications at Foundation, Advanced Certificate and Diploma level plus specialist short courses in Internal Communication (certificate/diploma level), Public Affairs Diploma and Crisis (Response) Communication Diploma. Senior professionals can apply for individual Chartered Practitioner status, where candidates are assessed against set criteria and breadth and depth of experience.

The CIPR supports the training and development of members through a comprehensive portfolio of face-to-face learning and development events, including webinars, which are especially helpful to overseas practitioners and those who are unable to travel to workshop events. Members of the CIPR are also encouraged to further their personal development through the Institute's continuous professional development programme. All learning and development is designed to advance the professional's career prospects, increase confidence and skills, provide theory to back-up decision-making and underpin practice and offer a more strategic and structured approach to PR.

CIPR Qualifications

There are several levels of industry-recognized qualification presently available through the CIPR.

CIPR Foundation Award in Public Relations The CIPR Foundation Award is a short starter qualification taught at A-level standard. It equips practitioners with the essential knowledge and skills needed to get started in public relations – from understanding the role of the PR practitioner to learning the basics of writing for the press and dealing with journalists.

It provides entry to the CIPR's higher-level qualifications and is aimed at school or college leavers; those considering PR as a career; those working in PR in a support or administrative role; and those interested in studying the Advanced Certificate but who do not yet meet the entry criteria.

The Foundation Award covers the basics needed to make a start in a career in PR. Assessment is via a three-hour examination involving a report, a news release exercise and an essay. Candidates study at approved centres across the UK.

CIPR Advanced Certificate in Public Relations This is for UK graduates of any discipline who wish to build a career in PR or for practitioners who have at least two years of PR work experience. It is delivered as a part-time, vocational course, designed for those in full-time employment, and gives students a solid grounding and understanding of PR theory and practice. Successful completion enables candidates to become a CIPR associate member, eligible to progress to the CIPR diploma. The Advanced Certificate is taught and assessed at level 5 of the UK (England, Wales and Northern Ireland) National Qualifications Framework (NQF).

Topics covered include: PR and its role in the organization; PR and communication theory; PR planning and tactics; writing skills; media relations; management skills and professional practice. The course comprises face-to-face class-based tuition (around eight days) plus five to six hours a week on independent study over the duration of the course. The Advanced Certificate is available at a number of study centres in the UK and overseas.

An Online Advanced Certificate is also available that combines an interactive e-learning programme with two (optional) full days of lectures and workshops in central London.

CIPR Diploma in Public Relations This gives working and experienced public relations practitioners the knowledge and understanding of theory and practice to develop as effective and efficient professionals, providing advanced capability in management and practice. It is taught and assessed at level 7 of the UK (England, Wales and Northern Ireland) National Qualifications Framework (NQF). A growing number of universities recognize the diploma in respect of their Masters' programmes.

Taught as a part-time course, the diploma is ideal for those in full-time employment and is suitable for experienced PR professionals without an industry-specific qualification and those who want to learn about the strategic roles and functions of the public relations practitioner.

To be eligible for the diploma the practitioner needs to have:

- a CIPR Advanced Certificate in Public Relations;
- a CIPR Internal Communication Certificate plus one year's full-time employment in PR;*

- a postgraduate professional qualification in a related discipline (eg Chartered Institute of Marketing diploma), plus one year's full-time employment (or equivalent part-time employment) in public relations;*
- a degree in business/marketing/management/communication studies, plus one year's full-time employment in PR;
- any other UK degree plus two years' full-time employment in PR;*
- a National Council for the Training of Journalists (NCTJ) Diploma plus either five years' journalism experience or three years' full-time employment in PR;*
- two years' full-time employment in public relations,* and the Communication Advertising and Marketing (CAM) Advanced Diploma in Marketing Communication;
- London Chamber of Commerce and Industry Examination Board (LCCIEB) five 3rd-Level subjects, including PR, marketing, advertising, principles and practice of management, plus two years' experience in PR;
- four years' full-time employment in public relations* and five GCSE passes, one of which must be in English language.

*Eligibility of PR employment is determined by the CIPR's qualifications department and needs to be of a sufficiently senior level.

Specialist short courses   The CIPR also offers several specialist qualifications, all of which are taught and assessed at Level 7 of the UK (England, Wales and Northern Ireland) National Qualifications Framework (NQF):

- *Internal Communication (certificate/diploma level)*

  This provides a solid grounding in all of the key concepts, techniques, theories and skills needed to develop effectively as an internal communicator. The syllabus covers: organizational culture and transformation; communication theory; strategic internal communication and engagement; planning and managing; setting the right tone – the fit between internal and external communication; using social media for internal communication; the role of communications in transforming organizations.

- *Public Affairs Diploma*

  Focusing on the process of policy formation and the wider corporate communications and reputational context in which public affairs operates, this qualification is grounded in public affairs practice and latest academic thinking. The syllabus covers the political landscape, trends and challenges; lobbying and campaigning; public affairs in the context of reputation management.

- *Crisis (Response) Communication Diploma*

  This qualification enables experienced practitioners to better understand why crisis damages trust and thereby affects reputation and how it might be mitigated. The course investigates relevant theories and practices including: crisis-prone behaviour and management styles; different levels and impacts of crises; the organization in society; issues management; reputation, its vulnerabilities and its opportunities; trust as an asset; relationships – why and how they can support or threaten; influencing strategies to avoid or avert a crisis; carrying out effective audits and research; the role, purpose and effectiveness of training for crisis management; the building and maintaining of effective crisis plans.

Continuous Professional Development (CPD) Continuing Professional Development (CPD) enables CIPR members to maintain, improve and broaden their knowledge and skills and develop the personal qualities required for their PR careers. The CPD year runs from 1 January to 31 December each year. Each year you will need to record 60 points of CPD activity by signing in to the CIPR website and accessing the online CPD system. You record activity to your CPD account by selecting from predefined activities in the database or by creating your own self-defined activities, and evaluating their effectiveness.

Accredited Practitioner Accredited Practitioner status is awarded to Members (MCIPR) or Fellows (FCIPR) who have completed either:

- two continuous years of CPD by accumulating 60 CPD points per year; or
- a CIPR diploma (CIPR Diploma, Public Affairs Diploma, Internal Communications Diploma, Crisis Communications Diploma); or
- a CIPR recognized Master's degree and are taking part in CPD.
- If you are an Associate (ACIPR) you can work towards completing your two years (120 points) of CPD and Accredited Practitioner status will be awarded when you upgrade your membership. Accredited Practitioner status is valid only for as long as you are a CIPR member and continue to participate in CPD.

Chartered Practitioner The CIPR's Chartered Practitioner Scheme awards Chartered status on an individual basis to members who have completed a rigorous assessment of their professional expertise. It is not only a benchmark for those working at a senior level, but a 'gold standard' to which all PR practitioners should strive to reach.

Full Members and Fellows who are participating on the CPD scheme and who also have at least 10 years' practitioner experience may start their application process at any time. Once they have passed and completed all three assessment stages – a statement of experience, a 3,000–4,000-word paper and interview – participants may describe themselves as CIPR Chartered Practitioners. By marking them out as practitioners at the top of the profession, this new status will not only benefit those who achieve it, but employers also will find it easier to recruit senior, experienced talent.

The Public Relations Consultants Association

Alongside the CIPR is the PRCA. The PRCA represents many of the major consultancies in the UK, and currently has over 250 agency members from around the world including the majority of the top 100 UK consultancies. The PRCA also represents over 70 in-house teams, including many of Europe's leading corporations and UK public sector organizations, as well as individual and freelance PR and communications practitioners.

The PRCA also offers training courses and professional qualifications.

PRCA Foundation Course This is designed to ensure that all new starters are trained in the core principles of PR, allowing them to be effective members of the team.

PRCA Online Certificate The PRCA Online Certificate is aimed at intermediate-level practitioners looking to progress their careers through a wide range of bite-size courses. The PRCA Online Certificate will give ambitious PRs the all-round skills to be effective members of the team and take on the challenges to progress to senior PR management roles.

PRCA Advanced Certificate This is designed for those who already have a good grounding in PR and are looking to advance their career in a structured and formal manner, creating a highly effective PR practitioner.

PRCA Diploma This is designed for those already at management level, providing them with the skills to lead their organizations more effectively and ensuring they are familiar with the latest management practices.

Client/consultancy contracts

From a client perspective, before holding a 'pitch' to determine which PR agency you'd like to work with – whether this is a new arrangement or whether you are looking to re-tender the PR agency account – it's prudent to carry out a company or bankruptcy search to ensure that the supplier is financially sound. This is especially true of smaller PR agencies or those that haven't been trading for that long.

Any PR agency agreement worth its salt should explicitly state exactly what the client wants otherwise it won't be clear what the PR agency should be delivering. In a nutshell, the PR agency agreement needs to cover the services provided; the standard of those services and the cost of the services delivered. And as the relationship moves forward, there should also be a clear process agreed for refining the PR services and deliverables under the agency relationship, which needs to be collaborative rather than dictatorial.

It's also unwise to rely on a clause that expects the PR agency to perform according to 'best practice' and it's preferable to spell this out in detail in order to describe the standard of services required. This is in everyone's best interests as it's fair, open and transparent and avoids ambiguity and misunderstanding that can so often creep into these arrangements.

If the PR agency has developed the description or narrative of the service to be delivered, then from a client perspective you need to ensure that it's 'fit for purpose' and meets your requirements. Ideally, the process of developing the service description should be collaborative, although this won't always be possible, for example, following an EU tender.

Depending on the value of the PR agency services being procured, it's worth considering inserting a provision by which the PR agency agrees that it has carried out its due diligence in relation to the services it will deliver and consequently it employs a 'no surprises or hidden costs' approach regarding the fees payable for those services. Most PR agencies now offer this as standard.

As a client, you'll want to avoid a situation where the PR agency claims that it didn't know that a particular circumstance existed and therefore wants to charge more for its services. You should also consider continuous improvement in agency performance and how the PR agency services can be benchmarked over the longer term. Many PR agencies now expect this to be the norm.

Another important factor is the location of the PR agency and where it's expected to perform and deliver its services under the agreement and the timescales for the delivery of those services. It's useful to draft an implementation plan with the PR agency in order to help manage expectations on both sides and maintain a workable relationship.

Although the implementation plan won't form part of the main body of the PR agency agreement it should include a list of meaningful milestones, the components of each milestone, any particular relevant considerations and dates for completion. The PR agency should be under a duty to mitigate any delay in achieving a milestone and the client should consider making time of the essence for delivery.

As part of the PR agency agreement, it's wise for the client to give itself enough flexibility to accommodate the changing demands of its employer, so the agreement needs to provide for a flexible change control procedure. As a client, it's prudent to take account of how pricing for these services will be accommodated as well as any additional consultancy time requirements.

Other considerations worth thinking about include:

1 The pros and cons of entering an exclusive PR agency agreement where the agency can't work for one of your direct competitors.

2 A mutual non-disclosure clause that protects the use of confidential information.

3 Copyright in the materials produced, such as photographs, artwork and other creative outputs as well as other intellectual property (IP) rights.

4 Attendance at weekly, monthly, half-year and annual reviews of the performance of the PR agency according to the milestones and the implementation plan agreed.

5 Engagement of an independent third-party consultancy to run an annual 360 degree review whose core objective is getting the most out of the relationship for the client and PR agency (usually with very large agency agreements).

6 Ensuring that any briefs (creative briefs should ideally be one page in length) are clear and unambiguous in order to save time and cost of re-doing work as well as producing better results faster and at a lower cost.

7 Payment terms (this can vary between 30–60 days for fees and 30–60 days in arrears for expenses) and ensuring that invoices are properly submitted in order to comply with invoicing and other financial control requirements as well as a penalty interest clause for late payments.

8 Warranties and indemnities for goods and services created by third parties.

9 Duration of the PR agency agreement as well as grounds for termination and what events would be fundamental breaches and what events would not amount to fundamental breaches of the agreement and are capable of being remedied.

10 Jurisdictional issues, choice of law and dispute resolution. In the latter, it's typical in PR agency agreements to have a dispute-resolution mechanism, such as escalation, and then mediation or arbitration where the costs are borne by both parties.

One final thought – if the PR agreement is one-sided then it's likely to be fatally flawed and more than likely will fail to achieve its true potential. (Kolah, A [online, accessed 30 January 2013])

Taking care of yourself

You need to look after yourself, physically and mentally. Here are 10 tips to keep you sane:

1 *Take it easy with technology.*

So many of us spent all day looking at one sort of screen or another – phone, pad, laptop, desktop, TV. It's easy to become a slave to technology. Take regular breaks away from your desk and from screens. Leave your desk and go and talk to people face-to-face. Let your eyes refocus, look into the distance, do some stretching exercises, read printed materials.

2 *Get enough sleep.*

It's easy to work hard, play hard and think that four or five hours will suffice. You need to be alert and on the ball in this job. Performance falls off if you are sleep-deprived. If you wake up in the middle of the night worrying about something, get up, have a glass of water and write down what's bothering you. You may just need to make a list and do a brain dump. If insomnia is a persistent problem it may be time to take a long hard look at the way you are working and be prepared to make a fundamental change if you need to.

3 *Drink lots of water.*

It's too easy to get so engrossed in your work that you forget to rehydrate. Get a water dispenser for the office or buy yourself a filter jug and keep it on your desk at work. Travel with a bottle of still mineral water in your bag. Drink a glass of water as soon as you get up, one before lunch and another before supper. Replace tea and coffee at meetings with water. Choose still rather than carbonated water, like TV journalists do – it's better for your stomach and stops you from gurgling!

4 *Watch the alcohol consumption.*

In this sociable business, it's easy to find yourself drinking almost every day, with colleagues after work, with clients or consultants at lunch, with journalists, at events, at receptions. This is especially easy of you are in a culture where drinking is the norm or even feels expected. You don't need to stop altogether but it is a good idea to stick to recommended safe levels, have a few alcohol-free days each week and replace alcohol with water or soft drinks whenever you can.

5 *Eat often but lightly.*

So you don't suffer from the after-lunch droop – keep a fruit bowl on your desk and snack healthily to keep energy levels high. Cut out the carbs, which can make you feel stuffed and lethargic.

6 *Learn about time management.*

Apply any helpful hints and tips to buy time for life after and outside work.

7 *Walk – everywhere.*

Up stairs, from floor to floor, from office to office, from the station to the meeting, from the meeting to the station. You may think that the taxi will get you there quicker, but traffic or roadworks can actually make your journey longer – a walk may take you just a fraction longer but it gives you time to think, to breathe and gives your legs a stretch. On business overseas, especially on long-haul flights, move about if you can or at least stand and bend and flex your legs every hour.

8 *Get involved with a sport as a player.*

It's not only good for you, it may also be a good opening gambit for conversation on social occasions and, if it's a team game, it gives you an excuse for a social get-together with clients or colleagues.

9 *Get a life outside of PR.*

Don't forget your partner/family/friends. Put birthdays and anniversaries in your diary, take holidays, don't take work home unless it really is an emergency, get a dog and take it for walks after work, get a cat and stroke it (good for the blood pressure). Be multi-dimensional and get passionate about something – try volunteering for a local charity or get involved with a local community project, take up a new hobby, learn a new skill, just do something you haven't done before and keep yourself interested and interesting.

10 *Stop beating yourself up – about anything and everything.*

This is especially true if you work for an organization where issues and/or crisis management are at the fore, if you are a perfectionist or if you work with colleagues or clients who are particularly demanding. And if you are a working parent this can be even more of an issue. Give yourself a break – a bit of time to think – or not to think – a treat, a space and reward yourself for working hard. Pat yourself on the back when you have done a good job and put mistakes down to experience. Learn to let go when you have done your bit. Don't carry guilt, regret or anger around with you. And be assertive when you need to be.

Finally, don't take yourself too seriously – yes, communications is an important job but it is just a job in the end. Few of us see PR as a vocation or have so little else in our lives that we want to spend every hour of every day doing it or talking about it. (You could get a little boring or come over as self-obsessed.) But don't take this advice if you are ambitious enough to want to become a PR guru, one of those people whose names are synonymous with the business, or if you want to make loads of money – in which case just knuckle down, focus on the business, get your name about, network at every conceivable opportunity and get to the top – and the best of luck to you!

Your action plan:

- Review the list of personal qualities and professional/business skills – measure how you are doing at regular intervals.

- Use this list during appraisals and discussions about your career development.

- Seek out learning and development opportunities to shore up weak areas or to acquire new skills.
- When you switch job, get promoted or get a new client review your development needs.
- Make sure you have an up-to-date job description and CV.
- Investigate whether a mentor or coach would be helpful – have an initial meeting to see how it might benefit you.
- Consider joining the CIPR. If you are already a member, make full use of the organization for networking and personal development. Consider studying for a qualification and join the Continuous Professional Development scheme.

04
Planning and evaluating public relations

Practical people want to get things done; they want to get on with it, to move into action and see results. Planning can feel like you are putting things off, that you are wasting time and prevaricating. I tell you this – planning saves time, is highly creative and sets you up for success. Whether it's a rolling communications programme designed to get people to drive safely, an annual fundraising event for a charity or a one-off launch of a new product, communications needs planning. Time spent planning is time well spent and will make your work as a practitioner more focused, the results more effective and evaluation easier. The old adage 'fail to plan, plan to fail' comes to mind.

There are so many benefits to planning. Professor Anne Gregory (2010) says that 'Successful public relations programmes do not just happen. They are the result of sound research, meticulous planning, and careful implementation.' She says there are practical reasons for planning. These can broadly be summarized like this:

- If you don't plan, you have no control.
- Planning provides a structure and particularly agreed goals against which performance can be compared. This is important whether you are an in-house team reporting internally to management or a consultancy reporting into a client.
- And you can start to think longer term, not just in the moment which can result in knee-jerk responses.

You focus your efforts on the objectives:

- You have to get right down to it and work out why you are doing what you are doing.

- You have a real purpose to the tactics you eventually undertake.
- You can take everyone with you if the direction and purpose are clear.
- You end up with a clear action plan with a defined goal.

You become more creative:

- Contrary to popular belief, a good plan sets up space for creativity, a space bounded by insight and with a clear goal.
- Planning allows for innovation, so people can come up with new ways to solve problems.

You reduce uncertainties:

- Change is a constant in our modern fast-moving world.
- Every organization, every sector faces issues, risks, unforeseen challenges – good planning includes contingency planning so you are forced to consider the 'mights' and 'coulds'.
- A solid plan builds in a consideration of risk and includes risk and contingency planning.

You use resources wisely:

- People's time is money – proper planning avoids time-wasting.
- You can predict when you need more or less resources and when you need additional help, for example agency or freelance support.
- You can allocate material resources and work out economies of scale to purchase effectively.

You co-ordinate effort:

- Your team knows where it's headed because the objectives are clear.
- You can integrate individuals, teams and departments across a network.
- Multi-disciplined approaches (eg marketing, advertising, public affairs, internal communications) are richer because everyone knows where they are now and where they are headed.
- You can avoid duplication of efforts and wasted effort.

You all feel better:

- Planning leads to a sense of order and discipline.
- Colleagues know what is expected of them and know what to do and by when.
- Consequently, everyone can do their best to achieve the desired results.
- Engagement is therefore stronger and productivity increases.

You become more competitive:

- because communications teams that fail to plan don't get results, don't celebrate success and don't win awards!

While in-house practitioners often assume sole responsibility for PR planning, if you are using them, there is a strong case for bringing in external consultants at the earliest possible stage. Planning developed as a specialized function in advertising agencies and has become one of the main services offered by major public relations consultancies. The objectivity from and range of resources offered by or through a consultancy can be invaluable in terms of asking the right questions, developing perceptions and gaining insight into the real communications issues faced by the organization. While evaluation is probably the principal way to demonstrate value for money and cost-effectiveness, it is perhaps more importantly a dynamic way of delivering management information.

Some organizations have more rigorous measurement and evaluation systems than others and this is particularly true in the public sector when the expending of taxpayers money is involved. Other organizations simply want to satisfy their directors that the budgets allocated to public relations are achieving specific objectives. There will always be a handful of organizations where the person at the top still judges the success of the PR effort in terms of the number of times his or her face stares out at us from the pages of the trade press or how many times he or she is interviewed on the *Today* programme every month, aside from any consideration of whether this is helping to meet the organization's communications objectives. But professional communicators recognize the importance of measurement and evaluation in PR planning. Measurement and evaluation should be viewed as essential – if this is not built into your plan how will you know if you have succeeded?

Used at its worst, evaluation will help justify defensively what the organization spends on communications expenditure. Used at its best it will encourage rational, analytical thinking that will enable the organization to improve on past performance and achieve focused and defined results.

In 2010 the seven 'Barcelona Principles' were published by the International Association for the Measurement and Evaluation of Communication, following a summit in (you've guessed it) Barcelona. These principles remain the central to any discussion about how we measure our effectiveness and corporate communicators:

1 Measurement and goal-setting are fundamental to any PR programme.
2 Media measurement requires quantity and quality measures; quantity measures on their own are useless.
3 Advertising Value Equivalents (AVEs) are not the value of PR.
4 Social media can and should be measured.
5 Measuring outcomes is preferable to measuring outputs.

6 Business results can and should be measured wherever possible.

7 Transparency and replicability are paramount to sound measurement.

The core idea is that research, measurement and evaluation are built into every stage of the communications process. That's not to say it is more important than having great creative ideas that cut through the noise of modern life. These disciplines are just as important, just often forgotten about, as they are sometimes a challenge for us. We'll come to this a little later.

Communications planning – writing a brief

Rigorous self-analysis is the starting point. An understanding of where the organization is now is essential for us to set a course to help us reach our desired destination. It's as simple as that. Spending time thinking is not a luxury – it is vital and will enable you to develop a brief that leads to a public relations strategy that is reasoned and logical.

You must be prepared to ask hard questions to flush out the important or hidden issues. The communications/PR brief is an essential piece of kit, whether you are going to use it internally, use it as the briefing document for a consultancy or write a brief for agreement with a client. These key questions will get you started:

1 The marketplace/environment:
- What market/sector/environment is the organization operating in?
- What are the prevailing dynamics? What are the key communications issues?
- Is the market growing or shrinking?
- What are the current market/sector shares?
- Which players are gaining/losing ground – and why?
- Who is winning the communications battle – and why?
- Who are the main stakeholders? Is this changing – and why?

2 The organization:
- What is the recent/distant history of the organization?
- SWOT analysis – What are the organization's Strengths and Weaknesses, and what Opportunities and Threats face it in the environment in which it operates?
- PESTLEE analysis:
  - **Political**

    What is happening politically in the environment in which you operate, including areas such as tax policy, employment laws, environmental regulations, trade restrictions and reform, tariffs and political stability?

- **Economic**

  What is happening within the economy, economic growth/ decline, interest rates, exchange rates and inflation rate, wage rates, minimum wage, working hours, unemployment (local and national), credit availability, cost of living?

- **Sociological**

  What is happening socially in the markets in which you operate or expect to operate, cultural norms and expectations, health consciousness, population growth rate, age distribution, career attitudes, emphasis on safety, global warming?

- **Technological**

  What is happening technology-wise that can impact what you do? How will it impact your products or services? Things that were not possible five years ago are now mainstream, for example mobile technology and social networking. New technologies are continually being developed and the rate of change itself is increasing. There are also changes to barriers to entry in given markets, and changes to financial decisions like outsourcing and insourcing.

- **Legal**

  What is happening with changes to legislation? This may impact employment, access to materials, quotas, resources, imports/exports, taxation, etc.

- **Environmental**

  What is happening with respect to ecological and environmental aspects? Many of these factors will be economic or social in nature.

- **Ethical**

  What is happening ethically and morally in the environment in which you operate, including examples such as supply chain management and child labour, animal experimentation, assisted suicide and so on?

  Also consider:

  - What is the organization's culture like?
  - What are the overall:
    - corporate aims;
    - strategic directions;
    - sales and marketing objectives;
    - existing/new products/services;
    - plans for the future?

- How does the organization see itself now?
- What vision does it have for itself in, say, the next 5 to 10 years?
- What will help the organization achieve its goals? What will stand in the way?
- Who are the key management players?

3 Communications:
  - How has the organization managed communications in the past:
    - in-house;
    - consultancy;
    - both?
  - What resources are allocated to communications? Is the person responsible for communications operating on his or her own on a day-to-day basis? How is the budget set?
  - What skills does the current team have? Are there any gaps/needs for communications/PR/general business training and development?
  - Is there an international aspect to communications management?
    - central coordination;
    - local implementation.
  - Who manages communications in the organization? Where do communications lie in terms of reporting structures?
  - What sorts of communications/PR has the organization undertaken (for example, corporate, consumer, B2B, etc)? What has worked?
  - How is communications/ PR viewed in the organization? What is its status? How does the rest of the organization relate to the communications team?
  - What is the internal relationship between communications/PR and the other marketing disciplines (advertising, sales promotion, direct marketing, etc)?
  - How is media planned? Are there audits to ascertain the best media to meet the objectives?

4 Communications collateral:
  - What materials does the organization currently have for the purposes of communications/PR?
    - Online press office – with logos, images, press releases, backgrounders and profiles on the organization, key personnel, products/services, video production to create content for the website and for media outlets.

- – Literature – consumer leaflets, corporate brochures, sales kits, branded materials, newsletters, bulletins, in-house and contract magazines – pdf format and print if audiences require this.
- – Printed press materials – paper, folders, background releases (for press conferences, when sending with product samples and other occasions when printed versions are preferable).
- – Branded merchandise – mouse mats, clothing, calendars, gifts, incentives, etc.
- Who is responsible for this? Is it communications/PR-led?

5 Research:
- What research does the organization have at its disposal:
  - – qualitative and quantitative;
  - – continuous and ad hoc;
  - – desk research;
  - – media coverage analysis – online, print, broadcast?
- Who evaluates? How are results reported, circulated and acted upon?

If the brief is to be given to a consultancy as part of a pitch or tender process, then the following additional information should be included:

6 Consultancy pitch process:
- What sort of response is required to the brief?
- What budget will be allocated to the consultancy?
- If 10 per cent is allocated to evaluation, how will this be deployed?
- What is expected at the pitch itself?
- When will the pitch take place?
- Who will be working on the business?

Once the brief has been written and interrogated then a response can be made in the form of a carefully considered strategic plan.

Best practice in communications planning

There has been more written about measurement and evaluation in public relations than any other aspect of the business over the past decade, particularly in relation to digital communications. *The CIPR Toolkit*, researched and written by Michael Fairchild MCIPR and first published in 1999, was revised and reprinted in 2001 and a 2003 edition looked exclusively at media planning, research and evaluation. An updated online version was published in 2010, which for the first time included guidance about digital media as well as tips on how to link PR measurement to what else is happening within organizations. It is indispensable for strategic communications planning, whether for a three-month launch campaign for a new product or a five-year corporate reputation programme.

The toolkit outlines five stages in planning. It is possible to look at them in a different order (although the audit is the foundation and always comes first). For example, you might start with a thorough description and visualization of your outcome or objective (and the technique 'Back to the Future' in Chapter 8 on creativity encourages this). Or you might start with the target for communications and get under the skin of the people you intend to engage with through communications (so look at Chapter 6 on audiences). The important thing is to make sure you do all five steps. These are:

1 audit;
2 objectives setting;
3 strategy and plan;
4 ongoing measurement;
5 result and evaluation.

Stage one – audit – which answers the question 'Where are we now?' and flushes out the key issues that the communications strategy needs to address

At the outset thorough research and analysis is needed to look at key communications issues and the current views, attitudes and behaviours of all relevant stakeholders. Some of this is likely to be included in the brief but other data-gathering techniques might include:

- Research (and lots of it) – brand tracking, online surveys, shoppers surveys, telephone research, qualitative and quantitative, continuous and ad hoc – this includes online research, usage and awareness studies, focus groups, vox pops, telephone research, postal questionnaires, etc.
- Stakeholder and target audience analysis – commissioned and/or desk research compiled by a research company such as Target Group Index (TGI), National Opinion Polls (NOP), Gallup, YouGov, etc.
- Informal discussion – with trade associations, opinion-formers, etc.
- Desk research – of reports and commentary on the market and the organization, eg Mintel, Datamonitor. Searching online is included here too.
- Media analysis – using National Readership Survey (NRS), Broadcasters' Audience Research Board (BARB), Radio Joint Audience Research (RAJAR), Metrica and other media-evaluation

companies and/or media packs – covering online media, blogs, broadcast media and print media.

- Media audit – getting the views of the media on the industry, sector, issues and/or the organization itself.
- Review of media coverage – simple or complex depending on need and budget.
- Incorporating your PESTLEE analysis.

All or any combination of these data-gathering techniques should be used at the outset of the programme, at regular intervals during the work, depending on budget availability, and at the end of the work to allow for evaluation. Planning is only as good as the quality and quantity of information that is put in. Don't make false economies by under-investing in information gathering. A properly researched plan will make the difference between wasting your budget on a campaign that fails to meet its objectives and one that hits its target.

This checklist might help you consider what research you need to do to gain that all important insight before you make any decisions about your communications objectives. We'll look at audience understanding in more detail in Chapter 6.

Insight methodologies checklist:

- Which methods are appropriate for your organization? Either (or both):
  - qualitative methods – useful for examining content (eg media comment, speeches, etc) and understanding why and how;
  - quantitative methods – eg to gain insight into how big or small an issue is; to answer questions like 'how often' and 'how many'.
- Are they affordable?: £ (low cost) – £££ (high cost)?
- Are they accessible?: ✓ (yes) or ? (possibly)?

Stage two – objectives setting – which answers the question 'Where do we want to be?' and sets the targets and goals for communications

Objectives indicate motion, either towards a stated goal or away from an existing position. They should be quantifiable and hence have some sort of measurable element. So the objectives you set for PR should always be SMART (Specific, Measurable, Achievable, Resourced and Timed) and should build on the organization's overall strategic direction and be synergistic with other business objectives. They should support the business strategy and, most likely, will focus on these sorts of areas:

- increasing awareness;
- educating, informing and generating understanding;
- supporting sales efforts;

TABLE 4.1 Finding out – research and audit tools

Affordability/ Accessibility	Considerations
Desk research £ ✓	**From public and private internal and external sources:** • Own and partners' research (eg research and development department, advertising agencies, etc) • Government data (eg National Audit Office, Office for National Statistics, etc) • Databases • Other examples from think tanks, business, universities, consumer bodies, trade associations
Digital £ ✓	**Relevant sites used by stakeholders and target audiences – monitored and analysed:** • Websites • Key bloggers • Twitter, Facebook, LinkedIn • YouTube
Verbal comment £ ✓	**Quotable quotes and testimonials from opinion-formers and influencers which might include:** • Informal/ad hoc feedback • Speeches • Media coverage, eg a business leader's views may be representative of the those of a sector • Verbatim • Spontaneous or elicited
Documentary evidence £ ✓	**Collection of supporting evidence from written and electronic correspondence and documents which might include:** • Transcripts of speeches • Legislation • Official documents

(Continued)

TABLE 4.1 (*Continued*)

Observations £ ✓	**One's own and others which might include:** • In-store observations • People watching • Anecdotal evidence
Media analysis (including digital) £ ✓	**To assess reach (amount – target audience), content (prominence and messaging) and effectiveness (accuracy, tone)** **Print/broadcast:** • Media name and type (eg radio station/TV channel/ website name and whether print, broadcast or digital) • Description – article/broadcast, eg announcement, interview with X, article about Y, etc • Journalist/presenter/blogger name • Date and time • Approx circulation/audience figures • Region, language • Favourability – positive, neutral or negative • Impact based on size and prominence • Accuracy – message repeated accurately or not; message understood? **Websites:** • Page views/impressions • Visits • Downloads • Search terms • Came from • Click through • Visitors • Hits • Time spent on page **Social media:** • Traffic/viewings • Interaction/comments • Audience delivery (eg number of followers) • Influencer interest/commentary (eg retweeting)

(*Continued*)

TABLE 4.1 (*Continued*)

Feedback or evaluation questionnaires (formal or informal collation) £ – ££ ✓?	**To assess the quality of an activity and its impact:** • About events: expectations, quality, satisfaction, relevance • About target audiences: media/channel usage, engagement in issue (previous and future) • Reaction: to messages already delivered (agree/disagree); informative, stimulating • Impact: eg change in knowledge, understanding, awareness, attitude, intention (eg will they discuss this with others?) *NB: questionnaires can be followed up afterwards (eg 3 –6 months later) and so allow extended communications opportunities*
Interviews • structured • semi-structured • in-depth £ – ££ ✓?	• Telephone • Face-to-face • One-to-one • Groups
Focus groups ££-£££ ?	• Logistics: location, number of groups, number of participants per group • Audience(s): definition and recruitment (eg incentivization) • Content: how to start and end, topic areas • Skills: eg facilitation
Public opinion polls/surveys (ad hoc, continuous/tracking or pre and post activity) £££ ?	• How: on the street, personally, e-mail, postal • Audience: who, how many • Content: getting the questions right, eg not leading respondents to a positive answer

- overcoming misunderstanding or apathy;
- engaging in debate and raising interest levels;
- reassuring, particularly after an issue has gone live or a crisis has occurred;
- confirming or challenging perceptions;
- changing behaviour.

AMEC's useful communications objectives funnel can help us understand where people are on an issue and where we want them to be. Look back at Chapter 2 and some of the key theories and you will find that setting communications objectives is all about understanding your audience and their psychological attitudes and current behavioural patterns.

Communications objectives should not:

- Include or infer *guaranteed* media coverage – professional communications practice will *enhance* the likelihood of media coverage but where there is a free press quality editorial coverage is not for sale.

- Include or infer inappropriate influence with political targets – for obvious reasons, not least because the PRCA Code of Conduct prohibits this.

- Cover up problems – if a communications practitioner believes there is any issue that may cause danger to life, health or has other implications for the organization's reputation, it is his or her duty to bring this to light immediately and take appropriate action.

- Promise direct sales – although professional practice will certainly support the sales effort and create a climate where sales can flourish.

I look at the case histories in professional publications, examples of programmes written up by clients and both entrants and award-winners for professional gongs and I remain disappointed that the objectives that are included are simply too vague and often include statements of strategy.

TABLE 4.2 AMEC's communications objectives funnel

No Awareness	Awareness	Knowledge	Interest	Preference	Action
I know nothing about this issue/ brand	That is something I have heard of – it is on my radar	I have enough information to be able to understand how this works	I am interested in this issue/ brand	I like this – I am primed to buy it or support it	I do something – I buy it, I speak out, I vote

The more we pay attention to objectives, the clearer the goal of our work becomes.

Here are just four examples:

Client 1 (consumer – voluntary sector organization)

To change negative perceptions among the general public about people with learning difficulties. (No – what perceptions exactly? General public is vast – is this what the research tells us? Do we have the resources for this? Over what timescale?)

A SMART objective might be to increase agreement with the statement that 'most people with learning difficulties can take on meaningful work' among managers in SMEs (currently only 23 per cent agree with this statement) over a two-year period, measured by a repeat of the survey undertaken this year.

Client 2 (consumer – retailer)

To generate increased footfall in our stores over the Christmas period. (No – is the increase by just one shopper? All stores? Or flagships? Locally or regionally? When does Christmas period start and finish? Is this a PR objective alone or will there be an integrated campaign using advertising and promotions all working towards achieving the same objective? Or will advertising and promotions be measured using sales figures?)

A SMART objective might be to increase the total number of shoppers entering our 50 top stores in major cities across the UK measured by our existing in-store Infra-red system, measured through the four trading weeks leading up to 24th December and compared to last year's result.

Client 3 (business-to-business – manufacturer of office equipment)

To increase awareness of our range of office machinery and stationery among buyers/procurement officers/office managers. (No – there are two product ranges here and the current awareness levels for each may be different so it's a compound objective. Also awareness might be enough but you might need to take people further along the objectives path towards action and purchase.

SMART objectives might be to maintain the high level of awareness of our stationery ranges among buyers/procurement officers/office managers (currently 95 per cent) while at the same time increasing their knowledge of our office machinery range (currently 22 per cent, aiming for 50 per cent) over 12 months, supporting a goal of increased sales of both ranges over 24 months.

Client 4 (business – public sector)

To position ourselves as the authority on overseas trade, able to support British businesses trade successfully in developing markets like Brazil, Russia, India and China. (This is not an objective at all – this is a strategy, a 'how to do' an objective – so what precisely are you trying to achieve?)

A SMART objective might be to increase by 25 per cent the number of enquiries coming to us from British companies in the design sector requesting our support and advice about trading overseas in developing economies over the next 12 months.

Stakeholders/target audience

You may have a short list or a long list of stakeholders that may include some and/or all from the following lists. Be focused in your selection and drill down to identify specific targets where you can achieve the most through more concentrated effort. Organizations working in an international context will have to take into account the audiences in each country they operate in. This means taking into account significant cultural, social and political differences and the media scene in that country. Budget availability inevitably focuses the mind in terms of agreeing priority audiences.

Internal audiences Always include this important group in PR planning – they can be your most ardent, loyal supporters and ambassadors or your most cynical and jaded detractors – this group might include:

- employees;
- management/directors/trustees;
- potential staff;
- supporters/members;
- unions;
- pensioners;
- suppliers (sometimes regarded as an internal audience by some organizations where they are working in close partnership);
- the influencers reaching these targets;
- the media used by these targets – websites, social networking groups, bloggers, newsletters, noticeboards, payroll communications.

Get internal audiences on side. Let them know what is going on. Where it is OK to do so (for example if an organization has a network of local groups), encourage them to be media-friendly, particularly if they might come into contact with the media themselves when out and about. Give frontline employees and those working in the field media training if you know they could be targeted by the media. Work with your human resources or training team to use the best systems and processes.

External audiences You will need to consider all possible external targets you are likely to have an interface and dialogue with. Some people say the media can be both a target (prioritized influential journalists from elite media coming top of the list) and a channel to reach audiences. So target audiences might include:

- Joe Public – broken down into broad groupings, which could include for example, consumers, women, parents, taxpayers, etc;
- professional groups, eg teachers, bankers, farmers, small business owners, etc;
- opinion-formers;
- pressure groups;
- the local/regional community;
- government and political targets – MPs, special and all-party committees, civil servants;
- customers/potential customers;
- business partners;
- international targets – for international programmes;
- financial targets – shareholders/owners, banks, financial advisers and agencies, the City;
- commercial and trade targets – suppliers, wholesalers/retailers/ dealers, competitors;
- influencers who will affect your target audience's opinions about you (eg midwives on pregnant women, teachers on children, accountants on small business owners, etc);
- the media used by these targets – websites, specific social networking sites, bloggers, print media, broadcast media.

Stakeholder mapping exercises can help get a perspective on which stakeholders should be prioritized on the basis of their spheres of influence. (Take a look at techniques in Chapter 6 on target audiences.)

Timescale

While communications/PR is a continuous and sustained process, specific briefs and campaigns may need short, sharp programmes. The launch programme of a new yogurt for example may require a short sharp 'burst' of communications activity to meet objectives relating to awareness and trial. But a corporate reputation programme is more likely to be longer term, structured over at least a one-year, but preferably a three-year period. Changing entrenched attitudes and prejudices, for example the assumption that all people with a learning difficulty cannot hold down a job, may need longer so be realistic about objectives and timescales. Use planning aids for timing and build in contingency time for approvals, holidays and seasonal and national events like Christmas and general elections.

Budget

PR is not free advertising. Achieving editorial media coverage requires resourcing – it doesn't come free. If you have a big job to do with communications, prioritize carefully during the planning process and tackle audiences in logical steps, one by one if needs be over the course of, say, three years. Don't try to do everything at once or you will only end up doing nothing particularly well. You will need to make budgetary allowances for:

- human resources – you and your in-house team, your consultancy(ies) and freelance support when you need it (eg when short-staffed, over peak periods and for maternity cover);
- operational costs – brought-in costs from third parties – including events management, photography, editorial promotions and expenses incurred in running them, monitoring/evaluation;
- administration – web updating, postage, fax, equipment, overheads – everything you need to keep the press office working on a day-to-day basis.

Messages/content

Having a clear sense of what you want to get across is essential for successful communications programmes. And while in the past this has often been referred to as 'messaging', perhaps now it's more appropriate to talk about content, as engagement comes with dialogue and two-way communications, not the one-way delivery of a message, which in the age of social media is ineffective.

That said, it will help you focus if you first think about what it is you want your audience to understand, consider and act on. So it's still worth defining your key messages so that they are understood by everyone (ie your spokespeople and representatives) who will be charged with delivering them to stakeholders. Prioritize them so the most important is delivered first. Keep messages simple – don't use complicated language or jargon. Go for messages that are motivating and memorable. Pare down your messages to a handful and really refine and hone them. Three is the magic number – more key messages than that and you start diluting their power and effect. You also make it much harder for your spokespeople to do their job effectively and confidently.

Summarize each key message with a keyword. Turning messages into compelling content is achieved by supporting those messages with evidence and examples so you can tell your story vividly and memorably, during presentations, media interviews and copy of all kinds, from blogs to annual reports. If you use key messages well they enable you to structure what you want to say before you say it and help you stay focused, and avoid drifting off the point.

Here's an example of three key messages for a 'beleaguered' retailer:

- Customer-led – everything we do, we do to meet the needs of our customers – eg our new wider organic range was launched in response to demands from our customers for everything from baked beans to olive paste.
- Quality – we will not cut corners or compromise on quality, eg our in-store bakery uses only the highest quality organic white and brown flour from Canada which gives better-tasting and better-textured bread, even though it does cost a little more.
- Staff-friendly – our staff are our route to our customers and we know that the better they feel about working for us, the better the service to the customer, eg our new staff uniforms have been designed to be more comfortable, more fashionable, more wearable.

In summary, the core message that must come through in every communications activity, every media interview, every leaflet, every blog post:

'We put people first.'

Keeping content fresh and interesting

Great editors and journalists are experts at creating great content – it's about making sure that the material will be found interesting by the listener or reader. In other words while your message is important, people won't listen unless they find something in it that they are able to engage with. So learn to package what you want to say in stories – irresistible, engaging, helpful stories. Stories that are well constructed, that are visual and descriptive, not just a list of facts and figures (although one killer fact can really help get a message across); stories that have a hero and sometimes a villain, and that have a problem or predicament at the heart of them that demands action and a solution. Because this is where you can deliver your message about your organization's policy, product, service.

Just as the media focuses on current events to help maintain relevancy and interest, so should you. Twitter is an immediate source of news and views that can help you link your message to what's happening now. Linking to current affairs can help get attention and connects your organization to the wider world.

Ideas for compelling content can also come from asking and analysing the questions you are asked by users of your service or your customers and clients. For example, to be able to say, as a utility company 'Our customers frequently ask questions about the services we provide and what they are paying for – so just think for a moment about your own home. Beneath your garden, driveway or path there are two rather important pipes that you should be aware of – a water supply pipe, which delivers water in your home from our main in the street, and a sewer pipe, which flushes all your wastewater into our sewers…'. Even sewage pipes can be interesting if you package the message in a story. In this way you are immediately showing you are people-focused and this is the most compelling content of all, as people love to hear about people in concrete and real examples.

If you have clear messages and can present them in a compelling way, then you may engage with your audiences and hence begin the process of dialogue. Social media makes this possible and desirable. Don't be afraid of discussion and dialogue – welcome it because it indicates people are interested! If people are prompted to agree and support you, terrific – if they are prompted to disagree or even oppose you, welcome this too. It means you have succeeded in engaging with them, they show that it matters to them and that they care one way or another and this gives you a platform for further debate.

Stage three – strategy and plan which answers the question, 'How do we get there?' and outlines the plan of action

The *Oxford English Dictionary* gives two definitions of strategy:

- The plan to achieve a long-term aim.
- The planning and direction of military activity in a war or battle.

Public relations strategy emerges from the careful analysis of evidence, the prioritization of audiences, and the clarification of the message – before any tactics are considered. Public relations strategy describes the overarching framework that defines how we will achieve those carefully considered public relations objectives. It is sometimes expressed as 'the big idea'. And it is always exciting if a 'big idea' can be arrived at, as this can inspire those responsible for its delivery. In the advertising industry, the creative strategy is the Big Idea.

Timescales also have an impact on strategic solutions. Some of us will be developing short campaigns, others of us longer-term programmes, and this in itself steers us towards quite different strategies.

In my experience, strategy usually needs to be expressed in written form for inclusion in proposal papers for wide-ranging communication purposes and may also be concentrated into a shorthand expression. For example, describing the strategy for Example two (long-term repositioning programme) in Table 4.3:

Communicate that we are the voice of authority in our sector by using our research capacity to show the breadth and depth of our expertise. We will seek face-to-face opportunities to present ourselves to influencers in the sector and will support this with the publication of interesting and thought-provoking reports that capture the imagination of the media and clients and customers.

TABLE 4.3 How objectives, strategies, channels and tactics may differ for different lengths of campaign/programme (adapted from Gregory, 2010)

	Example one: Single objective short-term campaign	Example two: Long-term repositioning programme
Objective	• Create spontaneous awareness of a new product among 75 per cent of target audience in first three months after launch (in support of sales objectives)	• Achieve acknowledgement (50 per cent of target audience) that organization is the market leader in the sector
Strategy	• Get respected, relevant media coverage, endorsing the product	• Position as industry 'voice of authority' using research expertise
Channels	• Niche and specialist press (print and online) • Social media: Bloggers, Facebook and Twitter	• Face-to-face • Print • Elite media • Social media
Tactics	• Press briefings • News story • Photography • Product testing • Competitions	• Publication of research reports • Literature • Speaking engagements • Blogs • Award scheme

In other words 'We are the most intelligent organization in the sector.'

Never omit statements of strategy from your proposals. They are not a repeat of the objective – they are a clear statement of the ways in which you will create awareness, generate interest and engagement and change behaviours. What influencing strategy will work with this target audience? This is where the theories of communications outlined in Chapter 2 are so helpful. It is also when creative thinking comes into play.

In my experience advertising agencies do this brilliantly while PR consultants do not. The clear statement of strategy is often missing and people jump straight to channels and tactics. When strategy is considered and included, there is a real focus and concentration.

Channels

We will discuss these in Chapter 7. Channels are chosen determined by what the audience uses, how many of the audience use the channel, what has the greatest influence on the audience and what your budget will stand. Channels you can use might include:

- face-to-face;
- word-of-mouth/multiplier endorsement;
- digital;
- media (social and traditional);
- print;
- audio-visual.

Tactics

Again this is when we use our creativity and apply it to the actuals – to so-called 'deliverables'. Again we'll discuss some of the practical issues in Chapter 7.

Tactics include:

- media relations – news stories, features, case histories, writing and responding to blogs, picture/video stories, letters campaigns, editorial promotions, etc;
- online activities – including virals, social networking groups, video and picture sharing;
- special events;
- competitions and award schemes;
- product launches;
- opinion-leader communication;
- educational programmes;
- research;
- corporate ID;
- sponsorship;
- publications/literature/websites/AV;
- seminars, conferences and hospitality;
- visits and press trips.

Stage four – ongoing measurement which answers the question, 'Are we getting there?' and helps review strategy to ensure corrective action is taken if required

The CIPR, AMEC and evaluation specialist companies have been working hard on this area of public relations for the past decade. Several important documents have been published that take us further forward. I don't propose duplicating what they say – instead I will summarize and make this as practical as possible to give you some ideas for effective monitoring.

Just remember that if you want to be seen as a professional public relations practitioner, you must measure the progress of your communications effort as you go. You should include observation and experience, feedback and analysis, social media and traditional media monitoring.

Each tactic should be measured and data collected throughout the activity period. You are likely to set up different criteria for each tactic, for example how many people visited the website, joined the online group, posted a comment, attended a conference, visited the stand, came to the specially hosted event, requested a leaflet/sample? If the data is collected in year one then a comparison can be made with years two and three to help work out whether a tactic continues to be useful and cost-effective. Research among delegates at an annual conference for example gives important information and can be used to determine whether awareness, attitudes or behaviour are changing over time.

How can you measure changing attitudes and behaviours? We talk about the measurement of inputs, outputs, outtakes and outcomes, and the last two are concerned with the changes effected in the target audiences. So collect this evidence as you conduct your campaigns and programmes and you have all the material you need to write a professional and satisfying evaluation report (which is what you do at Stage five).

Inputs

Background information and research undertaken at the audit stage. Some of this could provide benchmarks against which to measure later. Input measures include:

- the PR brief (the information on organization/sector);
- desk research and original research (that informed content of the agreed PR strategy);
- pre-testing (where messages and/or materials are checked prior to use).

Outputs

The messages that went out from the organization. This is a quantifiable measure analysing the degree of exposure of messages and the audience reach. It won't measure whether opinions or behaviour have been influenced. Many PR campaign measures are built around outputs. But this really doesn't enable us to show the significant impact of our work in achieving communications and hence business objectives. Outputs measures include:

- news issued and coverage monitored (media measurement);
- website (traffic analysis);
- events (who and how many attended?);
- research surveys (that have been used to inform the strategy and plan).

Outtake

Measures that tell us whether the audience is aware of our messages, understood and remembered them and the response this has provoked. This can be tracked online via tweets, blog comments or online community threads. Findings from representative samples of the target audience during the course of a programme can confirm that a campaign is working as intended or give a heads-up that we need to change tack. Outtake measures include:

- media commentary;
- online tracking of comments, feedback and engagement with audiences;
- qualitative/quantitative research to check understanding of and response to messages.

Outcomes

The most valuable but perhaps hardest to achieve measurements. Has the programme changed people's awareness, thoughts, opinions, feelings and behaviours? This gives concrete evidence tracing outcome to PR activity and the basis for assessing the return on the investment (ROI) of PR. When outcome is measured information can be fed back into next-stage planning and deliver greater value over time. You'll find more on measuring attitude and behaviour change in Chapter 6 on understanding audiences. Outcome measures include:

- Comparing the results with measures taken before the campaign/ programme commenced.
- Comparing results with the SMART objectives set.
- 'Hard' evidence (quantitative research, sales, numbers, a vote passed).
- 'Soft' evidence (qualitative research, observation, anecdotal).
- What did each PR/research method contribute?
- What was the return on PR investment for the whole programme and for individual components?
- What are the lessons for next time?

(Adapted from Macnamara, 2008)

Media monitoring

Media is generally defined as being online, press, radio and TV. But it also extends any published material such as report and accounts, government publications and news wires. Media measurement can be conducted on its own or in conjunction with other forms of research – for example, interviews with target audiences to see what extent media relations has influenced levels of awareness or opinion. It is important to measure both quality and quantity of coverage.

Print and broadcast media measurement usually takes into account some or all of the following measures:

- AVEs (or advertising value equivalents); although the third 2010 Barcelona Principle stated that 'AVEs are not the value of PR' the industry tolerates the use of AVEs mainly because people continue to use them. Jeffries-Fox gave us this definition:

  AVEs are calculated by measuring the column inches (in the case of print), or seconds (in the case of broadcast media), and multiplying these figures by the respective medium's advertising rates (per-inch or per-second). The resulting number is what it would have cost to place an advertisement of that size in that medium.

But editorial is not advertising. We usually say it's worth more and that's why we pursue the goal of positive media coverage. In fact some people multiply the value of coverage by a factor of three or four – or even more – because editorial coverage is read and remembered better than straight advertising. And how can you put a value on a three-minute interview on BBC 1 where there is no advertising rate?

PR and advertising do not perform the same role but AVEs imply that public relations is 'cheap advertising'. But no high-preforming media-buying agency would pay rate card figures when buying space for a client. And what about the times when the PR practitioner is attempting to reduce or prevent coverage appearing? What about negative stories, and an extensive story covering a range of topics, with only a passing mention of the organization in question? And how about coverage in an 'expensive' medium aimed at the wrong target audience?

- Volume of coverage – numbers of web pages, column inches, TV or radio interviews.
- Audience reach – how many of the target audience did you reach through the campaign? For example, was it 100 per cent or 70 per cent of all men aged 18–44? Was it 100 per cent or 50 per cent of all taxpayers? Or was it 100 per cent or 20 per cent of all financial advisors in London and the South East?
- Cost per thousand – the cost of the effort to achieve the coverage.
- Message delivery – did all three key messages get aired; only two – or just one?

- Slant of coverage – was it positive, negative or neutral? Believe me, neutral is a terrific result if coverage has been damning for the past three years.

- Where it appeared – did the coverage appear in *Media Guardian*, in print or on the website, as a recommendation by the world's most influential and best read blogger on the subject, in the sports section, in the local paper section, on the letters page of *The Tablet*? Each of these might be exactly the right, and therefore most valuable, positioning – or not!

- Photography – how do you 'read' media and what attracts your eye first on a mobile phone page or a web page or a paper or the TV? Images immediately attract attention so a photo/or moving image is going to gain greater attention.

Monitoring social media

Those of us who aren't geeks need a straightforward and practical way to assess the impact of our activities using social media as a channel. The clear presentation of such information is getting better all the time enabling us to 'read' the runes more quickly and easily with 'dashboards' summarizing key points increasingly used to make the task of evaluation simpler. The great thing about social media is that you can look at reactions in real time and get a sense of how things are playing out quickly.

Straight output measures include tracking blogs, forums, comments, tweets, online news, social networks and video for mentions of your organization, your client or your competitors. You can assess both quantity (the number of Twitter followers, comments, tweets, retweets, @replies, DMs) and quality (based on ratings, YouTube comments/ratings, and sentiment scores showing positive, neutral or negative trends). It is also possible to group total information into useful sub-sections so you could look at location, language or media type. Links and sources plus keywords can be segmented and assessed. This type of analysis can help to inform the PR programme, by identifying what people are saying about your organization or client and key issues and trends, to track active commentators, user responses, likes, comments and actions. This sort of monitoring means you can respond, build relationships, apologize, join in, laugh with your audiences and share ideas back.

Do be careful though of some tools that claim to measure online influence. Influence 'calculations' that show 'likelihoods that your brand is being discussed', authors divided by total number of mentions are often flawed and won't help you pin down the elusive idea of influence. Influence is not just a question of high numbers. Think of a UK Ambassador in a key country who has amassed 100 Twitter followers (hardly a large number when compared to Lady Gaga, with 35 million followers at the time of writing). But if those 100 followers include the prime minister and minister of foreign affairs of the country he or she is posted in plus respected local opinion-formers, academics and elite broadcast journalists then that's one hell of a result. Be clear when you use terms like influence (when in fact you mean popularity), authority (which is the power, knowledge and expertise of the journalist, blogger or tweeter) and influence (which is the strength of the ability that person has to persuade your audience to think, feel or do something). Get to grips with, understand and identify those who influence your target audiences. Are your customers among your Twitter followers or Facebook friends? Are elite influential media contacts quoting or linking to particular bloggers or tweeters? Or does a particular journalist/blogger/commentator/tweeter have an impact on purchasing decisions because he/she is a recognized authority (think of the energetic and entertaining restaurant critic Jay Rayner)? What about the influence of consumer reviews or by recommendations to family and friends? Technorati will give an influence score based on the number of blogs linking back to a particular blog.

Professional bodies, media measurement specialists and academics are all considering how to take such output measures and link them through to ultimate outcomes. For example, how a beauty product's high ratings and positive online comments starts a discussion that leads to purchase and further recommendations. One of the most difficult issues is whether different influences can be isolated and this can be tricky if an integrated campaign using advertising, sales promotion, direct marketing and public relations has been adopted. To someone who started her career in advertising this is not new. It's just now perhaps more of an issue with digital/social in the mix. Questions people ask include:

- Did ratings or recommendations lead to an increase in sales? Or requests for further information?
- Did positive customer satisfaction scores or comments lead to an increase in sales or sales queries?
- If a PR programme led to increased web traffic, what was the result of this traffic? More queries/sales/downloads/contributions to a campaign/signatures on a petition/comments for a public consultation?
- Did online comments provide feedback that has been used to inform strategy/improve products or services?
- Have perceptions or awareness levels changed as a result? Has this led to greater engagement between an organization and its publics/support for initiatives/changes in behaviour?

Social media monitoring

What does it all mean? (The glossary of terms in Table 4.4 has been reprinted with permission from CIPR Planning Research and Evaluation, 2010 Version.)

TABLE 4.4 Social media monitoring

Social media monitoring/social media listening/buzz monitoring	The practice of listening to the online conversations relating to a brand, monitoring and reacting to what is being said as well as where it is being said, who is saying it and how influential they are.
Influence	The power of one individual to affect the behaviour, perceptions, attitudes or opinions of others. In social media terms, influence is often calculated from a combination of reach and resonance.
Influencer	An individual who has the power to substantially influence the behaviour or opinions of others, often due to perceived superior power, wealth, social status, expertise or intellect.
Sentiment	The attitude of an online user towards a person, brand, product, etc, as expressed online.
Sentiment scoring	A methodology for showing how people feel about a subject or brand, often expressed in simple terms as positive, negative or neutral.
Human sentiment analysis	Human (or manual) analysis of a comment or post, aiming to determine the attitude of the speaker towards a brand or topic.
Automated sentiment analysis	Analysis of a comment or post, aiming to determine the attitude of the speaker towards a brand or topic.
Reputation management	The process of monitoring a brand's actions and others' opinions towards these actions in order to identify actions which create a positive response and those which create a negative response. The brand can then act (or react), taking actions which it believes will create positive responses in order to enhance its reputation.
Monitoring platforms	Online tools or services used for monitoring social media, often gathering data from multiple sources, to enable individuals and brands to track online conversations and make real-time interventions.

(*Continued*)

TABLE 4.4 (*Continued*)

Boolean queries	A form of words used to define the precise terms of a search query, for use either in search engines or social media monitoring tools. For example, 'Orange' AND 'mobile' NOT 'fruit' would produce results that include the words 'Orange' and 'mobile', but exclude those containing the word 'fruit'. Longer queries enhance data accuracy but can require the skills of professional analysts.
Dashboard	A user-friendly administration page that enables non-technical users to view and manipulate the data produced by a monitoring platform. Dashboards sometimes also allow users to create and manipulate data queries.
Mapping	Data mapping is a way of representing the relationships between data points visually, making it easier to understand. Mapping social media connections can highlight the common connection points – ie highly connected individuals.
Data mining	The process of filtering and analysing data in order to identify patterns.
Reach	The number of people that are exposed to your content once it is posted online. Reach is generally measured in simple terms, such as followers (Twitter), fans (Facebook), views (YouTube) or visitors (blogs).
Conversations	Social media conversations can be defined as any form of written online interaction. This includes a series of related comments, status updates, tweets or forum posts. The 'conversation' on a specific topic is measured as the total number of mentions of the defined keywords for that topic.
Keyword	'Keyword' is term taken from search engine optimization (SEO). Any word or phrase that is being targeted for optimization (in SEO) or used in a search query (in monitoring and analytics) is a keyword.

(*Continued*)

TABLE 4.4 (*Continued*)

Share of voice	'Share of voice is a brand's advertising weight expressed as a percentage of a defined total market or market segment in a given time period. The weight is usually defined in terms of expenditure, ratings, pages, poster sites etc.' (Wikipedia)
Share of conversation	Share of conversation is the percentage of the total conversation within a specific industry sector on a specific topic in a given time period that refers to the brand. This percentage is usually measured against competitors operating in the same industry.
Natural language processing	'Natural Language Processing' (NLP) is used by linguistics experts to enable computers to extract meaning, including sentiment and mood, from human language. Many social media monitoring services rely on NLP to make their data filtering more accurate.
Tone	In social media terms, 'tone' is used as a measure of sentiment, ie positive, neutral or negative.
Mood	Not to be confused with 'sentiment' or 'tone', which relate to the feelings expressed in a piece of content, 'mood' is descriptive of the state of mind of the author. It is often represented by smiles :)
Resonance	A measure of content popularity based on how many times and who shares it. Made popular by Twitter's 'Promoted Tweets', which are rated on a complex measurement of resonance.

Stage five – results and evaluation which answer the question, 'Did we do it?' giving direction to and informing future plans

Given that public relations and communications professionals have struggled to prove their contribution to business for years, we must pay attention to how we finally interpret the data we gather during the programme through monitoring. We must know how to report results and how to deliver a sound analytical evaluation that demonstrates we understand what worked and what didn't and so come up with even better recommendations for the future.

The contribution public relations makes is often required to be reported as a return on investment (ROI), particularly in the private sector where sales and profits are goals. If a monetary value is involved, this has the advantage of 'translating' public relations outputs or outcomes into language other members of the organization, or client personnel – like procurement people or finance directors – can understand.

To calculate ROI, the benefit (return) of an investment is divided by the cost of the investment; the result is expressed as a percentage or a ratio. So if £10,000 was spent (ie invested) on a public relations programme that generated £50,000 of sales, the ROI is 500 per cent or 5:1.

Return on investment is a popular measure because of its versatility and simplicity. If an investment does not have a positive ROI, or if there are other opportunities with a higher ROI, then the investment should not be undertaken. The calculation for ROI can be adapted to suit the situation – it depends on what you include as returns and costs. This flexibility has a downside, as ROI calculations can be manipulated to suit the user's purposes. So if you use ROI, make sure you understand what inputs are being used. And always factor in your own and any consultancy time, not just the costs associated with the campaign or programme. No two programmes are ever the same. At the end of a programme or campaign, measure your success in communications against the set objectives. If you have been measuring at every step of the way you are more likely to have been modifying tactics as you go, thus increasing the likelihood of success.

Analyse what went right and what went wrong honestly and without retribution. Life is about learning – the person who never made a mistake never learned anything. Learning the lessons both good and bad from every communications programme you undertake, will help future planning and improve the contribution communications plays in building and maintaining your corporate reputation.

When reviewing consider using:

- management reports – to demonstrate to your management team the value of public relations in the organization;
- case histories – to tell the story of what the campaign accomplished, and why it worked, in a graphic, narrative and engaging way – sell in to relevant media and include in newsletters;
- presentations – to show how the campaign worked – designed for target audiences like directors/shareholders/trustees/colleagues/partners or to present at staff meetings;
- awards – enter campaigns you are proud of for CIPR Excellence or PRIDE awards.

Planning and evaluating PR

CASE HISTORY: Stockport Council's 'CarbOff' campaign

Background

In August 2010, an E.ON report rated Stockport as third worst 'energy obese' region in England – seventh worst in the UK. Stockport Council had already signed up to the ambitious global 10:10 campaign, linked directly into the council's strategic priority to be 'a leading green borough'. But a radical action was required. The council consulted on attitudes to climate change and how residents would like to receive information on this subject. The communication methods used reflect the results of that consultation. In September the same year Stockport's CarbON-CarbOFF campaign was launched in partnership with the Energy Saving Trust (EST).

Situation analysis

While householders were generally sympathetic to green issues, there was poor awareness of the impact of carbon emissions and a general lack of understanding about what could be done on a practical level. Also householders were concerned about rising domestic energy bills.

Target audiences:

- 282,975 Stockport residents;
- 22,000 local businesses;
- voluntary and community groups;
- 4,000 council staff (approximately 70 per cent live in Stockport).

Communications objectives

The business aim was to make Stockport's population the best informed on reducing carbon emissions, so that emissions were reduced by 10 per cent by 2011:
1 To raise awareness among and educate the **fuel rich** (owner occupiers and landlords) about on how to reduce carbon emissions and save money via loft insulation, cavity wall insulation.

2   To raise awareness and inform **the vulnerable and those on low incomes** of the range of energy efficiency services available.

3   To educate **residents, staff and businesses** on how to save money in these hard economic times while reducing their own carbon footprints.

These objectives supported local and regional strategic sustainability targets.

Key Messages:

1   You can reduce your carbon emissions and save money by installing loft and cavity wall insulation.

2   There are lots of practical ways to save energy and money.

3   Log onto our website for more help and advice.

Strategy

The campaign focused on encouraging everyone in Stockport to reduce the amount of carbon they produced, while taking into account the prevailing economic climate. Ways to save money while becoming 'greener' were highlighted. Working with the Energy Saving Trust meant that Stockport could offer residents a good way to reduce their carbon footprint, while saving money. Loft or cavity wall insulation was offered at a discounted price (a potential 75 per cent saving).

Delivery plan

Demonstrably cost-effective communications techniques are essential when public money is being used. A budget of £15,000 was allocated – the equivalent of 5p per resident, plus the offering of savings on residents' energy bills of up to £300, with the uptake of loft insulation.

Channels and tactics:

- Display/print – advertisements on buses.
- Social media channels – Facebook, Twitter, YouTube and a blog featuring a resident's 'Nearly carbon neutral' project.
- Face-to-face/events.
- Roadshows at the local B&Q superstore.
- Linking with the global 10:10 campaign, Stockport Council marked 10 October 2010 with a 'Light Switch Off' of Stockport Landmarks – the Town Hall, Viaduct and Co-op Pyramid.

- media relations – local media *The Stockport Review* and the Council's own newspaper.

Additional effort was made to target people living in areas of social deprivation. As well as coverage in the council newsletter, distributed to approximately 9,000 homes, A5 postcards were produced and distributed at council centres, offering advice on debts and promoting the insulation offer. An internal communications programme delivered key messages to the council's staff on the intranet and via internal newsletters.

Results – outputs:

- Bus advertising – 1.2 million opportunities to see and 84.4 per cent coverage over the six-week campaign.
- Media coverage – regular stories covered locally in print and on broadcast media in which 100 per cent included the three key messages.
- Online – 1,332 unique visitors, 2,458 visits and 3,777 page views to the dedicated web pages.
- Face-to-face – 500 people attended the roadshow events.

Results – outcomes:

- The council reduced its carbon emissions by 11 per cent, surpassing the target of 10 per cent set in 2010, a reduction of 3695 tonnes.
- Around 400 enquiries were received for cavity wall or loft insulation to the Energy Saving Trust's hotline during the campaign, resulting in a 74 per cent conversion rate from referral to installation, enabling many local residents to reduce their fuel bills in future.

And afterwards

Inspired by this approach, the Greater Manchester Environment Commission mounted a similar campaign across Greater Manchester to all 10 local authorities.

Stockport Council won one of the CIPR's prestigious Excellence Awards the following year (2012).

(Source – CIPR Excellence Awards)

Practitioners seeking more information about PR-planning and evaluation should consult two excellent companion books, both in Kogan Page's *PR In Practice* series:

The first, *Planning and Managing Public Relations Campaigns: A strategic approach* by Anne Gregory (2010) is now in its 3rd edition and is fully updated with a 10-point plan for ensuring successful campaigns and programmes. Practical and easy to read, it takes the form of a step-by-step guide, covering in detail some of the areas I have summarized here including research and analysis and setting objectives.

The second is *Evaluating Public Relations* by Tom Watson and Paul Noble. Tom and Paul have revised and updated their terrific book (2014) so that it looks in detail at all aspects of evaluation from traditional media to the online environment. For those of us charged with demonstrating the value of PR (all of us?) this in-depth look at ways to gather and present results is hugely useful.

05
Public relations, marketing and related disciplines

How does public relations relate to and fit with digital marketing, advertising and sales promotion? Should PR take the lead, rather than advertising, in determining strategy? Do you need separate digital strategy or is digital considered a specialist communications channel that needs specialist management? Is public relations really defined as specialist media relations, added in to the mix once the other parts of the marketing strategy are in place?

I lecture and run workshops on Integrated Communications for the Chartered Institute of Public Relations. Integrated programmes, where every part is working together in a coordinated way, offer organizations the best return on investment. The target audiences see consistent, cohesive messages repeatedly. And this helps memorability and cut-through. People may even remember your message accurately!

But throughout my career I have been variously dismayed and delighted by the way other marketers have understood and interpreted the role and value of public relations within a marketing strategy. As a PR consultant, I have been introduced to clients by peers from other disciplines – particularly digital, advertising and sales promotion – who have confidently announced that PR would deliver 'free space'. Likewise I have worked with PR people who think marketing is a dirty word. Turf wars can break out, usually if fees are at stake.

PR can play a fundamental part in the success of a coherent marketing strategy. Difficulties come from misconceptions and ignorance. Everyone involved in marketing should make an attempt to gain at least a basic understanding about the other's discipline so that synergy is achieved. If your marketing colleagues accept that communications/public relations is about reputation, then pretty quickly they should arrive at the conclusion that it has wider scope than just achieving media coverage. The right communications plan will deliver much more – it will help shift attitudes, surround your product or service with more positive values and imagery than the competition and thus contribute to the sales effort. Plus it will enhance your organization's overall position in the marketplace. It may even have an effect on the share price.

When I worked in-house in a marketing team I was respected as a specialist in my field while still being an equal member of that team, which included digital marketing, advertising, sales promotion, direct marketing and new media specialists. This is the position we should strive for if we find ourselves working inside the marketing environment. It is incumbent upon all of us as public relations practitioners to make sure public relations is recognized as being a central part of a fully integrated approach to communications.

Consider a multi-discipline, integrated marketing course, such as those offered by Communications Advertising and Marketing (CAM). The Communications Advertising and Marketing (CAM) Education Foundation is a registered charity that offers qualifications in digital and offline marketing communications. In 2000 the CAM Foundation formed an alliance with The Chartered Institute of Marketing (CIM) and, since then, CAM qualifications are awarded by CIM. This means that the CAM diplomas go through the same quality processes as the diplomas offered by CIM with assessments and results validated by the CIM Awarding Body. Students come from right across the spectrum of agency, client and supplier backgrounds. They work in digital marketing, advertising, public relations, the media, market research, sales promotion and direct marketing and are from private, public and not-for-profit sectors. Consequently you get a good grounding, not just from studying with these people but networking with them too.

Definitions of marketing

Marketing is the management process responsible for identifying, anticipating and satisfying customer requirements profitably. (The Chartered Institute of Marketing [CIM])

NB The CIM definition looks not only at identifying customer needs, but also satisfying them (short-term) and anticipating them in the future (long-term retention). It's not just about selling, and this shows how much marketing has moved towards PR, a danger for the PR profession perhaps.

1) Marketing is the process by which an organization relates creatively, productively, and profitably to the marketplace. 2) Marketing is the art of creating and satisfying customers at a profit. 3) Marketing is getting the right goods and services to the right people at the right places at the right time at the right price with the right communications and promotion. (Kotler and Keller, 2010)

The right product, in the right place, at the right time, at the right price. (Adcock *et al*, 2001)

There will always, one can assume, be a need for some selling. But the aim of marketing is to make selling superfluous. The aim of marketing is to know and understand the customer so well that the product or service fits him and sells itself... ideally, marketing should result in a customer who is ready to buy. All that should be needed then is to make the product or service available, ie, logistics rather than salesmanship, and statistical distribution rather than promotion. (Drucker, 2009)

What is the marketing mix?

In the early 1960s, Professor Neil Borden (Borden, 1964) at Harvard Business School in the United States identified a number of actions that can influence the consumer decision to purchase goods or services. Borden suggested that all those actions represented a 'marketing mix'. Professor E Jerome McCarthy (McCarthy, 1960), also at the Harvard Business School in the early 1960s, suggested that the marketing mix contained four elements: **product, price, place** and **promotion**.

In popular usage, 'marketing' is the promotion of products, especially advertising and branding. However, in professional usage the term has a wider meaning that recognizes that marketing is customer-centered. Services or products are often developed to meet the desires of groups of customers or even, in some cases, for specific customers. McCarthy divided marketing into four general sets of activities. His typology became so universally recognized that his 'Four Ps' became legendary:

- **P 1 Product** –The product aspects of marketing deal with the specifications of the actual services or goods, and how they relate to the customer's needs and wants.

- **P 2 Pricing** – This refers to the process of setting a price for a service or product, including discounts. The price need not be monetary – it can simply be what is exchanged for the service or product, eg time, energy, psychology or attention.

- **P 3 Promotion** – This includes advertising, sales promotion, PR and branding and refers to the various methods of promoting the service, product, brand or organization.

- **P 4 Place (or distribution)** – This refers to how the service or product gets to the customer; for example, location, point-of-sale, placement or retailing. It refers to the channel by which a service or product is sold (eg online v retail), which geographic region or industry, to which segment (young adults, families, business people), etc.

These four elements are often referred to as the marketing mix, which marketers use to craft their marketing plans. The Four Ps model is perhaps most useful when marketing low-value consumer products. Services, industrial products, high-value consumer products need some adjustment to this model. Services marketing has to take into account the unique nature of services. Industrial or business-to-business marketing needs to take into account the long-term contractual agreements that are typical in complex supply chain transactions. And Relationship Marketing attempts to do this by looking at marketing from a long-term relationship perspective rather than individual transactions.

Is it seven Ps now?

As well as the standard Four Ps, marketing a service rather than a product calls upon an extra three, totalling seven, so known together as the extended marketing mix. These are:

- **P 5 People** – Any person (whether paid or volunteer) coming into contact with customers can have an impact on overall satisfaction. Whether as part of a supporting service to a product or involved in a total service, people are particularly important because, in the customer's eyes, they are generally inseparable from the total service. As a result of this, they must be appropriately trained, well motivated and the right type of person. Fellow customers or service users also come under 'people', as they too can affect the customer's service experience (eg at an exhibition, fundraising event, conference, sporting event, etc).

- **P 6 Process** – This is the process(es) involved in providing a service which can be crucial to customer satisfaction; the ordering and delivery process for example.

- **P 7 Physical evidence** – Unlike a product, a service cannot be experienced before it is delivered, which makes it intangible. This, therefore, means that potential customers could perceive greater risk when deciding whether to use a service. To reduce the feeling of risk it is often vital to offer potential customers the chance to see what a service would be like and how others have experienced it and benefited from it. This is done by providing physical evidence, such as case studies, testimonials and demonstrations.

Three new Ps for the 21st century (and all because of Web 2:0)

- **P 1 Personalization** – This is the tailoring of services and products that many of us now use through the internet. Early examples included Dell online and Amazon.com but this concept is expanding massively.
- **P 2 Participation** – This is the idea that the customer wants to participate in what a brand stands for, where a product or service should go (for example a new service or extension), even how it should be advertised. This idea is paving the way for more deep change in the way marketing is practised through 'democratization'.
- **P 3 Peer-to-peer** – This is about the powerful influence of networks and communities where people become advocates or recommenders of a service or product. Marketing started pretty much with a 'push' process (think of TV advertising, where once upon a time people passively watched commercials). These days, media has to be 'pull' – to attract potential customers towards it, because of the huge amount of choice available through a wide range of devices and channels. Peer-to-peer has reached its zenith through social networking and may be the most revolutionary force in the future of marketing. If you have ever completed a Trip Advisor review or consulted the website to check out customers' reviews of a hotel or restaurant you are part of this revolution in marketing. And think about how influential a respected blogger's opinions can be.

Marketing, communications and customer-relationship management

The decision-making process – whereby a prospect becomes a customer – comprises five main stages, moving from awareness through to buying and then liking and remaining loyal to a company, product or service. Marketing and communications work hand in hand at each of these stages:

1 *Realization* – whereby the prospect recognizes that he or she needs something. That something might be a face cream, a car or a pension. The need may be prompted because a previous item has gone past its sell-by date or has run out – ie repeat or substitute purchase – or a new need is established. New needs may be prompted by editorial coverage, blogger recommendation, point-of-sale advertising, sales promotion and so on.

2 *Information search* – whereby the prospect seeks information about what is available from manufacturers' literature, advertisements, editorial features, recommendations from trusted individuals (including journalists' reviews and blogs) or trawls his or her memory for stored information and past experience.

3 *Evaluation of alternatives* – whereby the prospect judges which is the best choice by evaluating information against a set of criteria which will include price, colour and other variables, brand name and values, availability and so on.

4 *Purchase* – whereby the prospect becomes a customer, convinced to buy as a result of successful marketing techniques.

5 *After-sales experience* – whereby the customer judges whether the decision to purchase was correct based on experience of using the product/service, its performance, possible loyalty schemes, comments on the internet, the aftercare received from the company and so on.

Cause-related marketing

Increasing numbers of commercial companies/government departments and good causes are recognizing that, by teaming up for marketing purposes, they can work together for mutual benefit.

Objectives for the commercial company/government department might be to:

● increase awareness, raise the profile and enhance the image of the organization, brand or service;
● increase goodwill and understanding;
● demonstrate social/ethical responsibility by associating the company with a relevant good cause;
● improve relationships with current stakeholders/customers;
● increase awareness among potential customers;
● gain competitive advantage/increase sales;
● boost employee morale.

Objectives for the good cause might be to:

● gain stature by association with a well-known organization or brand;
● draw public attention to and increase awareness of the cause;
● raise funds.

The best cause-related marketing campaigns engage with the consumer – according to research conducted by Business in the Community nearly 90 per cent of consumers are more likely to purchase from a company associated with a good cause. Conversely people are inclined to stop dealing with a company if they disapprove of their business behaviour. It is worth considering cause-related marketing whether you are a commercial organization/government department or a good cause as the benefits can be considerable.

With a strong supporting proactive public relations programme this sort of campaign can work very hard indeed. And don't forget to enter into a solid contract, even if you are dealing with a lovely, empathetic good cause. These days it's best business practice and an important management discipline.

Sponsorship

The objectives for sponsorship are virtually the same as those for cause-related marketing. There are masses of sponsorship opportunities:

- sports – from the Olympics and Premier League through to amateur swimming;
- arts – opera, drama, jazz and pop concerts, art exhibitions;
- broadcast – sponsorships of one-off programmes, short-run series, soap operas, weather reports on commercial TV and radio;
- online – websites, social networking sites, virtual communities, where branding is offered;
- publications – for example letters pages, special features and so on.

Sponsorship checklist

Key questions when assessing whether a sponsorship offers value for money:

- Does this sponsorship reach our target audience, fit with our planning and our objectives? (If not, stop right here!)
- Is this an entirely new project? Would we be the first to be associated with this activity? Who has gone before us and what benefits did they believe they derived from the sponsorship? What are the benchmarks?
- If an existing project, does this activity already get social and traditional media coverage?
- How are the sponsor credits handled?
- What proportion of our target audience does this reach?
- What opportunities to see/hear are afforded? What is the cost per head?
- Are we one of a number of sponsors?
- What does it really cost? It's more than just the price of the sponsorship – it's also manpower, time, accommodation and travel expenses, hospitality, advertising and special packaging.

When budgeting for sponsorship don't forget all the extras including:

- time costs – negotiation time, project management time;
- stand and display costs – design, build, erection, management and strike at every event;
- staff costs – salaries, temporary staff, uniform/costume, expenses, travel, accommodation and subsistence;
- product costs – samples, branded merchandise;
- promotion costs – microsite and social network management, TV/radio/press advertising, direct mail, posters;
- research costs – for post-sponsorship evaluation.

Product placement

This is where a product is prominently located so it is seen and registered (sometimes almost subliminally) by the target audience. You might for example want to place your soap powder on the shelf of the corner shop in a well-known soap opera. You might alternatively want to prompt awareness of your new fruit drink at a pop festival. On social networking sites applications allow for virtual product placement. Product placement is usually paid for and competitively negotiated. It is close to and usually involves some sort of sponsorship deal or reciprocal advertising.

Advertising

Communicators and PR people are sometimes asked to 'PR' the advertising execution itself. The issue here is that the advertising does need to be groundbreaking, substantially different, even revolutionary as just the announcement of a new commercial is not in itself highly newsworthy. That being said great new ads can cause a sensation on the internet and on broadcast media if they are supported by a viral campaign. The aim is to get the ad talked about and passed round.

Marketing through other channels

On many occasions, organizations need the positive involvement of a third party – a wholesaler, distributor or dealer – who has a face-to-face relationship with the ultimate customer. On these occasions the PR practitioner may be able to bring new perspectives to the marketing planning so that all communications routes are explored, including e-communications, newsletters, media relations and so on. Additionally the PR practitioner may find him- or herself getting involved with events, roadshows, conferences and seminars and may be responsible for the management and creative input.

Integrated public relations

Integrated public relations programmes require the coordination of two or more communications disciplines to achieve their objectives. Messages are coherent and cohesive and consistent across all disciplines and those responsible for delivery understand and can work with others pursuing the same overall objectives, working supportively, in a spirit of cooperation and trust.

Integration may mean the coordination of a number of specialist public relations practices (consumer relations, government affairs, internal communications, community relations, corporate and city/financial, etc) together with advertising, marketing and sponsorship.

The keys to getting this right are:

- Leadership – making sure someone has overall authority and decision-making responsibility.
- Cooperative team approach – zero-tolerance given to energy-tapping power struggles in favour of a respectful, honest and open win–win way of working.
- Strategy and planning – so everyone understands the objectives.
- Being creative – which makes the whole process more enjoyable and productive.

Checklist

Use public relations as part of the marketing mix to:

- Enhance other marketing and promotional activity.
- Reach targets who may be difficult or uneconomic to reach via other techniques.
- Reach targets face-to-face via seminars, events, displays, awards schemes and ceremonies, demonstrations, presentations, etc.
- Provide vehicles for more detailed messages or to present products in an unusual setting.
- Provide sampling and trial opportunities.
- Solve a particular short-term problem related to a product or service.

06
Understanding audiences

Definitions

Stakeholders

A person, group or organization that has interest or concern in an(other) organization. Stakeholders are – or can be can – affected by what the organization says and does. Stakeholders include directors, employees, unions, shareholders and investors, government and government agencies, suppliers and the local community where the organization operates. They are not all equal and need prioritization, different communications strategies, and will almost certainly be communicated with via different channels. Interestingly the term stakeholders has lost its allure of recent years, most probably because of its overuse (and it sounds a bit like a piece of jargon).

Target audience

A particular group of people, identified as the intended receivers of a corporate message or content.

Publics

Communities of people (whether or not organized formally as a group) that have a direct or indirect association with an organization (eg clients, customers, employees, investors, media, students, etc).

Introduction

So is it public, stakeholder or target audience?

People use all these terms often interchangeably. In the end we are talking about people; people we want and need to communicate with. Each one with his or her own views, beliefs, attitudes, prejudices and behaviours and whose views, beliefs, attitudes, prejudices and behaviours we may want to influence. Each person is a complex cocktail, a unique cluster of memories, values, beliefs, life experiences. And each has an educational attainment level, an income level, a family background, a point of view. We need to take all of these into account when we are planning our communications programmes.

In the 21st century, organizations can identify specific groups and communicate with influential individuals and opinion-formers in increasingly sophisticated ways, mainly thanks to digital technology. If you buy a packet of biscuits each week at a supermarket and use a debit or credit card to pay, the retailer and the manufacturer know precisely how often you buy that brand and what pack size and variety you prefer. Turning data into information is a huge industry and it means that organizations that want to target you know whether you are single, working, have children or buy biscuits once a week. On Facebook you give it all away anyway, as soon as you hit 'like' KitKat. And then factor in PayPal, online shopping, JustGiving and charitable donations. Our lives are open books.

With instances of identity theft increasing all the time, many people argue that privacy is impossible, that you cannot avoid being targeted. With governments digitizing all their services, voting going online and more and more people using digital platforms, few people in developed countries remain off the digital radar. Such is the reality of modern life. On one level this is disturbing, Orwellian, sinister. On another level, it is exciting and creative, timesaving, enabling people to connect like never before, enabling people to mobilize, to organize protests, even to bring about the downfall of hated dictators.

Here we'll look at stakeholder mapping and segmentation, research techniques and audience insight, consider a few psychology ideas and think about how PR professionals can use psychological insight to add value to PR programmes.

A note about international communications and international audiences

A country's culture has a huge impact on how PR is practised in terms of how audiences are segmented. This will dramatically affect what strategies, channels and tactics will work in particular circumstances. Among others Sriramesh and Vercic (2009) looked at the macrofactors that need taking into account and these include:

- the penetration of technology and its availability to individuals at home or work;
- a preference for electronic or face-to-face communication particularly for internal communications;
- the importance of hierarchy and power, where certain individuals, genders, professions command greater attention and respect;
- demographics, which are vastly different across the world and shifting rapidly, dependent on whether a country is developed or developing;
- split between those living in a rural or urban setting;
- the country's infrastructure, including its political economic and legal positions and whether there is a culture that permits and tolerates dissent and activism;
- the media scene – what mass media exists, what control is exerted on the media (by a country's rulers), how much media outreach is there and how many people have access to media of different types.

In two-way communications we look for ways to get feedback from our stakeholders, target audiences or publics. Feedback enables us to check whether our messages got through, whether they were understood and acted upon as we intended. Feedback also enables us to modify our message so we can communicate again, with a message that progresses things. The aim of two-way communications is mutual understanding.

Hallahan (2001) came up with a typology of publics to take into account the fact that some audiences are active and some are inactive but nonetheless should be taken into account when planning communications activities:

- aware publics (with high knowledge and low involvement);
- active publics (with high knowledge and high involvement);
- aroused publics (with low knowledge and high involvement);
- inactive publics (with low knowledge and low involvement);
- non-publics (no knowledge and no involvement).

Active publics are likely to be those groups and individuals with whom an organization can engage in a two-way dialogue because they are galvanized and already primed for engagement, whereas aware and aroused publics may be less well organized or able to debate the issues.

Thinking about stakeholders

For well-planned communications we first need to consider all the possible stakeholders – then we can think about targeting. First do your homework – bring together all the information you have at the start. This may come from past evidence, from online research looking at social networks, from surveys, questionnaires and other research sources. You could also invite small groups of stakeholders to meet together to discuss a subject so you can hear their views on a more qualitative level – this can also help to actively engage them with what you are trying to achieve.

Key questions

1 Who are the stakeholders? How many of them are there? Where are they? (These could be individuals or groups/institutions.)
2 What role do they play in the achievement of our business aims?
3 How should we classify/characterize/describe them?
4 What role do they play? Where are they located? What is their experience of our organization? What attitudes, beliefs and feelings do they hold? What behaviours do they display? What are their priorities?
5 What channels and media do they use and which influence them (including social and traditional media)?
6 What do they know/think/feel about us/our brand/our policy or issue?
7 What overall relationship do we have with them?

Stakeholder mapping – who's in the picture?

It is a really good idea to make a stakeholder map. You do this by using the information you have gained to create a visual representation of key stakeholders on a particular topic (people also sometimes call this an 'influence map') and this organizes information in a way that allows you to assess the whole situation. It helps you order your thoughts and assists planning your strategy and tactics. The technique of mapping, especially if it is done as a group exercise, helps everyone share and agree on what is most important.

Influence mapping

NB: There are no rules here – be as creative as you like with symbols, colours and shapes – do what's best for your team.

Step 1 Brainstorm every possible influencer on this issue – come up with the list in random order.

Step 2 Now organize this into some sort of ranking, most important at the top and less important lower down. You could do this in a pyramid for example. But again be creative – use any structure that works for you.

Step 3 Now indicate, perhaps using different coloured pens, any connections or overlaps. Be as creative as you like. If, for example, A clearly influences B then an arrow could be inserted pointing from A to B. If the influence is two way, indicate as such.

Finally complete a stakeholder analysis Once you have done a map you could then do more detailed breakdowns – this can visually represent whether stakeholders are positive or negative towards a particular issue and how much power they have in terms of influencing others. For example, for a hospital, stakeholders would include:

- patients – local people and those who have opted for treatment at this hospital from further afield;
- local MPs and the local council and councillors;
- patients' families;
- staff;
- unions;
- local media;
- local employers;
- local schools;
- local community and community groups (eg National Childbirth Trust);
- professional medical organizations (eg Royal College of Nursing).

FIGURE 6.1 Stakeholder analysis

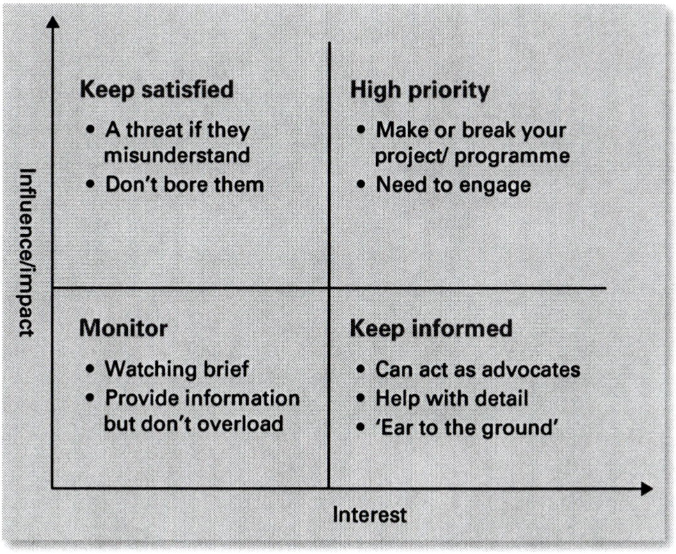

Then put the name of each stakeholder on a Post-it® note. Create a grid like the one in Figure 6.1, maybe on a flip chart.

Finally, place influencers in the appropriate segment.

What does this tell you? How does this inform your communications strategy?

CASE STUDY Audience segmentation – case history – Arts Council England

'Segmentation' is a research method where a given market is broken down into distinct groups that behave in similar ways or have similar needs. Segmentation can help organizations to understand their markets, identify groups of consumers they would like to target and develop products and communications that anticipate their needs.

Arts Council England conducted a major arts-based segmentation of English adults with the intention of enabling everyone to experience arts that enrich their lives. This piece of research looked at arts engagement across a very broad spectrum of arts events and activities, from opera to knitting, carnivals to video art.

Arts Council England's approach to segmentation had three key features:

1   It covered all English adults, not just a particular audience group – this enabled artists and arts organizations to understand their current audiences within the context of wider patterns of arts engagement, and to think about potential future audiences.

2   It was focused on the arts – existing population-wide segmentation tools (eg A Classification Of Residential Neighbourhoods [ACORN] and Mosaic – which are geo-demographic classifications of consumer types) are based largely on the socio-demographic characteristics of different groups. This segmentation was based on patterns of arts engagement and attitudes towards the arts to provide a tailored tool for arts communications in particular, allowing an exploration of lifestyle factors in the context of people's artistic lives, not vice versa.

3   It looked across the patterns of both arts attendance and participation – the events people go to see as well as the activities they take part in at home or with friends.

Arts Council England worked with research company Enlightenment (part of British Market Research Bureau [BMRB]) in four key stages focusing on an analysis of the patterns of arts engagement and attitudes towards the arts among English adults (aged 16 and over), based on data from a large-scale national survey of cultural participation. From this they were able to identify 13 arts consumer segments.

Arts participation – English adults

TABLE 6.1 Arts participation – English adults

Highly engaged in arts	Urban arts eclectic (5%)	Traditional culture vultures (4%)
Some engagement in arts	Fun, fashion and friends (18%)	Bedroom DJs (3%)
	Mature explorers (11%)	Mid-life hobbyists (4%)
	Dinner and a show (20%)	Retired arts and crafts (3%)
	Family- and community-focused (11%)	
Not currently engaged in arts	Time-poor dreamers (7%)	Older and home-bound (6%)
	A quiet pint with the match (8%)	Limited means, nothing fancy (2%)

(NB: The percentages refer to proportion of English adults in each segment. The nutshell descriptions speak for themselves really. It is really interesting stuff – go and find the full document and download the pdf http://www.artscouncil.org.uk/media/uploads/Arts_audiences_insight.pdf)

While this – and any segmentation – didn't have all the answers (eg it couldn't predict exactly how each individual in a given segment would behave nor could it tell an arts organization who is and who isn't engaging with its work) it is used to:

• increase collective knowledge about how people in England engage with the arts, putting individual projects into context;

- develop potential new communications strategies for increasing arts engagement and participation, so increasing and extending audiences;

- frame and inform the marketing of existing arts opportunities.

From stakeholder to target audience

There is an old adage in communications and that is 'start where your audience is'. Good advice – but only if you know *who* your audience is. Many people in organizations, when first asked, 'who is your target audience?' give me the answer, 'the general public'. Sorry, that's the wrong answer!

The *general* public is simply too vague, too vast and neither useful nor appropriate as a target. The Office for National Statistics estimated that, based on census night returns 2011, the population of the UK was 63.2 million. This is comprised of 31 million men and 32.2 million women. The estimated populations of the four constituent countries of the UK are 53 million people in England, 5.3 million in Scotland, 3.1 million in Wales and 1.8 million in Northern Ireland. The population aged 65 and over was 10.4 million (16 per cent of the UK population) in 2011. The House of Commons library recently estimated that the figure could exceed 70 million by 2026, three years earlier than previous official estimates. That is an awful lot of people.

If you plan to reach an audience that vast you'll need:

- an equally vast budget for communications;
- a remarkable news story (see Chapter 7 on what is news);
- a fabulous creative idea (see Chapter 8).

Even corporations with advertising budgets larger than many countries' GDP (think Coca-Cola or McDonalds) do not attempt to target 'the public'. We need to segment the public and prioritize audiences into interest groups, ages, locations. You might think council tax payers, voters, young people who will shortly become voters, young professionals, home owners, mothers, etc. This sort of drilling down gets you to specific targets.

There are also intermediaries; individuals, groups, communities and bodies of decision-makers who have influence over and are listened to by the ultimate target. For example, if we want to tackle childhood obesity ultimately we want to change children's eating habits, weaning them away from sugary and fatty food. The target is children whose diets increase the risk of obesity. The intermediaries include parents, because they have the greatest influence over their children's diets, and school caterers, who are responsible for the menus children are offered in school restaurants and cafeterias.

So as you can see this sort of clear thinking is essential for effective targeting of communications efforts and these questions will help you identify your target audience:

- Who needs to hear your message?
- Who has influence over your target?
- Who must be moved to action so your goals will be met?
- Who has the greatest impact on the outcome of your campaign efforts?

Most organizations have multiple target audiences, and there will be different communications objectives and possibly also tailored strategies for each of them.

Collecting the right data

Professionals make business decisions based on evidence, rather than assumption or 'gut feel'. Gut feel and instinct are powerful forces but we may be wrong and that may mean you wasting a great deal of time, effort and resources addressing the wrong issue. Audience research should be seen as an ongoing process, rather than an occasional, one-off event. Even a small audience research project can yield hugely useful information. Many research techniques are low budget. Any research is better than none at all and it does not have to be perfect. Do what you can afford.

You can use research to:

- Measure levels of awareness and understanding; prevailing attitudes and current behaviours.
- Assess the effectiveness of the programme or campaign.
- Gain insights that help set PR/communications objectives.
- Judge what channels and tactics worked best in a programme or campaign.
- Inform longer-term planning.
- Provide management information to clients and any sponsors or partners.

There are two categories of data collection: qualitative and quantitative.

Quantitative research tells you what is happening. It is associated with numbers, statistical analysis, large-scale studies, a specific focus, researcher detachment, and predetermined research design. It employs mathematical analysis and requires a large sample size. The results of this data shed light on statistically significant differences. One place to find quantitative results is in your web analytics (available in Google's suite of tools). This information will help you determine where contacts are coming from, how long visitors are staying on your site and from which page they are leaving.

Qualitative research tells you why something is happening. It is associated with words, description, small-scale studies, context and relationships, researcher involvement, and then more probing research design. Qualitative methods help to define problems and often use interview methods to learn about customers' opinions, values and beliefs.

Types of research

Primary research

Primary research is also known as 'field work' and it will help you meet your precise requirements. It can also be technical and expensive! The goal of primary research is to gather data you can then analyse about your target audience's levels of awareness, knowledge and understanding, preferences and opinions and behaviours. Primary research can include:

● Interviews (either by telephone or face-to-face)
● Surveys (online or by mail)
● Questionnaires (online or by mail)
● Focus groups gathering a sampling of potential clients or customers and getting their direct feedback.

Skill is needed to form questions and the work will be designed to meet the specific needs of your sector, context and issue.

Using social networks for primary research

By being active and participating in social media, you can create connections with your target audiences and turn them into powerful online focus groups. You can use your social media networks to ask for opinions, get feedback on new product ideas, to test policies, to get feedback on new packaging, to pilot ideas. By signing people up to your e-mail list, gaining readers for your blog, building followers on Twitter and fans and likes on Facebook, you can efficiently and effectively enlarge your potential research pool.

To set up a piece of online research:

1 Set your objectives – what do you want to achieve with this research?
2 What questions do you need to ask?
3 Devise a mechanism to collect responses.
4 Turn raw information into insight for decision-making purposes.

Doing qualitative face-to-face primary research – conducting a focus group

Even in this online world, there are still times when one or more focus groups will add considerably to your knowledge when you want to explore the views and attitudes issue of your target audiences. This is probably most true for internal communications. You could conduct a focus group yourself but it is worth thinking about subcontracting this to an experienced facilitator. There are a few practical steps required to getting this right:

- Write a brief that outlines what the purpose of the study is – what is being explored and probed and what outcome is required (eg information to enable a decision about a course of action relating to the communications programme) – depending on the issue it may be judged that several focus groups need to be conducted to make sure that:
  - the same issues emerge in each (so that you don't base conclusions on one 'rogue' group)
  - you have different types of audience that need to be questioned separately)

- Agree a facilitator (some people call this person a moderator or researcher) and brief them. You might also at this stage agree observers (likely to be those who will need to interpret and act on the findings) and brief them on how to behave during the groups (ie no participation and no unauthorized interruptions!).

- Recruit the participants – and this may require careful selection or randomized selection using a screening questionnaire (for example excluding atheists if you are exploring how best to promote religious practice). You may also need to consider if it will be necessary to offer an incentive to participate if the group takes place outside of working time.

- Working out the questions you want explored in the groups including whether any prompt materials are needed (for example mood boards, video clips, concept boards, layouts of proposed leaflets) and prepare a detailed set of guidelines to ensure the facilitator covers all required areas.

- Set up the room and check everyone can see clearly, that is has all the kit needed (eg screen) and that there is appropriate catering. You can hire a consumer lab that has a one-way mirror so observers can sit out of the group and are unseen (although participants must be told they are being observed, they soon forget about it).

- Run the group.

- Debrief on the session with the facilitator giving important information about what it was like to be with the group as tiny give-aways (usually body language clues) about people's feelings on an issue. Write up notes and a transcript if appropriate. Arrive at summary conclusions.

Secondary research

Secondary research is also known as 'desk research'. It is information that has already been published – in the widest sense of the word. It is useful, quick and often free, but may not be exactly what you need. Secondary research includes data from partners and allied organizations on the same target audiences, looking at surveys and polling results compiled by large polling and research firms, such as Gallup, who polls on current events, as well as smaller polls conducted by local newspapers and local groups.

These sites are useful when conducting secondary research about your target audience (NB: some give free data, some are US-based):

- Office for National Statistics (http://www.ons.gov.uk/ons/index.html).
- IPSOS Mori (http://www.ipsos-mori.com).
- Gorkana (http://www.gorkana.com).
- GOV.UK (https://www.gov.uk).
- Gallup (www.gallup.com).
- The Pew Research Center (www.people-press.org).
- Public Agenda (www.publicagenda.org).
- Research International (www.riusa.com).
- The Roper Center for Public Opinion Research (www.ropercenter.uconn.edu).
- TNS Intersearch (www.tns-global.com).

Using the internet for secondary research

The internet is a fabulous resource for communicators and you can gain enormous amount of information about people's views, attitudes and beliefs. Try any or all of these ideas:

- Use search engines to investigate issues, news, opinions, comment.
- Look at relevant bloggers' sites to see who is saying what about your sector.
- Set up alerts to pick up mentions of your product, service or issue.
- Listen to discussion threads to determine chatter about you, your issues, your competition.
- Use influence scores to pinpoint who you need to cultivate to be your brand ambassadors and to identify sector or industry influencers.

Four common mistakes organizations make when undertaking research

1. Using only secondary research

Relying on the published work of others doesn't give you the full picture. It can be a great place to start, of course, but the information you get from secondary research can be outdated. You can miss out on other factors relevant to your business.

2. Using only web resources

When you use common search engines to gather information, you get only data that are available to everyone and it may not be fully accurate or probe in-depth the issue you are interested in. To do deeper searches while staying within your budget, use the resources at your local library, university (if you can gain access) or business support organizations (for example Business Link).

3. Surveying only the people you know

Communications people sometimes interview only family members, colleagues and brand-users when conducting research. People close to you may not give you a clear and impartial view plus they fall into the wrong target audience profile – in other words they may not be a representative sample. To get the most useful and accurate information, you need to talk to a range of people, not just those easiest to get to.

4. Attempting to conduct a large-scale piece of research themselves

Use a reputable market research company if you are going to conduct large-scale research. They have the systems and process to make sure it is statistically sound and bears scrutiny when put to the media.

Psychological insight

We looked in Chapter 2 at some of key theories useful to communications practitioners. When thinking about audiences (and so that we can come up with strategies that help us achieve our communications objectives) PR professionals need to understand some basic human psychology.

What are values?

Values describe, and provide a means of talking about, what is important to us. They are the ideals we hold that give significance and meaning to our lives. Hence they underpin our beliefs and influence the decisions we make, the actions we take, and the lives we lead. Understanding values helps us to understand how we create our own reality and gives us insight into the personal realities of others.

Values have meaning only within a web of other values, not in isolation. For example, if I say that generosity is important to me, then you might expect that I will always be generous and giving. But, in fact, knowing that generosity is important to me will give you little idea as to whether I will always be generous unless you know the priority I place on generosity relative to my other values. If I place a higher priority on being liked than on generosity, then I may not give you honest feedback if I fear doing so would alienate you. This gets much more complex when our top 10 or 20 values are in play. It also means that people with shared values, but with different value priorities, may behave in radically different ways. People are so complex, aren't they!

The only reality we can know is the one that consists of the constructs we create for ourselves. Values, beliefs and experience are all constructs:

- Values are constructs that we hold as important to us. Values include concepts like equality, honesty, education, effort, perseverance, loyalty, faithfulness, etc. Our values are very much individual and they affect us at a deep subconscious level. Every decision we make is based on our values system. Values can be split into core values and secondary values:

  - Core values help us to resolve any hidden conflicts, remove stresses and give us a firm direction in life. Ultimately they are important for helping you move towards solutions and away from problems.

  - Secondary values are the values that we bring to the fore to use when certain situations arise. For example, you might make yourself suddenly more 'available' because you have a friend in need and this is because loyalty is something you value.

- Beliefs are constructs that we hold to be true. They are assumptions that we make about the world, that have come from what we see, hear, experience, read and think about. Beliefs apply not only how we see ourselves but also how we see other people. We tend not to question our beliefs because we are so certain about them and many of them stem from childhood. Our beliefs can be changed or turned round by 're-programming' our subconscious minds. Like values, our beliefs can be split into two different types; empowering beliefs and limiting beliefs:

  - Empowering beliefs help us to make changes confidently. We use our empowering beliefs to make decisions in what can often be a confusing or ambiguous world.

  - Limiting beliefs do the exact opposite. A limiting belief keeps us rooted in a particular position. Limiting beliefs are often based on assumptions that are not true. For example, saying you can't dance, or learn a language. If you spend a lot of time repeatedly saying that you can't do something then, for that time, it will be true.

- Experiences are constructs that give us a sense of reality. The way in which we see and experience the world – our own personal worldview – depends on how we interpret the outer world of nature, things and people, and also on our level of consciousness, which in turn depends on our value priorities.

Understanding values and beliefs – your own and those of others – is an important aspect of communications. If we have an understanding and appreciation of these we can encode our messages affectively to work with those values and beliefs. Planners and researchers in advertising world have been doing this sort of analysis for decades. We public relations practitioners have more recently come round to understanding the value of this discipline.

Think about your target audiences – what values, beliefs and experiences do they hold and what communications strategies might work best when you are communicating with them?

TABLE 6.2 Erik Erikson's psychosocial life stages

Erikson's psychosocial stages	Life stage/ relationships/ issues	Positive drivers	Negative drivers
1 *Trust v mistrust*	Infant mother/feeding and being comforted, teething, sleeping	Hope and drive	Sensory distortion/ withdrawal
2 *Autonomy v shame and doubt*	Toddler parents/bodily functions, toilet training, muscular control, walking	Willpower and self-control	Impulsivity/ compulsion
3 *Initiative v guilt*	Pre-school family/exploration and discovery, adventure and play	Purpose and direction	Ruthlessness/ Inhibition
4 *Industry v inferiority*	Schoolchild school, teachers, friends, neighbourhood/ achievement and accomplishment	Competence and method	Narrow virtuosity/ inertia

(Continued)

TABLE 6.2 (Continued)

Erikson's psychosocial stages	Life stage/ relationships/ issues	Positive drivers	Negative drivers
5 Identity v role confusion	Adolescent peers, groups, influences/ resolving identity and direction, becoming a grown-up	Fidelity and devotion	Fanaticism/ repudiation
6 Intimacy v isolation	Young adult lovers, friends, work connections/ intimate relationships, work and social life	Love and affiliation	Promiscuity/ exclusivity
7 Generativity v stagnation	Mid-adult children, community/'giving back', helping, contributing	Care and production	Overextension /rejectivity
8 Integrity v despair	Late adult grandchildren/ society, the world, life/meaning and purpose, life achievements	Wisdom and renunciation	Presumption/ disdain

Erik Erikson and life stages

The psychologist Erik Erikson's research and theories (Erikson, 1966) helped to broaden and expand psychoanalytic theory. Erikson contributed to our understanding of personality as it develops over the course of our lifespan. Erikson had a strong interest and compassion for people, especially young people, and also because his research was carried out among societies and communities very different from the more introspective world of psychoanalysis.

Erikson arrived at the theory of life stages (Table 6.2). It is a powerful model, accessible and relevant to modern life, helping us understand how personality and behaviour develop in people. Erikson's psychosocial theory is widely and highly regarded. His theory is useful far beyond psychoanalysis – it's useful for *any* application involving emotional intelligence, personal awareness and communication – and it is helpful when considering target audiences and their drivers and concerns.

Think about your target audiences – what life stage they are at, what the concerns and motivations are and so what communications strategies might work best when you are communicating with them.

There are many more models that give you psychological insight. Be curious and interested in people – arguably you can't be good at communications unless you have a deep interest in people, how their minds tick, how their hearts flutter.

This all links into the development of PR strategies that work, building in research to investigate attitudes and beliefs at the planning stage and then being creative in terms of how the communication is encoded and presented.

Myers-Briggs Type Indicator® (MBTI®)

The Myers-Briggs Type Indicator® (MBTI®) personality questionnaire was developed by the mother-and-daughter team, Katharine Cook Briggs and Isabel Briggs Myers and was first published in 1962. They based the questionnaire on the theory of Swiss psychiatrist Carl Jung, in order to provide understanding of people and appreciation of the differences between them. MBTI describes different preferences – ways of behaving, processing information and making decisions. Individuals can adapt these styles when required, but they will be at their most comfortable and effective when able to use their preferred choices. There are four different dimensions, when looking at preferences:

- **Extroverted/Introverted (E/I)** – whether you gain more energy from the company of others or from being on your own.
- **Sensing/Intuitive (S/N)** – whether you prefer to focus on individual specific and concrete details or the 'big picture' when learning new information.
- **Thinking/Feeling (T/F)** – whether you are ruled more by your head or by your heart when you make decisions.
- **Judging/Perceiving (J/P)** – whether you prefer a planned and structured approach to completing tasks or you prefer to take a more relaxed, 'take it as it comes' approach.

The questionnaire gives you a four-letter type indicating your preferences (for example my preferences are ENTP). While the questionnaire gives an individual personal feedback, you can use these ideas to think about audiences' likely needs when devising public relations strategies.

This can be very helpful when considering communications with particular professional groups where there is a high proportion of a particular preference. For example, if your audience is one of engineers, who often have an ISTJ preference set, you would make your communications more detailed and systematic. While if your audience was one of volunteers, where the preference for making decisions is more based on values than logic you would frame your interventions with a greater focus on emotion than logic.

It can also be very useful for planning internal communications, where it is possible to judge preferences.

Neuro Linguistic Programming for public relations practitioners

NLP is a behavioural model and set of skills and techniques founded by John Grinder and Richard Bandler in 1975. NLP studies the patterns or 'programming' created by the interactions of the brain, language and body that produce both effective and ineffective states and behaviours.

Neuro refers to the brain/mind and nervous system of the human organism through which each experience is gathered via the five senses or (in NLP-speak) representational systems: visual (pictures); auditory (sounds); kinaesthetic (feelings); olfactory (smells); and gustatory (tastes). Experience is processed, coded and retained as memories.

Linguistic refers to the content that moves across and through these pathways and so is about language, symbols, words, metaphors and also the nonverbal communication systems through which our neural representations and experiences are coded, ordered and given meaning.

Programming refers to our ability to organize these parts (sights, sounds, sensations, smells, tastes, and symbols or words) and the way such content is directed, sequenced and connected by each of us to produce our individual thinking patterns and behaviours (the programmes we run inside our brain) that are our experience of life.

The skills and techniques were derived by observing the patterns of excellence in experts from diverse fields of communication, including psychotherapy, business, hypnosis, law and education. NLP theory helps us understand how to encode communications so that our messages stand the best chance of making it through and being decoded as we intended.

NLP developed ways of eliciting strategies from an individual and making the more useful ones available to others. Teaching strategies often incorporates elements of trance to assist use of imagination so NLP courses usually include hypnotic language. NLP allows us to notice the *process* of our thinking as separate from the *content* of our thinking. NLP gives us choices about how we think, which inevitably make it easier to change what we think and the behaviours that follow.

I became an NLP Practitioner and then Master Practitioner some years ago and found that much of what good communicators do is presented in a few NLP ideas, the most important being:

Multi-sensory language

As we use our five senses to make sense of the world, so we can enrich our written and spoken communications by using sensory language.

Visual words and phrases

TABLE 6.3 Visual words and phrases

• See	• Illuminate	• Hazy
• Look	• Twinkle	• Sparking
• View	• Clear	• Crystal clear
• Appear	• Foggy	• Flash
• Envision	• Focused	• Imagine
• Appears to me	• In light of	• Up front
• Beyond a shadow of a doubt	• Looks like	• Well-defined
• Clear-cut	• Make a scene	• I see what you mean
• Dim view	• Mind's eye	• Make a show of
• Hazy idea	• Plainly see	
	• Under your nose	

Auditory words and phrases

TABLE 6.4 Auditory words and phrases

• Hear	• Rings a bell	• Overtones
• Listen	• Be heard	• Unheard
• Sound(s)	• Resonate	• Question
• Make music	• Deaf	• Attune

(Continued)

TABLE 6.4 (*Continued*)

• Clear as a bell	• Manner of speaking	• To tell the truth
• Describe in detail	• Pay attention to	• Tongue-tied
• Earful	• Power of speech	• Unheard of
• Express yourself	• Purrs like a kitten	• Word-for-word
• Give an account of	• Outspoken	• Are you listening to what I am saying?
• Hold your tongue	• Be all ears	
• Idle talk	• State your purpose	
• Loud and clear		

Kinaesthetic words and phrases

TABLE 6.5   Kinaesthetic words and phrases

• Feel	• Throw out	• Unbudging
• Touch	• Turn around	• Get a handle
• Grasp	• Hard	• Solid
• Get a hold of	• Unfeeling	• Suffer
• Tap into	• Concrete	
• Make contact	• Scrape	
• All washed up	• Hand-in-hand	• Pain in the neck
• Boils down to	• Heated argument	• Pull some strings
• Chip off the old block	• Hold it	• Sharp as a tack
	• Hot-headed	• Slipped my mind
• Come to grips with	• Keep your shirt on	• Smooth operator
• Control yourself	• Know-how	• Start from scratch
• Cool/calm/collected	• Lay your cards on the table	• Stuffed shirt
• Get a handle on		• Too much of a hassle
• Get a load of this	• Moment of panic	
• Get in touch with	• Not following you	• Topsy-turvy
• Get the drift of		• Underhanded

NLP model of questioning and listening

We think so much faster than we can talk and we think many more thoughts than we can ever speak. When trying to find out what someone is thinking we cannot read their thoughts directly, we can only access their language (both verbal and non-verbal). So much is lost in translation, from lightning-fast thoughts and memories to a few mumbled words. If we want to know what someone is thinking (what NLP-ers call 'deep structure') we have to start with the clues in the language the person is using (what NLP-ers call 'surface structure') and then ask questions to fill in the blanks.

When people construct sentences they will often (as an unconscious process) delete a great deal. Instead of referring to someone by name they will say, 'he said' or 'they did'. We could then ask 'who specifically?' Similarly if someone says 'I am useless at finances', an additional question like 'in what way specifically?' or 'tell me why you say that' can fill in some of the missing information. Good questioning helps people find out what assumptions they are making, which examples of success they are overlooking, which useful bits of information they have missed out; rather than just assuming that what someone says is the whole truth and nothing but the truth. See Chapter 11 for more on this.

'Artful' language

The hypnotherapist, Milton H Erickson (1901–1980), was observed by Grinder and Bandler in the 1970s (see Grinder and Bandler, 1993) to find out how he so successfully influenced people to help them give up addictions, repair relationships and improve the quality of their lives. Erickson used language in a particularly skilful way. He used stories and metaphors to get his message over. He also used whatever style was appropriate to his client rather than using just one preferred style (which is what many skilful communicators do). Great communicators tell stories and adapt their written and spoken style to suit their audiences. What came first, NLP theory or great communications practice?

Creating rapport

Rapport is when two people are 'in tune with each other', or 'on the same wavelength', or 'seeing eye to eye'. When two people are in rapport then they are able to communicate with maximum effectiveness and clarity. There is also no such thing as 'bad rapport'. Again great communicators do this instinctively. See Chapter 11 on body language and mirroring and matching.

Drawing this all together – developing strategies for public relations

I have attempted in this chapter to get you to think inside the head(s) of your target audience, or public, or stakeholder – whoever matters to you when you are considering your approach to public relations and communications.

Once you have a thorough sense of where they are in terms of your issue, your brand, your organization you have a starting point for planning both proactive and reactive communications. Let's finish with an example that brings this all together. It's one that demonstrates the importance of deep understanding of the audience.

In 2013, the government announced that all dogs in England must be microchipped by 2016. The intention was to reduce the number of stray dogs. Government figures show more than 100,000 dogs are dumped or lost each year and it's estimated that this costs the taxpayer and welfare charities £57 million per year.

According to the Pet Food Manufacturers' Association there were an estimated 8.5 million dogs in the UK in 2013. A quarter of all households include at least one dog. That's a huge number of dogs that need microchipping.

Audience insight gained through extensive desk research, talking to pet owners and animal welfare charities showed that dog owners believed that microchipping would be painful for their beloved dogs, would take a lot of time and be costly. Yet the vast majority of dog owners would do anything for their dogs – dogs are seen as members of the family. This audience insight was the starting point for the Department for Environment, Food and Rural Affairs (Defra) communications plan to announce compulsory microchipping of all dogs in England by 2016.

To encourage people to get their dogs microchipped Defra focused on the benefits of this measure for them *and* their dogs. Who wouldn't want to make it easier to be reunited with a much-loved pet if it went missing?

The campaign did not feature ministers and officials – it featured dogs and their owners. It focused on dogs being members of the family and told stories of lost dogs and how microchipping enabled dog and owner to be reunited quickly and easily. It also showed dogs being microchipped with friendly vets demonstrating that the procedure is quick, easy and painless. Social media enabled dog owners to get involved and tell their stories for the benefit of other dog owners because everyone loved talking about their dogs. Dog owners themselves, not a government department, endorsed the scheme and told others why microchipping is part and parcel of being a good, responsible pet owner. Defra partnered with the Dogs Trust who promoted #chipmydog on Twitter to their 67,500 followers, tweeting about the announcement, answering microchipping questions and addressing concerns. Other influential tweeters such as the British Veterinary Association adopted the hashtag to widen the reach. Twitter was used to drive traffic to a new Facebook page co-created with the Dogs Trust. Owners were asked to tweet pictures of their microchipped dogs which were then posted on the Facebook page. Quickly a gallery of some seriously cute dogs was created, which proved to be a great way of drawing people to the page and then finding out more about microchipping.

Dog owners listen to other dog owners and to empathetic vets, so videos fronted by Dogs Trust vets were loaded onto YouTube. These films showed how quick and easy the microchipping procedure is. More videos of dogs reunited with their owners, thanks to microchipping, were encouraged, rein-forcing the idea of dog owner talking to dog owner.

Whenever a policy is announced that requires people to act, it's essential people can easily find out what they have to do and that the message is as clear and easy to understand as possible, especially, as in this case, when the public in question (dog owners) come from every background and from every part of the country and are any age. So clear information went live as soon as the announcement about microchipping was made. Links with dog charities and the British Veterinary Association ensured that information was consistent wherever people looked.

This case history demonstrates that Defra put the dog owner at the heart of the communication process. The communications team ensured that the strategy was entirely coherent, with dog owners talking to dog owners, and using cost-effective channels and tactics to get the message across. At the time of writing, the campaign has delivered impressive results – with num-bers of dog owners getting their dogs microchipped increasing since the campaign was launched.

07
Using the right communications channels and tactics

Once you are clear on your target audiences, the messages and the strategy you can begin to assess what channels and tactics will be most effective. A channel is the medium you use to send and receive messages, while the tactics are the practical outputs you then create which are delivered via the channel. Channels have more or less significance depending on the sensory impact they have (ie vision and sound, plus smell, taste and feeling) with, as a rule, face-to-face/one-to-one communications being most and print channels being least impactful and memorable. As a side note, research studies, investigating the lasting impact of social media, are probably something we should all look out for and pay attention to.

Channels for impact

MOST IMPACTFUL
    Face-to-face – one-to-one
    Face-to-face – group
    Live event
    Cinema
    TV/Video
    Photography
    Interactive digital (internet including social media)
    Non-interactive digital

Radio
Printed word
LEAST IMPACTFUL

These days, channels are often categorized like this:

1 *Owned channels*, eg your own website (or corporate website), your own newsletter, your own events, all of which you have control over.

2 *Paid-for channels*, eg Google AdWords, pay-per-click (PPC), promoted tweets, banner advertisements, etc (largely the domain of advertising and promotion although PRs should have an awareness of how other disciplines are using channels).

3 *'Rented channels'*, eg your Twitter handle (or company Twitter account), your LinkedIn page (or company page), your Google+ page (or company Google+ page) – rented because if Facebook/YouTube/Twitter close, you have no control over it.

4 *Earned channels*, ie editorial coverage in the media (trade press, national newspapers, broadcast and accompanying websites), plus independent bloggers and the commentary of influencers (eg analysts). Bear in mind you can earn negative as well as positive coverage!

You increase the probability of your message and your content being seen if you use a channel that your target audience is already using, uses a lot and trusts. Consider the impact and influence of the channel and its ability to not only reach the right people with the right content but also to enable a two-way dialogue. This is a matter of research, careful planning and analysis. Consider measurement tools to monitor the effectiveness of the channels and tactics used and potentially how improvements can be made, where/if required, as the programme progresses.

So, as part of the planning process, ask yourself the following questions:

● If you already have a number of channels set up, review them regularly – are they still effective?

● How do you measure them for effectiveness?

● Does your target audience still use the channel? What have they shifted to?

● Are you using the channel for research and for listening to your audiences, as well as for getting messages across?

● Has a channel been superseded by another, more effective communication tool?

Digital is often considered first these days because it is fast, comparatively inexpensive and enables a two-way dialogue, but it should not be considered in isolation. Established so-called 'traditional' channels, particularly media and face-to-face engagement, remain highly influential. Nor can print, in the form of leaflets, brochures and reports, be discounted as these items remain key for some audiences and for some communications situations where detailed information is required or when targets do not use other channels.

PR professionals have to adapt faster to changing situations, particularly at a time when traditional and digital are transitioning in relative importance from one to the other. A recent Business and Professional Women's (BPW) Foundation study (BPW Foundation, 2011) noted that by 2025, Generation Y (ie those born between 1978 and 1994) will make up roughly 75 per cent of the world's workforce. Young people have always driven new ideas into the corporate world, challenging management structures that have been carefully built by older generations. This time it's the combined impact of social networks, cloud computing and mobility, aligned with globalization and economic uncertainty that makes this situation uniquely different.

All PR practitioners must keep themselves updated by reading, researching and experimenting with social media, virtual communities and collaborative tools. As communication channels evolve this will keep you adaptive, inventive and very employable.

Digital

So let's look at digital first (where I have also considered audio and video) and then move on to traditional media, face-to-face and finally, print. Related to this chapter is Chapter 9, which covers visual communications techniques which, while obviously related, demand separate consideration.

Websites

Let's start with your own website. This is the first place that your customers or potential customers will visit to find information about you. Larger corporations will have an in-house specialist or a design consultancy to address the technical aspects. These days it is typical to have your website set up to be interactive, ie it allows visitors to perform tasks and get a response from the website, rather than just view information. This includes adding comments, asking for responses, registering for a newsletter, podcasts, latest news, searching for information and buying products. Interactivity makes the communication process circular. A website with a clean layout style, coupled with legible font colours, will have the edge over a graphically heavy website, with poor legibility. Great content is vital to give visitors what they want as quickly as possible. The messages your website conveys reflects your brand and the service you offer to visitors in the real world.

Whatever your budget, these few important checks will help you make your website work as hard as it can so your target audiences want to read and engage with you. Test your site often to make sure visitors have a great user experience:

1 Your website must be **easy to find**. Most of us would like our organizations to come top of the list of results when people search for our sector, product or issue. Search Engine Optimization (SEO) is the process where web pages are designed, built and modified with search engine results in mind. The goal of SEO is high placement (preferably first place) in the organic listings of search engines (especially Google). SEO is a branch of search engine marketing and involves paying attention to the many factors involved in a search engine's algorithm. This includes on-page elements (such as meta tags and internal linking) and off-page factors (such as the number of back links coming to a site, which is used to build Page Rank). Consult an expert IT consultant as they will ensure that your website is consistently in the first 10 search results.

2 People want fast answers when they go to websites so make access as **easy and fast** as possible. In my experience, the 'three-click rule' has always helped, eg you're only ever three clicks away from getting the information you desire. Visitors to your site want to get to the content they need quickly. Attention spans are shortening all the time – you have at maximum three seconds to download your web page to a visitor. The home page should be as clear as possible to read and understand. On a technical level your designers should use coding that delivers content at speed.

3 Providing your audience get what they want and like what they get, people return to websites – and tell their friends about them. This is because the best websites have **great and relevant content.** This is the most important factor of all and will determine whether your site is valued and visited repeatedly. Corporate and campaign-related websites should engage, inform, educate, entertain and sometimes, even challenge. Review and refresh content frequently if you want return traffic, to be bookmarked as a favourite site and to be recommended to others by visitors. Make sure there are good blogspots. Use images, video, podcasts, webinars and web conferences to deliver a rich online experience to visitors.

4 An **online press office** that has current and archived press releases, media-ready background information and cleared, copyright-free photography is another must for interactive websites. Most journalists and analysts will use this online resource to check facts, use imagery for company relevant articles, so keeping it up-to-date is essential.

5 By following **good design conventions** you will make your website a pleasure to use and to return to. The majority of people read left to right, starting at the top and working down to the bottom, as confirmed by my eye tracking studies carried out by usability consultants. Text should be left aligned. Every page should link back to the home page. 'Contact Us' should appear on every page,

particularly for commercial sites. Likewise 'Join the debate' or similar 'calls to action' should appear on every page if you want interactivity and comment. If you have one, the 'search' box should appear in the top right of the screen. On bigger sites this is both a basic and an essential feature. The search function needs to be extremely accurate, because search is generally a last attempt to find something on your site. Monitoring what people are searching for may be extremely important to your organization. Also remember to check the brand guidelines to ensure consistency.

6 Better to go for **simple graphics** than overly sophisticated ones. Remember that nowadays people are more likely to review your site on their smartphone or tablet than on a PC. People are savvy about the internet now and know that moving images and flashy graphics are likely to support advertising messages so go easy on these elements. Avoid using Flash sequences that may take time to load and add time to a visitor's search. (The 'skip intro' button is allegedly one of the most clicked-on buttons of the internet). Search engine spiders are unable to read flash files so you are also reducing the likelihood of achieving a high placement on a search. Get good designers who understand the internet's mechanisms to design the website for you but make sure you can edit the website yourself every day so you can keep it as up-to-date as possible. Make sure your website looks great but isn't over the top. Some websites with overly clever graphics are too hard on the eye and may make getting to the information too hard for the user. Err on the side of simplicity and remember it's the content that matters.

7 Give **control** to your website visitors to allow them to tailor their experience to suit them. Offer them different font sizes, particularly if you know your target audience includes the elderly or those with visual impairment.

Your website checklist:

- The site is easy to understand, use and navigate.
- It speaks the language of your target audiences (and that is not necessarily the 'corporate voice').
- Every page can be viewed in multiple browsers, eg Safari, Firefox, Chrome, Internet Explorer, etc.
- The website is mobile and tablet-enabled and works with the key mobile operating systems.
- Badges with links to your social assets (such as Facebook, Twitter, LinkedIn and Google+) are added prominently on your front page.
- There is no need to scroll sideways.
- The purpose of each page is clear to the reader.
- Any action you want the reader to take is clear, eg the 'three-click rule' to locate what you want to find.

- The reader can quickly identify areas of interest.
- The important information is at the top of each page.
- There is a clear focal point on each page.
- Use headlines and pictures to get attention quickly.
- The layout is clear – use bullet points and white space to make reading and scanning easy.
- The design (colour palette, typeface, logo and other devices) follows corporate brand identity guidelines.
- Comfortable colour combinations (backgrounds and text) enable text to be read easily (dark text on light background vs light text on coloured background) – take care with text over photographs.
- Any page downloads quickly (within three-to-five seconds).
- Use columns for text, avoiding text across the entire landscape screen.
- The copy is reader-orientated and has a clear aim – right style, right content , right structure.
- All copy is as concise and as brief as possible.
- Appropriate use of 'white space' above and below headline.
- Headlines are attention-grabbing.
- Moving graphics/animations are used for a reason not for whim or novelty.
- Minimal clutter on the page – not too many logos, badges and flashing signs or banners.
- Pages are Search Engine Optimized (SEO).
- All pages are tagged.
- Interesting articles, whitepapers, reports, etc can be easily 'socialized' through Twitter or 'shared' via LinkedIn, Facebook, or Google+.

Social media

Websites and online tools which allow users to interact with each other in some form – by sharing information, opinions, knowledge and interests – are all broadly known as social media. Social media involves the building of communities or networks, the amplification of ideas or content and collaborative engagement. At its essence are an openness, immediacy and transparency that directly challenges closed hierarchical systems. Just look at how social media was used during the Arab Spring to see how easily and rapidly it got round and overtook traditional media channels.

The enormous and rapid growth of social media initially caught many individuals, businesses and governments off-guard. Many were found to be ill-prepared to deal with the required openness and transparency needed in a newly information democratized and globalized 24/7 world. Most now are adapting to this new way of operating and some are also realizing the competitive advantage that can be gained by effective employment of social media.

We PR practitioners need to work with our HR counterparts to create social media best practice guidelines for both our organizations and the individuals working in them. These guidelines should also be updated every six months (at least) to ensure that these channels are not 'abused' or 'mishandled' – either deliberately or unintentionally. Organizations that apply the traditional methods of dealing with the media to social channels can get into trouble. That doesn't mean that the 'rule book' can be completely disregarded as there are areas – both legally and in terms of best practice – that still apply whether dealing online or offline.

Public relations practitioners have an ethical and professional duty to set standards. The Chartered Institute of Public Relations published a Social Media policy paper in 2012 giving advice for professional communicators who want to use and work with social media. One of the key points to remember is that reputation is holistic and that it is not possible to sustain one image created through conventional media alongside a completely different one created through social media. Old and new media interact – and messaging needs to remain consistent.

Social media tools facilitate communication, engagement, transparency and trust among stakeholders and target audiences. These tools are complementary (and can be integrated) with traditional communication activities and are used extensively by organizations who recognize the importance of effective social communication – where it is relevant and will help to achieve specific communications objectives.

Social media does pose some issues for PR professionals. The convergence of social media, mobile devices and cloud-based information systems means that your next generation of employees, partners and customers will be brought up expecting real-time collaborative engagement – aligned to this, businesses and governments will evolve analytical systems to harvest the 'Big Data' produced by the convergence of social, cloud and mobile. This is happening now, so this should make the selling of the idea of using social media to our less enthusiastic colleagues easier.

While we can get to grips with the basics and be reasonably effective, we sometimes can't manage digital alone – we may need specialist consultants and companies to help us maximize our internet presence in terms of the technical side, search engine optimization and so on. If you have them, your in-house specialist team or outsourced consultancy will help with all of the technical aspects, like set up and coding. A mass of information is available on the web if this has to be more of a DIY approach, because you are a small company or a not-for-profit organization.

If you don't have social media/digital experts in-house, review what can be handled by an agency or yourself and be realistic about what can be achieved – ie set realistic expectations. I would urge all PR practitioners to keep themselves updated by reading, researching and experimenting with social media. It is a vast subject and one that is probably best understood by looking at the internet and researching how ideas are developing – the sheer quantity of information can be overwhelming.

Fortunately there are many thought-leaders who share best-practice and good ideas so it might be worthwhile following and setting up alerts on a handful of them. This will enable you to keep up-to-date. The majority of social media sites are easy to use and many have video tutorials to assist self-learning.

There are a large number of established and emerging social media sites, but I would suggest that these are the most important social media channels:

- Facebook;
- YouTube;
- LinkedIn;
- Twitter;
- Google+;
- Wordpress (for blogging).

Blogging

Anyone can be a blogger and there are millions of blogs. There will be millions of new bloggers today and there will be millions of new ones tomorrow but it's only the ones that are read and respected that matter. Successful blogging has lots of benefits to business.

According to WordPress there are 76,158,445 WordPress sites across the world. Each month users produce about 40.5 million new posts and 50.3 million new comments and over 409 million people view more than 14.4 billion pages (http://en.wordpress.com/stats/ accessed 27 February 2014). HubSpot's 2012 State of Inbound Marketing Report found that smaller businesses plan to spend dramatically more of their budgets on social media and blogs than large businesses and that 57 per cent of companies with a blog have acquired a customer from their blog.

Blogs can be a very successful marketing tool and an excellent way to communicate with staff, investors, members of your industry, journalists and prospective customers. That's why it's important that you get it right – if you've made the decision to start a blog immerse yourself in it and make sure you're committed to making it a success. Readers are savvy and can see through obvious 'corporate-sells' or 'PR hype' so be careful of the positioning and messaging. Also remember the 'right to reply' – far from being afraid of this it is an excellent way to encourage debate and discussion allowing you to explain your ideas, policies, products.

The blogger who writes brilliantly, who is an expert focusing on the subject you are particularly interested in (for personal or professional reasons), who entertains and challenges can be just as compelling a commentator as any professional, elite journalist. However, the writing style used for long-form magazine articles or short-form news is not quite right for a blog. We cover this in Chapter 11.

There are several aspects of blogging that should concern all communications professionals:

- Is it going to be a regular blog?
- Will it only be used as a 'push' marketing channel or will it encourage a two-way conversation?
- How do we identify and communicate with influential bloggers relevant to our issue/product/sector?
- How do we create, write and maintain blogs that support and add value to our communications strategy, eg do a group of people take turns to write the blogs for the CEO, CTO, CIO, etc?
- How do we market our blogs so the target audience and stakeholders are driven to them – will this be 'socialized' via the corporate Twitter, corporate website, or by individuals or both?

With all this in mind, have a look at blogging sites and see what works, what doesn't and also check out how your customers and other target audiences communicate to their end users using blogs.

Identifying and communicating with bloggers

Most people don't have the time to spend hours surfing the net for relevant blogs and often go to them as a result of a friend, colleague or traditional media recommendation. People tend to gravitate to blogs where the authors are discussing issues that are of interest to them, whether they hold the same or different opinions. As readers participate more in blogs, they find out about other blogs by clicking on the profile of other contributors. You can start to search for relevant blogs on search engines like Google, in just the same way you would look for a website. However you might just get popular sites, not necessarily what you are most interested in.

When you look at a blog, look at the profile of the writer. The name is not as important as a description of the blog and its purpose. Cross-reference the blogger's name against their LinkedIn profile. Find out if they have a Twitter handle, then follow them. For the bloggers you discover as thought-leaders or influencers, create Twitter Lists on key subject areas – this allows you to build real-time intelligence feeds.

Follow links from a respected blog. And before subscribing, track and read the blog for a while to see if it is pertinent to you and your organization. For most people, it doesn't matter how few or how many posts a blogger writes each week providing they are interesting and well written. When you are satisfied that this blogger is for you, put it in your 'blog roll', ie your blog directory. Organize the blogs you want to read using RSS feeds or use Twitter Lists for aggregating the bloggers you discover as subject-matter experts or thought-leaders – this allows you to build real-time intelligence feeds.

Get involved by engaging in dialogue with the blogger, perhaps on a topic that is relevant to both of you. Make sure you treat highly regarded bloggers with respect. Ask them if they would like to receive information and media stories about your organization, its products and/or services. Don't automatically send press releases or other materials, unless you want to provoke a hostile response, which you undoubtedly will if you assume they are bound to be interested in what your company has to offer. This about is about building relationships; it is not a sales ambush.

More recently some PR agencies have experimented with 'Google Hangouts' for bloggers, in place of press conferences. Keene Communications trialled this for a travel client where travel bloggers are hugely influential. The aim was to develop a conversation between the organization's VIPs and the key bloggers. Broadcasting across YouTube and Google+, selected bloggers watched a live video stream and posed questions directly to a government minister and the CEO across Twitter, Google Chat, Google+ and YouTube. With questions being answered every 30 seconds this permitted a level of engagement with travel bloggers that would have been lacking in a traditional press conference, where there is a pecking order and the most senior journalist could hold court. 'Google Hangouts' demolish hierarchy and are immensely casual.

Creating and maintaining blogs

Blogging is a serious endeavour and you have to put time into it to do it well. Infrequently updated and poorly written blogs reflect badly on an organization's brand reputation and the individual. So create a good quality blog that people want to read and that can be 'socialized' (ie shared). Remember that this is an opportunity for organizations to encourage their employees to re-tweet company information safely – like a 'brand advocate'.

Blogs are momentary and like everything else on the web, borderless, so make sure you keep materials fresh and potentially global. When you have committed to launching a corporate blog, select one or two people to act as gatekeepers/editors. The role of the gatekeeper includes:

- reviewing blog posts and ensuring that they are all in line with the communications and strategy goals;
- ensuring the content of the blog is factually and grammatically correct;
- monitoring comments and replies posted by readers;
- discovering blog-worthy topics and tasking them to the bloggers;
- flagging posts and comments that may need involvement from managers and PR;
- ensuring consistency with any current marketing or sales campaigns.

So who writes the blog? There is an etiquette to blogging that infers blogs should be authentic and written by the person who claims to be the author. An organization's blogs may be written by anyone – the chief executive, the director of operations, the research director, the head of communications, a customer, a case history, you – or all of these. Some blogs are anonymous – to protect identity when material is sensitive (for example a charity for domestic violence might want to get a victim to write about her experiences and it would be sheer folly to reveal names).

As far as corporate content is concerned, if there are agreed 'no go' areas define what these are very clearly – otherwise give bloggers freedom to express their views, negative and positive, on approved areas. No content should be obscene, defamatory, profane or hateful. Also refer or cross-check with the organization's tone of voice (if one is available). Then build the personality of the blog you want to roll out. Bloggers should not only write about their organizations' challenges, thought-leadership agenda, etc but also include topics like economics or business as such issues have a wider appeal – and of course, in order to engage with their customers, what challenges affect them in business. This will demonstrate empathy, understanding and knowledge. Posts that are genuinely helpful and incisive work much more effectively than product/service plugs.

Join the blogging world by engaging with other people's blogs first. It is, in fact, the main way to drive traffic to your own blog and to develop your blog brand in the blogosphere. Pick a handful of blogs relevant to you – blogs that are industry-related and have significant influence and reach. Read and comment on them regularly. Send your readers to other blogs too – don't be anxious about whether they'll come back or not. This is blogging etiquette. They will return to your blog providing it is good enough.

Readers want to feel that they know and can trust you. The blogger has to come across as a real person, not a faceless organization or a sophisticated communications professional. So develop a natural and personal voice (or voices, depending on how many of you are posting). Be authentic, opinionated and unafraid to say what you think. Corporate speak has no place here. If you are advising a senior person in your organization make sure they understand this. Don't just proofread what they write; make sure they understand how important it is to be 'real'.

Write good plain, correct English. It will read better and won't give critics ammunition to criticize you with. Check spelling, grammar and punctuation. Don't rely on your PC's spell checker – remember to get your posts proofread and corrected before posting. Look at the hints and tips for style in Chapter 11. If someone points out a factual error in your blog, check it and correct it immediately if appropriate. Thank the person who corrected you in the amended post. Again this is good blogging etiquette.

Some of the best bloggers post every day including weekends. If you work in a fast-paced sector your organization may be posting five times *per day* or even more. If it's an authoritative blog, three to five times per week is more usual. If that sounds a heavy load, take heart – posts can be short, and you can write them in advance.

Most people don't have the time or patience to read through reams of text, especially on the web and when reading on a smartphone or tablet. Two or three paragraphs are sufficient, longer depending on the complexity of the subject or the type of target audience you are appealing to with more detailed articles.

Don't use your blog as a substitute for advertising. Blogging isn't the right form for this. If and when you do mention your product/service, be explicit and honest about the fact that this is your own product/service you're mentioning. Keep the post short and link straight to the product page on your main web site instead of writing about it in detail in your blog. Don't stick to the same format every time or fit all your blog posts into a set template. This will make your blog look, sound and feel boring. Add visual interest with photographs, graphics, graphs and lists. Lists are simple to create and are highly effective for social book-marking and media sites such as Digg or del.icio.us. For example:

- Top 10 hints/tips;
- A-Z of *xx*;
- Companies' top 5 favourite *xx*.

If your blog's goal is to promote you (and your organization) as an authority, interview other prominent bloggers in your industry/sector. Your own organization's credibility will improve by association. When appropriate, link to previous posts from your blog in the main text of new posts. Do this judiciously. This works well for search engine optimization purposes and keeps readers on your blog for longer.

Just because a given post is no longer first/on the front page doesn't mean that people aren't still reading it. Review and revise old posts, improving and updating them as you go.

Not every post has to be wonderfully original. Other people's blogs can be and are often the main source of inspiration for good bloggers. Feel free to use ideas or content that you've read about in blogs or from any other source like TV and press – this is fertile ground. But never simply copy and paste other people's content. Re-write it in your own words and link back to the source of the content. This is ethical and as an additional benefit will increase the traffic to your own blog. Better than re-hashing content you've read elsewhere is to voice your own opinion on the issue, either agreeing or disagreeing with another blogger.

In the same vein, if you've come up with a great post or a great piece of information, encourage other bloggers in your network to use it (and link back to you). Again, it's about community and the etiquette peculiar to the blogging world. There's no such thing as an exclusive in the blogosphere – it is all sharing, changing, evolving, amplifying, debating.

Read and reply to what other people are saying in response to your posts. From a public relations point of view this is very important feedback and will help flush out important issues and opinions that can inform your communications strategy. You may unearth a rich vein of sentiment or opinion that is worth building on or challenging.

If you have genuine news to break on your blog, great. Otherwise avoid it, unless you've got a particular angle or opinion on a news story that had appeared elsewhere. People read blogs for opinion, not for breaking news. Remember blogging is only one aspect of digital and an 'exclusive' should be complemented with other vehicles, eg press release, tweet, LinkedIn announcement, etc.

TABLE 7.1 Successful blogging

Qualities of a good blogger
- Ability to 'listen' to the audience
- Passion for the topic
- Ability to communicate their personality online (not everyone can actually do this)
- Perseverance and commitment
- Good writing skills
- Sufficient time to do the job properly?

The corporate blogger's tasks
- Write posts
- Incorporate or write with key stakeholders in mind
- Reply to comments from readers
- Monitor other blogs in the sector/industry
- Comment on other blogs
- Keep up-to-date with industry news
- Build relationships with other relevant/influential bloggers

A corporate blogger's posts should be
- Industry-relevant
- Appealing to stakeholders/target audience
- Transparent and honest
- Personal and entertaining
- Related to what's going on in the blogosphere

Promoting yours or your organization's blog
- SEO
- Via the front page of your website
- Sharing via Twitter, Facebook, Google+ and LinkedIn
- Use your e-mail signature to promote the blog via a click-through
- Use Google Analytics to provide tracking and statistics

How people use social networks

I reckon I won't need to explain this to you, as you are highly likely to be a private user already. However, here we are talking corporate use not private use so there are some important considerations for us as PR professionals.

Just to recap then, there has been a huge and rapid rise in the number of social networking sites in recent years. They are now a mainstream communications technology for many people. These sites offer people new ways to communicate via the internet, via laptop, PCs/Macs, tablets or smartphones. The best-known examples include Facebook, LinkedIn, MySpace and Bebo. Sites allow you to create your own online page and profile and to construct and display an online network of contacts, often called 'friends' or 'connections'. Users can communicate via their profile both with their 'friends' and with people outside their list of contacts.

Many politicians, academics, journalists, ministers of religion and celebrities are users of social networking sites, some for personal and some for professional reasons. As professional communicators, why would we want to use social networking sites? Why might our organizations need to understand how they work as a communications vehicle?

The means by which UK consumers can communicate has transformed over the past five years, as new digital devices and services such as smartphones and social networking grow in popularity. Ofcom has produced Communications Market Reports since 2004 and these explore UK adults' personal communications preferences and use and produce some fascinating results.

The press release launching the 2013 Ofcom Communications Market Report, reported huge growth in the take-up of smartphones and tablets. The report paints a picture of a nation of media multi-taskers, transforming the traditional living room of our parents and grandparents into a digital media hub. People are still coming together to watch TV in the living room – 91 per cent of UK adults view TV on the main set each week, up from 88 per cent in 2002. But an array of new digital media is now vying for their attention. People are streaming videos, firing off instant messages and updating their social media status – all while watching more TV than before.

These activities are mostly carried out using smartphones, with over half of adults (51 per cent) now owning these devices, almost double the proportion in 2011 (27 per cent).

At the same time, tablet ownership had more than doubled in the past year, rising from 11 per cent of homes in 2012 to 24 per cent in 2013. The average household now owns more than three types of internet-enabled device, with one in five owning six or more.

Over half (53 per cent) of UK adults are now media multi-tasking while watching TV on a weekly basis. Watching other content on a different device is one of these activities.

A quarter (25 per cent) are regularly 'media meshing' – doing something else but related to what they're watching on TV. Examples of media meshing include talking on the phone (16 per cent) or texting (17 per cent) about what they're watching, using social networks (11 per cent) or 'apps' to communicate directly with programmes (3 per cent). Younger people are most likely to use other media while watching TV (74 per cent) with 44 per cent media meshing.

The impact of media meshing was seen during the 2013 Wimbledon Men's tennis final, with 1.1 million people worldwide tweeting 2.6 million times using hashtags associated with the tennis final. Of these tweets, around 80 per cent came from mobile devices.

The other major social phenomenon driven by digital devices is 'media stacking'. Half (49 per cent) of people use their smartphones and tablets for completely unrelated activities while watching TV every week – such as surfing the net (36 per cent), social networking (22 per cent) or online shopping (16 per cent).

Women are significantly more likely to media multi-task weekly (56 per cent compared to 51 per cent of men), as are those with children at home (66 per cent).

While the average household owns at least three types of internet-enabled device, the TV set in the living room retains its importance. People are increasingly reverting to having just one TV in their household – 41 per cent of households in 2012 compared with 35 per cent in 2002. In the first quarter of 2013, half (52 per cent) of 5–15 year olds had a TV in their bedroom. This compares to seven in ten (69 per cent) in 2007. And the proportion of UK adults viewing via the main TV set has increased from 88 per cent in 2002 to 91 per cent in 2012. The trend is for tablets to replace additional TVs in the home.

Live TV accounted for 90 per cent of all viewing in 2012, with the average viewer watching just over four hours of TV a day – 15 minutes more than in 2008. Viewers are also enjoying bigger screens in the living room. 'Jumbo' TV sets (43 inches and over) accounted for 15.8 per cent of sales in the first quarter 2013, a 4.3 percentage point increase on 2012.

Tablets are also supporting the continued popularity of watching TV live, with more than half (57 per cent) of tablet audiovisual content viewers watching live TV at least weekly via this device.

Previous Ofcom research studies indicated that, in terms of attitudes and behaviours towards social networking sites, social network users fall into five distinct user groups:

1 *Alpha socializers* (a minority) – people who use sites in intense short bursts to flirt, meet new people, and be entertained.

2 *Attention seekers* – (some) people who crave attention and comments from others, often by posting photos and customizing their profiles.

3 *Followers* – (many) people who join sites to keep up with what their peers are doing.

4 *Faithfuls* – (many) people who typically use social networking sites to rekindle old friendships, often from school or university.

5 *Functionals* – (a minority) people who tend to be single-minded in using sites for a particular purpose.

Non-users also appear to fall into three groups, based on their reasons for *not* using social networking sites:

1 *Concerned about safety* – people concerned about safety online, in particular making personal details available online.
2 *Technically inexperienced* – people who lack confidence in using the internet and computers.
3 *Intellectual rejecters* – people who have no interest in social networking sites and see them as a waste of time.

Research has shown that people use social networking sites in different ways. For many the importance of a well-developed profile page is crucial. Profiles often contain detailed information about the user, even though it is not compulsory to include this. Users enjoy customizing their profiles, posting photos, watching video content, playing online games, and in some circumstances, experimenting with aspects of their personalities.

Building a profile enables users to develop a wide online social network using the communications opportunities this presents. Users enjoy the process of building a social network, collecting a list of 'friends' and using this list of friends to browse others' profiles. Social networking sites stretch the traditional meaning of 'friends' to mean anyone with whom a user has an online connection. So a 'friend' includes people who the user has never actually met in person or ever spoken to.

Unlike 'real world' friendship, online 'friendships' and connections are also displayed in a public and visible way via friend lists. This public display of friend lists means that users often share their personal details online with people they do not know at all well. These details include religion, political views, sexuality and date of birth that in the offline world a person might share only with close friends.

The underlying point of social networking is to share information. But the risk is that leaving privacy settings open means that the user cannot control who sees their information or how they use it. So what does this all mean for us as PR professionals and for our organizations?

Communications and PR practitioners' role is to create, maintain and protect reputation. We may be generating awareness of our organization, our services and our products. We may be working in an issues-based environment – politics, religion, philosophy, academia. Here everything is ideas, policies, concepts, discussion. This plays out well in the social networking arena where people link, have common interests and values.

However, we may have, again dependent on our organization, a more traditional marketing role and may be responsible for building up a customer or client base with the ultimate goal of driving sales. Social networking sites now carry huge amounts of advertising and are huge generators of advertising revenue. If you have an overt sales message you may need to buy the space. If you are seeking the equivalent of editorial coverage on social networking sites, you have to respect the social networking environment. It is not a place to be blatant about marketing communications. You must learn and play by the rules. In my experience, I would work with your marketing colleagues to see how yours and their programmes could be integrated for such advertising (eg banner ads) as this will not only support consistent messaging but also save on budgets too.

Social networks provide heaps of opportunities to learn about people you might want or need to communicate with, either as a group or on a one-to-one basis. Read profiles to understand what people like, who they know, what causes they support and potentially what influences their buying decisions. You may want to find out about people who are using your product or service, or who may be using a competitor's product or service. You can build relationships and offer opportunities for people to try out a product they might not be currently using. Key point to note, is not to be aggressive. Pay attention to profile information, tweets, blog posts and so on.

Get to know some of the people you want to link to on social networking sites. This will require an investment in terms of time and some companies now recruit people to manage this function as a discrete discipline. Users of social networking sites will accept messages from a source with which they have built up a relationship already. Trust to some greater or lesser extent has been established. It's not just the equivalent of a hard, cold call. Unsubtle cold calls in social networking situations just don't work and may even stimulate a very hostile and negative response.

Social media and social networks are collaborative. So give to get – give ideas and be helpful, be human and, in terms of style of communication, be informal and even entertaining. Generosity works in social networking. In many respects it is just like any other form of marketing, in that you are building relationships with customers and finding out what they want and need so you can design your products and services accordingly – and then tell them you have responded.

All sorts of marketing and communications professionals are beginning to play with social networks, creating groups on social networking sites with specific interests and concerns. I think these brands and organizations are worth looking at to see how they use Facebook effectively:

- Marmite (https://www.facebook.com/Marmite);
- The Foreign Office Travel Information (https://www.facebook.com/fcotravel);
- Crohn's and Colitis UK (https://www.facebook.com/crohnsandcolitisuk).

Recruitment of specific sorts of consumers, encouraging support, voting for and against particular issues – think about what is right for your organization but make sure you do the groundwork first so that when you do start to make inroads into social networking sites you do it with skill. The aim is to find and unite supporters and give them something of value.

Virtual communities

An online or virtual community is the gathering of people in an online 'space' where they come, communicate, connect, and get to know each other better over time. The community is what its members make of it. Social networking sites create online communities through special interest groups. Other specific virtual communities exist too.

Online communities enable people to:

- **Socialize** – (social networking) to 'meet' others, to play, to share ideas, to take an interest in each other. Communities like this often focus around bulletin boards and chat rooms.
- **Work together** (business) – distributed work groups within companies and between companies use online community to build their team, keep in touch and even work on projects together.
- **Work together** (community – geographic) – local communities can communicate and work together as virtual communities. Community groups such as voluntary groups, football teams, school groups and others have used online communities to provide forums for information and discussion.
- **Work together** (issues) – virtual communities have been very important to people who share interests in issues and causes. Political issues, environmental issues, religious groups, people dealing with certain diseases, people studying together... all of these can form a nucleus for an online community.
- **Have topical conversations** – online salons and discussion forums bring together communities of people who enjoy conversations about topics and shared interests. Forums may have topics like relationships, business and finance, health, hobbies, religion, music and international issues.

For example, virtual communities can bring together:

- ethnic groups (eg black and ethnic minority);
- families/heritage (eg the MacDonald clan);
- geographical groups (eg Chinese diaspora across the United States);
- illness and/or disability support groups (eg diabetes patients);
- intellectual discussion groups (eg humanists);
- issues-based groups (eg gay, lesbian, bi-sexual, trans-sexual groups);
- members' groups (eg National Trust);
- political groups (eg Green Party);
- professional groups (eg public relations practitioners);
- religious groups (eg Liberal Jewish Movement);
- self-employed networks (eg HR people in West London);

- special interest groups (eg steam engine enthusiasts);
- workers (eg teachers).

Building an online community

First identify your community purpose and goal and be clear about it to community members. It may be for example to campaign for an issue, effect a change in government policy or to repeal a law and may therefore only exist until its objective is achieved. Internet access, access costs, computer and browser types, geographic and time zone issues all affect the type of community you build. You may have a group of people who all have high internet connection costs, or who don't have web access. In this case e-mail and newsletters may be a better bet than trying to get people to 'attend' online conferences, for example. This is especially true if you have a geographically diverse group with international time zone disparities where it is immensely difficult to get people together at the same time.

Do you want a public or private community? If you want to attract new and diverse people or supporters (for example to political, philosophical or religious ideas) a public community is more appropriate and these days may be best set up on a social networking site as a special interest group.

However, sensitive or private issues (for example an illness-support group or a business workgroup) are best discussed in a private forum that you would set up and manage yourself using a website which requires some kind of application to be made or requirement to be met before access is granted.

Private communities are safer from disruptive individuals who can make life difficult for everyone. They're good places for business workgroups, for illness-support groups, and for families, as well as groups discussing sensitive or private subjects. However, it can be difficult with private communities to get enough members to create critical mass. Public communities have more potential for growth and diversity. It is all about your communications aims.

There are a few key questions that will help you think about how your virtual community should work:

- Will your users be visiting from home or from work? Home users:
  - may not have broadband;
  - often have slower connections;
  - may not have state-of-the-art equipment;
  - don't have technical support available to them.
- Workplace users:
  - may have faster connections;
  - probably have newish computers and software;
  - are more likely to be Windows users;
  - are more likely to have technical support available to them.

- Will your users be in one time zone or not? This could affect your ability to run 'well-attended' live events (despite the fact you can always record webinars and load up to be watched later, as this somewhat defeats the object of a community where everyone can participate in the moment) and so on.
- How many visitors are you anticipating?
- Are there any physical limitations that your users share (sight impairment, mobility restrictions, etc)?
- How technologically savvy are your users? Will you need access to shared software so you can collaborate? And will most of your users speak the same language… or not?

The answers to these questions will determine how you proceed. The good thing is that the convergence of mobility, cloud computing and social networks is driving the development of a new range of low-cost or free unified communications services that will answer these questions. Google is the market leader in this brave new world with the launch of Google+.

The Google platform now allows businesses and individuals to create a Google+ page, build a following and interact with different circles. It has many similarities to Facebook, and some commentators have labelled it a just another social networking site, but as you explore its capabilities you will realize it is a potential game changer due to its integration and exploitation of search algorithms, collaborative tools and unified communications.

The first thing to do is create a profile for your Google+ business or personal account. For business accounts, sign up with a company or team Gmail address rather than an individual one. This means it'll be more accessible and multiple people can log in to interact and contribute to the page.

On the Google+ profile page you can include a profile picture and tagline. Before you start promoting your Google+ page, it's worth customizing your page beyond the basic level. You can do this by sharing some good quality content as links as soon as you've set up your account. You can also add recommended links under your 'About' section. This will generate more traffic and prompt other people to add you to their circles.

Image-based content like photos and infographics work well on Google+ as lots of individual images can be shared by multiple users. When you share content and links, ask others to share it within their circles. This is similar to asking people to retweet on Twitter. It is easy to do on Google+ and will ensure that your content is amplified quickly.

The 'circles' feature on Google+ is perhaps one of the key differentiators of the social networking site which makes it stand out from Facebook or Twitter. Once your profile has been customized, you can start adding people to your circles. Your circles can be split up into various groups such as family, acquaintances, and work colleagues.

Because Google+ allows you to categorize the people you connect with into circles and groups, you're also able to customize who can see and access your shared content. You'll also be able to see what other people are sharing in your related circles depending on their settings.

The Google '+1' button is a useful tool for sharing and generating awareness to posts. If you '+1' something, this shows you give it your approval. You can then comment or share the post with your circles. Your '+1's' are collected and stored in a special tab on your page. You can either share this tab or make it private.

If you have posts that gain a lot of '+1's' then it shows it is useful and worth reading. People are more likely to click on your content giving you an improved click-through rate. These can be embedded onto other websites much the same as the Facebook 'Like' button. Although this is just another sharing button, the importance of it should not be overlooked. It provides an effective call to action and will drive traffic to content.

Google is aggressively using SEO benefits to entice webmasters and bloggers to engage with Google+. Google Authorship is how Google authenticates and will increasingly begin to 'trust' you as a quality source of content. Google Authorship is the easiest way to take advantage of the SEO benefits of Google+. Doing so will allow the author's picture to show up next to his or her blog posts in Google search results, causing higher rankings and click-through rates.

Google's search tools mean that it can help you network better within the site. Google also gains an advanced insight into all your interests, what you are sharing and which contacts are most valuable to you. This means Google+ will be able to rapidly analyse trends and interactions.

Google also has an 'Events' feature that allows Google+ users to send out customized invitations to anyone regardless of whether they are Google+ users or not. It syncs with Google Calendar and shows up automatically when a user confirms for an event. In addition to sending out invites to webinars, work functions and launches, Google Events can also send out invites for Google+ Hangouts (I have already referred to Keene Communications' use of this on page 136). Google+ Hangouts, is a group video chat service and it is this component that completes the game-changing capability of Google+. Google Hangouts are easy to use and you can choose which groups of people you want to invite to your Google Hangouts session, making it easy to start a video conference in seconds.

To get started with Google Hangout, users need to install the Google Voice and Video plugin. This lets you use video in Hangouts, Gmail, iGoogle, and Orkut (another social network owned by Google). The plugin takes around 30 seconds to install. Each hangout session can hold up to 10 people using video.

When creating a hangout, you can choose which group of contacts, or circles, you want to invite to your video chat. A post will then appear on all relevant streams letting people know that a hangout is happening and it will list all the people currently participating.

If you've invited fewer than 25 people, each will receive an invitation to the hangout. Also, if you invite users who are signed into Google+'s chat feature, they'll receive a chat message with an invitation to the hangout. Users who have been invited to a hangout but try to start their own, receive a notification that there's already a hangout going on. Then, they get asked whether they want to join the existing session or create their own. Each hangout has its own web-address that can be shared, making it easy to invite people to hangouts.

Google Hangouts is a great alternative to Skype when it comes to hosting larger, but informal, video chats, especially since group video chat on Google is free while Skype charges for it.

Google Hangouts has Google Drive and YouTube integration, which means you can share documents and video with all the other invited participants. Combined together all these capabilities offer businesses the ability to use content, collaborative technologies and unified communications to achieve competitive advantage.

Twitter

As a public relations professional I can only imagine that if you haven't used Twitter you have only just come out of a 10-year coma. Twitter is *the* global breaking news channel. The hotly anticipated stock-market debut of Twitter in November 2013 exceeded expectations and a stampede for shares sent the company's value to more than $24 billion (an extraordinary debut for a company that had never made a profit).

Twitter is a short message communication tool (the 21st-century telegram) that allows you to send out messages (tweets) up to 140 characters long to people who subscribe to you (followers). Your tweets can include a link to any web content (blog post, website page, pdf document, etc) or a photograph or video.

People follow (subscribe) to your Twitter account, and you follow other people. This allows you to read, reply to and easily share their tweets with your followers (retweet). In the social media, Twitter is classified as a microblogging tool because of the short, disconnected messages it distributes. It shares features with the most common social media tools (Facebook, Pinterest, LinkedIn, Google+ and YouTube). However, it's the differences that make Twitter a very powerful communication tool.

A tweet is like a short Facebook status update. However, with Twitter, every tweet arrives at near real-time in every follower's feed. Twitter allows you to share photographs and provide commentary like Pinterest, but with Twitter, it's much easier to have conversation around a shared image.

While LinkedIn is based on trust relationships (and two-way agreements), Twitter allows you to follow anyone. This is a useful mechanism for following and targeting thought-leaders and prospects.

Twitter also allows you to organize people into lists similar to Google+ groups.

Your Twitter account and profile are the foundation of your Twitter presence and it's important that your Twitter site has the same brand values as your other online assets. Make sure brand continuity is maintained by choosing an account name, images, colour schemes and backgrounds that are consistent. Perhaps the most important factor to consider is your Twitter 'tone of voice' – does your brand or business have a voice or perceived personality? Make sure your corporate 'tone of voice' is replicated in the vocabulary you use to tweet. Nothing defines your brand on Twitter more than your account username. This name appears next to all of your tweets, and is how people identify you on Twitter. The settings section in Twitter enables you to easily upload photos and images, select colour schemes and add text descriptions to customize your profile.

So having created your profile, using the Twitter search tool to identify keywords related to your interests, this will provide a list of relevant Twitter feeds. Search through the results and then follow the other Twitter users who interest you – essentially by clicking on the 'follow' button you subscribe to read what they share.

Twitter has best practice guidelines on the rules of following – choose who to follow wisely and take the time to select the most interesting and relevant people.

As a general guide, start following people in the following categories:

- your customers;
- your business partners;
- your competitors;
- trade organizations or professional organizations for your industry;
- journalists and analysts for your industry (really important in terms of dovetailing this with your approach to traditional media);
- innovators and thought-leaders in your industry.

This process can be made more powerful by using Twitter Lists and creating lists with these categories – lists provide a powerful real-time intelligence feed on your industry. Engaging on Twitter is different from every other social media site. It's a real-time and continually updating environment. Don't panic when you first join, simply follow interesting people, listen to the conversations, click on interesting links and gradually start to engage.

There are five ways to engage using Twitter:

1 *Tweet*: a message you send out to everyone who follows you.

2 *@Reply*: a message you send out as a reply to a message you received.

3 *Mention*: a message you send out that mentions another Twitter username.

4 *Direct message (DM)*: a message you send privately to another Twitter user. (NB: You can only send a DM to someone who follows you.)

5 *Retweet (RT)*: a message created and sent by someone else that you share with the people who follow you.

So what should you talk about on Twitter?

If you share useful and relevant information, promote innovative ideas and are prepared to answer questions, you will attract followers, advocates and potential customers. Twitter is a great tool for driving traffic to your other social networks. Shortened hyperlinks can be added in a tweet and an interesting call to action in a caption can encourage clicks on the link.

To amplify all potential touchpoints, add your Twitter handle to the social media account information on your other social networks and also encourage people to share your website and blog content on Twitter.

The microblogging and real-time news capabilities of Twitter also make it a natural and popular channel for the rapidly growing global audience using mobile devices, tablets and smartphones. When this is combined with the capabilities of 3G, 4G and mobile broadband, it is no surprise that video content is becoming increasingly popular on Twitter.

You can add videos to your Twitter timeline, but you must first upload them from YouTube, and then link to them in your tweet. If your company has a YouTube channel with video content it is very easy to share this content on Twitter. A huge benefit is that Twitter allows you to play a video within the tweet and without leaving the platform – this makes for a very compelling user experience.

Twitter recently launched a new video service called Vine that allows you to take short, six-second videos and play them on an endless loop inside Twitter – this could be useful for communicating complex messages in a visual way to a global audience.

Another way to extend your potential Twitter audience is the use of hashtags. When you see a tweet with a hashtag, click on the hashtag to see a list of all tweets that include the same hashtag. This capability is really useful for events and conferences.

Remember the following Twitter tips:

- The more tweeting you do, the more engagement and clicks you'll get.
- Tweeting keyword-enhanced, good content throughout the day will attract followers specific to your industry/interests.
- Build your Twitter following by following those who follow companies/people similar to you.
- Use #hashtags to amplify your content.
- 'Favouriting' tweets acknowledges others and earn you followers.
- Use scheduling tools like HootSuite to broadcast tweets at peak times.
- Twitter Lists provide real-time intelligence feeds.
- Making some (not all) of your Twitter Lists public drives traffic to your profile and gains you followers.
- Branding your Twitter page like you would your website will help grow your following.

- Engage with key influencers in your industry by following them.
- Tweets with visual content can earn you more followers.
- Reference original source authors by including a 'via @tweeter' at the end of the tweet.
- Tweet when your audience are most likely to read your tweets.

Video and audio

People and organizations are discovering more creative, efficient and direct ways to engage with their target audiences and are producing their own programming. Podcasts enable anyone to engage in digital audio – and video – broadcasting. Some podcasts are professionally created by media organizations like the Press Association, while others are produced by creative individuals with just a PC or digital voice recorder or camcorder plus microphone and headphones.

Audio Podcasts

Podcasts cover a huge number of subjects – digital news, your HR director explaining new employee policies for internal corporate communications, political comment on a live issue, or even how to get a boyfriend via YouTube. Podcasting is not controlled and it is free to create and distribute. It is a great way to get a message across in audio video format.

Think of podcasts as mini radio programmes; so a podcast might be a talking head speaking or reading (well) on a subject; it could be a discussion between two or more people. It could take the form of an interview. To create a podcast, plan what you want to achieve and who the podcast is targeting. What will the listener want? The content is entirely determined by you, taking into account what will work well for the listener. Radio programmes often have some kind of identifying introductory sound, like an ident, a jingle or a distinctive piece of music. Podcasts should be no longer than 20–30 minutes. If it is all talk, limit each topic to about five to eight minutes, split up with the ident or jingle and then move to the next topic. Keep it fluid. Importantly, watch issues of copyright if you are using music that is in copyright in a commercial context.

Video programming

Forbes Insights conducts primary research designed to support both strategic and tactical decisions for business executives. According to Forbes (2014), executives are embracing opportunities to communicate, to research products and services, and even to make direct purchases from suppliers through mobile websites and apps. Smartphones are ubiquitous, and, increasingly, tablets are emerging as a device of choice for transacting business, poised to soon supplant standard desktop and laptop PCs. Importantly, video is becoming the critical information source for senior executives, heavily influencing global buying decisions. In fact Forbes states that 75 per cent of executives watch video once a week with more than half forwarding the videos they watch.

YouTube used to be the place where you could watch comedy videos, catch up TV, etc but now it is seen as another communication channel that organizations can set up themselves – for free – and easily too. Once you have a small library of videos that you can add to on a frequent basis, consider setting up a YouTube channel. This is used by government departments, commercial organizations and not-for-profits.

Great examples include:

- Department for International Development (http://www.youtube.com/user/ukdfid);
- Cancer Research UK (http://www.youtube.com/user/cancerresearchuk);
- Diageo (http://www.youtube.com/user/DiageoCareers).

Again you can promote it through the channels outlined previously, eg Twitter, RSS, etc. So every time you upload a new video, promote it via these vehicles. YouTube is an ideal vehicle to 'live track' views, comments (that will also need responding to) and which videos are popular (and which ones aren't). Understandably budgets in smaller organizations are limited so out of necessity these videos may need to be produced in-house, whereas larger ones may seek out professional support. In my experience, videos should be no more than four and a half minutes long (and ideally less than three minutes). This will keep your messages succinct and the viewers watching to the end.

Whether videos are produced in-house or via a professional agency, prior to filming consider the following:

- What are your communications objectives?
- Who is the target audience?
- Once you have clarified the above, draft the creative treatment (or storyboard) – just like a TV programme or film.
- What is the tone of your film, eg tearjerker, comedy, documentary?
- What is the background to the person being filmed? Make sure it is consistent with the tone you want to convey.
- What is the clothing of the person/persons being filmed? You may notice on news programmes that people wearing striped ties or checked jackets seems to strobe, so plain clothing is always best. But you may want your 'cast' to dress in a particular way to underpin a specific point (one of the UK's female ambassadors dressed in bikers' leathers and sat on a Triumph bike to help promote British trade in New Zealand).

Many broadcasters have found this an ideal way to attract and retain audiences both nationally and across the globe, eg BBC iPlayer, and as smartphones and tablets get smarter and so do network bandwidths, this will also make it easier for organizations to use this video as much as other more traditional vehicles. Content is created using digital recording equipment. A software programme enables you to edit and then upload your video. Windows Media, ePodcast Creator, Audacity and audioBoo are all good and widely available examples of software programmes.

Once you have an edited programme, it is loaded onto your website. Make sure the videos are marketed so people know where to find them and how to download them or subscribe to them automatically. Aim to make them entertaining, lively, educational, good viewing and listening – this is what makes people pass them on and ask for more.

If you want to reach a much wider audience, consider the following ways to 'push' your audio and video:

- Publish on your own website.
- Tweet via your corporate handle.
- Publish your MP3s file on a blogging service, like blogger.com.
- Share your podcast on podcasting.com or the iTunes Podcast Directory.
- Using the URL from your corporate website, create a RSS feed (Really Simple Syndication). There are two ways to do this – either code it yourself (http://www.rss-specifications.com/), or simply download software that will enable you to create and manage your feeds (using for example feedforall).

Your own TV channel?

Independent of YouTube you could consider setting up your own TV channel either for your internal audience or your external audiences. Think of CIPR TV. This can be highly effective providing you approach it professionally, in terms of quality standards, but it is likely to require a considerable investment in terms of time spent on it to get it right. That is not to say it has to be glamorous and glitzy, but it must be watchable. (There are so many examples of terrible use of video on the web... so beware!)

- If you decide it is right for you you'll need to invest in some kit and that should include: internet connection (of course); video equipment such as camera, microphones, sound equipment, sound mixer and lighting, an internet TV hosting service, video encoding software and a video stream supplier.
- Build a website to host your TV station. You can also upload those same videos on YouTube and Google.
- Build a virtual studio – consider the background, colours, branding, seating and camera angles.

- Start producing your TV programmes based on the types of audience you are targeting. Approach programmes as a producer would by writing the script first, doing thorough pre-production (ie planning how you will make the programme including using a storyboard), handling production (the filming/recording part) and then completing in post-production (editing and finishing the programme with titles and captions and so on).

- Always put your audience first in terms of creating something interesting that others would want to watch.

- While in theory you can upload any size of video, don't bore people. You are more likely to get and keep people's interest with programmes of between 5 and 15 minutes than 45 minutes (you are not Steven Spielberg... are you?).

- Publicize your programmes. Send e-mails with the URL or link to your channel so that people can watch your uploaded videos. Get people to subscribe to watch future programmes.

  Whatever you decide, make sure it doesn't turn into a party political broadcast by your CEO (grey men in grey suits are not what you want). So have a look at how admired organizations have approached this, how your customers and competitors have gone about it and how you can differentiate yourself, but most importantly to gain some inspiration and avoid mistakes.

Shooting your own video – top tips:

- Always use a tripod. It prevents shaking and gives you confidence to focus on the shoot. If you don't have a tripod, use the cupping elbow technique where the non-filming hand supports the elbow of the filming arm. Alternatively, seat your subject and rest the camera on an appropriate surface to offer stability.

- Try and get as quiet a room as possible to film in. The sound is very limited on small cameras so you need to be in a quiet place and close to your subject. Air conditioning can ruin the sound on a recording, as can mobile phones. Before you start filming, stop and listen to the noises around you. Are there any constantly, low sounds? If so, move. One-off noises like aircraft can be dealt with, but constant 'hums', eg from air-conditioning may make your recording useless. Small video cameras may have poor microphones, move in close or use pin-microphones. If you can't avoid noise, show the source of the noise in the background.

- Don't film in portrait. Film in landscape and get people to speak directly to the camera. If you're asking them questions, ask them to repeat the question in their answer. You'll unlikely to want your voice in the piece and it will make the videos self-explanatory. For example: 'Six months' means nothing to the viewer. 'I lost my baby six months into the pregnancy' makes (tragic) sense.

- Think about your background. Make sure it adds to what you are filming about. For example, if you were filming a piece about trains you would try and get a train or station in the background. Don't film at significant landmarks if you've not sought permission.

- Make sure your subject is lit, they must be the brightest object in the frame. A simple trick is to turn them fully or partially towards the window. Do not set your subjects against white walls or windows. You'll wash them out or make them a mere shadow.

- Don't film too close to the individual's face. Try and get a mid-shot with their neck and shoulders visible and focus their eyes.

- Try and avoid obstructive clothing: hats, coats, or clothing-labels. Politely ask the individual to remove their name badge/staff badge.

- Press 'record' five seconds before you actually want the filming to commence. You'll be more relaxed and the camera won't shake just as the subject starts talking. Leave a few seconds at the end before turning the camera off.

- Film general shots in support of your interview so when you are editing you have footage to package together with the interview and make it more visually appealing. Use a tripod and avoid zooming in and out.

- When filming general shots try to get a wide shot, a mid-shot and a close-up shot of the same thing so you can vary your shots when editing.

Taking your own photographs – top tips:

- **Get to know your camera.** Have the camera set to the highest pixel resolution. Take some practice shots – experiment beforehand. Take spare/charged-up batteries with you at all times.

- **Spend time thinking** about the pictures you need. Make a shot-list.

- **Look around you.** Try to make the best use of your surroundings. Avoid cluttered backgrounds; and try to photograph people in context where possible.

- **Try to use the best available light.** If shooting outdoors, try to do this in the morning or evening. Keep the sun behind you and slightly to one side. If indoors, try to move your subject near to a window; and try to avoid using flash.

- **Get great portraits.** Get people's names, titled for captions.

- **Get close to the action.** Get in close with a wide-angle lens; and use the zoom on your camera – but remember when you zoom in, it gets harder to keep the camera still.

- **Take a moment to frame your composition.** Look through the view-finder (if the camera has one). It's easier to frame an image this way. You can crop pictures but get the best you can in the camera.

- **Think about your point of view.** More dramatic pictures come from being above or below your subject, looking up or down at the subject – can you get an interesting vantage point to lift this shot above the ordinary.

- **With group shots focus on one person, one face and make sure he or she is looking down the barrel of the camera –** to give human interest and intensity.

- **Hold your breath when taking a picture.** Hold the camera with both hands; and rest against a wall or any available surface to help steady yourself.

- **Always take lots of pictures.** You can always delete the ones that don't work!

RSS

If you regularly post content to your business blog or website and want to increase your audience reach, consider RSS feeds. RSS is an acronym for both 'rich site summary' and 'really simple syndication.' It is a subscription service that summarizes and delivers the titles, summaries and links of your content in a digestible format to your subscribers.

RSS feeds push out your website and blog post content in bite-size portions into your subscribers' RSS feed aggregator tools – such as NetVibes, NewsGator, Yahoo, and Atom.

The best reason to have an RSS feed available on your website is that it keeps content fresh, constant and alive for your readers. When users subscribe to a feed, they see content sorted by most recent to oldest in their content streams and they can get more information when something matches their interest.

Subscribers need to know you have continually fresh content to offer, so review past posts and be sure you have a consistent content schedule before implementing an RSS feed. As new content continues to be published, the aggregator will check your RSS feed and update their feeds accordingly.

Creating an RSS feed on a website or blog is frequently done with do-it-yourself sites, such as WordPress. If you have a website designer, they can easily incorporate the feed on your site.

Once your RSS feed is implemented it will also drive traffic as RSS feeds are attractive to search engines and the more your content shows up in search engines, the higher your site will rank. This strategy can be enhanced by using SEO on headlines.

Traditional (aka elite) media

PR has for many people and for many years literally meant Press Relations. Whether you're in-house or a consultant, media relations has been the single most important aspect of the job for all of us, once the communications strategy and plan has been formulated. The achievement of positive or at least balanced media coverage in the media most watched, listened to and read by our target audiences was the goal, as editorial coverage was judged to be more valuable than paid-for space (ie advertising). This was because viewers, listeners and readers believed and trusted journalists as experts and authority figures, who would present them with news, views and content that was topical and true. And much of this remains true.

But the huge changes in the media landscape are changing the way we PR professionals work with media, including the relative importance we place on media as a channel to reach our ultimate audiences. Integrity has been called into question with the phone hacking scandal and the resulting Leveson Enquiry, leading to the Royal Bill affecting how the media operates, legally and ethically. So journalists are perhaps less trusted than they were.

Then we have the impact of digitization, changing the business model for media companies. Paywalls, free media, consumption of news online and for free, have all led to news organizations (newspapers in particular) shedding staff over the last couple of decades. Because multinational corporations control newspapers and need to maximize profitability, the focus has shifted from investigation and reporting to increasing audience (ie reader/listener/ viewer numbers). This is in pursuit of shrinking advertising revenues, much of which has diverted from traditional to social media. With fewer journalists employed and less time available for investigative journalism, content is sought from press agencies, from trusted sources and direct from organizations' PR teams. It has been argued that media has perhaps become *too* dependent on public relations for the supply of content for web pages, to fill air time, to deliver column inches.

The debate about the future of journalism and the direction the media is going in rages. Does printed news have a future at all? Is the local newspaper dead in the water? Do communicators and their organizations even need to think about media relations any more when they can use the internet and social media directly to accomplish objectives related to awareness and education?

Despite this soul-searching, the role of journalism in society is surely a crucial one – professional journalism 'shines a light in dark corners', exposes corruption, summarizes and reflects upon events, entertains and provokes thought. Democracy and a free media go hand in hand and I would argue that, as long as we have a free media, as long as we want to understand what is really going on in the world, as long as we have journalists whose opinions and reflections are listened to, whether they are writing for an online news site, a printed publication or a script for a radio or television broadcast, then the public relations professional must be able to engage with the professional journalist.

Journalists can be cynical about and critical of PR people, mainly as a result of PR people not really understanding how media and journalists work. However, most journalists appreciate those of us who *do* bother to understand how they work – and they are prepared to work with us. Indeed the power some big PR consultants and consultancies wield means that, as the primary point of contact between an organization and the media, PR professionals control access not only to a great deal of information that journalists need but also to individuals they want to interview. This gives some of us tremendous negotiation power when talking to journalists.

Ethics and the media – post-Leveson... where now?

There has been a whole load of soul-searching about media practice over recent years with the phone-hacking scandal and privacy invasion. Many media professionals think that their integrity has been brought into question, with some fearing that the result will be the suppression of good investigative journalism.

In my experience journalists understand the 'contract' that exists between them and their audience. They know that, if trust is broken, that relationship is severed. (Paradoxically it goes back to reputation – what we PR professionals are in the business of building, protecting and repairing.)

In the book *After Leveson? The future for British journalism*, edited by John Mair (2013), Phil Harding, former controller of editorial policy at the BBC, argues that ethical awareness and practice is established at the start of a journalist's career, with good training and mentoring. He goes on to say that this must be underpinned with mid-career learning and development for senior journalists (those who play a crucial part in editorial leadership: in print the people who give assignments to reporters; in broadcasting, those responsible for daily output) as these people get little or no training since those early years when they first entered the profession. Harding says, 'Regulation is what *you can and can't do*; ethics is what you *should do*.'

At the time of writing the Royal Charter on press regulation is in consultation process. Make sure you get a copy of the charter when it is finalized.

CASE HISTORY   The BBC

Whenever I travel anywhere in the world, for business or for pleasure, I ask people 'what do you think of the BBC?' The answers are overwhelmingly positive. 'Wonderful'; '... the best journalism in the world'; 'a lifeline for those of us in countries where the media is suppressed...'; 'OK a bit liberal middle-class, middle-England but who cares when its programming is so brilliant...'; 'a trailblazer across the planet.'

The BBC has had its difficulties – take the Hutton report and then the Jimmy Savile scandal and its repercussions. It is however attempting to recover its reputation with the publication of a set of editorial values which everyone – its journalists, editors, producers, backroom staff – is asked to work by. These editorial values form an impression of a media organization that is doing all it can to behave ethically, in the best interests of the public. Here are those values:

1   *Trust*

Trust is the foundation of the BBC: we are independent, impartial and honest. We are committed to achieving the highest standards of due accuracy and impartiality and strive to avoid knowingly and materially misleading our audiences.

2   *Truth and accuracy*

We seek to establish the truth of what has happened and are committed to achieving due accuracy in all our output. Accuracy is not simply a matter of getting facts right; when necessary, we will weigh relevant facts and information to get at the truth. Our output, as appropriate to its subject and nature, will be well sourced, based on sound evidence, thoroughly tested and presented in clear, precise language. We will strive to be honest and open about what we don't know and avoid unfounded speculation.

3   *Impartiality*

Impartiality lies at the core of the BBC's commitment to its audiences. We will apply due impartiality to all our subject matter and will reflect a breadth and diversity of opinion across our output as a whole, over an appropriate period, so that no significant strand of thought is knowingly unreflected or under-represented. We will be fair and open-minded when examining evidence and weighing material facts.

4   *Editorial integrity and independence*

The BBC is independent of outside interests and arrangements that could undermine our editorial integrity. Our audiences should be confident that our decisions are not influenced by outside interests, political or commercial pressures, or any personal interests.

5   *Harm and offence*

We aim to reflect the world as it is, including all aspects of the human experience and the realities of the natural world. But we balance our right to broadcast innovative and challenging content with our responsibility to protect the vulnerable from harm and avoid unjustifiable offence. We will be sensitive to, and keep in touch with, generally accepted standards as well as our audiences' expectations of our content, particularly in relation to the protection of children.

6   *Serving the public interest*

We seek to report stories of significance to our audiences. We will be rigorous in establishing the truth of the story and well informed when explaining it. Our specialist expertise will bring authority and analysis to the complex world in which we live. We will ask searching questions of those who hold public office and others who are accountable, and provide a comprehensive forum for public debate.

7 *Fairness*

Our output will be based on fairness, openness, honesty and straight dealing. Contributors and audiences will be treated with respect.

8 *Privacy*

We will respect privacy and will not infringe it without good reason, wherever in the world we are operating. Private behaviour, information, correspondence and conversation will not be brought into the public domain unless there is a public interest that outweighs the expectation of privacy.

9 *Children*

We will always seek to safeguard the welfare of children and young people who contribute to and feature in our content, wherever in the world we operate. We will preserve their right to speak out and participate, while ensuring their dignity and their physical and emotional welfare is protected during the making and broadcast of our output. Content which might be unsuitable for children will be scheduled appropriately.

10 *Transparency*

We will be transparent about the nature and provenance of the content we offer online. Where appropriate, we will identify who has created it and will use labelling to help online users make informed decisions about the suitability of content for themselves and their children.

11 *Accountability*

We are accountable to our audiences and will deal fairly and openly with them. Their continuing trust in the BBC is a crucial part of our relationship with them. We will be open in acknowledging mistakes when they are made and encourage a culture of willingness to learn from them.

SOURCE http://www.bbc.co.uk/guidelines/editorialguidelines/page/guidelines-editorial-values-editorial-values/

How media works

Newspapers, television and radio stations now broadcast breaking news on the web 24 hours a day, updated every minute, accessible to a world-wide audience, with pictures, video and audio. In a sense the old boundaries between print and broadcast have broken down – radio stations use photographs, newspapers use video, TV channels use text. Convergence is the name of the game.

Although circulations are inevitably declining as more and more people consume news online, **print media** remains an important and prolific sector. With online news media carrying breaking news, many printed versions of national press now concentrate on background features, colour pieces, exclusives and special add-ons that offer something different to the reader. There is a journal or magazine for everyone and everything; general interest consumer magazines, specialist press for experts and enthusiasts, professional journals, business and corporate titles.

Some glossy magazines offer compact, 'travel-sized' versions. Some new 'magazines' are launched online with no print version at all. Newspapers and magazines do not simply have websites they also have app versions for subscribers who wish to consume online It is all about what the consumer wants and what makes commercial sense. Behind it all is the commercial imperative to sell – and thence to sell advertising space – in order to make profit. Publishers think of themselves as content creators, regardless of the platform they use.

In this country virtually everyone can access to the web on their phones, at school, at university, in cybercafés, and the penetration of PCs at home via broadband is reaching saturation point. (Recently I had the strange experience of *not* having internet access, when I rented a cottage in the Pennines. But I went for lunch at the local pub… and hey presto! Wi-fi with my jacket potato and I was able to read the BBC headlines on my iPhone!) Yet in other countries across the world newspapers remain hugely important particularly where access to the web is restricted or non-existent.

While a significant number of young people say that they never watch it anymore, **television** remains a huge influence. The key aspect of television that makes it so powerful is the combination of sight and sound. Audiences are still huge, although more fragmented. On the other hand, the proliferation of specialist channels via satellite and cable has resulted in the ability to reach defined target groups, for example those interested in film, travel, history and children, the Asian community and so on. If people aren't watching TV as it is broadcast, they are certainly watching it later via iPlayer and other on-demand services. Internet television means you can watch YouTube films every evening, instead of the regular TV channels, if that's what rocks your boat.

Radio is ubiquitous – cheap, instant, accessible digitally on any phone, PC or Mac. It remains a very effective medium for discussions and debates, for the airing of issues and points of view. In remote and poor countries, radio is *the* medium of choice with solar-powered radios and phone chargers enabling connection to the outside world.

News agencies offer central and widespread dissemination of breaking news to reach international, national and regional news organizations. Every news outlet subscribes to the Press Association here in the UK and receives fast, accurate information, access to text, photographs and videos. For some PR practitioners news agencies offer the potential for the most widespread dissemination of information.

As I write there are new initiatives in media driven by technology, by commercial imperatives, by influences in the financial markets. Nothing stays the same in media and communications professionals need to keep abreast of developments by reading, by researching and by experimenting with new methods and channels as they become available.

Working with journalists' work

More and more communications practitioners are coming into the profession direct or from marketing and so have never worked as journalists. This can be a problem – the main complaints heard from elite journalists about communications people is that 'they just don't understand what news/what journalism/what my job is', 'they can't get the facts turned around in time' and 'they don't know the difference between news and corporate puffery'. We need to put ourselves in the journalists', the researchers', the producers' shoes. We have to understand what they need and want from us and square this with what we are trying to say about our organization.

The fundamental issue is that there are several agendas at work. These are:

- The target audience's agenda – what's in it for me? Am I really interested in this? Do I need or want to know about this? (If I don't, I may go to a different website/stop buying this magazine/paper, switch channels.)

- The journalist's, producer's, editor's agenda – is this relevant and will it therefore appeal to my readers/viewers/listeners? Is the feature right for our readers? If it's bad news, our readers/viewers/listeners have a right to know. If we don't get it right for our readers/viewers/listeners, we could lose circulation/ratings. Is this an exclusive that will help me build my own reputation? Will my editorial values be compromised if I pursue this story?

- The media owner's agenda – will this bring in the readers/listeners/viewers? Ie the higher the number, the higher the advertising rates we can set and the greater the income and profitability.

- Your organization's agenda – how can we get our message across through the media? How can we improve our awareness and favourability ratings through positive media coverage? How can we minimize and contain any negative media coverage?

In order to build relationships with the media on a day-to-day level we have to understand the journalists' agenda and work towards meeting their objectives while also achieving our own objectives.

The first thing to get right is prioritization. Each one of us must be clear and targeted, focusing on the media that is key to our own organization, to the sector we operate in and that is read by, viewed by, or listened to by our defined audiences and stakeholders. I would always start with a key 'hit list' the 10–20 media that are essential to us and with whom we want to build relationships.

Once we have our 'key media', then further refinement is necessary. Print journalists, photographers and broadcasters are frequently grouped together and referred to as 'the media', but we need to tailor our approaches to suit individual requirements.

Then find out about the way different journalists work. Talk to them, do your research, ask the right questions, read what they write and read about the media. If you are not interested in the media maybe you are not in the right job!

Broadcast media

When working with **television and radio** we need to remember a few issues and practical points:

- People watch TV and listen to radio news, documentaries and current affairs programmes to be informed. But the rest of broadcast output is essentially entertainment.
- It's a high probability that, if your organization appears on broadcast news, you will do so as a part of a 'news package' – these are a particular form of storytelling (see below).
- Consider the range of broadcast opportunities available, over and above news. These include:
  - Magazine programmes – for example *The One Show*.
  - Chat shows, interviews and discussions.
  - Serials, soap operas and series – where a storyline about, for example, a social issue would be both natural and appropriate for the characters (eg a story about female genital mutilation appeared in *Casualty* in April 2012 and created a great debate).
  - Current affairs programmes like *Panorama*.
  - Interviews (consider radio days with specialist radio production companies, where they pre-arrange a series of interviews for your spokesperson with a number of radio stations over the course of a day, all undertaken from one studio location).
  - Generic footage – which may be used to illustrate a story (for example airside at Heathrow).
  - Prizes – for example in quiz shows.
- Logistics are complex, and must take into account camera and sound crew availability, pre-production (ie planning and research), location finding, interviewee identification and arrangement, lighting, post-production, etc.
- While some TV is still live, much is pre-recorded – this means if you accept an interview you can do several takes (but you must still be a competent spokesperson – there are many examples when producers used poor takes to imply the spokesperson was incompetent or

evasive). This is less true of radio where there is a higher proportion of live broadcasting. (Radio is a remarkably responsive medium, broadcasting weather warnings, traffic issues, and getting information across about emergencies immediately.)

- Documentaries and current affairs programmes can be made months in advance of their transmission so they may not be broadcast to suit your timings, if they broadcast at all. Similarly interviews/footage/recordings may be held over for use at a date later than originally planned.

- Editing can change meaning, sometimes dramatically – so be prepared for this. (I think it is a calculated risk when assessing whether to take part in pre-recorded filming/recording.)

- If we agree to be being filmed, do we have the answers to these questions?:

  - Why do they want to film?
  - What format is it going to be edited into? (eg news package, documentary, pre-recorded interview).
  - Who do they want to film?
  - What do they want to film/photograph?
  - When do they want to film/photograph?
  - Who and how many people will be filming/photographing?
  - What equipment will they be bringing?
  - Do they have liability insurance?
  - How long will it take?

News packages

Watch the news at 10 pm tonight and you will see a series of news packages. Each story selected for the broadcast (based on news values – see page 167) is 'packaged' so it is easily understood by the viewer. Let's say it's a story about the Budget – it will in all probability go something like this:

> Anchor in the studio introduces the story in about 30 seconds. Package opens with establishing shots of the Chancellor leaving No 11 with his little red box, the House of Commons, the Chamber, accompanied by a voice-over (the political or economics editor) explaining the main issues.

Then we see and hear an extract from the Chancellor's speech, and it will be a sequence highlighting the main issue from the Budget.

This cuts to a series of graphics showing ups and downs, where taxes and allowances rise and fall, and will include fuel duty, alcohol (the impact on the price of a pint or a glass of wine), personal tax allowances, pensioners allowances and family credits). In other words the winners and losers.

Cut to a financial analyst praising the Chancellor's clever moves, with a soundbite of around 12–20 seconds.

Then a sequence of shots of an average family, settling on a mum and dad sitting on a sofa with their two children. Mum provides another 12–20 second soundbite about the negative impact of the Budget on their household finances.

Finally the news package concludes with the journalist doing a piece to camera summing up the story and a final shot of whatever has caused the most interest – family tax credits or that significantly more expensive pint of beer.

See what I mean? All TV news is packaged like this. So if you plan to sell-in to broadcast media what are you offering them? In short probably generic shots of your key issues, your products and services, and then interviews to allow editors to gather great soundbites.

Selling-in stories to the media

Whether for print, online or broadcast here's my advice for selling-in effectively and confidently:

- Make sure you have a genuine story!
- Write your story up first (as a news release or a feature synopsis) so your thinking is straight – try to think about all the other questions the journalist might ask not covered by the release (especially the ones you don't want them to ask and that you don't want to answer!).
- Allocate the right time to make a call (specific time of day, day of week to suit media – broadcast media; current affairs – three or four weeks ahead; TV news – up to one week ahead; radio news – a day or two before; print daily news – just one or two days before; monthly print magazines, maybe up to six months in advance for features-based stories).
- Rehearse before you do it for real.
- Have your diary/calendar and a pen at hand.
- Have the right numbers to call plus the names of the right people you need to speak to.
- Have all of your materials at hand – story, back up materials, e-mail text to follow, etc plus your contact details.
- Think about your aim again – why are you making the call? What do you need to accomplish?
- Make note of any questions that you need to ask.
- If you feel nervous or uncomfortable take a moment to visualize the conversation in your mind and take a few deep breaths.
- Think about how you'll capture the journalist's attention – what's likely to work best – and then pick up the phone. You might choose in preference to send a well-composed e-mail. Or even write a letter (fine for some print media, especially if is about something a little

way in the future or if you intend sending a product sample at the same time).

- Make sure to turn off or away from screens, music, or other distractions when making media calls.

- Remember that putting things off only makes it worse. Just get the calls done and you'll feel much better.

- Make the calls!

- Most calls start with 'Hi this is _____ ____. I'm calling from ____ ____.'

- Explain what's in it for them, eg 'I've got a story about...', or 'I've got a features idea for...'. Talk conversationally, not artificially, and leave out sales talk and corporate puff.

- Ask which way they'd rather receive the story and other support materials.

- Get the story to them – but don't harass or say 'When will you be using it?' – remember the final decision isn't up to reporters but to their editors.

- For broadcast tell them about the filming opportunities – and ask if they would especially like to film (and make sure you make it possible!).

- When you are finished with the call take time to thank the other person and reiterate the important information, ie 'Thanks___ ___. So I'll send ___ and ___ and we can talk later today, once you've had a chance to read it this through.' Or, 'Thank you and I'll see you on ____.'

- Make a note of and action all follow-up tasks/appointments immediately.

What makes good content?

The media is looking for stories, not simply corporate information, and people in the media get mightily irritated by non-stories being touted about by communications and PR people. The very first thing you need to develop is what the best editors and journalists have and that is a real understanding of what makes news content – and what does not. You need to be sure that you have stories worth contacting the media about, otherwise it is a wasted effort and moreover may affect your reputation and impact on your ability to build relationships with the media. In this respect, you need to act as a consultant to your clients and advise them when their story is not up to scratch or needs more news value to work.

In 2001 Leeds Metropolitan University (Harcup and O'Neil) conducted a study looking at what makes news, the sorts of factors that determine whether a story is collected, selected and included by news media. The study identified 10 major factors:

1 *Magnitude* – how BIG is this story? Here in the UK? On the world stage?

2 *Relevance* – how relevant is this story to our readers/viewers/listeners?

3 *Power elite* – does this story involve royalty, politicians, lords, police, lawyers, anyone in authority?

4 *Celebrity* – is this a well-known face? Someone who is an icon, for whatever reason? Someone our readers/viewers/listeners will recognize and want to know about?

5 *Entertainment* – will this amuse our readers/viewers/listeners? Does it make us laugh? Does it break the monotony of everyday life?

6 *Bad news* – how will this affect people? Is there fault here? Is there someone to blame? Are there some dramatic pictures?

7 *Good news* – do we have a hero? Is this a cure for a disease we would like to see eradicated? Does this make life noticeably better?

8 *Surprise* – well I never knew that! That's amazing!

9 *Follow-ups* – a year since... five years since... What's happened in between? What's changed since then? What happened to the people involved?

10 *The news organization's agenda* – we have a liberal/well-educated professional/conservative/working-class audience so this story plays well with us.

So then, to ensure you have a good news story that news outlets will want to collect and select, ask yourself the following five questions. The more of these five elements you have in a story the more likely it is you've got a fighting chance; the lower the score, the more you should consider reworking your story, representing it perhaps as a feature or using it on your own website or in your own newsletter;

1 Is the story **topical/timely** (just happened/about to happen)? News travels immensely quickly and is old immediately. So assume recent means today and tomorrow but never yesterday. Look out for hooks to breaking and running news stories – what is your organization's point of view on this subject? Do you have a new angle you can offer? How do you respond to a news story that breaks today where you have a significant perspective to offer? Not all news stories are created from scratch on the day. Of course some stories appear out of the blue (especially dramatic breaking news about disasters, deaths and murders) but many are the result of forward planning and careful preparation. Newsrooms have diaries to help teams plan what is coming up. Preparation allows journalists to do their research, contact potential interviewees, create scripts and also allows TV and radio editors to allocate resources (ie film and recording crews). So plan ahead so your news stories relate to, capitalize on and exploit what will be happening in the next year.

2 Is the story about a subject or issue that is **relevant** to our readers/
viewers/listeners? As a rule, the more people it affects, the more
newsworthy a story is. This means it needs to be seen as relevant,
important and interesting to first the journalist and then the ultimate
target audience. This is an important question because it helps to
focus on both the stakeholders and the media most likely to be
interested in the story, so you direct your effort where you are most
likely to be successful. For example, the launch of a new beehive will
be irresistible to the news editor of *Beekeepers Monthly* but may fall
on stony ground if sent to the consumer editor of *The Times* – unless
you know he is a keen amateur beekeeper or that honey will taste so
different or the story is fantastically quirky.

3 What is **unusual** or even better **unique** about this story? The clue is in
the word **NEW**s – a good story is unusual – people haven't seen or
heard this before. That's why they will be interested – this is not
familiar, not the same old, same old... there is an unusual angle or
aspect, there is a new creative element. Think *Guinness Book of
Records* – first time, last time, one-off event, largest, smallest,
youngest, oldest, fastest, slowest...

4 Where is the **tension**? All stories – soap operas, novels, operas, films
– need inbuilt tension to work and grip the audience. Is there **trouble**
or **tragedy**? Or is this story about a **triumph over tragedy**? These all
add that vital tension to the story. Journalists are trained to look at
the other side of the coin. A press release from an organization only
gives that organization's point of view. The professional journalist
will ask, 'Who would take a different stance? Who would oppose
this, challenge this, take issue with this?' These questions are asked in
the interest of impartiality, so there is no bias. Journalists love a story
where they can act as champions of the public, campaigning for the
right to information. Publishing material 'in the public interest' fuels
media interest and commitment. Truly interesting stories have
dramatic tension that comes from two or more parties in opposition
or from engaging in a struggle. If the story is something your
organization doesn't want to talk about, it's probably a 100 per cent
bona fide genuine news story. Randolph Hurst, the newspaper
magnate, famously said, 'News is what someone does not want you
to print – the rest is advertising.' The best news stories are laced with
crisis, conflict and/or controversy. The good news is that most skilled
practitioners – and the brightest and most responsible management
teams – can turn a PR disaster into a positive opportunity if they act
swiftly and deal honestly with the media.

5 Where is the **human interest**? Real news is all about people – news is
created by and affects people. Celebrities do of course attract
media interest, especially if a photocall is offered. But real people,
who have done something heroic or extraordinary, who have an
important or interesting story to tell are just as good, in fact

usually better. However do not assume that the media will find your chief executive interesting just because he thinks he is important. If he isn't interesting but dull, charmless or arrogant, don't use him as a media spokesperson. It's the organization's reputation that is at stake and the spokesperson projects the values and character of the organization. Get an outside consultant to help you deliver unpalatable truths to senior colleagues if you daren't risk your job.

The news-gathering process

Once you are certain you have a story, you can consider how you maximize the chances of it achieving coverage. In terms of gathering content, the same basic three-stage process applies: collection, selection, rejection.

Regardless of platform, media organizations need content and news intake is centralized on the news desk. The news editor takes an initial look at news just in. He or she will be using criteria to identify the news his/her organization wants; it's the first stage of selection.

Once selected the editor briefs a journalist/reporter, who will be asked to follow up a story. The brief may be for him to follow up a particular angle or to find more openings. Only senior and seasoned correspondents have free rein to pursue stories themselves. The majority of journalists work to briefs given to them and agreed by their editors.

With thousands of news releases being circulated every day from many sources the competition for selection is intense. Virtually every organization has wised up to the value of positive media coverage, from government departments and multinationals to small- and medium-sized enterprises and even the very smallest of local charities, and this has made the PR practitioner's job even more challenging.

Hard news stories – an earthquake, a terrorist attack, a high-profile death, a new treatment for cancer, the conviction of a child killer, derailed commuter trains – will bounce all but the most robust PR stories out. Even the tightest PR plan can't legislate for this. The lesson is don't simply target the news desks – be ready to get your story to the specialist correspondents, relevant freelancers, specialist media and specialist bloggers.

It has been estimated that over 80 per cent of media stories produced by PRs are deleted by the media. Many only receive a cursory glance, regardless of whether they are delivered as e-mails, faxes or through the post. Write well, sift out non-news and put out good newsworthy material. (Post is sometimes still used, if you are sending a product to a journalist for sample/ review for example and that sample needs printed information to go with it.)

When you have made a good contact in the media, then you can go direct to the journalist with a story. On these occasions you can choose to give an exclusive and may be able to offer an enticing one-off in-depth interview that will give the journalist the competitive edge. This may be an important and persuasive plus point when the editor weighs up the story's value during the selection/rejection process.

If you are not the source of the story, but it involves your sector in general or your organization in particular, you may be contacted by the journalist and asked for a response. You may be prepared for this and have pre-prepared 'lines to take' or it may hit you out of the blue. You may find yourself shifting into damage limitation mode using principles of issues or crisis management. The journalist may ask you to confirm or deny facts and is likely to seek direct quotes. Your organization may be called upon to be an expert witness and journalists may come to you to obtain information they can't get elsewhere.

If on the other hand you have been proactive and put a story out which has elicited a reaction and pick-up, then you should be prepared for any follow-up that is required. Journalists tend to pursue a line of enquiry that reflects their own knowledge, feelings and emotions about the subject in question. Consequently journalists questioning styles vary enormously and they may ask superficial or very probing questions. Journalists generally don't want to haul you over the coals and the Jeremy Paxman/John Humphrys style is pretty much reserved for spokespeople representing organizations that are in the middle of a difficult situation. But you may be asked questions by an inexperienced journalist so be prepared to make things easy to understand and to simplify complex information.

In terms of making it through the selection stage, you will need to be fast and efficient and respect deadlines. You will also be expected to provide competent spokespeople, background information, still images and video at the drop of a hat. Once the journalist has all his/her information, he/she will write the story. He/she is likely to be under pressure and won't thank you if you fail to deliver on time, give incomplete or incorrect information or pester him/her for feedback. The professional journalist will also check and verify facts and information with his/her sources.

The journalist never works alone. Once the story is written it will be passed to the news desk or news editor where it is edited for the first time. This might mean being binned in its entirety, rewritten by the editor, shortened or returned to the journalist for amendment, development or a complete rewrite.

Once the story is accepted, the subeditors have traditionally* taken over – their job is to ensure that the paper version gets to print and the online bulletin goes out quickly. They will also be responsible for ensuring that the house style is followed and that the news items fill the space available. So it's at this stage that the story may be shortened (or 'subbed'), photographs, videos and other images (for example satirical cartoons) will be added and again accuracy is checked. The subs also write the headlines. The article may still carry the name of the journalist who originally wrote it (the 'by-line') but it will not look entirely the same as the piece he submitted. It is unfair to blame a journalist if the story has been severely hacked about and appears

---

*I say 'traditionally' because the role of subeditor appears to be being phased out, again a resultant factor of changes in the media business. This function is being absorbed by journalists and editors and by the technical team who make up the web pages.

to give a distorted view of the issue. The editing process needs to be rigorous particularly for online presentation so anything judged as not adding substance to the story or that is factually doubtful will be cut. Selection and rejection are intertwined and there are hurdles all the way along the process.

Corporate expectations about media coverage need to be carefully managed – the organization which expects lengthy news coverage of a new product may be sorely disappointed if a piece resulting from what was a lengthy interview with the chief executive is brief. But providing the main message is there and it is in the right media reaching the right target, you should count a news piece of even just a few lines as a great success, providing it's in the media you really want.

There are so many media outlets that it's impossible to have good working relationships with absolutely everyone. These days it's quality not quantity that counts. Journalists and media-bods are frantically busy and, while the offer of a slap-up lunch at the newest and hottest restaurant in town may sound appealing, few people working in the media have either the time to spare or the inclination for a jolly with a stranger if there is no real story in the offering. Lunch works best when you have got to know someone a bit first and have the basis for a good hour's chat with the passing across of decent material. And lunch is the place for relaxed chat and industry gossip too. Start the ball rolling with this suggested action plan:

- Identify the top 5–10 media titles/stations/websites where you would like your organization to achieve coverage.

- Study the titles/stations/websites carefully – read them, watch them, listen to them regularly and work out where your organization could fit and where you might be able to tell your story.

- Research names of editors, journalists, bloggers, presenters and researchers on key subject areas/programmes – follow them on Twitter, monitor what they say about your industry or sector, you or your competitors, issues and news.

- Approach these named individuals by offering an informal meeting over coffee/tea, or a drink, so that you can introduce yourself and your organization. At the meeting hand over a short reference press pack with the website address. If they can't/won't meet you for a meeting send them well-written information. Give them your website address, your Twitter handle and Facebook page reference and any other social networking details. They may chose not to follow you but you have at least offered them this way of connecting.

- Try to make contact not less than once every three months. Invite them to informal events, one-to-one briefings, etc and feed them stories, picture and feature ideas regularly.

- Make yourself accessible: return calls from journalists as soon as possible. Journalists work under the tyranny of deadlines and the demand of editors for new stories.

- Be as helpful as you can. Even if you can't give them the information they need at that time, be as charming as possible.
- Be friendly but beware of over-friendliness that takes you across professional boundaries.
- Never say 'no comment'. It always sounds like you are guilty or avoiding the unpalatable truth.
- Never lie. The lie becomes a story and your reputation and that of your organization will be seriously damaged. If you can't tell the truth then don't tell a lie. If you give a piece of incorrect information, correct it as soon as you realize.
- Thank them if they write about your organization favourably.
- Don't harangue if they criticize but do take note and act on fair criticism. No one has editorial control apart from the editor.
- Have less formal meetings with them (eg coffee, lunch, drinks) when you feel you have the makings of a relationship based on trust and respect.

Hints and tips for working with broadcast media:

1 Listen to the radio and watch TV and online news outlets: study how others do it. Good programmes to study are:
   - *Newsnight*.
   - The *Today* programme.
   - *The Andrew Marr Show*.
   - *Channel 4 News*.
   - *Five Live* news bulletins.
   - As far as news is concerned there are obviously diary stories – scheduled weeks or months before – alongside the breaking news stories. If there is one programme you judge to be the best to reach your target audience (for example *Newsnight*, the *Today* programme, *Woman's Hour*) make sure you listen to or watch most editions. Then when you do make contact you can do so confidently and knowledgably.
   - Other perhaps more consumer-led opportunities exist for getting your message across when hard news is scarce – obviously you need a good angle:
     - Seasonal and thematic campaigns, for example dovetailing into the Christmas season, Valentine's Day, summer holidays.
   - General feature programmes.
   - Discussion shows, chat shows and phone-ins.

2 Make sure the story you have to tell meets the 'is it news?' criteria and is highly people-orientated. Have case history subjects ready to tell the story like it is.

3 Watch your timing: regular programmes have weekly planning meetings. Consider long-term sell-in for exclusives giving plenty of planning time and involving the programme throughout.

4 Identify the right person to talk to: forward-planning teams, producers, reporters, correspondents and intake.

5 Look for opportunities particularly in slow news seasons: Bank Holidays, Christmas, New Year, or school holidays (bear in mind you need to make yourself available to do this well).

6 Always call before sending any material – then make sure you have a text to e-mail immediately.

7 Write specially crafted material for radio and TV – standard 'press' releases don't work. Write crisp and colloquial material that reads well aloud. For TV write a 'TV Advisory' which focuses on the visual elements and has all the elements that will make a story work as a TV package: what video film is available, what filming opportunities are available, interviewees and statistics or key facts. And for radio, write a 'Radio Story Advisory', including notes about spokespeople and possible sound effects.

8 Create pre-recorded video footage of broadcast quality to support stories where footage would be hard to obtain for the broadcasters – this will increase your chances of coverage. Obviously this costs money, so set aside a budget.

9 Select the right spokespeople for each: make sure they are trained and have two or three main messages that they are comfortable and familiar with.

10 Be prepared to work unsociable hours to suit radio and TV production schedules: the *Today* programme for example runs between 6 am and 9 am each morning and interviewees need to be there at least 40 minutes before live interview – which could mean a 4 am wake-up call!

Press conferences

- Press will still sometimes come out for conferences but far less often than in the past as there are fewer people to cover, they are all working under pressure and they don't want to waste precious time.

- Don't have a press conference unless the news is staggering or you are in the middle of issues or crisis management and the eyes of the media are on you.

- Work out how much it will cost per head either to hold a press conference or go out on a series of one-to-one briefings (frequently yields better results in my experience) or consider a Google hangout (see page 147).

- Try out the idea of the conference – before committing yourself – with three or four journalists. If they aren't interested, don't go any further. You know you are onto a loser.

- Bill the event as a press reception, if you want it to be a lower-key and informal occasion, largely held for networking purposes.

- If you do proceed, only invite the media likely to be interested.

- Choose a date that doesn't clash with another event, a competitor's event or a national occasion. Avoid school holidays if you are after consumer journalists, many of whom have children, unless you offer a crèche or entertainment for the children too.

- Make sure it's held at a time that will suit the majority of those you want to attend. Find out what time will suit your key contacts.

- If you are going for a press reception, these are usually held over breakfast, lunch, drinks or dinner and may feel much more like a party than a business event.

- Choose a venue that will suit the majority. Unusual venues may be beautifully creative but may be hopeless for access and travelling.

- The press conference is for the press – it is not a 'jolly' day out for management. Only have as many people as you need to do the job and give then all a specific role – no viewers, passengers or hangers-on – and never outnumber the journalists on the day.

- Call those invited the day before to confirm numbers for catering, not to harass them to come.

- Many people still use a 'signing in' book on the press desk to act as a record of attendance but also for security purposes, although journalists and photographers sometimes manage to slip in without recording their presence, especially if it is a busy conference.

- Expect people to tweet and provide a Twitter handle and hashtag for the event.

- Post materials on the online press office immediately after the event.

Setting up a press office

Press offices come in all shapes and sizes. Some small organizations can manage perfectly well by allocating the press office function to a properly trained member of staff on a part-time basis. Others need a full-time, dedicated team of people working 24/7, particularly if you are working for high-profile international organization. Press officers typically provide press briefings, statements to the media, crisis-handling, lines to take and support for spokespeople. A press officer needs good relationships with colleagues, alongside sound media judgement, good writing skills and the ability to pre-empt the media and prepare accordingly. It also helps if you are creative and ready to think of imaginative ways to approach a story or get coverage.

Great press officers are resilient and also calm in a crisis as a busy press office can be quite a challenging place to work. The function may be subcontracted fully or in part to a PR consultancy. Form should follow function. To help decide what sort of press office you need to set up, you need to ask yourself:

- Are you operating in a high interest/high issue or low interest/low issue sector? The more high interest/high issues you have, the more reactive resources you will have to allocate. And the more low interest/low issues you have, the harder you are going to have to work to gain media interest.
- Are you stimulating coverage with proactive initiatives or are you in mainly reactive mode? The more proactive you are, the more effort you may need to make and the more media interest you will generate.
- What are the aims and objectives of the press office and its press officers? The more aims and objectives, the more effort and people will be needed.
- How do you brief press officers on what is happening in the business so they are competent to handle press enquiries confidently and competently?

Practical hints and tips:

- While there are agencies and news release companies who handle mass distribution of releases via e-mail, err on the side of the 'less is more' rule – target media tightly for better-quality coverage.
- Journalists go to Twitter feeds and websites for background information on organizations, as well as to pick up previous news and to get the name of the public relations officer (PRO). So make sure your online presence is working hard for you.
- Follow key journalists on Twitter.
- Go to meet journalists whenever you can – and try to take a look backstage at their offices – it can be enlightening, helping you realize what sort of pressures and environment they are in.
- When working with the broadcast media, all the same rules apply.

Make sure journalists understand the basis of any briefing at the outset:

- 'This is "on the record"' – 'Everything I say can be reported, along with my name as the source and the name of my organization.'
- 'This is "off the record/unattributable"' – 'I am telling you this and you can use the information but do not identify me as the source or allow it to be traced back to me.'
- 'This is for background only/not for use/in confidence' – 'I am telling you this but it is between us and you cannot use it. The reason I am telling you this is that, if you don't know this information, what you write will make no sense/be misleading/be a completely daft piece that will later be found to be incorrect.'

Press office checklist:

- Location:
  - facilities and equipment;
  - ISDN lines;
  - internet access.
- People:
  - the scope of the role of the press officer(s);
  - social media responsibilities especially monitoring selected journalists on Twitter;
  - web-editing;
  - sector experience;
  - consultancy/freelance support;
  - admin/PA support;
  - training needs.
- Resources:
  - press materials – digitized;
  - photo library – digitized;
  - video footage – digitized;
  - spokespeople – media trained;
  - video/audio kit;
  - other collateral;
  - samples service for journalists.
- Communication and information:
  - dissemination of information throughout the organization;
  - website and journal reading and circulation;
  - Press lists;
  - media- and web-monitoring;
  - media coverage reports.
- Budget:
  - capital costs – kit and equipment;
  - running costs;
  - salaries/fees;
  - operationals – press events, reception, lunches, etc.
- Evaluation of press office activities:
  - media evaluation;
  - journalists' feedback.

- Launching and marketing the press office:
  - internally to colleagues;
  - externally to media;
  - externally to other third parties – partners, suppliers and customers.

Media contact log – checklist

All proactive calls to or reactive calls from media should be logged so that action can be taken and a record kept of interactions. Typical information taken should include:

TABLE 7.2   Media contact log – checklist

Date of call Call received or made?
Name of journalist/researcher? Which media? Staff or freelancer? Contact details Phone E-mail Twitter handle?
Website/publication/programme
Deadline
Enquiry
Information given
Further contact required?
Date story is likely to appear (if known)
Name of person taking/making call
Details passed on to

- 'This is an important point because…'
- 'What this all boils down to…'
- 'The heart of the matter is…'
- 'What matters most in this situation is…'
- 'And if we take a closer look, we would see…'
- 'I think it would be more correct to say…'
- 'Another thing to remember is…'
- 'What I've said comes down to this…'
- 'Here's the real issue…'

Performance   Your general manner is important. If you are nervous, it will be reflected in your voice and may make you come across as 'shifty'. You need to come across as cool and collected – even if you don't always feel that way. Breathe deeply – watch the expression on your face. Always smile for an upbeat interview and a show a serious face for a serious issue.

Conflict makes great broadcasting and the presenter may attempt to 'provoke' you to make you sound combative. Be assertive (you'll need to be sometimes just to get a word in) but not pushy. Empathy is essential if you are in discussion with someone relaying their personal experience or talking about an issue or crisis that involves people.

No matter how obnoxious your co-interviewee, guard against appearing aggressive or smug. It may be helpful to remind yourself that the audience (which really matters) and sitting in front of a PC catching up on the day's news, are watching TV on the sofa with the kids, are listening as they drive home from work or are doing the washing-up.

You don't need to be defensive. If, for example, an assertion or allegation is made which, in your experience sounds hugely unlikely, feel free to say that in all your experience you've never come across similar incidents and bridge to a positive point you can make with confidence.

Ten rules for spokespeople appearing on radio and TV:

1   There is only one rule really and that's *prepare, practice and perform.*
2   Check logistics and fellow speakers:
    - Where are you supposed to be and when?
    - Transport: are they providing? (They should do.)
    - For TV will they be providing make-up? (They usually do.)
    - Will it be live or recorded for later transmission? Live means that you have a good opportunity to get your messages across without later editing.
    - Who are you up against/with? Will they be hostile or on side? Get your bridging phrases ready.

- What's the composition of the studio audience if there is one? Pitch the message so they feel involved.
- If the filming is in your office what backdrop should you use? (Bear in mind the camera operator will look for best lighting and composition.)
- If part of a package, what is the story likely to be and who else will be filmed?

3 Get your key messages clear in your head before you get to the studio or the crew get to you: make sure you get them in.

4 Check names of presenter(s): don't get it wrong.

5 Dress comfortably but reasonably formally for television:
- Men: to convey authority, wear a dark suit, pastel shirt with a colourful (not striped) tie or to communicate the work of the organization, clothes to suit (for example high-visibility jacket for emergencies, bright clothes for deaf people's projects, branded t-shirt/sweatshirts for promotional stories).
- Women: for authority, wear a jacket with skirt or trousers (your bottom half isn't usually on display) or again clothes that communicate the work of the organization if you are in the field. Avoid black as it drains the colour from your face. Pastels are usually kinder. Avoid big jewellery: it's distracting on screen.
- Glasses: don't wear them if you can manage without, but not if so doing makes you squint or peer.

6 Communicate well and with energy and enthusiasm:
- Remember to use language that people – both audience and viewer – will understand and *never, ever* use jargon. If your spokesperson will explain the issue better in a language other than English, tell the interviewer this and try to offer a translator.
- Statistics can be very dull but if you have a really strong killer fact that enables you to 'paint a picture' – like '7 out of 10 handbags bought in the UK are produced by children under 10 working in sweatshops in developing countries' – then use it.
- Use examples and anecdotes to bring your story alive – this makes the message more memorable to the listener/viewer.

7 Speak a little more slowly and – if you can – more deeply than usual: it helps convey authority (especially for women). Also think about your breathing and try some deep breathing before the interview.

8 Don't take any documents with you: rustling paper sounds dreadful in front of the microphone, is distracting in front of a camera and will certainly trip you up.

9 Forget the microphone or camera and try to keep the level conversational and lively, as if you were explaining your subject or point of view to a friend in the pub over a pint or over a cup of tea.

10 Much of the magic is in the performance as broadcast media is largely entertainment, so try to enjoy it, be enthusiastic and passionate about your subject and your organization and this will translate. If they like how you perform, producers and researchers may invite you back again and give you another chance to get your message across using these powerful media. And in time you develop the position of authority on your area – the first choice for comment if the issue goes live. The aim is to get into the journalist's/ researcher's/producer's contact book.

Thinking like a journalist – what will they ask in interviews?

As a rule, short questions are better than long ones, simple questions are better than convoluted ones, and clear questions are better than fuzzy/ambiguous ones. That said journalists who are trying to control the interview, have it in for you (or are inexperienced and trying to be clever!) may ask you long, convoluted, fuzzy and complex or compound questions, especially leading questions. These are the questions journalists most often use.

Open questions – that allow initial expansion and development:

- Exactly what is…?
- Tell me about…?
- What made you…?
- Why do you think…?

Closed questions – that get the facts and clarify:

- Did you…?
- Are you…?
- What's…?
- How many…?
- How much…?
- Where…?
- Who…?
- When…?
- Why…?

Leading questions – which are a sub-section of closed questions:

- You're a Conservative, aren't you?
- How did you react? Were you furious?
- How much money went missing – more than a million pounds?

Assumptive questions – which can be annoying or, if phrased well, get into interesting areas:

- Are you married or single? (When the answer may be neither.)
- Were you educated in a grammar or private school?

- When did you last take drugs?
- How many redundancies will there be?

Direct, suggestive or loaded questions – which are somewhat manipulative:

- What sort of person would disagree with the campaign to make foxhunting illegal?
- It's proven that alcohol cause all sorts of social problems so why should manufacturers be allowed to continue to freely promote their products?
- Gandhi said non-violent protest was the only way – don't you agree?

A few interesting questions that get a new perspective on a person:

- What's the most important lesson you've learnt?
- How would you explain that to the man or woman on the street?
- What three words would you use to describe yourself?
- What makes you angry?
- Who's been your greatest influence?
- What's your favourite quotation/saying?

Look for questions used in interview features on television, in newspapers and magazines. Simon Hattenstone of *The Guardian* is excellent in terms of asking original questions. Study him and other excellent journalists to get a sense of how they build their stories.

Traditional media – checklist:

- Do we know what is going on within the organization to deliver a flow of news stories and features to the media?
- Are we following key journalists on Twitter and reading their copy/watching or listening to their programmes?
- Do we have good news stories:
  - new product;
  - new company – acquisition or merger;
  - new person;
  - new contract;
  - new investment;
  - new research?
- Do we have good features? Or could we provide the following features-based content:
  - expansion and development of a news story;
  - review of organization's products and/or services;
  - interview with or think piece from organization's figurehead;
  - market/sector analysis or developments in the sector;
  - educational backgrounder;

  - tried-and-tested feature;
  - regular columns, eg advice and letters' columns?
- Are all our media materials well written? (See Chapter 11.)
- Is the media tailored for different media sectors and target audiences?
- Are our media contact lists up-to-date?
- Which named media could we deliver this story to in advance, to stimulate greater quality media coverage?
- What is the best route(s) out to the media we are targeting:
  - one-to-one briefings;
  - Twitter;
  - e-mail;
  - press conference/online press conference/press reception?
- Do we have good images:
  - digital pictures – stills and video;
  - portraits of key personnel and spokespeople;
  - products;
  - generic shots;
  - all captioned?
- Do we have enough samples/literature for media distribution?
- Are the spokespeople fully briefed and media-trained?
- When should a particular story be released:
  - share price and other corporate sensitivities/regulatory issues;
  - distribution in place;
  - spokespeople available?
- Is the press office staffed/switchboard briefed?
- Who will manage media relations out-of-hours and are contact details up-to-date?
- Is there a need for other briefings to ensure co-ordination:
  - internal;
  - suppliers;
  - distributors/dealers;
  - customers;
  - opinion-formers?

Face-to-face

Despite the fact that we do so much online, face-to-face communication remains the most impactful channel to get your messages across. It enables you to create multi-sensory experiences, using vision, sound, taste, smell and touch, all of which make an interaction more memorable and 'sticky'. Face-to-face events with a communications purpose, linked to other marketing activities, can be powerful channels to deliver important and sometimes complex messages to key target audiences, helping to build reputation in a very close-up and personal way. This is the right forum to communicate the importance of an issue, to give new information, to project the values and stature of the organization, to demonstrate how the organization respects and values the views and opinions of the invited target audience.

But with people being as busy as ever and with time-management courses preaching the need to prioritize, potential attendees will ask always 'is this event really one I need to attend?' Skype, webinars, online satellite conferences enable us to communicate without leaving our offices. We don't ever need to shake hands any more, share a drink or move from the comfort of our offices... or do we?

The point is that social networking does not satisfy all human needs for interaction, whatever the fans of it say. People will go to events – and in great numbers – providing it is clear what is in it for them, that logistics are attendee-friendly and that invitees have enough notice to get themselves organized to be there. Human beings will always need contact and, as less and less contact takes place on a day-to-day basis, so relevant, appropriate and tailored face-to-face events become even more important as a way of keeping in touch. And they will use social networking to say they are attending and to talk about their experience while they are there and after they have gone home.

Whether you are organizing a round table discussion for 10 or 12 business gurus, an advisory panel meeting for a group of the country's top neurologists or a public meeting to discuss a local planning application, the central principles remain the same. However, for large events, unless you have particular expertise or have your own special events team in-house, I would at the outset urge you to consider using a special event organizer. Their extensive experience will help ensure that your event runs smoothly. Indeed when you are putting together your communications strategy an initial consultancy session with a special events organizer may give you new and creative ideas about how the inclusion of appropriately designed events might deliver considerable added value to your programme.

When thinking about face-to-face you'll need to take into account the pros and cons of face-to-face engagement:

Pros:

- Face-to-face communication is, as I mentioned, the most direct and, arguably, the most memorable and powerful method of reaching the stakeholder.

- There is focus on the theme or issue – 'background noise' and day-to-day distractions are reduced.

- There is time for complex information to be presented and discussed in detail.

- Online and satellite links can network participants in any number of locations or countries.
- Social networking enables people to amplify their experiences.
- You can demonstrate corporate openness about a sensitive issue on a public platform (although this needs careful managing).
- The stakeholder can be made to feel special/important – 'this is just for me/us', 'my opinion matters'.
- If you 'own' the event (ie you are the organizer) you have ultimate control over content, format and style.
- If you are taking part in an existing or new event organized by a third party, your organization, product or service will be associated with the values of that event and organizer.
- Smaller organizations may derive status by being associated with an event which puts them in front of a wider or more prestigious audience.

Cons:

- You will have to work within or negotiate parameters set by third parties if you do not own the event.
- Unless you resort to online techniques, events require people to take time away from the workplace and/or home – not only the stakeholder attending the event but also your own staff.
- The cost-per-head is usually higher than other PR tactics.
- You may have to hire and train external contractors to provide management and additional staff.
- There are often complex logistical issues to resolve – the bigger the event the more likely it is that you will need to think about subcontracting to a reputable event-management specialist.
- You need to plan well in advance – sometimes a year or more – to secure speaker opportunities, the best stand positions, hotel accommodation, etc.

Conferences and exhibitions – designed to bring a large number of people together to discuss common issues. Associations and unions may also bolt on an annual general meeting for members and use the exhibition facilities to generate income. These may be sponsored – and therefore owned – by the organization or it may be an event where the organization is playing a subsidiary role, with, say, a stand or exhibit, the sponsorship of a fringe meeting or taking up a speaking platform. If it is owned by the organization, this is probably the most complex event scenario and one where an event/conference management company should probably be called in as soon as possible. There may be an overt sales objective or the main aim may be to reach a large number of individuals, representing an important target market, to build bridges, gain opinions and undertake research or to reassure after a difficult period.

Sales conferences – designed to motivate the frontline sales team. Usually includes performance data and encourages competition between sales teams, Often used as a briefing meeting to tell the team about new products and services they will be expected to sell and so may show new advertising, etc. May also include training sessions on sales or customer service. May be residential if the sales teams work from home. The communications team is sometimes asked to help organize part or all of these events.

Internal staff events and briefings, etc – designed for internal communications purposes, sometimes one-offs, sometimes as part of a change management programme, sometimes regular, routine events that happen quarterly/annually. May be held on- or off-site – obviously there is far more control of on-site events – quite apart from the fact that they are usually cheaper. May involve a large number of people or smaller groups. May be phased over a period of time to get to all staff over a region or over the country.

Online – or virtual – events – at their simplest form a webinar, at their most sophisticated a multi-site entertainment extravaganza for a private audience, with the look and feel of a TV show. Used when it is judged impossible to bring opinion-formers and influencers from all over the country together – for example doctors or Business Link advisors – or when people are based in several different countries. Can also be used as part of an internal communications programme for international companies. Virtual events enable people to gather together where some or all of the attendees are not physically in the same location but are connected in a common environment. The common environment might be one of many types but is usually enabled through the use of computers and the internet. Many people are now experimenting with virtual events for communications purposes, often to stretch budgets but also to access and attract reach audiences that would otherwise remain hard to reach.

You may have virtual events that are on-demand or live. On-demand services/sessions are when content is available online and can be accessed as and when demanded or required by the viewer or listener. Live services usually cannot be replayed, as the broadcaster will transmit the programme content or service at a certain point and once the broadcaster stops the live service, the viewer or listener cannot access the content. You may also have *live simulated*, when pre-recorded activities/sessions are set up to run at a specific time and date (and are not publicized as being pre-recorded) and are followed by a real-time live Q&A.

These are the main types of virtual event:

Webcast – transmission of an audio or visual or a combination of audio-visual media file either live or on-demand over the internet. Webcasts generally use the streaming media technology, which broadcasts the content from a single source to multiple viewers or listeners simultaneously. Do I need any extra hardware? A webcast will require a headset or speakers to listen to the audio script or the version as a part of a media file streamed on the internet. It does not require any extra high-end hardware other than your PC speakers.

Slidecast – a set of slides broadcasted on internet with the synchronization of video and audio effects. Slidecast will facilitate the multiple viewers to see the deck of slides simultaneously in a multimedia presentation format, uploaded on a single source.

Virtual trade show/online trade show – this is a combination of some of the most successful elements of a live trade show collected and translated into a multimedia file format and broadcasted or transmitted on the internet. Virtual trade shows allow the exhibitors and sponsors to reach their target audience round the clock. Some are run over a short time period (one to three days usually) and others are open for months.

Virtual expo/online expo – an online virtual exposition hall accessible over the internet. It is a multimedia format that gives the real-time experience of visiting and moving (in 2D or 3D) around in the virtual exposition hall and booths using arrow keys on your keyboard. Available to visitors online round-the-clock, though there are usually specific times that the exhibitors are present in their booths and you can chat with them.

Virtual job fair/online job fair – as it sounds, an online job fair that gives the potential employers and employees access to up-to-date job openings and company profiles through online booths/stalls that attendees can visit similar to the virtual exposition. This can be one of the most cost-effective techniques used to attract employees, saving time and travel costs.

Webinar – the transmission of an audio and visual media file scheduled at a particular time or on-demand over the internet. The content comes from a single source to multiple viewers simultaneously. A webcast will require a headset or speakers to listen to the audio.

Virtual meeting – a live event or meeting that is done using a virtual platform generally available from one of the virtual event platform companies, custom-built or hosted on a virtual world like Second Life (SL) perhaps in a virtual conference centre.

Audiocast/audio conference – a telephone-based conference consisting of a presentation that will usually include an audio-based question and answer session.

Virtual (or synthetic) world – most often used for gaming (though can be used for conferencing and text-based chatrooms) a virtual world, like Second Life, is a computer-based simulated environment. Users inhabit and interact with animated figures called avatars. Avatars are usually depicted as textual, two-dimensional, or three-dimensional graphical representations, although other forms are possible.

Hybrid event – when a mixture of a physical event and a virtual event is offered, usually running simultaneously and with overlapping content and interactive elements.

Awards ceremonies – the culmination of a project that involves a competition or a nomination/voting system, involving peers (like the Oscars), fans (like the Brit Awards) or specific groups with a vested interest (like parents, invited to vote for their Teacher of the Year). There are thousands of awards ceremonies every year and these are often, in specific industry sectors, associated with or sponsored by media – often the main industry trade press title, for example *WhatCar?*'s Car of the Year Awards or, in our own industry, the CIPR Excellence or *PR Week* Awards. These can surround an organization with 'warm glow' and can help drive awareness of a brand name (Man Booker Prize) or an issue (National Training Awards). Pre-publicity is vital – and television coverage may be part of a sponsorship package. Event logistics may be complicated, particularly if there is to be complex staging, music and lighting – a prime example of when an events management company should be called in.

Seminars and workshops – have many purposes and can be tailored to suit many target audiences, from graduates entering a profession to experienced people who want to sharpen their practice or skills set. Because they involve smaller numbers that a lecture, the cost-per-head will be higher. However, the opportunity to drive key messages home in depth – and to perhaps achieve a change in perception or behaviour – is greater. These sorts of events also enable you to recruit ambassadors to perhaps act as advocates for your organization and to speak with knowledge and experience – people who understand you and the sector you operate in and the specific issues facing your sector. Cost-effective webinars can also be considered here.

Private breakfasts, lunches, round tables or dinners – used to gain information from and to network with selected individuals. Only suitable for small groups where the interests are shared and where the tone is informal and intimate. A prestigious board room occasion for 8–12 VIPs including an important guest of honour, sector guru, elite journalists, a respected speaker and chaired by an experienced facilitator can work well to attract important targets, to create a powerful forum for discussion and debate and to generate opinions for future communications, media, promotional and marketing use.

Lectures – designed to bring together opinion-formers and influencers and packaged so that the organization is surrounded with positive values and kudos. Think Dimbleby Lecture or TED talk. Suitable not only for organizations with a serious academic or research-based orientation but also for professional organizations where theory can be brought alive and even made sexy via a whizzy and entertaining presentation. May be a launch platform for new report or paper. Can be treated as an opportunity for networking and may be followed by a drinks party and canapés. May be used to offer exclusive media-relations opportunities to highly desirable media targets.

Press conferences and photocalls – for example, on-site after a rail crash or to announce the launch of a new treatment that will reduce the risk of developing cancer, or featuring a celebrity supporter. Only consider a press conference if the news you have to deliver is really strong, the issue your organization is involved with is in the headlines or you have an A-list celebrity supporter. Photocalls can be useful if your visual subject is strong or, again, you have engaged the services of an A-list celebrity.

Parties – which may be to celebrate the launch of a new perfume, to mark a significant anniversary for an organization, to open a new restaurant, to kick off or conclude a sponsored exhibition, sports event, concert or festival. If the story is really newsworthy or has an amusing or quirky angle, the more you increase the chances of achieving media coverage. A-list celebrity attendance might tip the balance, but don't bank on it.

Using events to get the message across

PR consultancy Kaizo won a CIPR Excellence Award in 2012 for the use of events as part of a launch programme for the sweetener Truvia®. The Truvia® Voyage of Discovery transformed over 400 square metres of the roof at London's most iconic retailer, Selfridges, into a magical pop-up island and boating lake (which metaphorically represented the birthplace of key ingredient stevia and recounted the unique journey taken by the Truvia® brand to becoming US category-leader). Two thousand public tickets sold out within two hours of going online and 200 journalists and influential retail customers and potential partners attended. Ten TV slots, including *Daybreak*'s weather reports, added to over 500 million opportunities to see the brand launch.

Top tips for event management

TABLE 7.3   Top tips for event management

If you think you can achieve your objectives in any other way, don't have an event
Use your common sense and don't underestimate how much planning and organizational time is needed
Secure the venue first – provisionally book three if you must but do this first
Give people plenty of notice – send out dates for diaries four to six months or even a year ahead if you want VIPs – follow up with invites
Get a great online presence using Facebook and Twitter
Brief staff on duty carefully – on the day these people are your organization's ambassadors
If you are including breakout sessions and workshops build in time for people movement on the day
If you can, make it a weekend event as hotels and conference centres are less busy and may be willing to negotiate on price

(Continued)

TABLE 7.3 (*Continued*)

Invite guests and partners for a better attendance level

If there any more than 50 guests consider subcontracting to an event management consultancy – delegate properly and let the event management company liaise with the venue, etc

Make events interactive and participative – people like to express opinions and to have a chance to share ideas rather than be lectured at – let people Tweet and Facebook

Treat everyone you have invited as an individual

Event management checklist:

Planning:

- Has this been done before? Do we have any benchmarks? Did we achieve our objectives? If not, why not? How can we improve?
- What are our objectives for this event?
- What type(s) of audience(s) and how many are we targeting?
- How do we make this event attractive to and relevant to them? How can we make it a 'must attend' occasion:
  - location and ease of travel;
  - date and time;
  - content?
- Content – what do we need to include:
  - speakers;
  - celebrities and/or chairperson;
  - audio-visual (AV);
  - display;
  - giveaways/delegates packs/papers/digests/event 'newspaper', etc;
  - competitions?
- Are there any networking opportunities?
- Critical path – up to the event and including any follow-up?
- How much will the event cost, in total and broken down by:
  - set, stands and/or displays – space costs, design and build, equipment, transportation and storage, samples, prizes, giveaways and gifts, branded merchandise;

- supporting hospitality and complementary events – eg press reception, business briefing, private drinks party, sponsored dinner – venue hire, catering, speakers, entertainment, set/branded backdrop;
- design and print – all materials, eg packs, leaflets, invitations, etc;
- staffing – fees, accommodation, catering, travel, celebrity/speaker fees if required;
- marketing – Facebook/web page, advertising, leaflets/flyers;
- sponsorship?

Action:

- Guest management – invitations, RSVP monitoring, joining instructions, accommodation, management on the day including stewarding, goodie bags, gifts and giveaways.
- VIP management – speakers' briefing, chairman's notes, breakout session format.
- Event management – booking, liaison with venue, recce, access, room layouts, set/stand design and build, set-up, set strike and get out, print materials, catering.
- Staff management – hire additional staff, staff briefing, transport and accommodation, corporate clothing/dress code.
- Web page – how does this need to be handled so guests can engage with the event from the start?
- Media relations – media invitation and press desk/press office management, at exhibitions and conferences, press day attendance.
- Support materials – literature, brochure/catalogue copy, advertising.

Evaluation:

- Review event as soon after it has taken place as is practicable.
- What went well and what could have worked better?
- Write a summary report so that lessons learnt are captured for next time.
- Circulate that report to management and anyone who has an interest in the event.

Print

PR professionals still need to create and produce well-designed materials to support their communications activities. We can't rely on digital/social media, traditional media or events to deliver every message to every audience. Just think of these examples:

- A housing association communicating improvements in services to its residents, some of whom are elderly, some housebound (this needs a simple newsletter).
- A not-for-profit organization seeking to gain volunteer mentors for local young people (this needs a well-sited poster carrying a phone number and e-mail address).
- An awards event where attendees include the great and the good whom we believe don't spend much time using social media but who will be captive for three hours (this needs an impressive programme for the event).
- A retailer whose staff spends all day serving customers and do not have access to the internet at work and may not have it at home (this may need a quarterly staff magazine).
- An organization with staff who speak English as a second language and do not have access to the intranet (this may need a bilingual staff newsletter).

Even if you don't actually print materials yourself, you will go to pdf stage so that your audience can either read on screen or print it themselves if they prefer.

Printed materials PR professionals usually have some responsibility for include:

- leaflets and brochures;
- newsletters;
- reports and reviews;
- posters.

Writing a design brief

There is more on this in Chapter 9 when we are thinking about different visual communications techniques. Regardless of whether you are going to undertake the design in-house yourself or are going to commission print design from a graphic design consultancy, you'll need a design brief. The starter question is: what do we need this for?

Think about your audience:

- Who is this aimed at?
- Why are you communicating with them in the first place?
- Why are you communicating with them in print form?
- What do you want them to be thinking/feeling/doing once they have seen this work?
- What are they thinking/feeling/doing about this issue now?
- Have you seen any pieces of work recently that did a similar thing well?

Think about your message:

- If you can only get three points across to your audience, what would they be?
- And what would you tell them to convince them?
- What tone of voice would you take?

Think about the practicalities:

- Is there anything that absolutely has to be included?
- Is there anything that absolutely mustn't be included?
- How is this piece of work going to be distributed?
- When is it needed for? Are there other key deadlines you should know about?
- How many do you need?
- What's your budget?

Think about managing the project:

- Have an idea of your timeline working back from when things need to be delivered. Printing and art working takes time, so plan it out from the start.

Designing print materials yourself

- **Planning** – With aims and objectives in mind, sketch out the design. Even a really rough sketch can help you identify potential problems and save time. Also make sure you have a realistic timeframe for your project if you are printing and distributing the material too.
- **Think about your audience** – Who is your audience? How are they going to see the final product (print or on screen)? Is English their first language? How do you want them to react? If you consider all this during the initial stages of the design process, your project will be better, simpler and quicker overall.
- **Get inspiration** – Do some research on similar products. Has anything like this been done before? Look outside your own organization for inspiration: check Google for reports, newsletters and materials produced by other organizations. Collect print materials you admire and think have done the job well. Learn from them.
- **Consistency** – If you don't have corporate identity guidelines, create some and remain consistent to them, in terms of font (style, size and colour), colour palette and proportions. Keep tables the same weight and size.
- **Less is more** – Don't pack your design with too much information: white space can increase the impact of your message. Think about

how people are going to see it. No one likes to read too much: ensure that your design has an impact by keeping it simple.

- **Colour** – Consider using tints of a single colour to keep the design looking consistent and clean. Colour can look one way on screen and be totally different in print so take care of this especially when thinking about your logo.

- **Align everything** – Simply aligning the elements of your design and keeping your layout evenly spaced will immediately improve how it looks. Most designers use grids to start their designs and ensure they are well aligned and balanced.

- **Images** – We cover this in more detail in Chapter 9. The key thing is to think about your images and what they help you say. Make them work with the copy. Clipart is sometimes used by not-for-profit organizations to save money but it does look cheap and unprofessional – and it is also a bit of a cliché. Use images that tell your story.

- **Test it out** – Ask a colleague to take a look and give you their opinion. This is a great way to pick up errors, as it's easy to get too close to your work to notice the obvious mistakes. If the design is intended as a rough to give to a professional designer allow him/her to use their expertise and accept their suggestions for improvement. And always test out a print version, don't just rely in the screen appearance.

Further reading

For practitioners who want to get deeper into social media I recommend *Public Relations and the Social Web: How to use social media and Web 2.0 in communications* by Rob Brown (2012). This book explores the way in which communication is changing and looks at what this means for communicators working across a range of industries, from entertainment through to politics. The book examines emerging public relations practices in the digital environment and shows readers how digital public relations campaigns can be structured. With a detailed look at communication channels such as blogs, wikis, RSS, social networking and SEO, *Public Relations and the Social Web* is essential reading for students of public relations.

08
Creativity in public relations

Creativity is intelligence having fun. **EINSTEIN**

C reativity is having ideas and its sister innovation is turning those ideas into reality. Just like in Shakespeare's *As You Like It* where Celia comes up with the good idea and Rosalind embroiders it and makes it work. Creativity is a desire to find a better way to do things, including things you do already, and to find new ways of working too. It involves looking at things in a different light and exploring new boundaries and possibilities. Creativity usually manifests in people who are curious and who take an interest in what goes on around them.

Creativity is a subjective gut thing and it's hard to measure. An idea that means one to thing to one person means something completely different to another. There's lots of subconscious and emotional intelligence in creativity. As a result, it has always been a challenge to sell creative ideas to accountants and super-rational clients who want to see evidence – before they commit – that this will sell, transmit an idea, persuade people to behave differently. That said, there are so very many examples of brave creative ideas that have transformed communications programmes, given them wings so that ideas have taken off in a way no logical, rational message never could have.

In public relations and communications creativity helps us solve problems and arrive at original combinations of words and pictures that have emotional and intellectual impact. Creative communications gives the message stand-out and memorability, makes it something people want to talk about, generating dialogue, impact and visibility. Effective creativity ensures that the message is seen, gains attention and prompts word-of-mouth exchange; people pass the message on, people are attracted to the message, like it and respond to it. It's about devising the right tactics – online, printed and experiential – to communicate the right message to your target audience of stakeholders. Creativity that seeks to be simply 'whacky', merely done for effect, is not what we are after although generating lots of ideas (some of which should be whacky!) is a goal of creativity – because the best ideas come out of having LOTS of ideas.

Let's take an example of a great creative campaign, a marketing case history for Procter & Gamble (P&G).

CASE HISTORY

In 2003 the company's traditional men's toiletry brand, Old Spice, introduced a body wash for men. Many other men's brands, including Nivea for Men, subsequently entered the market and with so much competition Old Spice's market share nose-dived. A further threat to the brand was the launch of Dove for Men, launched at the US Super Bowl in 2010. Creative thinking was needed and Old Spice looked for a way to protect its market share and, initially, to generate excitement among men who were not currently Old Spice purchasers.

The company needed an idea that would make it stand apart from the competition. Research had discovered that 60 per cent of men's body washes are purchased by women and so female shoppers had to be the prime target for the communication. Now if you are a normal sort of person you don't spend much time thinking about let alone talking about the product you use in the shower. It's a pretty low interest subject. But the brand team was certain that simple brand awareness/recognition would not be enough. What was needed was to get men and woman talking about body wash, and the virtues of a manly-smelling body wash (Old Spice) over a 'lady-scented' brand. All those new entrants into the market lacked masculine credentials. So Old Spice was able to position itself as the champion of 'manly-scented' shower products. If you wanted to 'smell like a man' there was only one choice and that was Old Spice.

This smart creative thinking led to the creation of 'The Man Your Man Could Smell Like' and the creation of the archetypal spokesman for the situation: a crusader against 'lady-scented' body wash, whose sexy, charismatic character appealed to both men and women. His 'look at your man, now back to me' dialogue practically forced a conversation between women and their partners.

'The Man Your Man Could Smell Like' first appeared on YouTube and Facebook a few days before launch of Dove for Men at the Super Bowl game. The advertising agency scooped up Super Bowl-related terms (like 'Super Bowl commercials') to drive traffic over Super Bowl weekend. With these tactics in place, online buzz for 'The Man Your Man Could Smell Like' was at its highest level just as the Super Bowl game was finishing. By the time the commercial appeared on television – 24 hours later and in a much less expensive timeslot – many people assumed that it first been aired during the Super Bowl.

After the initial launch period, the strategy shifted gear to get both sexes talking about the campaign. Instead of buying media space in heavy male environments like sports games, P&G went for audiences of men and women watching together. These included programmes such as *Lost, American Idol* and cinema during Valentine's Day weekend.

In a short amount of time 'The Man Your Man Could Smell Like' became a cultural phenomenon. Millions saw the advertisement, dozens of people parodied it. Media coverage about 'The Man Your Man Could Smell Like' was achieved on *Oprah, The Today Show, Good Morning America* and ESPN in the US. This was reflected too in international coverage.

In July 2012 a follow-up campaign, 'Response' was launched. This was a short two-and-a-half-day event when 'The Man Your Man Could Smell Like' recorded 186 personalized messages to Old Spice fans who commented on YouTube, Twitter, Facebook and more. Everyone wanted to ask 'The Man Your Man Could Smell Like' a question. All great fun. All generating enormous amounts of online discussion.

To generate more online buzz for this interactive effort, digital specialists identified influencers who had already admired the campaign and shown affection for the work. This included Ellen DeGeneres, Perez Hilton and Kevin Rose (the founder of Digg). Old Spice for Men has repositioned itself, secured its market share and created a unique personality and profile in a crowded market place, as a product for smart guys, and outsold the competition.

OK it's advertising but it tells us a lot about creativity. I love this campaign because it's smart and clever and funny and got people talking. We need ideas like these in public relations. Creative thinking helps us arrive at ideas that cut through the noise of modern life so that our target audiences pay attention to our companies, brands, our policies, our issues, our messages. We have to find ways to encourage creativity and nurture it. And we need to encourage it in ourselves.

Many people believe that they are not creative. That's simply not true – we were all children once and we all played and imagined. We are all creative but sometimes we work in organizations or even cultures where creativity is not a priority and not nurtured. It can be hard sometimes to be freely creative if you are working in-house and for a bureaucratic risk-averse organization – the public sector, say, where tax-payers are funding communications work. (*No frivolousness please!*) I would argue that you need to be even more creative in these circumstances as a great idea may have huge impact (remember the 'Best Job In the World' campaign for the Queensland Tourist Board?) If you work in a consultancy it's likely that creativity will be recognized as a key part of the job. In fact clients often hire consultancies to do their creative thinking for them. The good news is that creativity can be learnt and developed. All that is needed is the will. It is a wholly powerful and practical part of a public relations practitioner's skills bank.

Big ideas about creativity

In the workshops I run on creativity, I usually introduce participants to a few ideas about how we think to get them started. Many of these ideas have similar features. The first is about whole brain thinking. Roger Sperry, who won a Nobel Prize for his research on how the brain works, first suggested that the left and right sides of the brain were responsible for different functions:

- The left hemisphere for logical and rational thinking, the processing of verbal and practical information, judgement, evaluation, reasoning, systems and analysis. It's also where we control our speech. It is ordered and looks for realism.
- The right hemisphere is the non-verbal, visual and pictorial and emotional part, where we process images, create symbols and see colours. Intuition, recognition and comprehension happen here. It is also the part of the brain where dreams are processed. This is the creative side of the brain.

As communicators we need to use both sides of our brain. It is easy to see why. We need to think logically when we plan, monitor and evaluate, when we write messages and deliver them verbally and in written form. We need to think emotionally when we encode our messages using images, symbols and colour (see Chapter 9 on visual communications)

Edward de Bono (de Bono, 1969), the great writer and lecturer on how we think, gave us the terms 'lateral' and 'vertical' thinking. I like to describe lateral thinking as digging small holes in lots of different places to come up with many ideas and solutions for challenges where there is no right answer. Brainstorming and other techniques to get the grey matter working are used to stimulate lateral thinking. Vertical thinking on the other hand, is when you drill down more and more deeply for the single right answer. You use vertical thinking, for example when you are looking at research to arrive at a conclusion. Again we need to do both types of thinking as communicators.

In the same vein JP Guilford (Guilford, 1959) came up with divergent and convergent thinking, divergent thinking being the opening up of thinking, where multiple answers are possible, innovation and unusual, original ideas are required. Convergent thinking is linear and logical, a closing down of ideas to a single correct answer. We use divergent thinking to come up with lots of ideas and convergent thinking to narrow down all the options to one that we go with.

The key factors that determine how creative we feel we can be are parental influence in childhood, education, work environment, our home and family and our attitude to play and leisure. Our culture will also have an influence, encouraging creativity or not. Compare an art director working in an advertising agency on Madison Avenue with a bureaucrat working in North Korea. Compare these pen portraits of two different organizations:

TABLE 8.1 Portraits of two different organizations

Organization 1	Organization 2
We think mistakes are bad/not tolerated	We think it can be done
There is a blame culture	We welcome new ideas from all
We don't want to look foolish	We ask 'why?'
We don't want to upset tradition	We dare to be different
We are introspective	We are outward-looking
We don't step out of line	We don't get into a rut
We don't take risks	We make time to think
We hire people like us	We take an opposite view
We don't like change	We look at things from many viewpoints
We see things in black and white	We see the world in colour

Which one is likely to be the organization that comes up with new ways of working? Which one is likely to evolve and grow? Which one is likely to be the place that's most fun to work in?

The creative process

Graham Wallas (1926) and other commentators said that there is a clear process for coming up with great ideas and novel solutions. I'll describe it based on how we apply it in our business context:

1 *Pre-work* – we need to write ourselves really good clear briefs, with a crystal clear summation of what the problem or opportunity is that public relations needs to address. Delving into research, particularly motivation and influence theories regarding our target audience. Defining our problem or opportunity tightly is the first step to great creative ideas. For example, we might end up with the statement:

> We need to educate men and women aged 25–54 and in lower socio-economic groups about the health risks associated with obesity. We want

to persuade them to change their behaviours in terms of diet and exercise. We have found that they are so preoccupied with the business of daily life and earning a living to support their families that they do not factor in time for themselves.

2 *Idea generation* – we come up with all sorts of ideas using creativity thinking techniques, group brainstorms, individual 'daydreaming'.

3 *Frustration* – or 'the Groan Zone', when we have come up with loads of ideas yet don't think we have found the right solution.

4 *Incubation* – this is 'downtime' when we might sleep on it and it is a vital part of the process. Our clever brains still work on a subconscious level.

5 *Illumination/inspiration* – then something clicks. We recognize what will work and is likely to be a great solution. We use convergent thinking to narrow down and polish up the idea we select.

6 *Verification* – finally we test the idea and we might invest in focus groups if we will be mounting a big campaign and spending lots of money. If it's a media campaign idea we might talk to a friendly journalist or two and try it out as a concept. Or we might run it past other colleagues not involved in the communications aspect of the business.

It is always a challenge to sell creative ideas to people who are ruled by rational thinking. Forces against creativity include colleagues who like to play it safe and having few resources (people and cash) available. But when an organization is up against innovative competitors or is seeing media interest declining then maybe it's easier to make the case for creative bravery.

Twelve ways to wake up your creativity and solve problems

Journalist: 'Mr Burton, to what do you attribute your success?'
Tim Burton: 'I don't stop myself.'

We spend so much time at work using rational and logical thinking. I often ask people I am mentoring, 'When was the last time you were asked to use your imagination at work?' and 9 times out of 10 the answer is 'I can't remember – I don't think I ever have been.'

So it's no wonder that our creative abilities get rusty and we think that emotional and perceptual thinking is not what we do at work.

Excellent original thinking is exactly what you need when you want ideas and are developing campaigns and programmes to give them stand-out. There are lots of great ways to get the brain going. Here are 12 techniques I often use to come up with ideas for my own business and for my clients.

They are all fun and so people think they are playing when engaged in them, when in fact they are actually working hard and coming up with lots of great ideas. As I said earlier you can't have a great idea without having lots of ideas.

One – brilliant brainstorms

Some organizations have stopped using brainstorms, saying they are simply not effective. That's because they are often poorly facilitated so they are dull or – even worse – a chance for louder, more extroverted members of the team to show off and dominate proceedings. A noisy brainstorm can be hell for an introvert but a well-run brainstorm is terrific and generates lots of good ideas. These are the rules:

- Brainstorms work best when there are between 6 and 12 people. It is hard to keep everyone going if there are more than that in a group. Too few participants and it's not a rich enough cocktail to get a variety of ideas.

- If everyone is from the same team you may run into 'group think'. So don't just have everyone from the same work area – get in others with different perspectives from different parts of the organization. A good mix of personalities works best so aim for a mix of ages, genders and experience.

- Hold the brainstorm in a decent room – people's ideas flow better in natural light. Create a welcoming environment. I always play music as people assemble. I bring in coloured pens and paper and table-top toys like balls, Rubik's cubes, snowglobes and so on, so people immediately get the idea that they are allowed to 'play'. Make sure you are not interrupted and there are no distractions.

- Appoint a skilled facilitator and a scribe. Don't let the most senior person act as facilitator. Even if he or she is well liked and respected, it can stop others contributing. It might be better to have an independent facilitator who can encourage input from everyone and stop one person (including the boss) from dominating.

- Set either a strict time limit for the brainstorm or a target number of ideas – or both (eg 'We're going to generate 100 ideas in the next 30 minutes. Then tomorrow we will select four or five really good ones.')

- Express the goal as a question and don't make it too detailed as this will cut down free thinking and ideas generation (eg 'How can we get men and women aged 25–54 to take action and reduce their weight?' Rather than 'How can we get men and women aged 25–54 to take action and reduce their weight, using traditional and digital media?') and write it down on the wall as large as possible.

- Give individuals a chance to think – introverts particularly respond to this as they would rather think quietly on their own. State the problem and let people think on their own for five minutes and write their ideas down. Then get started. (Or you could tell people the question before the session and ask people to think about it before they come along, and to write down their ideas and bring them to the session.)

- I usually warm people up with a simple game like, 'Come up with as many new uses for… (a paper cup, a brick, a sheet of paper, an egg…) in three minutes.' Or sometimes I show them a slide show and play some music and ask them to pick their favourite picture and tell the group why they liked it.

- Then consider using an idea generation game (like the others in this chapter) to get people thinking more fluently. Suspend judgement from the start and all the way through.

- In order to encourage lots of crazy ideas, ideas should not be criticized, 'dissed' or evaluated. All ideas, every one, must be captured and written down. Enforce this rule rigorously. Apparently one learning and development consultant issues water pistols; anyone who is critical gets squirted.

- You want lots of ideas – as many as possible in the time allocated. Brainstorming is one the few activities in life where quantity improves quality. You need stacks of energy. Mad ideas that are completely unworkable are often the springboards for other ideas that can be adapted into great ideas. And good ideas often come after daft ones have tickled and stimulated your brain.

- End on a high note – thank everyone for their energy and input. Mention again one or two of the best, most inventive or funniest ideas. People love short, high-energy brainstorms that lead to actions. So don't finish the brainstorm with vague promises of what comes next – get on with it as soon as you can afterwards.

From brainstorm to action plan – three ways to whittle

So you have a long list of all sorts of ideas. Now you need to whittle them down to reach an action plan. You may also find that combining ideas gives a brilliant and unique solution:

1 A quick way of reducing lots of ideas to a few is to give each person five sticky stars that they can award to the best ideas – one star to five different ideas or all five stars to one idea. Total the stars and select the best for development.

2 Put each idea on a Post-it® note so that they can easily move ideas around and then put ideas into three groups: 'promising', 'interesting' or 'reject'. If any of the promising ideas are no-brainers – so appropriate and good that they should be implemented straight away – these are actioned immediately.

3 Other people use a high/low impact, high/low difficulty matrix where the list of solutions is transferred to a grid like this:

TABLE 8.2 High/low impact, high/low difficulty matrix

High impact	Low impact	
1 High impact, low difficulty – highest pay off – significant results with lowest investment	**2** Low impact, low difficulty – easy to do, basic stuff – but will it make much of a difference?	Low ↑ Difficulty
3 High impact, high difficulty – hard to implement but could give a brilliant result with important consequences	**4** Low impact, high difficulty – discount these ideas altogether	↓ High

Two – mighty metaphors

A metaphor is where you compare a situation or object to something completely different and try to identify any similarities. It helps you break away from your normal thought patterns and recognize connections that you would not normally identify.

The human mind always subconsciously links one object to another. This helps in comprehension and in recall. So, techniques such as metaphors, similes and analogies are a conscious extension. The problem or opportunity you have defined… what is it like? What does it remind you of? The world is full of metaphors:

- 'All the world's a stage…' (Shakespeare)
- 'This is a crisis. A large crisis. In fact, if you've got a moment, it's a 12-storey crisis with a magnificent entrance hall, carpeting throughout, 24-hour porterage and an enormous sign on the roof saying, "This Is a Large Crisis."' (Ben Elton/*Blackadder*)
- 'You are my sunshine.'

I once had a client who had a brilliant mind but was quite explosive and difficult to manage. My team and I came up with the right metaphor and it helped us to come up with some practical solutions (see Table 8.3).

You can also use fairy stories, myths, fables and legends. I was a rather plump child and not the prettiest little girl. I loved *The Ugly Duckling* and felt it was 'my' story. One I could learn from and one that gave me hope. Stories are wonderful for stimulating creative thinking.

You can also do a story rewrite. Think about a fairy story, myth, fable or legend you know well. Think about how that story is similar to your present situation. Cast the characters. How could you change the narrative and so change the story? What happens to the characters now? Play with alternative storylines. What does that tell you?

TABLE 8.3 Using metaphors in problem-solving

Problem	Question	Ideas
Sarah is a great client with lots of energy and passion but she can get a bit nervy and tetchy. She also speaks really quickly and sometimes her thinking comes across as a stream of consciousness. So we sometimes misunderstand what she is saying and we think this makes her cross.	So what – or who – does she remind us of? (a metaphor or simile) **Answer** She reminds me of my two-year-old niece – a really bright kid who needs constant stimulation – what do I do with her?	Play with her (ie engage with her) Look her in the eye when she is talking (ie listen carefully and concentrate) Give her a book or toy that will occupy her (ie make sure she gets enough to read before and after status meetings) She might be tired and needing some downtime (ie make sure meetings don't go on for too long) Give her a cuddle (ie pay her attention) Make sure she is not hungry (ie take her out for lunch or if there is no time bring fruit into the meeting)

Three – picture this

Chance, out-of-context events shake up and challenge habitual thinking. The juxtaposition of a randomized picture or word with our problem or opportunity generates new connections in our mind. This can often produce an instant 'Eureka' moment of insight or intuition. (Apparently Newton got the idea of gravity when he was hit on the head with an apple while sitting under an apple tree. We don't need to sit under trees and wait for apples to fall – creative thinking techniques shake that tree by creating chance events.)

Because we are visual beings, pictures set off powerful associations. Random associations create great ideas. I make my own random picture cards by getting lots of pictures and they come from anywhere – magazines, advertising, the web, books, postcards. Choose pictures without text to allow a more right brain approach. My cards include pictures of animals, art, people, landmarks, natural scenes and abstract designs. I mount these onto card so it's like a deck of cards that can be shuffled and I pick a card at random. Focus on it – really concentrate. What does the image tell you about your problem? How does it connect to your problem? Anything the picture kicks off in your mind? The crazier the idea the better: Don't give up. Take at least 10 minutes – some people like to do an initial five minutes, take a break and then come back to it again – but don't be tempted to discard it for a 'better' picture. And don't select a picture to suit your problem.

For example, if I were considering the problem of how to educate men and women aged 25–54 about the health risks associated with obesity and I got a picture of Big Ben, I might come up with:

- Time – obesity shortens lives or 'don't leave it until it is too late'.
- The tower isn't Big Ben – Big Ben is the enormous bell inside – alarm bells must ring when you get to a certain body mass index.
- Big Ben – could we create a character called Ben and tell a story about the trials and tribulations of being a big man?
- It's a tower – you have to climb towers... obese people get out of breath easily – perhaps we could create a story about a father who is always out of breath and can't play football with his little son.
- Numbers 1–12 on the clock face – a 12-step programme to get your weight to a healthy level.
- And so on and so on...

Four – right here, right now

This is a similar technique to 'picture this' except that you concentrate on the objects which are in the room you are in. Look around you – select a few objects and spend three minutes on each one. What does the object tell you about your problem? How does it connect to your problem? Anything the object kicks off in your mind? The crazier the idea the better. In this room as I write I can see:

- a smartphone;
- a stapler;
- a wastepaper bin;
- a fashion magazine;
- a block of Post-it® notes;
- a rubber cow;
- a rucksack;
- a pencil;
- a mug of cold tea.

Five – ask the oracle

Various cultures over the centuries have used oracles. The purpose of these oracles was not so much to foretell the future but to help the user delve deeper into their own minds:

- The ancient Greeks used the ambiguous predictions of the Delphic Oracle.
- The Chinese used the I Ching.
- The Egyptians consulted the tarot.
- In Scandinavia runes were used.
- North American Indians used medicine wheels.

You can create your own oracle by doing three things:

1 Ask a question. This focuses your thinking. Write your question to focus attention.
2 Generate a random piece of information. Random selection is important, as the unpredictability of this new input will force you to look at the problem in a new way.
3 Interpret the resulting random piece of information as the answer to your question.

The important thing is to have an open, receptive mind. It is not logical but it is powerful and a way to get that wonderful brain working in a different way. The real insanity as Einstein said is 'doing the same thing over and over again and expecting different results.' This way you will certainly get novel results.

Six – random words

This is a simple creative technique, widely used to create new ideas. Because the brain is a self-organizing system, and very good at making connections, almost any random word will stimulate ideas on a subject. Look at the associations and functions of the word, as well as the word as a metaphor.

Ways to generating random words:

- Lucky dip – create a bag full of hundreds of words written on small pieces of paper, cardboard, poker chips, etc. Close your eyes, put in your hand and pull out a word.
- Open the dictionary (or newspaper) at a random page and choose a word.
- Chose the third noun on any random website
- Make up your own list of 60 words. Look at your watch and take note of the seconds. Use this number to get the word.
- Photocopy the list in Table 8.4 and randomly stick a pin in to any one word.

It is important to use the first word you land on. Don't 'select' a word you think you 'like' better. Once you have chosen the word, list its attributions or associations with the word. Then apply each of the items on your list and see how it applies to the problem at hand. Try it out on these three:

- You are looking for ways to improve your internal communications and your random word is APPLE.
- You want to create a new eye catching leaflet for doctors' surgeries that gives information about diabetes. Your random word is LEAF.
- You need to come up with a new campaign that draws attention to the dangers of binge drinking. Your random word is PASSPORT.

TABLE 8.4   Idea-generator: a list of random words to spark creativity

Aeroplane	Bridge	Earth	Hammer
Air	Butterfly	Egg	Hat
Airport	Button	Electricity	Hieroglyph
Album	Car	Elephant	Horse
Allotment	Carrot	Eraser	Hose
Apple	Cat	Eyes	Ice
Arm	Cave	Family	Ice-cream
Army	Chair	Fan	Insect
Baby	Chess	Feather	Junk
Backpack	Chocolates	Festival	Kitchen
Balloon	Circle	Film	Knife
Banana	Circus	Finger	Leaf
Bank	Clock	Fireworks	Leather jacket
Barbecue	Clown	Floodlight	Leg
Bathroom	Coffee	Flower	Library
Bathtub	Comet	Foot	Liquid
Bed	Crystal	Fork	Magnet
Bee	Cup	Fruit	Man
Bird	Cycle	Fungus	Map
Bomb	Desk	Game	Maze
Book	Diamond	Garden	Meat
Bottle	Dress	Gas	Meteor
Bowl	Drill	Gate	Microscope
Box	Drink	God	Milk
Boy	Drum	Grapes	Milkshake
Brain	Ears	Guitar	Mist

(Continued)

TABLE 8.4 (Continued)

Money	Record	Shop	Tennis racquet
Monster	Restaurant	Shower	Thermometer
Mosquito	Rifle	Signature	Tiger
Nail	Ring	Skeleton	Toilet
Navy	Robot	Slave	Tongue
Necklace	Rock	Snail	Torch
Needle	Rocket	Software	Torpedo
Onion	Roof	Solid	Train
Paint	Room	Spectrum	Triangle
Passport	Rope	Spotlight	Tunnel
Pebble	Saddle	Square	Typewriter
Pepper	Salt	Staircase	Umbrella
Perfume	Sandwich	Star	Vacuum
Pillow	Satellite	Stomach	Vampire
Pocket	School	Sun	Videotape
Post-office	Sphere	Sunglasses	Vulture
Potato	Spice	Swimming pool	Water
Printer	Spiral	Sword	Weapon
Prison	Spoon	Table	Web
Purple	Sportscar	Tapestry	Window
Pyramid	Sex	Teeth	Woman
Radar	Ship	Telescope	Worm
Rainbow	Shoes	Television	X-ray

Seven – borrow a brain

When we have a problem or opportunity and don't know how to crack it, we may ask a person whose judgement we value to help us with it. I always ask my husband if I get stuck – he sees the problem from a different perspective and comes up with new ways to crack the nut. It is all about thinking like someone else and in the process releasing you from the usual way you think. Fantastic when you have been thinking logically and rationally about an issue for a long time.

You can do this on your own or in a team. First define your problem or opportunity, then pick a person (even better do it a couple of times with different characters):

- at random (see my list below to get you started);
- someone who is as far away from you as possible in terms of opinion and outlook on the issue;

TABLE 8.5 Borrow a brain: how would the following solve your problem?

Your doctor – Neil Armstrong – Jeremy Paxman – Gandhi – Victoria Beckham – Mr Spock – Barack Obama – Batman – Boris Johnson – David Bowie – Homer Simpson – Winston Churchill – your mother – a spider – Oscar Wilde – Dalai Lama – Mr Bean – Danny Boyle – Isambard Kingdom Brunel – your three-year-old niece – your favourite teacher – Mo Farah – a carpenter – Dexter Morgan – Diana, Princess of Wales – Charles Darwin – Queen Elizabeth I – John Lennon – Horatio Nelson – Margaret Thatcher – Professor Stephen Hawking – Eric Morecambe – Dawn French – Walt Disney – Father Christmas – Sir Steve Redgrave – Bob Geldof – a train driver – Robbie Williams – Geoffrey Chaucer – Sir Richard Branson – Bono – Johnny Rotten – your dog – Dirty Den – Adele

- someone you admire or love;
- someone you dislike;
- a profession (a cook, a train driver, a teacher, an optician, an ambassador).

Now spend some time getting under the skin of the person. Their attitudes, values, thoughts, feelings and beliefs. If you are working as a group explore this together.

So how would these people solve your problem? How would they approach it? What would they do about your problem? What would be their communication style? What messages would they send?

Eight – cocktail bar

Here we randomly combine elements to come up with novel solutions, like discovering great new cocktails. Use a table like the one below. Complete the table, selecting appropriate column titles for the problem you are exploring and with as many rows as audiences.

Randomly combine numbers and letters and see what ideas the combinations give you.

Example – ideas for communicating how to eat healthily (and reduce levels of obesity).

A 1, B 2, C 10, D2 and E 7 – Reach ordinary working men with a flyer to their place of work that shows them where to get healthy food nearby – inspire them with the idea that to lose a bit of weight is easy by choosing a salad, not a burger, at lunchtime.

TABLE 8.6 Cocktail bar: combine the elements to come up with a creative solution

	A – Audiences	B – Locations	C – Emotions	D – Meal occasions	E – Channels
1	Sedentary men	Home	Happy	Breakfast	Website
2	Working women	Office	Depressed	Working lunch	Television
3	Children	Shop	Surprised	Tea	Facebook
4	Teenagers	School	Anxious	Dinner	YouTube
5	Mothers	Hospital	Angry	Sunday lunch	Radio
6	Fathers	Pub	Creative	Packed lunch	In-store sampling
7	Grandparents	Supermarket	Content	Birthday dinner	Flyer
8	Families	Church	Apathetic	Restaurant	Magazine
9	Older couples	Park	Frightened	Motorway service station diner	Conference
10	Retired people	Train	Inspired	Fast food pitstop	Leaflet

Nine – back to the future

When we plan in a rational, linear manner we sometimes choose a route we've gone down before and the plan can be a little formulaic. Starting with the outcome can shake this up really effectively. So-called 'back planning' sets you free from the limitations you may normally place on ideas. It encourages you to think in different directions and helps you see a clear way of achieving your goals. It is a creative visualization technique.

To do this:

- Visualizing your goal, your end point and success – draw it out, create a storyboard, describe it energetically, write a front page press story, feel it has really happened (If you saw the wonderful *Inspiration* film used in the bid presentation in Singapore for the London 2012 Olympics it's pretty clear they used this technique).

● Ask 'What did I do to achieve this?'

Repeat asking this question until you have captured all of the things you need to do to achieve this result. This reversal can be very liberating and oddly takes off the anxiety we can feel when we are planning forward.

Ten – sleep on it

As we said earlier our brains work on the subconscious level all the time. So take advantage of your brilliant brain by using this technique. (I have asked a team to do this the night before a conference and it not only was a talking point it also resulted in at least three really great ideas the following morning). Just five steps for this:

1 Put a notepad next to your bed.

2 Set your alarm 15 minutes earlier than usual.

3 Ask yourself a question before going to sleep.

4 Write down any thoughts, if you wake during the night.

5 Take time, after you wake in the morning, to review your thoughts and write down any ideas that you have.

Each step is important. The notepad next to the bed allows you to write down your thoughts while they are fresh in your mind. Similarly, asking yourself a question, before going to sleep, directs your mind to the issue or problem. If you do not do this, your subconscious will bounce about on lots of different issues not relevant to your problem. Setting your alarm 15 minutes earlier gives you time to capture thoughts. Most people jump out of bed in a rush to get ready for work, with the *Today* programme for company and don't spend any time just tuning in to their subconscious creative thoughts. The writing down of thoughts makes sure the ideas don't drift back into the subconscious and so get forgotten.

Eleven – green light, red light, blue light

This technique is great for encouraging honesty, helping teams develop great communications and arriving at good ideas particularly when the programme or project has been running for a while. (You can use it to tackle interpersonal conflict situations too.) Of course it doesn't take the place of methodical measurement and evaluation of communications but it can get a good discussion going that can result in new ideas. You focus on just three questions and you can give this task to people before a group session takes place so they can think about it in advance:

1 What is working well? Something we should CONTINUE – give this a green light.

2 What are we doing that isn't working? Something we should STOP and give the red light to.

3 What should we put in place to improve? Something we should START and give a blue light to.

Twelve – wake up and smell the roses

There are loads of things we can do for ourselves that restore personal energy and creativity. Working hard can knock the stuffing out of us so try these few simple ideas to get your mojo back:

- I once worked with a girl who ate the same sandwich every day, did the same journey to work every day, read the same newspaper ever day – she did that for the four years I worked with her and she was the single most non-creative person I have ever worked with (not surprisingly she was a very good office administrator, not a PR professional). To be creative you need to think differently and you can do that by breaking your routine. Do something new every day. Don't wear a metaphorical uniform. The psychologist Erich Fromm said that we should be born every day; so look at the world every morning through a child's eyes, as if for the first time. What do you see?

- If you spend a lot of time facing a screen, take lots of breaks. Apparently the ancient Romans said you could restore your equilibrium by taking a walk 'into the green' – in other words by going outside. Sit in the sun, sit under a tree, look at some flowers. If the weather permits, take off your shoes and socks and feel the grass between your toes. Just a short blast does wonders for your mood and creativity. (PS: don't do this if you have hay fever!)

- Go into your nearest fruit shop and stimulate your senses with the waft of oranges or strawberries, basil and coriander. Or visit a perfumier or pharmacy. Smells awaken your creativity and trigger memories too.

- Read poetry – you may never have done so since school – try it again now. See how poets capture a mood in a few words. I love the haiku, the poetry equivalent of a tweet. Originally a Japanese form of poetry, a haiku is an ultra-short poem of just 17 syllables over three lines, which uses imagery to convey the essence of an experience of nature or the season, and links this intuitively linked to the human condition. Here are three examples by Basho Matsuo, the first great poet of haiku in the 1600s:

  An old silent pond...
  A frog jumps into the pond,
  splash! Silence again.

Autumn moonlight –
a worm digs silently
into the chestnut.

Lightning flash –
what I thought were faces
are plumes of pampas grass.

- Look at bold, bright colours for a few minutes. These change your mood. Blue and green reduce stress levels, yellow energizes and red stimulates.
- Flip through magazines and books. Pictures, colours and ideas will give you sparks and switch your attitude.
- Laughter cures all ills as far as I am concerned – authentic, flat-out, raw laughter will make you feel brilliant. Spend time with people who make you laugh, watch stand-up comedians and films that tickle your funny bone. A really good laugh improves your breathing and energizes you as much as exercise. And keep a smile on your face. You make other people feel better too.

Summary

All too often PR people spend a huge amount of time looking at screens, doing the admin, fiddling with detail at the end of a process. We need to learn from advertising, design and marketing professionals and give ourselves time to think freely without boundaries at the start of the process of problem solving. Creative thinking helps us to solve everyday problems but is especially important when we are devising novel solutions to public relations problems through strategies that enable us to communicate in an interesting and fresh way about our organizations. Make sure you build in time for creativity in your work and that you encourage it in others too.

Finally take a look at award-winning campaigns to inspire you to be brave and bold – the CIPR's Excellence Awards, PRCA Awards, PRWeek Awards and CorpComms Awards all offer inspiring case histories demonstrating new ways of cracking old problems.

09
Visual communications

Any PR professional needs to be able to use still and moving images to improve and enhance communications work. The fast pace of digital communications means we need this skill more now than ever before. Recent survey results from ROI Research (Spring 2013) suggested that almost half of respondents were more likely to engage with brands on social media if they posted pictures – much more than if links or status updates are included.

Human beings take in information about the world using their five senses. Crucially, and unless we are visually impaired, most of us use our eyes before we use our ears. Apparently human beings process images 60,000 times faster than words. We recall information presented as images six times more easily than text. Images transcend language so for those of us working internationally, effective visual communications becomes even more crucial. A visual message, with a caption, may have the greatest power to change hearts and minds. Think of the unforgettable Pulitzer award-winning photograph of terrified children fleeing a napalm attack in Vietnam – some people think this image changed public and political opinion about the war and helped to bring it to an end. A visual may be all we need to get the message across and have the desired dramatic impact with stakeholders.

Visual communications works on subconscious physiological and psychological levels. Graphic designers, art directors, photographers and typographers have all had extensive technical training so that they can come up with concepts and create executions that have a huge and lasting impact. As a PR practitioner you may not have that professional training but you do need to develop an appreciation of what elements make good visual communication. You need to work with colleagues and suppliers to get to the best possible creative solutions for communications programmes.

Visual communications includes stills photography, moving images (live, animation or even a mixture of both), signs and symbols such as brand devices, graphics and so-called infographics (broadly translated as graphs and charts).

Infographics present complex information, data or knowledge quickly and clearly and now appear every day in traditional and social media. They are especially good at presenting information that would be unwieldy in text form. Inforgraphics have real impact in social media where the right infographic can stimulate extensive sharing among interested communities. Take a look at the marvellous *Information is Beautiful* by David McCandless (McCandless, 2009) for lots of ideas and inspiration.

Considerations about light, colour, composition, content, cultural cues and perception all need to be taken into account. Take a look at an article on the BBC's website about how we see colour – fascinating (http://www.bbc.co.uk/news/science-environment-14421303).

Images can be analysed though many perspectives, for example these six major perspectives presented by Paul Martin Lester, professor at the Department of Communications at California State University, Fullerton:

1 Personal perspective – when a viewer has an opinion about an image based on their personal thoughts. Personal response depends on the viewer's thoughts and values individually. This might be sometimes in conflict with cultural values. Also when a viewer has viewed an image with a personal perspective, it is then hard to change the view of the image on the viewer, even the image also can be seen in other ways.

2 Historical perspective – an image's view can arise from the history of the use of media. Through time, the sorts of images we see have changed, largely because new and different media have come onto the scene. For example, pictures edited using computer software (eg Photoshop) look quite different to images that are made and edited by hand using craft skills.

3 Technical perspective – when the view of an image is influenced by the use of lights, position and the presentation of the image. The right use of light, position and presentation of the image can improve the view of the image. It can make the image look better than the reality.

4 Ethical perspective – from this perspective, the maker of the image, the viewer and the image itself must be responsible morally and ethically to the image. This perspective is also categorized in six categories: categorical imperative; utilitarianism; hedonism; golden mean; golden rule and veil of ignorance.

5 Cultural perspective – the cultural perspective involves the use of symbols: the use of words that are related to the image, the use of 'heroes', etc in the image, give the image symbolic meaning. The cultural perspective can also be seen as the semiotic perspective.

6 Critical perspective – the critical perspective is when the viewer adopts a critical approach towards the image, and criticisms may be made in the interests of society/from a societal viewpoint. This differs from any personal perspective. (It's worth reading Lester's work if you are interested in these ideas (Lester, 2012).)

Photography for PR

You may be planning photography to support a marketing communications campaign or thinking about photographs to gain editorial coverage. Persuasive photographs get attention and make a brand, an event, an organization memorable. Our eyes go straight to photographs on the page especially those of people – and we tend to look into the eyes of the subject. We register strong colours quickly, especially red (that's why warning signs all over the world are painted red). And our eyes go to familiar shapes (like circles and crosses), and recognizable symbols (like flags and signs). We can't help ourselves – it's a combination of physiological reflex, perceptions and symbolism.

Bear in mind people have become wise to the value of the image. If you are offering a photo to support a media campaign it will have to make the grade. Ten years ago the picture editor of the *Daily Telegraph* was receiving 5,000 images a day – now it's more like 50,000 on a busy news day. Your picture has to be brilliant if it is to be selected by a high-traffic website or the print version of a paper. (*Unless* it is the only existing and available image of an event – in which case it may be used.) A picture editor scans all the pictures he or she gets very quickly and, equally swiftly, will make a decision about which will work on the screen or page. So make sure you create and submit pictures that gain attention and work hard for you. These few tips will help:

- Words and pictures work together so make sure you have a strong story to support a photo, as well as a strong photo to support the story. Think pictures when you are writing your story. As the picture editor of the *Daily Telegraph* remarked recently in *PR Week*, 'a picture may punch above the weight of the story it represents, but it has to be a knockout image'.

- Make sure your subject is interesting. I recently asked one of my clients to bring out all the photos they had taken in the past year for their organization; men in grey suits… more men in grey suits… men shaking hands on deals; men sitting around tables; men standing at podia making speeches. You may have to take 'official shots' for protocol reasons (like a line-up of ministers) but think 'story'. Some might be included in business-to-business media but only the most exceptional (eg biggest trade deal ever between the UK and China) would be selected for a media website or print version.

- You should take lots of pictures – think about a different picture, appropriate for each media type you are targeting.

- You may be interested in photography (I hope you are!) and be quite competent using the camera on your phone. Don't do the photos yourself! Trained, experienced photographers with media experience look through the lens differently, thinking about composition, lighting, point-of-view. The only exception is citizen photojournalism, where an amateur was the only person present to capture the images of an event as it happened, whether that is a riot, a bomb blast or a meteorite. On these occasions quality matters less than the raw drama of an eyewitness's record of a moment in time.

- Likewise if you have a picture no one else has, this will increase the chances that your shot will be used by a media organization, especially if offered as an exclusive.

- Brief professional photographers properly. Discuss what would work with them and ask them for their ideas. Let them be creative – they are interested in creating photos that are selected not rejected as they make money that way.

- Professionals will use the right format for media. Images sent in the right format to news organizations drop directly into picture desk picture browsers. But photo editors cannot use zip files.

- Give your photo a better chance of selection by timing it well. Avoid clashing with big events like the Oscars and Royal weddings where picture content will be given over to famous faces, red carpets and designer gowns. The time of the day when you offer the photo is important too – while online is refreshed through the day and night, printed daily versions go to press at around 5pm so if your organization's fantastic photo comes through at 4pm hold until the next morning. And news organizations work weekends so sending in a photo on a Saturday or Sunday (you may have to work the weekend…) can produce great results in terms of media coverage.

- Branding in an image is acceptable (Red Bull do this brilliantly), but clumsy, artificial, over-the-top branding looks too much like advertising. If you want editorial be very careful. Use the caption to explain brand involvement.

Visual aids

Visual aids help audiences, particularly those listening to the delivery of information, to understand what is going on. Visual aids range from hand-outs to PowerPoints. Selection of the right visual aid is dependent on the presenter and the audience (speakers usually have a preference but importantly the audience's needs should come first). Used badly a visual aid can be anything but – the wrong visual aid can distract from the message and confuse and exhaust the audience. So, as with all things planning ahead is vital.

Types of visual aids

Objects

The use of objects as visual aids involves bringing the actual object to demonstrate on during the speech. For example, a speech about a new smartphone would be more effective by bringing it in – and maybe showing it on a big screen.

Pros: The use of the actual object is often necessary when demonstrating how to do something so that the audience can fully understand procedure.

Cons: Some objects are too large or unavailable for a speaker to bring with them. And some are just too small (hence the need for projection).

Models

These serve in place of an object that can't be brought into the session. Examples include architectural models, the core of the earth, a human skeleton.

Pros: Models serve as substitutes that provide a better example of the real thing to the audience when the object being spoken about is an awkward size or scale for use in a demonstration.

Cons: Sometimes a model may take away from the reality of what is being spoken about and quaintly miniaturize it . For example, the vast size of the solar system cannot be seen from a model, and the actual composition of a human body cannot be seen from a dummy.

Graphs

Bar graphs, line graphs, pie graphs, and scatter plots – all help present complex information in a way that the audience can get their heads round.

Pros: Graphs help the audience to visualize statistics so that they make a greater impact than just listing them verbally would.

Cons: Graphs with too much detail overwhelm people and turn them off.

Maps

Maps are often used to show differences between geographical areas or to show location.

Pros: When maps are simple and clear, they are excellent. For example, a map showing the relationship of one political system with its neighbours or a new school illustrating its proximity to residential areas.

Cons: Again it's detail. Include too much and people can lose focus on the key point.

Tables

Tables consist of columns and rows that organize words, symbols, and/or data.

Pros: Good tables are easy to understand. They enable the comparison of facts and so can help gain a better understanding of the issue – for example a table showing numbers of reported cases of human trafficking into Europe through the Polish borders over the past three years.

Cons: Depending on the graphic design skills of the creator, tables can look dull. Or again they can be too dense with too much information. Don't use a table if the audience has to take a lot of time to be able to understand it. And a table hinders understanding if the type is too small, or the columns are not drawn evenly.

Photographs

Pros: Photographs are good tools to make or emphasize a point or to explain a topic. For example, when explaining the laying of sewage pipes or how pistachios are grown, a photo enables the audience to understand what things look like and how they work. A photograph is also good to use when the actual object cannot be viewed for legal or ethical reasons (eg a picture of smuggled drugs). Local/regional photos can make the point that the issue is relevant here and to you.

Cons: Small photographs are hard to see and so can irritate and distract.

Drawings/diagrams/artist's impressions

Pros: All are really helpful when photographs can't show exactly what needs to be explained. They can also be used when a photograph is too detailed and hence distracting. (Classic example – a diagram of the circulatory system is more effective than a photograph of the same thing.)

Cons: If it's not drawn carefully and correctly, a drawing can be ineffective, look careless and unprofessional.

Chalkboard or whiteboard

While new chalkboards and whiteboards are flexible and convenient, they are not a panacea! I have used these in international classrooms and lecture theatres and the main issue for me is that you have to turn your back to the audience and so break eye contact. It's tempting to draw and speak at the same time and so you do both less well!

Poster board

Posters are underrated as a visual aid. Posters carrying charts, graphs, pictures, or illustrations can hang around for a long time. And this means that audiences may see them frequently, just right for a dramatic health message (for example, 'Use a condom' in a clinic in Africa). Take care on production so the paper quality is robust enough.

Handouts

People keep good handouts and this helps them remember messages. Be careful when you hand them out though – handing them out during a speech may mean people concentrate on the handout not the speaker and you have lost them. But be considerate of your audience. I work with many people for whom English is a second language and the handouts help them follow what is going on. Be led by the audience and use your judgement. If using a handout, it's best to hand it out just before you reference it. (NB: Most speakers including academics say handouts are fine (even necessary) for a 45–60-minute talk, but NOT required for a 10-minute talk.)

Video excerpts

I often use video clips in speeches, presentations and lectures to gain attention and demonstrate a point. The movement and colour, music and action of video wake people up and can be used to add emotion and life to a subject. There are a few aspects that require care – first a video that includes audio means the speaker will not be able to talk. It might be OK but it could break up the speech. Second if the video is hugely exciting and interesting, by comparison the speaker may appear boring! The key to showing a video during a presentation is to make the transition to video a smooth one and to only show very short clips. Finally (unless it's a video of David Beckham, the Prime Minister or the Queen who just couldn't be present) never use video to replace an actual speech.

PowerPoint

PowerPoint presentations can be an extremely useful visual aid, especially for longer presentations. For 5- to 10-minute presentations, it is probably not worth the time or effort to put together a PowerPoint. For longer presentations, however, PowerPoints can be a great way to keep the audience engaged and keep the speaker on track. Just make sure it's not 'death by PowerPoint' with slides containing too much detail (see earlier comments relating to tables and graphs and charts). Use PowerPoint as a VISUAL AID, not as a way to deliver every word of your script.

Ideas about visual communications from an art director

I asked Roger Sealey, who I have worked with for years (and been married to for years too!), to give me a few thoughts about visual communications based on his long career as an art director in advertising. He has worked for all the big agencies including Ogilvy's, M&C Saatchi, Leo Burnett and Publicis and has more recently helped some forward-thinking PR companies like Fever too in terms of cracking visual communications challenges. He's really down to earth, while also being a whizz on visual communications. These ideas summarize what he thinks we PR people should think about:

- 'A picture paints a thousand words' goes the old saying, and these days when our world is so full of words demanding our attention, pictures are more important than ever.

- We're all encouraged to write from an early age. Writing is serious study. Pictures are not. Pictures are play. (English is an academic subject. Art is often something that non-academic students do.)

- We read words in a rational logical way and whether we realize it or not we have to work at reading them. But we can glance at a picture and get a feel, a tone, a message seemingly without having to try.

- Over centuries, pictures and imagery have been used in many, many way to communicate.

  - There were (and still are) house and pub signs. I love the sign in Prague – the house of the swan – http://www.personal.psu. edu/tmh1/Prague/HouseSigns/pages/whiteswan_jpg.htm and http://traveldk.com/prague/topten/house-signs). And we have the Crown and Anchor, the Red Lion, the King's Head, which had symbols or pictures so that illiterate or semi-literate people – or presumably drunk people too – could find them.

  - The barber's pole, the pawnbroker's balls – all visual communications.

  - Throughout history dress and decoration have been used to communicate status or authority, state coaches and liveried uniforms, the red coats of soldiers, the tall hats of Bow Street Runners.

  - The elaborate loops and scrolls of written script on Royal proclamations and official documents.

  - The simple austerity of Puritan churches, the over-the-top decoration in Catholic ones.

  - Every nation, every religion has used visual communication to impress, to awe, to control.

- And visual imagery doesn't just mean pictures, with the invention of moveable type and the development of different fonts, letterforms started to have different character. So some typefaces would be seen as friendly and others as authoritarian.

- Diagrams and maps, graphs and charts can help to explain information to us in a more palatable way. Take a look at London Tube maps of 1908 compared to the iconic map by the brilliant Harry Beck, created in 1933. What a guy. (http://en.wikipedia.org/wiki/ File:Tube_map_1908-2.jpg and http://www.tfl.gov.uk/assets/images/ general/beckmap1.jpg)

- In the 19th and 20th centuries, with the development of printing, film and television, and then with digital media, visual communication has developed and is used everywhere.

- When did you last see a newspaper with no picture on the front page? (http://www.guardian.co.uk/news/datablog/2011/sep/26/data-journalism-guardian)

- Have you ever gone to a web page that's wall-to-wall words and decided to look at a different site?

- Pictures or imagery interest us. They break the monotony of the world of words. They communicate in a different way. Pictures can work on their own to communicate a story; with words (so that the picture without the words would be meaningless and vice versa) or as a decorative accompaniment to words.

- Some pictures have even changed the way we looked at the world (http://brainz.org/10-war-photographs-changed-world-forever).

  Iwo Jima was the first piece of Japanese national soil to be captured by the Americans – hence the area was heavily fortified and required four days of bloody battle before its mountaintop, Suribachi, was captured. The battle persisted for a whole month, in which three of the flag raisers were killed. In 1951 the picture was used by Felix de Weldon to sculpt the USMC War memorial just outside Washington DC.

- Sony Bravia – 'Balls' commercial – rolling coloured balls down the streets of San Francisco – endline 'Colour like no other'. A film like no other. (http://www.youtube.com/watch?v=-zOrV-5vh1A)

- Decorative menu cards (http://www.utterlyengaged.com/illustrated-menu-cards/)

Of course, how you use pictures to communicate, whether they communicate on their own, with words, or as a purely decorative element, will depend on what it is you're trying to communicate. If you're working in news and you have an important person visiting your city, then you'll probably want to have a picture of that person so that people can instantly recognize them. But who the person is and the reason for their visit will determine what sort of image you choose. If the person is a respected politician, you might show them formally shaking hands with the mayor of the town. If it's a comedian or a celebrity they might be having a beer and a laugh with the locals, or meeting local people in a shopping street. And it's probably a photograph or a piece of video.

If you're designing a website about cakes and confectionery, you might want a decorative illustrative approach. What you're trying to communicate will determine what imagery you use and what style you adopt.

Commissioning pictures, using stockshot libraries, working with photographers, designers and illustrators and taking photographs and video yourself

Some professional photographers and directors charge thousands of pounds a day. But in our age of digital video and photography we all have cameras on our phones.

A wonderfully composed and colour-balanced high-resolution photograph might be the only thing that will work for your job. But sometimes a piece of video shot on a phone or a simple cartoon scribbled on a Post-it® note might convey your idea more suitably. Visual communication doesn't always have to cost a fortune.

Illustration

Where do you start? Maybe children's storybooks – for me Janet and John books and Ladybird books. Styles of illustrations that appeal to children or illustrative styles that remind us of our childhood.

How do I put this furniture together? IKEA style instructional illustrations, or Haynes Car manual illustrations that explain how things work.

Cartoons. Jokey swiftly drawn illustrations. Or anarchic desperately scratched ones.

Also consider:

- painstaking botanical studies of fruit and flowers;
- vivid flat colour silkscreened holiday posters;
- craftsman made and precisely crosshatched etchings;
- traditional subtle washes of watercolour.

If you're going to commission illustration you need to think about what style of illustration is right for you to underpin the ideas you're trying to communicate. A style can say as much as what the picture's actually of.

Photography

Look at portraits. A person on their own, smartly dressed, looking straight into the camera, so looking straight out at you the viewer. A serious, sincere, 'trust me' look.

Two people together. Looking at each other. Looking like they like each other. Smiling and shaking hands, or touching. They've just met and want everyone to know that they're going to work together for you.

Where are these people? Are they in an office, in a street, in the countryside?

How people are posed for a photograph, how they are dressed, their body language, where they are, you need to think about all these things when you commission or resource a photograph.

Now look at product photography. Do you want the product to be in a natural environment, as if it's in use or is about to be used? Or do you want it to be on a neutral background in isolation?

There are many other things to consider with photography. Black-and-white or colour or enhanced colour? Do you want movement in the shot? Should it look like an amateur snap? Would it be better shot from an intriguing point of view? Should it look like art or photo-reportage, ie a news picture?

Remember, whatever you're photographing, the better you can define and describe what sort of picture you need the better chance you have of getting what you want.

Specialist photography

- As well as people who concentrate on photographing people and still life, there are all sorts of specialist photographers out there: fashion, music, cars, food, animals, children, landscape and aerial photographers.

- Anyone can take a picture, but some subject matter calls for specialist knowledge. Make sure you know who's the best in the business in your sector.

Stockshot libraries

- Budgets are often tight, so sometimes we might need to use library pictures. Stockshot libraries hold vast collections of photography and illustrations and you can browse and chose pictures online.

- This obviously saves you the time and trouble of finding the photographer or illustrator who's right for your job.

- There are rights-managed and royalty-free shots. Rights-managed means that the price will vary depending on what you want to use the picture for. Royalty-free means that the picture is ready and available for sale and the price you pay will depend on the resolution of the image you require.

- There are downsides to using stockshot libraries. Some things like fashions, haircuts, computers, televisions and cars, go out-of-date very quickly, so if your picture contains elements like this you might be better off commissioning photography. Also, stockshots are taken by photographers working without a specific brief, and if you have a particular requirement you could find yourself searching forever and never finding the picture that suits your needs exactly. Whereas by commissioning a picture you can get precisely the picture you need.

- If you're looking for specialist pictures, there are specialist photo libraries too. These and their catalogues are easy to find on the internet.

Retouching and manipulation

- Photoshop is a marvellous tool, but be careful if people say they can sort it all out in post-production.
- Try and get as close to the picture you want in the camera.
- If you present the image as a piece of editorial then manipulation is unethical and could land you in hot water with misrepresentation.

Research

With any design or visual material it's very easy to do some research. Look what's been done before on a computer. If you're selling outboard motors look at how other people do it. If you're reporting on a state visit look at how other people have done it. It might not be right but it'll give you an idea of how to do or not to do it.

Collect images, finished designs, colours, anything you think relevant.

Briefing designers

- When you're briefing a designer or illustrator or photographer, never assume that they know what you want. Tell them about what you think you need, if they don't think that what you want will work, they'll tell you, then hopefully you can work together to find what's achievable.

- When you're putting together a design think about what's most important and least important in your design. What do you want people to look at first? Aim for a clean and neat look. Make it easy for people to understand where to look. Don't hide your communication.

- Don't be embarrassed to draw a diagram of what you have in mind, it's often easier to talk to a designer with a rough scribble than try and explain everything in words. And don't be worried if you can't draw, most designers can't either.

- With folding leaflets, get a piece of paper and fold it, and write what goes where.

- Look at the piece you are considering as if you know nothing about it. Try to see it with fresh eyes.

- Think about what someone who knows nothing about what you're trying to communicate will make of your design. It helps with the brief and helps you judge the final version.

- There are many elements that dictate the overall look and feel of a design.

- Try to be clear what sort of tone you are after. Serious, jokey, homemade, precise, etc. Consider colours carefully – there is a great deal in the psychology of colour, most of it to do with physics, with the wavelengths of colour and the effect this has upon us physiologically:

  - Being the longest wavelength, red is a powerful colour. Although not technically the most visible, it has the property of appearing to be nearer than it is and therefore it grabs our attention first. Hence its effectiveness for warning signs and traffic lights. Bright red is a danger sign, a bargain basement colour, a 'look at me' colour. Red raises the pulse rate, giving the impression that time is passing faster than it is. It can also activate the 'fight or flight' instinct. It is stimulating, lively, friendly. At the same time, it can be perceived as aggressive and 'in your face'.

  - Being a tint of red, pink also affects us physically, but it soothes, rather than stimulates. (Interestingly, red is the only colour that has an entirely separate name for its tints. Tints of blue, green, yellow, etc are simply called light blue, light green etc.) Pink traditionally represents the feminine principle and little girls in particular. But too much pink is physically draining and can be somewhat emasculating.

  - Blue is the colour of clear communication. It has an establishment, traditional, intellectual, authoritative feel. It affects us intellectually more than it does physically. Strong blues will stimulate clear thought while soft blues calm the mind and aid concentration. Blue is the world's favourite colour, the colour of the sea and sunny skies.

  - Yellow is stimulating. The right yellow lifts spirits and self-esteem; it implies confidence and optimism. But the wrong tone can make us feel anxious and even nauseous.

  - Being in the centre of the spectrum, green is the colour of balance – a more important concept than many people realize. Green strikes the eye in such a way as to require no visual adjustment and so it is immediately more relaxing and restful. Green reassures us on a primeval level – when the world about us contains plenty of green, this indicates the presence of water and so little danger of famine.

  - The shortest wavelength is violet, often described as purple. It is introvertive and encourages deep contemplation, or meditation.

It has associations with royalty and the church and is used to communicate the finest possible human qualities. Being the last visible wavelength before the ultra-violet ray, it has associations with time and space and the cosmos.

- Since it is a combination of red and yellow, orange is stimulating and reaction to it is a combination of the physical and the emotional. It focuses our minds on issues of physical comfort – food, warmth, shelter, etc – and sensuality. It is a 'fun' colour.
- Pure grey is the only colour that has no direct psychological properties. It is, however, quite recessive. Unless the precise tone is right, grey has a dampening effect on other colours used with it.
- Black is serious, weighty. It is essentially an absence of light. It communicates absolute clarity, with no finer nuances. It can communicate sophistication and uncompromising excellence and it works particularly well with white.

(Crozier, WR (1996) The psychology of colour preferences. Review of progress in coloration and related topics, *Coloration Technology*, **26** (1): pp 63 –72)

● Though of course it depends how and where you use these colours. So think about colour carefully and what it might say or imply about your product or service.

What does your typeface say about you?

Typography is a particularly wonderful branch of graphic design – and typographers are a particularly wonderful breed of professionals.

A typeface is the specific letterform design of an alphabet and a font is a collection of all the characters of that typeface, including capital letters and lowercase letters, numerals and punctuation marks. Thousands of fonts have been created by renowned typographers, designers and type foundries over the centuries and new typefaces are being created every day. Typefaces can be the most important feature of text. The right typeface gives a whole load of subliminal messages, that can either delight or deter the reader, in print or on the screen.

The development of the corporate image is arguably down to a careful and consistent use of typography – think about *The Times* newspaper, the BBC, Apple. All are recognizable partly because of their distinctive typographical style, used consistently over time. Sometimes the character of a font comes from the typeface being very familiar to us because it has been used extensively by one product or service (easyJet use Cooper Black for example).

Typefaces have characters. Sometimes this character comes from the shapes of the letters themselves. Take a look at these six examples; what do they 'say' to you?:

Powerful, Practical Communications   Arial

Powerful, Practical Communications   *French Script*

Powerful, Practical Communications   Comic Sans

Powerful, Practical Communications   Times New Roman

POWERFUL, PRACTICAL COMMUNICATIONS   STENCIL

𝕻𝖔𝖜𝖊𝖗𝖋𝖚𝖑, 𝕻𝖗𝖆𝖈𝖙𝖎𝖈𝖆𝖑 𝕮𝖔𝖒𝖒𝖚𝖓𝖎𝖈𝖆𝖙𝖎𝖔𝖓𝖘   𝕺𝖑𝖉 𝕰𝖓𝖌𝖑𝖎𝖘𝖍

Arial conjures up thoughts of documents, French Script has a feel of the nailbar, Comic Sans reminds us of children's party invitations, Times makes use think of news, Stencil reminds us of the stamp on a crate side, and Old English has the feel of a Robin Hood film poster.

Deciding on the right typeface is very much a matter of instinct. You need to decide what tone you're trying to get across and go from there. One of the major considerations is whether you use a serif or sans serif typeface. Serif typefaces have letters with extra flourishes, like handwriting. With sans serif (literally without serif) typefaces letter forms have cleaner lines, there is greater prominence given to white space and they tend to look more austere and less decorative. There are also handdrawn forms and these tend to look more homemade and less formal.

Choosing the right font requires a basic knowledge of the breadth of options and a core understanding of how effective typography functions. When you are given the opportunity to re-brand or update your brand, consider typefaces that convey a mood and reflect your brand positioning, differentiating you from the competition. You'll also need to think about all the ways you will apply your typeface and how it will translate in different sizes and colours as well as in black and white. Above all it must be legible.

Your typeface needs to be flexible and easy to use, and it must provide a wide range of expression. With an estimated 200,000 fonts to choose from, there will be a typeface that supports the tone of your communication, the personality and brand values of your organization and the message you want to convey.

Finally limit the number of fonts that you use for greater cost-effectiveness as you need a licence to use particular fonts (unless you are using open-licence fonts).

10
Public relations essentials for issues, incidents and crises

Introduction

Sustained corporate and financial communications mean that we – and the media – are now interested in organizations, in the rises and falls, the successes and failures, the good guys and the bad guys. Organizations make news and the most interesting news is peppered with elements of controversy or conflict, tension and human interest, intrigue and, almost best of all, cover-up. Taking into account that corporate ethics and responsibility are hit topics and very widely discussed (think Enron) and we can see that, unless it gets things right, there's trouble ahead for the organization who behaves badly... or is perceived to have done so. The media spotlight is on organizations, whatever the sector, whatever the business when the hard stuff happens. The organization that finds itself in difficulties, commits real or perceived misdemeanours or causes harm to human life, animal life, the environment is certain to find itself making headlines in the media and on social networking sites immediately and globally.

Some organizations call in the communications team when the issue is about to break or when the crisis has taken place. It's too late. The definition of public relations talks about a planned and consistent approach and this is just what issues and crisis management is all about – preparation before the event and competent performance when it – whatever it is – goes live. No organization can afford to ignore this planning. You need to think ahead so you can think on your feet. The reputation which you have worked so hard to build and nurture should be protected in the event of the unexpected.

Be scrupulous about your preparation and interrogate both the broad issues facing your sector or industry in general and then the particular issues facing your organization:

- What are the worst things that could happen as a result of your corporate activities?
- How would your organization respond?

When an issue breaks or a crisis occurs, do not ignore your own responses, which may include:

- physical effects – raised heart rate, sickness, the shakes, 'fight-or-flight';
- psychological effects – anxiety, fear, anger, guilt, sadness, paralysis.

Issues, incident and crisis management put people under particular stress. This is a 24/7 job and you'll need to be ready for every eventuality. Good planning for issues and crisis management will help you take action when you may feel paralysed by events.

If your organization faces an issue or crisis, friends may desert you if you fail to communicate properly as they may feel they will be tarnished by association. Foes may use the opportunity to gain a competitive advantage or even put the boot in. They will give their version of the story if you don't talk to the media and you can be certain they won't do you any favours. Don't go underground and never, ever say 'no comment'. You are abdicating your corporate responsibility.

Organizations facing an issue or crisis tend to behave in or of two ways – they either take a negative approach (we have something we must minimize/ignore/cover up because it will threaten our reputation – let's say nothing) or they see the positive side (we must face up to this and be proactive as this will help to rebuild/enhance our reputation – let's tell people what's happened and what we are doing about it). You can work out for yourself what's the more helpful strategy and what's more likely to set the scene for recovery.

You need the buy-in of your top management team in issue and crisis planning. When the going gets tough and corporate reputation is at stake, the senior team will need to get involved and lead by example, demonstrating that they are taking this seriously. The reputation of the organization is ultimately their responsibility.

The purpose of this chapter is to help you think *now* so that you can act positively when you need to. We will look at the preparatory stages necessary for good issues, incident and crisis management and then the main practical issues and the immediate action that is needed. The good news is that it is all common sense, tempered with liberal doses of pragmatism and humility and a strong willingness and ability to communicate.

Definitions

Are we dealing with an issue, an incident or is it a crisis?

Dictionary definitions imply an issue is less dramatic than a crisis – the difference is rather like that between a chronic illness – which goes on for a long time – and an acute condition – with a rapid onset and potentially equally rapid conclusion. And an incident is a flash point that may develop into something else with even more serious consequences:

- *'issue'* – a topic of interest or discussion – an important subject requiring a decision – (legal) the matter remaining in dispute between the parties to an action after pleading;
- *'incident'* – an event with potentially serious consequences – that may result in a crisis, and may involve many people, be violent in nature or may be of political consequence between countries;
- *'crisis'* – a crucial event or turning point – an unstable period especially one of extreme trouble or danger. An unpredictable event that is a major threat to your company, an entire industry or to stakeholders.
- And then there is the emergency. There are two main differences between a crisis and an emergency; an emergency is usually localized so doesn't affect a whole industry and, unlike a crisis that alters the entire way an organization operates, an emergency is a temporary disruption. Most organizations recover fully from an emergency.

Many communicators have offered other definitions for example

'issue – unexpected bad publicity'

'crisis – an issue in a hurry', 'a serious incident which has or will affect human safety, or is threatening to life and/or health and/or the environment'

The newspaper magnate William Randolph Hurst said that, 'news is whatever someone, somewhere does not want published.' A major issue can be at least as damaging to an organization as a crisis. If we ignore this fact we ignore a great truth – that the professional and effective daily handling of an issue, sometimes over months and years, is as critical as the immediate handling of a dramatic incident.

While risks and issues are not the same, issues-management and risk-management processes do overlap. This happens when issues emerge from risks associated with an organization's product, service, policy or some other aspect of its operations. For example, the debate around the effective communication of risks associated with prescription drugs. The United States' pharmaceutical industry has been widely criticized for inadequately communicating the risks of many popular and widely advertised drugs. The risks themselves and then the lack of communication about those risks have drawn criticism from the public, media, advocacy groups and regulators. It all comes down to the perception that the drug companies were willing to put profits before people. And this caused an issue!

Risk audit and analysis

The first step is a thorough audit of the organization's interests and activities to flush out risk areas and vulnerabilities. You can call in specialist risk managers to help with this process if your organization is particularly large or complex. Risk managers seem to be particularly good at defining the potential financial impact that loss of reputation might have on your organization or brand and this seems to help focus corporate minds on the subject! Some organizations have an ethics panel or ethical review process. This may be a good forum to tap and a fertile place to harvest ideas about issues your organization may be facing.

Use the following list of questions to get you started – you should brainstorm others and be forensically thorough. You must be completely honest – it's usually the issue that has been swept under the carpet that proves to be the most problematic.

TABLE 10.1 Risk audit and analysis sample questions

What are our main industry/sector issues (eg ethical trading, mechanical failure, transparency, health and safety, 'excessive' profitability, etc)?
Are there any legislative issues that would have an impact on our ability to conduct our affairs (eg tax measures, employment law, export restrictions, etc)?
Are there any global issues that could have an impact on the way we conduct our affairs (eg commodity prices, environmental changes, war zones, disease, sanctions, etc)?
Is there any area of our operations that could give campaigners cause for concern on any level? Is our industry or sector or organization being targeted by pressure groups (eg ethical, environmental, human rights, animal rights, etc)?
Are there any issues relating to the integrity or good character of our management team/staff/consultants/suppliers/past employees?
Are there any issues regarding our premises or sites (eg health and safety, security, machinery, upkeep, etc)?
Are there any issues regarding the quality of our work/products/services (eg repeat customer complaints, product failure, withdrawal)?
Have we ever had an issue in this organization in the past? How did we handle it? Has the problem been resolved? Could it recur?

A word on 'wicked problems'

Climate change, fighting terror, financial meltdowns, long-term infrastructure projects like road and rail systems, pension provision, forced migration, drugs smuggling, people trafficking, pandemics, world poverty, humanitarian disasters, human rights abuses, freedom of speech... all huge issues, sometimes called 'wicked problems'.

In 1973 Horst Rittel and Melvin Webber, professors of design and urban planning at the University of California at Berkeley, published an article entitled 'Dilemmas in a general theory of planning'. Here they coined the term 'wicked problem' to distinguish the toughest problems that defy solutions from simply hard but otherwise ordinary problems. Rittel and Webber (1973) said wicked problems have these 10 characteristics:

1 *There is no definitive formulation of a wicked problem.* It's not possible to write a well-defined statement of the problem. (You can do this with an ordinary, hard problem.)

2 *Wicked problems have no stopping rule.* With a wicked problem, the search for a solution never stops. (With ordinary, hard problems you can tell when you've reached a solution.)

3 *Solutions to wicked problems are not right/true or wrong/false, but good or bad.* Deciding a course of action – a solution – to a wicked problem is largely a matter of judgement. (Ordinary, hard problems have solutions that can be objectively evaluated as right or wrong.)

4 *There is no immediate and no ultimate test of a solution to a wicked problem.* Solutions to wicked problems generate other subsequent unexpected consequences over time, making it difficult to measure the solution's effectiveness. (You can assess immediately if the solution you have applied to an ordinary, hard problem is working.)

5 *Any single proposed solution to a wicked problem is a 'one-shot' operation; there is no opportunity to learn by trial and error, so every attempt counts.* With wicked problems, every solution has consequences that cannot be repealed or undone (whereas proposed solutions to ordinary, hard problems can be tried and stopped if unsuccessful).

6 *Wicked problems do not have an exhaustively describable set of potential solutions, nor is there a well-described set of approved operations that may be incorporated into the plan.* Ordinary problems come with a limited set of potential solutions, by contrast.

7 *Every wicked problem is essentially unique.* An ordinary problem belongs to a class of similar problems that are all solved in the same way. A wicked problem is substantially without precedent; experience does not help you address it.

8 *Every wicked problem can be considered to be a symptom of another problem.* While an ordinary problem is self-contained, a wicked problem is entwined with other problems. However, those problems don't have one root cause.

9 *The existence of a discrepancy representing a wicked problem can be explained in numerous ways.* A wicked problem involves many stakeholders, who all will have different ideas about what the problem really is and what its causes are.

10 *The planner has no right to be wrong.* Problem-solvers dealing with a wicked issue are held liable for the consequences of any actions they take, because those actions will have such a large impact and are hard to justify.

PR professionals often have to deal with how an organization tackles and discusses wicked problems, particularly in terms of policy development and international relations. Wicked problems really never go away – they are always bubbling under, morphing, circulating. And if we are organizations for whom wicked problems are part and parcel of how we operate, we need policy statements, holding statements, Q&As (questions and answers).

Issues management

Every organization, large or small, for-profit or not, struggles with issues that affect the way they do business. Learning how to spot, and take part in shaping issues can strengthen your brand equity and give competitive advantage. Many issues never become full-blown crises. But an issue can affect and hinder your business. Managing them well ensures your business can continue to operate and be profitable as the environment changes.

An issue, trend or condition developing in your industry has the capacity to change how you do business and that change might be positive or negative. If positive your communications strategy should be to maximize the potential to enhance your reputation. If the change is less good then your communications strategy should seek to minimize reputational damage and to respond as constructively as possible. While the issue is live it's important to be resilient, persistent and tenacious.

To manage an issue effectively you need to be on top of things and that means monitoring both online and elite print and broadcast media. You are looking for warning signs, and you want an early warning!

This information then needs to be interpreted so that trends can be identified and tracked over time. You need to assess whether the issue has gained traction, how this might play out over time and this may require external and expert analysis alongside scenario-planning. You need to focus on how the issue might affect trading conditions, profitability and how business is conducted. Messages and holding statements representing your policy on

TABLE 10.2 Monitoring online, print and broadcast media: a checklist

Online	Traditional
• News and business wires • Blogs • Professional associations, special interest groups, and government archives • Twitter • Facebook • Other forums connected to your business and customers	• Newspapers • Business magazines • Network news • Trade journals • Stakeholder opinions • Government publications (especially if your company is regulated)

the issue should be crafted and these need reviewing regularly as the issue evolves.

Once you have honestly faced up to the issues within your sector and your organization, you can start thinking about future planning. If it is a problem that concerns only your organization, then do something about it immediately. If you can't solve the problem immediately then prepare a plan for doing so with timescales and responsibilities clearly outlined.

You need to see issues management as a positive and proactive process, not a reactive process of damage limitation. Proactive issues management enables an organization to stay on top, to be seen as taking the lead, to even take the position as a leader and authority and to gain a competitive advantage. Issues flare up again as a news story with the release of new research, another similar case, a vividly told case history, a story circulating on the internet, a related overseas incident. This in itself poses problems for the communications practitioner and for the management of the public relations process. As news is passed across the internet as soon as it happens, you must accept that you will not always be in control. But you can be proactive.

Some large corporations have discrete in-house teams whose sole job is issues and crisis management. In some instances the responsibility for issues management is devolved to a communications/PR consultancy. Many organizations don't have the budget for this and so need a workmanlike practical strategy to handle issues in-house. If you are responsible for issues management on a day-to-day basis within your organization, I offer you the following checklist to help make a start – this can be tailored to suit your resources. You may need to outsource some of the elements if you do not have the right skills or resources in-house; again this will be based on priorities.

Do your research

For each one gather lots of intelligence – from the internet (from bloggers, social networking sites, online media, competitor press offices, etc) and from print and broadcast media, from your colleagues, from your network. Assemble past commentary and evidence on the issue including research and reports (for example government, scientific and opinion polls). Make sure you look at the archives not just this year's commentary and you should look for cycles and patterns and so on. Some issues have a distinctly seasonal pattern, others are about areas and regions where parts of the country or the world are particularly 'live'. The best and most professional organizations have many years of data on issues that really matter to them. At the time of writing there is a live and serious crisis in the food industry relating to the supply chain. Any responsible and prepared supermarket will have a position on how food is sourced.

Get monitoring in the present

Who is saying what to whom – who are the influencers and the amplifiers? Look at the messages that are circulating and what response is elicited. You need to determine who is on-side – who is friend and who is foe, those for and against you and the issue. Bloggers and commentators with large followings are particularly important, as are pressure groups. They know how to mobilize and are both responsive and proactive, fast off the block and highly influential.

How often should you monitor? Well it depends on the issue really. Some organizations monitor every day – twice a day – while others take a look each week. Monthly monitoring suggests it's not a live issue.

Agree the key messages on this issue

Most organizations have so-called 'holding statements', policy statements or 'lines to take' on issues. Your messages should be consistent and coherent with these. The 'rule of three' works here too so try to keep messages to a maximum of three to four at most. Your messages need to be written simply and use persuasive and vivid vocabulary. No jargon, science-speak, marketing guff or government whitewash. Get those messages out to anyone acting as a spokespeople, on their mobile devices. Allow messages to be adapted to suit circumstances and audiences. Make sure messages are updated frequently.

Create useful materials and support collateral – these include:

- A Questions-and-Answer (Q&A) document – a basic tool for the management of issues, asking all and every question(s) a journalist might ask, particularly the difficult ones, and constructing the optimum corporate answer. This document can then be circulated to all spokes-people and may also be edited and used with other targets. The key messages should feature strongly. The Q&A may also be cut down to produce a FAQ (frequently asked questions) which could be edited for wide distribution, included in your own organization's blogs, sent to bloggers and posted on your website.

- Holding statements – on the issue that are updated regularly as the issue develops.

- Supporting documentation – the organization's own reports and papers about the issue, which can be used in discussions with journalists. Write them for e-mailing.

- Background press materials – which should already be created and available for day-to-day media work and which are already posted in your online press office.

Get your people mobilized

Select your issues management team and spokespeople. The team would normally include:

- chief executive/chairman/managing director;
- PR /communications director;
- relevant members of the senior management team with particular knowledge of and/or responsibility for each given issue;
- the organization's bloggers;
- media-handling advisors, press office, webmaster-consultants as well as in-house teams;
- select spokespeople – choose three or four – I would recommend:
  - the most senior person – eg CEO/MD;
  - the most knowledgeable person – eg scientist, expert;
  - the most charming person – eg anyone who is sincere, authentic, takes a brief well and who could be the public face of the organization;
  - an independent spokesperson who could act as an advocate if the going gets tough.

Use materials to brief them and put spokespeople through their paces with presentation skills and media training focusing on the issue – include simulated interviews – press, TV, radio. Make sure they de-jargon and speak in layman's language.

Include your own people

Make sure your own people – including national account managers, customers, suppliers and other closely involved or directly affected third parties – and make sure they know what is going on and understand the key messages. You may need to communicate with colleagues and contacts around the world if this is broader and bigger than the domestic. Keep people posted by e-mail, on social networking/ virtual community sites, via tweeets if you use Twitter, via your intranet, extranet.

Keep up the dialogue

Look for and create opportunities to make your point assertively – via your blog and on other blogs, at conferences, speaker platforms, features, chat shows, documentaries.

Of course there may be instances where you judge that it is better to take a reactive rather than proactive stance – in which case refrain from proactive tactics and simply respond where necessary. If you get your issue management right, not only is your reputation protected but you may also help to enhance your organization's standing and develop a profile for your spokespeople and bloggers as experts and commentators.

The lifecycle of an issue

An issue always moves through a four-part cycle, even though that cycle has significantly speeded up thanks to digital communications. Knowing where you are in that cycle will help you plan your communications strategy:

Part one – potential: While there is no clear and present issue on the horizon, the conditions for one to arise is evident. There may be significant media commentary. But the public, stakeholders, regulators or your industry do not define the issue.

Part two – emerging: At this stage the media, the public, your stakeholders or your industry and regulators clearly define and name the issue. Additionally, the issue is applying pressure to your organization. Potential change is on the horizon.

Part three – live/crisis: So this is when a crisis hits. A issue becomes a crisis when there is a public outcry for change, media scrutiny and regulatory involvement. Stakeholders are well aware of the change, and the organization or industry in crisis is experiencing significant loss in reputation and brand equity, as well as profit.

Part four – dormant: After a crisis has subsided, it moves into a dormant stage, which is the end of the cycle of an issue. At this point media interest subsides and regulators back off. The organization or industry is likely to have changed fundamentally.

Understanding the cycle issues move through can help you prepare messages for each stage. The point with issue management and knowing its various stage is to control an issue before it becomes a crisis.

Crisis management

Many of the principles for issues management are carried into crisis management – but there are some additional considerations, as detailed in Table 10.3:

TABLE 10.3 Crisis management principles

Statements – write them

In crisis management you need to get a basic statement together immediately which covers facts and may also include key messages. This should be available for immediate use on the internet. You will need to update the statement frequently as more information becomes available. The first time a statement goes out it is likely to be very short, containing basic facts only. This should be updated after the crisis management team meet to decide strategy.

What are the key facts? What happened, when did it take place, where did it happen and who is involved? Why and how may be questions that have to be left while an investigation takes place.

Involve and negotiate with insurers and legal advisors. There can be considerable tension here about making public statements that may communicate what you need to say but which legal advisors believe could imply acceptance of responsibility when no one yet knows who is to blame. Keep in mind your objective – to protect and repair the reputation of the organization with its stakeholders – and use this as a yardstick when working with other advisors. But always:

- Express your concern to victims and their families and give reassurance about what you are doing as an organization in response to the crisis

(Continued)

TABLE 10.3 (*Continued*)

- Tell people what action you are now taking – management team are meeting now, our specialists are travelling to the scene, we are about to launch an investigation, a review of procedures – practical actions include anything which demonstrates that you are taking this seriously and doing something about it
- Use an unblemished record to underpin messages that this is a one-off, your organization is not a past offender
- Let people know where and when further information will be available
- Direct people to the website for more information

Stakeholders – identify them

Agree priority stakeholders – these may include:

- Emergency services – police, fire, hospital, ambulance
- Those immediately affected – eg involved parties' families and colleagues
- Staff, customers, partners, retailers, suppliers, legal advisors, insurers
- Local MPs, local community
- Media – regional, national, international, local as appropriate and as available
- Social networking sites – which may be effective in order to reach the target group affected
- The general public

Decide who should contact each stakeholder group and what briefing materials and which channel they should use

Crisis team – assemble them

This may be the Issues Management Team but may also include other specialists, eg:

- Operational experts
- Health and safety experts
- Site management and security teams

Get them together as soon as possible – it may have to be via audio or video conference – if on-site then in a private and quiet room where they can discuss strategy

Crisis management strategy – agree it

Examine the nature of the crisis by asking the following questions:

- Is there a more fundamental problem?

(*Continued*)

TABLE 10.3 (*Continued*)

- Are we at fault?
- Is there an inherent weakness that makes us vulnerable?
- How can we correct this?
- If we can't, how can we prepare for a similar situation?
- Is there more to come?
- What is the worst-case scenario?
- What will the stakeholders think/feel?
- What are the timing implications?
- What is at stake regarding our reputation?
- Are there any advocates willing to speak for us?
- Are there any third parties involved?
- Is this a fragment of a bigger story?
- Can the crisis be contained?
- What action do we need to take now?
- Who will take it?
- When will we next meet?

Crisis communications strategy – agree it
Decide on your action plan by asking the following questions:

- How proactive/reactive do we need to be?
- What targets do we need to communicate with and how shall we accomplish this?
- What media need to be briefed?
- How do we do it? – online (always and first); video, photographs/visuals, social networking sites, bloggers/written; e-mail/face-to-face; press conference/one-to-one press briefings
- What do we post on the web immediately? What video footage do we need to create?
- Do we need an emergency phone line for relatives to get more information?
- When do we go proactive?
- Who fronts for the organization?
- What do they say?

If a press conference is required:

- Prepare media briefing packs
- The most current statement

(*Continued*)

TABLE 10.3 (*Continued*)

- Backgrounders on the organization including; history, aims, objectives, major documents (eg annual report); financial position
- Policy statements
- Biographies of spokespeople and other board directors
- Provide visuals if required or manage requests for photography/ filming
- Identify sites and brief site managers immediately – photographers will head straight for crisis sites without asking for permission
- Digital photography – eg sites, products, workforce, customers
- Video footage – digital moving images for immediate loading online

Practical issues – resolve them

- Crisis communications team – working room/crisis HQ
- Don't use the chief executive's office – create a dedicated space as the communications team needs 100% access
- Try to locate this on the crisis site – have an emergency communication kit ready to roll for crises 'on location' and check it is up-to-date at the end of every week. Use as much technology as you can to support communications – web-enabled mobile phone, wi-fi laptops with e-mailable materials ready to go (remember mains cables, rechargers or spare batteries for electronic equipment – it's important to maintain this press facility as, if your electricity supply has gone because of floods or fire, etc, you will need battery backup power)
- Background press releases loaded and ready to e-mail, digital video and stills camera, portable printer, corporate literature and backgrounders
- If you are working on site specify a conference room that can be seconded for crisis – make sure this has complete connectivity – ISDN lines, phones, e-mail and web access
- Consider extra resourcing needs for the crisis HQ including staffing. Make sure there are flip charts, markers, Blu Tack and refreshments available at all times

Internal communications – brief team

- Your staff are your best and closest ambassadors. Keep them aware of developments as they occur. Use tweets, texts, anything that works for your organization

(*Continued*)

TABLE 10.3 (*Continued*)

- As far as media are concerned, all staff should be briefed as part of their induction that all media calls should be passed to the press office. Switchboard operators have a particular role to play in media management during a crisis
- Give switchboard staff briefing and instructions for media calls
- Pass media to in-house or external press office
- Use a media enquiry form if staff end up taking a media call, eg out of hours and pass to the crisis team immediately

Social media for issues and crisis management

Providing you have a social media strategy already in place and are using social media channels to build followers you can mitigate a crisis faster than you would otherwise be able to, in terms of effective crisis communications. Your crisis plan should include a social media strategy, arguably as the first aspect of external communications to tackle when the crisis hits. You need to discuss and agree how you will handle, and who will be responsible for, your website and digital channels (blogs, social media sites, video, and photo channels). You cannot leave it to the web editor or social media editor – as messaging must be agreed at the highest level as part of reputation management.

Consider options ahead of any real crisis and make sure people know the rules of the game in these changed circumstances. When bad news or an emergency suddenly strikes, stakeholders usually go to your website – which in turn links to your social media channels – for the latest update. Given the momentum inherent in crisis situations you have no time to build a new crisis site from scratch. Instead, a prebuilt dark site can be 'turned on' as required.

The dark website can replace the normal website, can be linked to the normal website via a display on the home page, or the dark site can have a completely new URL, based on the most likely/obvious search terms. A dark site helps position you as the primary source of information about the crisis and this in turn can help suppress or at least control speculation and rumour. It also usefully signals to the news media that you intend to provide timely, accurate information (and so encourages them to come to you first for balanced coverage).

This transparency shows you are confident and competent, taking corporate responsibility quickly and professionally. Stakeholders will also make assessments based on this response. When your own website becomes a source of credible information, it translates directly into trust. Not communicating is seen as hiding, which frequently escalates the crisis online.

During normal operations, websites promote a company or organization and its products or services. But during a crisis, stakeholders want, need and expect different, specific and consistent factual information from a trusted source. That information should cover:

- prominent and frequently updated facts about what has happened and the organization's response;
- any special instructions telling anyone affected by the crisis what they must or must not do;
- what steps are being taken to get the situation back to normal;
- relevant background information describing the organization, the causes and impact of the crisis, promoting a clear understanding of the situation;
- contact information for the news media;
- contact information for members of the public affected by the crisis;
- regular fact- and action-based updates.

Two important pages for crisis management communications are a 'Frequently asked questions' page and a virtual press office where text, pictures and videos can be downloaded.

With large-scale crises there is often a huge amount of information coming in and going out so everyone needs to understand how to handle a crisis online. Everyone responsible for social media channels should receive crisis training and take part in a crisis simulation, using a social media simulator (see below).

Issues and crises have predictable rhythms and cycles, as discussed earlier (Potential, Emerging, Live, Dormant). So get an appreciation of where you are with the crisis and how the media will respond.

As Chris Syme (2013) says in her excellent post 'How to use social media to manage a crisis' (http://socialmediatoday.com/chrissyme/1540966/how-use-social-media-manage-crisis):

> Monitoring the chatter around your organization should be part of
> your everyday social media operations. You may already use HootSuite
> or Google Alerts on a daily basis. But once a crisis hits, you may need
> something more powerful. An application that is set up specifically for this
> purpose will serve you better in a crisis. Look for an application that can
> handle a high number of data entries, identifies influencers (both positive
> and negative), and analyses sentiment, volume, and escalation. Make sure
> it can export information, as this will save you time so you don't have to
> produce manual reports for the communications and leadership teams.
> There are many such analytical tools, including Brandwatch and Meltwater.
> If your budget won't accommodate the cost, then you may need to bring in
> an experienced monitoring company for the duration of the crisis. (Adapted
> from Syme, C (June, 2013))

She goes on to say that when monitoring a crisis online you could analyse the following:

- Volume: Monitor the number of posts on the crisis each hour by channel. Keywords you monitor may vary, but as a minimum watch the brand stream and any other keywords associated with the crisis. Keep an eye on Twitter as hashtags develop and monitor them as well. Also, to get a sense of balance, track the number of crisis mentions to non-crisis mentions.

- Escalation: First look at the number of crisis mentions to non-crisis mentions. Make sure this is on a timeline graph so you can see escalation at a glance. Escalation is a key indicator of when you should speak to the public. If a crisis is escalating quickly, it will require more interaction with stakeholder groups. Also track escalation by sheer volume and sentiment. Faster escalation requires faster and more frequent communication.

- Sentiment: Some monitoring tools record sentiment. Although they're not exact, Radian6 and Meltwater Buzz for instance both have tools that let you change sentiment tags on a post or help the application determine the ratings with keywords. Use a positive (+), negative (–) and neutral (0) rating for both brand and crisis mentions. It's important to separate brand issues from crisis issues. Sometimes a crisis can trigger online criticisms and conversation about routine brand issues that are nothing to do with the crisis itself.

- Influencers and detractors: Make sure you track influencers by frequency of posting and shares. If you have time, you can even check on people's social graphs or Klout scores. If you have important pieces of information, you may want to reach out to key positive influencers to help you spread messages. Remember that detractors are different from haters. Know how various online social communities operate in a crisis and factor them in accordingly.

(Adapted from Syme, C (June, 2013) How to use social media to manage a crisis, socialmediatoday.com)

Once you have a grip on where the chatter is, address the crisis on the channel that is buzzing about it. So if it's on Twitter and Facebook, go there with your messages. Don't use a traditional press release for social media work.

Issues and crisis management training

Depending on budget consider the following to sharpen your issue and crisis handling skills:

- External courses on issues and crisis management – which may give you additional perspectives on the subject and which usually include relevant case histories.

- In-house training – for PR and management teams who would be responsible for handling an issue or crisis. Useful as a team-building exercise particularly if the issues and crisis team is drawn from disparate parts of the organization or several sites are involved.
- Media training for spokespeople – preferably with some input from or interviews with a working journalist. Can be held on-site or in studio and would cover TV, radio, studio and down-the-line interviews and soundbites.
- Regular 'roadtesting' for spokespeople – simulated and surprise media interviews on the phone with a 'journalist' – with feedback and suggestions for improvement.
- Crisis simulation – to test the processes on-site. May also include a simulated press conference.
- Social media simulators – software that simulates social media debate via a number of commonly used social media platforms including Twitter, Facebook, blogs, video and online media sources. Often backed up by role-players who simulate citizen, media and community reactions in a realistic, real-time scenario, from scurrilous hashtag rumours to nasty phone calls.

Issues and crisis management and external consultants

There are times when an organization simply cannot handle its own issues and crisis management. Maybe the in-house team is too small, maybe they don't have this sort of experience, maybe they are too busy on other projects or are on holiday or maternity leave, maybe they just need some expert independent, external reality-checking.

If you accept that issues and crisis management is a vital part of reputation management – and therefore the communications function – and you know or suspect that you will need an external consultant if the going gets tough, then get them in now. You may already use a consultancy – as a rule it's usually best to use existing partners, providing they have top-up issue and crisis-management capabilities as they will know your organization and sector already. They may have indeed included a contingency for issue and crisis management as part of their overall communications planning and budgeting.

But don't wait until the issues are smothering you or the crisis has broken. It's just too late. If you are making a new appointment, get someone on board who understands the nature of your industry or sector and who has had experience dealing with your sort of issues and crises. Involve them in the planning stage, have short but regular update meetings. Pay them a retainer if you have to so that they are on call when you need them.

There are a number of consultancies which specialize in issue and crisis management. It may be worth considering one of these if you have a particular need where this sort of specialist support will deliver added value. Otherwise full service consultancies and corporate/public affairs consultancies usually employ three or four senior consultants with issues- and crisis-management experience. You could also develop relationships with freelancers who are on the whole very flexible and cost-effective (BUT bear in mind they may not be available when you need them). It's a question of shopping around to find the best fit. As far as fees are concerned, issue and crisis management has higher value attached to it and so daily or hourly rates are likely to be higher than you might expect to pay for a straightforward consumer, business-to-business or corporate communications campaign.

One final point

Clients and colleagues often ask me what about a crisis manual? Surely we need one?

I don't think so. There was a time when it seemed sacrilegious to make such a suggestion. Many consultants made a stack of money selling them to clients – and I have helped to write one or two of the things in the past. Most communications teams had one of these weighty tomes on their shelves.

The 'thud factor' of the crisis manual was used both to satisfy the anally retentive and to prove to unbelievers that this was a really serious subject, not one that could be treated lightly. Luckily we don't need to sell the concept as hard as we used to. We – and by this I mean management – generally acknowledge that issue and crisis management is vital and we all know what happens when organizations get it wrong (BP or RIM, the owners of BlackBerry).

Crisis manuals once tried to include every scenario that might befall an organization – staff abusing vulnerable residents, fires at warehouses, chief executive having an illicit relationship with chairman's son, computer systems going down – and had 10 pages of instructions about how to deal with each crisis. Some weren't crises at all and many scenarios were the product of feverish brainstorms held under pressure late at night. Inevitably the crisis that did occur varied wildly from the imagined scenario, so much so that the template proved little more than useless.

Manuals became unusable and unwieldy because they tried to combine procedural instruction with communications priorities. There is undoubtedly a place for procedures manuals but these are quite different to quick-response communications plans that need to swing into action immediately.

We work fast, we work remotely and we can't carry a 300-page manual round with us – although this could now be loaded onto a pad, smartphone or a password-protected USB stick. But there isn't the time to plough through an encyclopaedia when news is breaking every second on Twitter.

Finally crisis manuals need updating and many of those dusty old volumes had contact details and names of folk who had long since left the company or been transferred to Bogota. The bigger the organization, the bigger the admin problem.

The truth is that, as I said at the outset, it is all down to planning in advance and then performing on the day. If you go through the issue audit you will identify those areas where you are most vulnerable and where planning is necessary. Then follow through the processes I outline above, making sure that issues and crisis management is alive in your organization not something you did once and filed away, just in case. You should end up with holding statements and questions and answers – which should be lodged on a secure site and be accessible for all those responsible from anywhere in the world.

These days the following three items are needed, given to the relevant people (ie those that need to know) and available to them in the form that works best. Update and reissue them every other month and be absolutely methodical about this:

1 A key contact list which has phone numbers, including home and mobiles, and e-mail addresses – if you can, organize this list so that spokespeople responsibility is clear and you can call the right person quickly when there is a crisis or an urgent media query or opportunity.

2 An issue and crisis communication action checklist – compile your own based on the checklists in this chapter. Try not to exceed the equivalent of a couple of sides of A4.

3 Key messages – as discussed earlier.

Evaluating issues and crisis management

So it's all over... how did you do?

First of all it is a mistake to think it is all over. Issues run and run and may come to the fore at any time. Follow-up news coverage of the results of an inquest, public inquiry or private prosecution all serve to resurrect the memories of the crisis. For those worst affected it never goes away. A year, 10 years, 20 years after the event and parents may still be grieving a drowned teenager, a woman may still look in a mirror and see the scars from the train crash, a widower leaves flowers where the train went off the rails. Anniversaries make strong human-interest news stories. This is a reality and you need to plan for it. Make sure you have a statement ready about how things have progressed since that time, what action you have taken, what good news came from bad.

But you can evaluate the process. You can review qualitatively the way you handled an issue or crisis. Did you follow the process? Do you get some reflections from a trusted journalist? What were the outcomes? Should you review the issues and crisis management procedures? This will tell you if the processes and procedures are right for your organization and whether your team is working well.

You can qualitatively and quantitatively evaluate media coverage. Where did it appear? How fast did the story travel in all media – on Twitter, on online media, radio, TV, press? Which bloggers and journalists wrote about you fairly, what did elite, respected and influential media say about you – good and bad – how big was the story; how many bloggers, viewers, listeners and readers may have registered your organization's name and involvement in the story and, vitally, did your messages get across?

And you can track sales figures and share prices. These will tell you whether there has been any commercial impact. You can also track correspondence into the organization via your website and by post to gauge how individuals, perhaps representing interested groups and other organizations, have responded.

For the communications professional the key issue is whether your reputation has been damaged or enhanced in the long term by these events. To be absolutely certain, you must look at continuous tracking. To do this really well and to be able to extrapolate the most value from the data, put monitoring in place now and measure at regular intervals, before, during and after the events in question. This may take the form of qualitative or quantitative studies among one or several key stakeholders, perhaps those most vital to your organization. Only then can you be certain you have met your objectives.

Issues and crisis communications – checklist

TABLE 10.4 Issues and crisis communications checklist

Do	Don't
Plan	Wait for it – whatever it is – to happen
Communicate	Bury your head in the sand or say 'no comment'
Communicate simply – cut the jargon	Muddy communications with irrelevant jargon, management-speak or too many facts and figures
Get management buy-in	Make it just a PR-only issue (it's a much wider issue)
Get in help – more in-house resources or a consultancy, if you need to	Struggle on with inadequate resources

(Continued)

TABLE 10.4 (Continued)

Do	Don't
Train the team together	Assume people will simply understand a written communication
Demonstrate that public interest/ safety is main issue and empathize with the people who have been affected	Come over as an arrogant organization with commercial concerns as the key driver
Look for cooperation and conciliation	Engage in conflict or head-to-heads with victims and relatives, media or opponents
Learn from the experience – change working practices, review, track reputation	Put it in a box at the end of the day and forget about it
Work fast – use technology, social networking, the internet to get the messages out to as many of the target audiences as possible as quickly as possible	Put it off until tomorrow

Further reading

For practitioners who know that issues and crisis management will be a major part of their role, I would recommend as further reading one of Kogan Page's PR In Practice series Risk Issues and Crisis Management in Public Relations: A casebook of best practice by Michael Register and Judy Larkin (2008). Not only does it go into more detail in terms of ideas and strategies for the handling of risk issues, incidents and crises it also has a wealth of fascinating case histories to learn from, drawn from the public, private and not-for-profit sectors.

11
Essential skills for the PR practitioner

Introduction

In Chapter 3 we considered the qualities and attributes needed to be a successful public relations practitioner. Here we look at some specific practical skills we need to develop and polish throughout our professional careers. These are:

- writing skills;
- interpersonal skills;
- briefing skills;
- listening and questioning;
- positive body language – essential for building rapport;
- assertiveness – essential for all PR practitioners in their role as consultants, whether internal or external;
- presentation skills.

Writing

'Be sure your words are better than silence.' (Confucius)

How much time do we spend reading, either online or in print, or both? I reckon half my professional life is spent reading what others write and the other half is writing what I want people to read! As PR practitioners we have to produce many different forms of written materials, ranging from e-mails, proposals/recommendations, reports, award entries and case histories, through to invitations and letters. Most of us are responsible for our online content and this includes web pages, tweets and other social media updates, blogs, comments and frequently asked questions.

Most of us still produce printed materials and need to be able to write (and sometimes edit) annual reports, leaflets and brochures, and our in-house magazine. The main written materials we all are required to create are to support our media relations activities, and these include holding statements and 'lines to take' for issues, situation updates for crises, background information for journalists, news stories – in full as press releases and then as a headline tweet, features/feature materials and opinion pieces. And don't forget crisp photo and video captions. Finally, some of us also write for speaking and this covers scripts for videos, speeches and presentations.

Writing is probably the single most important practical skill you need to be a competent PR professional. Many books have been written on the subject of writing for communicators but it all boils down to:

Being clear; being concise; being correct; being compelling.

This applies whether you are writing a tweet, a blog, a 1,500-word feature for a trade magazine or your annual report that will get printed or presented as a pdf.

If you ask UK news editors and journalists how many pieces of communication they receive every day from their sources and contacts, including tweets, e-mails and direct messages, they'll frequently answer 'at least 80 a day' with some reporting many, many more; some say thousands of pieces of material. The news reporters at the Press Association in London file hundreds of stories every day, from big breaking news to showbiz and human interest stories ready to use online or in print. (This doesn't include their photo and video output.) How many pieces of communication do you filter every day? How many does your target audience?

How do we decide what we are going to read if we can't read everything? It's estimated that one in six editors assess whether they are interested in reading on based on the name of the sender and the headline. A further five out of six assess on sender, headline and first paragraph only. (We all read like this don't we, whether we are reading a blog, a news story or a feature? Because we can't read everything that comes our way we are likely to weed out the stuff that doesn't seem relevant to us and that is painful to read.) Many journalists say they want 250 words max on a new story – they will ask for more if it captures their imagination. I have asked journalists all round the world these same questions and these are pretty consistent responses. How do you decide what to read and what to 'bin/delete'? How does your audience decide whether to read past the first line and make it to the end?

PR professionals need to focus on four aspects of writing to get better and faster in terms of consistent quality of output:

1 purpose;
2 style;

3 structure;

4 content.

While many of the observations and recommendations I make here relate to writing for the media (because we have to do a lot of this in our profession) the principles apply to all writing.

Purpose

Before we write anything at all, there are two questions we must ask ourselves:

1 Who's the reader? (Or, for oral delivery, the listener?) And

2 What's my aim?

As far as the reader is concerned make sure you have a really clear idea of your reader. I often have a picture in front of me when I am writing of my target audience (for example when writing material for university students I have a picture of one of my nieces on my desktop to inspire me). It's useful to consider:

- Readership (how many people will read this? How many followers? How many will buy or access online? In other words, circulation figures).
- Readers' ages – if there is a bias – as this also indicates life stage and likely priorities.
- Gender dominance – if there is one.
- Educational attainment – as this affects writing style.
- Where they work (trade) or live (consumer).
- Job titles (trade) or interests (consumer).
- Budget available (trade) and disposable income (consumer).
- Time spent reading the publication/website – again as this affects style.
- Political/religious/social and ethical affiliations – which will have an impact on angle and content

With aims, when we are writing for public relations purposes we should be pursuing clear communications objectives. But the first objective must surely to be understood! If we are writing for the media we are probably first of all trying to get our story selected as opposed to binned. We will be interested in gaining positive or at least balanced media exposure. Sometimes our objective may be to minimize coverage. Ultimately we may be seeking to create awareness of and interest in our product, idea, company, or to persuade/sell/ gain support or to educate the target audience, enhance our reputation, or communicate expertise. We might be seeking to change opinions or even to precipitate action or change behaviours.

Style

'The short words are best, and the old words are best of all.' (Winston Churchill)

So you have a clear idea of your reader and your purpose. Now you can think about style, because style is determined by both of these factors. Respecting our readers, we should aim to make professional writing as clear and as concise as possible and, as far as possible, a pleasure to read. Can the reader readily understand it or is it a struggle to plough through? Is it full of language that he has look up because he is uncertain of meaning or even totally unfamiliar with a word? Are the sentences so long he has to read them several times to make sense of them?

Style also embraces correctness. The issue is of course what exactly is correct? Spoken language changes and evolves all the time with changes in written language gradually following on afterwards. The rules for what constitutes correct writing tend to stay the same for longer.

Change is usually slow but in recent years we've seen the pace of change in both written and spoken language accelerate because of the internet and technology. We all start in different places too and every one of us learnt to communicate using language in different ways. As a London child with a Scottish father and an English mother, my speech patterns and vocabulary differed from my West Indian and Polish classmates. We pick up words and expressions from everyone we play and work with and we get new words from other languages (baksheesh, sabbatical), by combining words ('brunch' from 'breakfast' and 'lunch') and by shortening them ('phone' from 'telephone'). Proper names and brand names drop into common use too (Hoover, iPhone).

Sometimes language is used by groups to mark them out as different and special: the first time I worked with diplomats I wondered what they meant by 'interlocutor'; meeting senior military people I pondered on their use of the expression 'kinetic removal'; working with a not-for-profit organization media-training young men from South London to help them explain the phenomenon of gang membership required me to learn their vocabulary and then teach them a new vocabulary, if they were to explain why families need to be aware of the signs. So vocabulary needs special consideration because it can be purposefully used to either alienate or include.

While there seems to be no one single correct answer to the question 'how many words are there in the English language?' if you include derivations, words that are joined together, medical and scientific terms, Latin words used in law, French words used in cooking, German words used in academic writing, Japanese words used in martial arts, Scots dialect, teenage slang and so on the publishers of the Oxford English Dictionary (OED) reckon it could be around 750,000. Yet we only use a tiny proportion in everyday speech – some people say our day-to-day repertoire consists of just 2,000 plain words. So if we want to be quickly and easily understood we should use those plain old words we speak to each other every day as far as we can.

Many of the changes that occur in language start in young adulthood and if we think about how digital ideas spread this fits with changes to the way information is disseminated. As young people interact with others their own age, their language changes and includes words and constructions very different from the generation before. Some words and constructs are fashionable and only last a year or so, others catch on and change language permanently.

You may work with those who are wedded to what appears to be old-fashioned, pedantically correct English – people who were educated in a formal and precise way. They really do have a point. Not only do incorrect grammar, spelling, punctuation and usage errors undermine your authority and reputation, making you look ill-educated and ignorant, they also can confuse and even change meaning. Take a look at these examples and you'll see what I mean:

- King Charles walked and talked an hour after his head was cut off.
- King Charles walked and talked; an hour after, his head was cut off.
- The Panda eats shoots and leaves.
- The Panda eats, shoots and leaves.
- The Panda eats, shoots, and leaves.
- The girls like spaghetti.
- The girl's like spaghetti.
- Your welcome.
- You're welcome.
- A woman without her man is nothing.
- A woman, without her man, is nothing.
- A woman: Without her, man is nothing.

George Orwell (1903–1950), journalist and writer, was passionate about clear, direct writing. His 'six elementary rules' (*Politics and the English Language*, 1946) are robust guidelines, used in the teaching of journalism, to help writers develop a good, plain style, suitable for public relations purposes and all kinds of business writing – from press releases to consumer leaflets and business proposals:

1 Never use a metaphor, simile or other figure of speech, which you are used to seeing in print (ie avoid mind-numbing clichés).
2 Never use a long word when a short word will do (ie don't be pretentious).
3 If it is possible to cut out a word, always do so (ie edit, edit, edit).
4 Never use the passive when you can use the active (eg passive – the car was driven by Jim; active – Jim drove the car).

5 Never use jargon, a scientific word or a foreign phrase if there is a straightforward English equivalent.

6 Break any of these rules sooner than say anything outright barbarous.

In today's hip-hop-happening world, this roughly translates to: Cut the crap and keep it simple and direct.

The Plain English Campaign was set up by a feisty Liverpudlian woman who was sick and tired of pompous and wordy government forms that ordinary people couldn't understand. Take a look at their website, there is a fantastic set of resources available to download (www.plainenglish.co.uk).

Also look at *The Economist Style Guide* – I have it on my desk in printed form and I also consult it online: http://www.economist.com/styleguide/introduction. It is a really beautifully written guide, terrific if you love the English language – witty, intelligent and wise, a fantastic resource to help you develop a good writing style for public relations.

Always make sure you are a champion of good, plain English whatever you write.

Sentence length

To make your writing as easy-to-read as possible, go for sentences that are between 15 and 20 words in length. That said, aim for some variation. If you only write short sentences writing can be monotone, staccato and boring. Too many long sentences close together are hard to read. Sentence variation is also about variable syntax too. More complex sentences, moving away from a simple subject-verb-object order ('The man drove the car.') by using modifiers ('The man, a previous client of mine, drove the car.') or dependent – independent clauses ('Since I once worked with him, I recognized the man who drove the car'). You can use more complex sentences (and in literature very complex sentences abound) but again think about the reader and the purpose. Most usually for public relations people the full stop is our friend.

Assessing style

You can use online The Gunning Fog Index, which is a readability test designed to show how easy or difficult text is to read. It uses the following formula:

Take a sample of text of around 100 words.

● How many sentences? – Work out the average number of words in a sentence – A.

● Count the number of words of three or more syllables – include numerals, exclude proper nouns (this is the percentage of words of complex words) – B.

● Add A and B together and multiply this by 0.4 (why this figure I do not know!).

● This gives you a number – the Gunning 'Fog' Index. The Gunning Fog Index gives the number of years of education that your reader hypothetically needs to understand the paragraph or text.

The Gunning Fog Index formula implies that short sentences with everyday vocabulary achieve a better (lower) score than long sentences written in complicated language. The London and *New York Times* have an average Fog Index of 11–12, *Time* magazine about 11, *The Sun* around 7 or 8. Typically, technical documentation has a Fog Index between 10 and 15, and professional prose almost never exceeds 18.

Punchy writing

To ensure readers read to the end, make sure your style is lively, with variation, and with concrete and colourful vocabulary. Grey boring writing makes for heavy going.

'Concretize' your language. (Sorry – it appears to be an American term for making writing more, well, 'concrete'!) This means getting meaning or images across in a precise and imaginative way. For instance, by using stronger, more evocative verbs when describing an action to add weight and colour. So instead of, 'The woman walked aimlessly across the street,' write: 'The woman strolled across the street.' Concretizing language means also 'particularizing' nouns as well. Instead of, 'I ate a sandwich...' write: 'I ate a cheese and pickle sandwich...' Suddenly you have a much stronger picture because it's not generic. (This is very helpful if you are talking to people – for example selling-in a story to a journalist by phone – as it plants an image quickly in the mind.)

Onomatopoeia is also useful for waking up grey prose. (Onomatopoeia is when a word that sounds like its description is used, for example: 'crash,' 'splash,' 'boom', etc.) When describing something that has a sound effect, use onomatopoeia: 'The thunder boomed in the distance' or 'the children splashed in the water.' Immediate impact and colour is added.

In creative writing modifiers and adjectives are useful to add colour, especially when describing senses – sight, touch, scent, taste and sound. Use modifiers to describe any of the senses: sight: 'his dark and mottled skin,' 'the sky was the colour of steel'; touch: 'the dog's coat was oily,' 'the prickly grass'; scent: 'the rancid odour of stale sweat,' 'the floral scent of her cologne'; taste: 'the pasta was too salty,' 'the pear was sweet'; sound: 'the deafening music,' 'the honeyed singing'. Your readers see, hear, taste, touch, and smell what you are talking about in your writing. This is really helpful if you are writing for radio or for presentations. By making ideas colourful and concrete, you make them real. (One note of caution however – if you need to edit copy it's often the adjectives that that have to go.)

Get rid of wordiness and pretentiousness. Readers do not have the time to wade through repetitive and affected writing. In my experience pretentiousness comes when a writer is showing off his or her intellectual abilities. We are not writing novels or poetry or academic papers – we are writing to get a message across quickly and powerfully. So choose words that are simple and clear. This does not mean that you shouldn't broaden your vocabulary (varying your word choices avoids repetition.) but pretentiousness doesn't clarify your prose so much as makes it overlong, confusing and grey.

What gets the message across more effectively?

'Laura's oblique narrative discombobulated Michelle.'

'Laura's rambling note confused Michelle.'

A note on spelling/using the right word:

- Keep a notebook with you all the time and write down words you spell or use incorrectly.
- Keep a crib sheet of words you know you tend to get wrong or have a block on.
- Refer to your list.
- Always use spellchecker/dictionary/thesaurus.
- Team up with a spelling buddy or mentor.
- Use same techniques we used to use at school, ie spelling exercises:
  - Write down the word correctly.
  - Look – at word structure and letters.
  - Cover – and memorize.
  - Write – again.
  - Compare – with the original.

Parts of speech

It's helpful to remember these for sentence construction. Remember to keep sentences short to aid understanding (15–20 words max) and paragraphs too, dependent on reading occasion. There are eight categories of parts of speech:

TABLE 11.1 Parts of speech categories

Part of speech	Definition
Noun	The name of anything: • Concrete – something you can see and touch, *eg a cat, a laptop, a mobile phone* • Abstract – qualities, *eg honesty, goodness, humour* • Proper – real and specific people, places and things, *eg Barack Obama, London, The Royal Albert Hall*

(Continued)

TABLE 11.1 (*Continued*)

Part of speech	Definition
	• Collective – things which form a whole, *eg team, flock, crew, herd, committee* • Verbal (sometimes called gerunds) – denoting an action, *eg walking, running, jumping* • Common – anything which cannot be classified as abstract, proper or collective
Pronoun	Used in place of a noun. Useful as they help avoid repetition of nouns. Main types are: • Personal – *I, we, they* • Possessive – *Yours, theirs*
Adjective	Used to describe, qualify or limit a noun. Used next to a noun or linked to a noun by a verb, *eg the talented Mr Ripley*, and *Mr Ripley is talented*. Several classes. Only use sparingly for business writing
Verb	Doing, being or having words, which give meaning to the sentence – and every sentence has one!
Adverb	Used to modify or qualify a verb, adjective or even a whole phrase or sentence, *eg below, always, badly, now, soon, then, always*
Preposition	Used to show the relationship between one thing and another in a phrase or sentence, eg cat *on* the mat, room *with* a view, baby *in* the cot. There are also prepositional phrases, *eg instead of, in spite of*
Conjunction	Used to join words and phrases, most common being *and*. Poor business writing often includes too many unconditional conjunctions, *eg provided, if, unless* which can lead to overlong sentences and lack of clarity
Interjection	Eg Forget it! – not recommended for business writing

I was taught this little rhyme at school – I found it in one of my old school notebooks recently and was reminded how much I'd enjoyed learning parts of speech as a kid – and I hope you find it fun and helpful too.

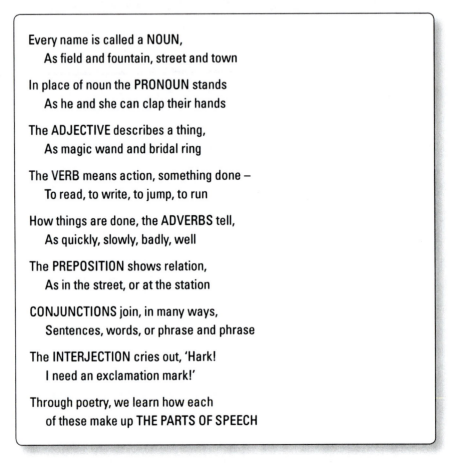

Every name is called a NOUN,
  As field and fountain, street and town

In place of noun the PRONOUN stands
  As he and she can clap their hands

The ADJECTIVE describes a thing,
  As magic wand and bridal ring

The VERB means action, something done –
  To read, to write, to jump, to run

How things are done, the ADVERBS tell,
  As quickly, slowly, badly, well

The PREPOSITION shows relation,
  As in the street, or at the station

CONJUNCTIONS join, in many ways,
  Sentences, words, or phrase and phrase

The INTERJECTION cries out, 'Hark!
  I need an exclamation mark!'

Through poetry, we learn how each
  of these make up THE PARTS OF SPEECH

Punctuation

People often get confused about what's right and wrong especially with apostrophes. Although I generally get it right, sometimes I get my wotsits in a twist too so use Table 11.2 as an easy reference (I have this pinned on my noticeboard in my office).

Content

You understand your reader. You know what your purpose is in writing. You have thought about the style that's right. Now you need to ensure you have compelling content. Something that will get a reader's attention and keep it.

TABLE 11.2 Correct use of punctuation

Punctuation mark	Usage
Full stop .	• Use plenty to keep sentences short.
Comma ,	• Use as an aid to understanding. Too many can be confusing. Use them to break up a long sentence and only where the break is a natural one.
	• Use two commas, or none at all, when inserting a clause in the middle of a sentence. Do *not* write: *Use two commas, or none at all when inserting...* Or *Use two commas or none at all, when inserting...*
	• If the clause ends with a bracket, which is not uncommon (this one does), the bracket is followed by a comma.
	• Do not put a comma before *and* at the end of a sequence of items *unless* one of the items includes another *and*. Thus: *Its main exports were oil, carpets, textiles and pistachio nuts.* But: *Its main exports were oil, carpets and textiles, and pistachio nuts.*
	• NB: The Oxford comma, also known as the serial comma, is an *optional* comma before the word 'and' at the end of a list: *We sell books, videos, and magazines.* It was traditionally used by printers, readers, and editors at Oxford University Press. Not all writers and publishers use it, but it can clarify the meaning of a sentence when the items in a list are not single words, *eg These items are available in black and white, red and yellow, and blue and green.*
Colon :	• Use 'to deliver the goods that have been implied in the preceding words' (Fowler, 1994), *eg They brought gifts: gold, frankincense and myrrh.*
	• Use before a whole quoted sentence, but not before a quotation that begins in mid-sentence, *eg She said: 'It will not work.' He retorted that it had 'always worked before'.*

(Continued)

TABLE 11.2 (*Continued*)

Punctuation mark	Usage
Semi-colon ;	• Use to mark a pause longer than a comma and shorter than a full stop. • Use to distinguish phrases listed after a colon if commas will not do the job clearly, *eg They agreed on three points: there should be a salary freeze until June; it should apply to all staff, including directors; and holiday entitlement should be reviewed for junior members of staff, including graduate trainees.* • Use for antithesis or contrast, *eg Man proposes; God disposes.*
Exclamation and question marks ! ?	• Limit use in business writing.
Apostrophe	Showing possession. • Use normal possessive ending 's after singular words or names that end in s, *eg boss's, Jones's.* • Use it after plurals that do not end in s, *eg children's, businessmen's, media's* • Use the ending s' on plurals that end in s, *eg Danes', bosses', ladies'* including plural names that take a singular verb eg, *Barclays', Reuters'* Showing omission. • Use to show that some letter (or letters) have been omitted, *eg can't, I'm* NB: The most common error is *it's* – the possessive pronoun which does *not* need punctuation and so should be *its. (eg [of a book] its cover [of a chocolate bar] its flavour [of a play] its length.)*
Dash –	• Use to break up a sentence, allowing the writer to emphasize a point without appearing too repetitious, *eg after the presentation – the last in the process – the client will tell the consultancy the outcome of their deliberations.*

(Continued)

TABLE 11.2 *(Continued)*

Punctuation mark	Usage
	• Used to introduce an explanation, amplification, paraphrase or correction of what comes immediately before it. • Can be used alone if the phrase comes at the end of the sentence.
Brackets (or parentheses) ( )	• Similar use to dashes. Useful to contain an aside which might otherwise interfere with the grammatical construction of a sentence • If a whole sentence is within the brackets, put the full stop inside. Square brackets should be used for interpolations in direct quotes, *eg 'Let them [the poor] eat cake.'*
Quotation marks ' ' " "	• In business writing use single quotation marks round the names of things, *eg 'The Guardian'.* • Double quotation marks go round direct quotes and speech.

So what do people want to read? Again I ask every copywriter I work with, every journalist I meet and any blogger I talk to what makes interesting content. The answers are always variations on the same themes:

'Something that is relevant to my readers... something that is useful to my readers... that will engage them... or entertain them... something different or unusual... stories that tell me about the human condition, that are about real people and their struggles... a bit of drama, away from the everyday... something that is happening now or imminently...'

As a basic rule, when news editors select their stories for the day they are looking for stories that:

- are topical and timely (fits within the timeframe and involves change);
- are relevant to the audience;
- are unusual, unpredictable and best of all unique;
- have the necessary tension/drama (which can come from trouble, tragedy, triumph and triumph over tragedy);
- are full of human interest, because all news is caused by or affects people.

According to Jonathan Grun, the editor of the Press Association, a good story is simply one people want to talk about. And if people talk about it, its effect and reach are magnified.

In 1965 Johan Galtung and Marie Ruge identified what they called 12 'news values', factors that help determine whether a story would be covered in the media and make it through the editing process, judged to be worthy of inclusion. Even today virtually any media analyst's discussion of news values will go back to this list, initially intended as an analysis of coverage of international events. Look at news breaking on Twitter and you'll see these news values haven't changed. This also helps us understand whether the story we've been given by our client has legs or not:

- Frequency – What is the time-span of an event and how will it 'fit' the frequency of the broadcast or print media's cycle? Motorway pile-ups, murders, plane crashes qualify as they are all immediate, short order and so fit the rolling news schedule. These sorts of events are also pretty straightforward, not requiring detailed explanation. Long-term trends are not likely to receive much news coverage – this is more appropriate for features-based exploration.

- Threshold – How big is an event? Is it big enough to make it into the national or international news?

- Unambiguity – How clear is the meaning of an event? Media tends to go for simplicity (unlike novels, where multiple threads and complexity keep us reading). This is why motorway pile-ups, murders and plane crashes work – the meaning is instantaneous and immediately grasped. (In 2000 Peter Preston in *The Observer* quoted the results of a US survey conducted by *The Columbia Journalism Review*, which revealed that the single most frequent reason why stories don't appear is that they are 'too complicated'.)

- Meaningfulness – How meaningful will the event appear to the viewers and readers? We Brits will find meaning in stories about what is happening in the UK, then Europe and the USA. But we will find less meaning in stories from other countries and cultures. That is also true within our own society, where minority groups receive proportionately less coverage.

- Reference to elite nations – Closely related to the last factor, where nations culturally closest to our own will receive more coverage – France receives more coverage than Ghana, Scotland more than Peru. This occurs not just with political and conflict coverage, but also in disasters (apart from when large numbers of British nationals are involved; and this is also partly affected by the fact that major news organizations have reporters already stationed in Europe and the United States so that when a story arises there's someone there to cover it.)

- Consonance – Does the event match media expectations? Journalists tend to have an idea of the so-called 'angle' they want to report an event from, before they get there.
- Unexpectedness – 'Dog bites man' equals no news. 'Man bites dog' equals news. An unpredictable event is a news story.
- Continuity – The running news story allows media organizations to develop a theme and use resources already put in place to cover the original event.
- Composition – Where an editor will judge whether the bulletin's or paper's content needs balancing, by for example dropping a foreign news story in favour of more domestic news. A major event seizing a huge amount of attention (for example the death of Margaret Thatcher) will mean that there will be a 'round-up' of less important stories.
- Reference to elite persons – Naturally VIPs attract media attention. VIPs include political leaders, royalty, celebrities.
- Personalization – Events happen because of people's actions. Confrontations between the government and the opposition are presented as battles between two sparring partners.
- Negativity – In 1978 the journalist Edward Behr published his memoirs, memorably entitled *Anyone Here Been Raped and Speaks English?* The title was inspired by the crass question put to a group of white women by a US journalist as they were trying to get out of the war-torn Belgian Congo.

Bad news is good news because bad news sells – more clicks, more viewers, more readers. Bad news dovetails with other news values as it may also be big (as in a major natural or man-made disaster, like an earthquake or a terrorist attack) and so may be unexpected and is also usually unambiguous.

Allan Bell in *The Language of News Media* (1991) made a few further additions to Galtung and Ruge's news values, additions which reflect the media's way of working:

- Competition: the commercial pressure to get to a story first and to get an exclusive which enhances a news organization's prestige and reputation – and which may attract additional readers and viewers.
- Co-optation – A story that can be connected, interpreted and presented together with a major story, for example a British person who survived an earthquake who is later found to be a drugs mule would amplify the meaning.
- Prefabrication: – If a story is already written and available as a press release, on the news agency wires, etc as this provides an easy supply of stories for media outlets with reduced resources.
- Predictability – A story will more likely be covered if it is prescheduled and diarized so it can be researched beforehand.

Academics Harcup and O'Neill's (2001) later study of the UK national press, listed the following news values:

1 *The power elite*: stories concerning powerful individuals, organizations or institutions.
2 *Celebrity*: stories concerning people who are already famous.
3 *Entertainment*: stories concerning sex, showbusiness, human interest, animals, an unfolding drama, or offering opportunities for humorous treatment, entertaining photographs or witty headlines.
4 *Surprise*: stories with an element of surprise and/ or contrast.
5 *Bad news*: stories with negative overtones such as conflict or tragedy.
6 *Good news*: stories with positive overtones such as rescues and cures.
7 *Magnitude*: stories perceived as sufficiently significant either in the numbers of people involved or in potential impact.
8 *Relevance*: stories about issues, groups and nations perceived to be relevant to the audience.
9 *Follow-ups*: stories about subjects already in the news.
10 *Media agenda*: stories that set or fit the news organization's own agenda.

Twitter – hints and tips for avoiding bad and ensuring good content

Poor content:

- What you're eating for lunch.
- Random things you are doing (unless it is immediately relevant for your readers to act on). Occasional personal posts can humanize an organization but frequent, breathless, 'Guess what I'm doing?' updates are indulgent and boring.
- Complaining and ranting.
- Bad-mouthing people.
- Unsubstantiated new-age advice and homilies.
- Hard selling.
- If using Twitter as a business tool, avoid political or religious content.

Good content:

- Each tweet has one idea.
- Mix tweets so they are different – about blog posts, news articles, pictures, videos.
- Useful information people act upon immediately.

- How-to suggestions.
- Use lists, such as:
  - six tips;
  - five ways, and;
  - nine steps.
- Use the imperative form, such as:
  - do...;
  - don't... and;
  - join.
- Create time limits such as:
  - 'Today only';
  - 'Last chance', and;
  - 'Available until...'.
- Use quotations (but only if they fit your brand values).
- Include a (shortened) URL link when appropriate.
- Re-tweet and give credit to the original source by including that person's @twittername.

NB: The sorts of tweets that get most retweets are:

1 Breaking news.

2 Warnings and alerts (eg 'Storms expected today').

3 Quotes or statements (eg 'You can avoid reality, but you cannot avoid the consequences of avoiding reality.' 'Content is NOT King; relationships are King').

4 Links to fun, relevant ideas (eg 'Quiz: How addicted to Facebook are you?' or 'Would you pass the PR Professional test?' and polls).

5 Information summaries.

6 Key topic warnings/tips, 'secrets', dangers, etc (eg 'Did you know you can be suspended for failing to ...?', 'Top 10 Tips for PR Professionals for 2015').

7 Resource summaries (eg a list of useful/new/clever PR evaluation tools).

Structure

You have a clear idea of the reader and your aim and you understand what style is right. You know what content is compelling. Now you can consider the form of the writing to give it structure, the scaffolding if you like, which gives it order and logic and enables the reader to follow easily.

All writing needs a beginning, a middle and an end. The beginning needs to get a reader's attention; the middle needs to keep interest and build desire to continue; the end, when writing for communications purposes, tends to be a call to action of some description.

Let's look at four of the key forms of writing professional public relations practitioners need to master: tweets, news stories, features and opinion pieces:

1 Tweets

  - Hardly any structure at all as it is simply a headline, told in 140 characters (but 80 characters are ideal to encourage retweeting).

  - Use hashtags to classify or categorize your tweets. For example, if you're tweeting about PR use '#PR,' and your tweet will show up in Twitter search results relating to that subject.

  - To get viewers to click through, your tweets are likely to include a shortened URL.

2 News stories (aka press releases)

  We should structure our news stories as a journalist would – so something like this:

  At the top:

  For immediate release: [date]

  (If you want the media to use the story as soon as they receive it)

  or

  Embargoed for: [time/date]

  (This is a good way of giving journalists time to prepare and to ensure they don't use it until a specified time.)

  Headline:

  Make it direct and short and don't try to be so witty or clever that the meaning of the story is obscured.

  Paragraph 1: Summarize the story – who, what, where, when and why. All key information needs to be in this paragraph.

  Paragraph 2: Put in more details to flesh out the story you have outlined in the first paragraph.

  Paragraph 3: Quotes from you or someone relevant to the story. Don't try to cram too many points into one quote – each quote should make one point.

  Paragraph 4: Any extra relevant information.

  Put the word 'ends' at the end of the story.

  Finish with 'Notes for Editors':

  - Provide background information in case they run a longer story.

  - Outline what you have to offer: pictures, interviewees.

  - Outline any additional relevant information or facts and figures, but keep it short.

And finally contact details:

- Make sure you supply numbers where you can be reached day or night. This can make the difference between your story being covered or not.
- Include telephone number(s), e-mail, website, twitter handle.

3 Features

Features go beyond the reporting of facts to inform, educate, help, entertain, persuade and amuse. PR professionals write them for internal publications, for trade and specialist media and for websites. There are five common types of feature:

- **Profile**

Individuals or two or more people, eg pop groups, comedy writers, board of directors:

- first person (ghosted);
- reported (third person);
- edited down from notes and voice recording into Q&As;
- in reply to a set of questions;
- NB If the subject is dead these are obituaries!

- **Product story:**
  - one product or a round-up of several/many;
  - described, compared, tested.

- **Background feature:**
  - putting news in context;
  - news feature – hybrid between news and feature;
  - colour piece – describing events as they happen(ed); funerals, revolutions, sporting events, etc.

- **Opinion piece (comment):**
  - the backbone of most publications;
  - leaders/editorials/comment pieces;
  - think pieces;
  - columns/regulars;
  - diaries.

- **Advertising supplements/special issues:**
  - annual/quarterly features lists showing what's planned;
  - your sector/industry and your client as part of that;
  - you may be the supplier of material to the publication's feature writer – or you may be writing as the writer.

Features also have add-ons – like charts, checklists, timelines and so on.

Features have distinct beginnings, middles and ends.

Beginning – a really strong and motivating introduction to hook the reader:

- provocative, intriguing, shocking;
- narrative/anecdote;
- descriptive/scene setting;
- a question that grabs the reader;
- a quote;
- a startling fact;
- a surprising event;
- 'did you know that…?'

Middle – keeps reader going and flows from point to point:

- intelligent analysis;
- reliable, fresh facts and statistics;
- 'must know' facts;
- links – last sentence has a word used in first sentence of next paragraph;
- 'heralds' – first sentence of the paragraph is a clue to what the following paragraph is about.

End – rewards the reader for making it to the end:

- a final statement or quote;
- a final anecdote;
- a rhetorical question;
- call to action, asking the reader to think, feel or do something (could be to sign up, visit a website, read a new book, etc).

4 Opinion pieces

Here's a classic structure for an opinion piece (following the rules of rhetoric). Start by putting forward an opinion or argument (eg 'Fox-hunting should be banned/legalized'). Then set out the opponents' point(s) briefly. (If you don't then the necessary tension is left out. You need the opposing view to argue against.) Then demolish the opponents' point(s) with your points:

- point one – plus evidence;
- point two – plus evidence;
- point 3 – plus evidence.

End with a conclusion and a call to action (to vote a particular way, make your feelings on the subject known, write to your MP, boycott a manufacturer, etc).

Further reading

If writing is an area you feel you need to look at in more detail, the marvellous book *Writing Skills for Public Relations* by John Foster (2012) is now in its fifth edition. It's an excellent read apart from being full of helpful hints and tips for PR professionals. It is a wide-ranging guide to style and technique for all written communication. From the do's and don'ts of English grammar, to jargon and clichés, to the important legal considerations, Foster advises on how to write concisely using jargon-free language while avoiding overused words and phrases. There is guidance on policing house style with emphasis on consistency and advice on punctuation, headlines and captions.

As I mentioned earlier, I would recommend *The Economist Style Guide* – it's a hugely entertaining and valuable book, packed full with helpful hints and tips to help you develop your writing style. And you can access the content via *The Economist*'s website too.

Interpersonal skills – and briefing skills

Building rapport by listening, questioning and observation of body language

As communications specialists we are likely, through our careers, to work with a wide variety of people, particularly colleagues and clients. We may also need to conduct research with target audiences, by interviewing them on a one-to-one or small group basis. We may also need to work with and interview case history subjects in order to obtain material to write up afterwards. So skilful questioning and listening, along with competent note- and minute-taking, are all essential skills.

We may take a brief in a relaxed and supportive environment on an aspect of business that requires a planned and proactive communications strategy. Or we may take a briefing when an issue has gone live or an incident has taken place where people are rushed, anxious and concerned, where we are expected to come up with a professional, immediate reactive response.

Some briefings are excellent and all the information is there: a written version supplements a verbal briefing; there is complete openness; questions are answered thoroughly. Other briefings are partial, thin on detail, assumptions are made, the verbal briefing is poorly delivered, and sometimes the person taking the brief is – and feels – less senior and so potentially rather intimidated so the right penetrating questions may not be asked or assumptions may go unchallenged. Mistakes get made this way, hence the ability to handle a briefing professionally and competently is vital.

Listening

During a briefing we often need to get a lot of information out of people quickly and efficiently. And to do this we must be active listeners as well as skilled questioners. We must be able to concentrate on what's being said and to sometimes draw out what really matters. We need to hear what the client – whether an internal or external client – is anxious about, is excited about and what the core business issues really are. Listening is an active skill, not a passive exercise. Listening is more demanding than speaking, in terms of concentration. Because we lead busy lives, we can be distracted by other thoughts and this can get in the way of good listening. You have to get into the right frame of mind to listen.

There are three levels of listening:

- Peripheral listening – done at subconscious level, formal and informal situations, eg at party, restaurant – 'cocktail party syndrome' (when we hear our name, if it's spoken across a room at some distance).

- Apparent listening – we do it all the time – it might look like we are listening but we are not really concentrating.

- Active listening – concentrating on the message being transmitted by trying to understand not only what is being said but how and why it is said:
  - interpreting;
  - understanding;
  - evaluating;
  - reacting;
  - planning;
  - responding.

Most people talk at around 125 words-per-minute but we think at four times that speed. So listeners have spare mental capacity (which they could use to make useful notes I guess) but which in practice means they can also 'go off on one', their minds can wander, they daydream and are distracted... unless they concentrate and listen actively.

People feel unimportant, insignificant and disrespected if they sense their ideas, concerns, feelings and not being paid close attention or being taken seriously. But not only can the working relationship suffer, the ineffective listener can simply get things wrong! If you ask a question and get the answer you were expecting, you make assumptions and so miss some enlightening, new or additional important information. If you are busy getting your next question together in your mind you won't be listening to the current answer.

Listening well

Prepare to listen. If you can, do some research/reading before you go into a briefing session. For example, read last year's PR programme, an annual report, the latest media coverage and so on. Get into the right frame of mind – win–win is what you should be aiming for, even if previous meetings with those briefing you have been challenging. Observe participants' body language and speed of speaking (to pick up clues about areas of concern, urgency and any anxiety). Don't make assumptions but observe and 'tune in' to the people involved.

Sit to see. A fundamental point but having clear visual contact will aid concentration. Don't forget that placing your back to the sun means that the person you're listening to may not be able to see your eyes or facial expressions clearly. Likewise you want to see them clearly too. We gain so much more information if we 'listen' to body language too (see page 287).

Avoid distractions. Apart from worrying about how much you have to do, other distractions can interfere with concentration: open-plan offices, external sound, glass walls, television screens and mobile devices that people can't get their eyes – and attention – away from; your to-do list may be terrorizing you too. Be careful about these interfering with your concentration when you are listening.

Show empathy and build rapport. At the opening stages of a briefing it's useful to show empathy so that rapport is built with the other person. Empathy is an attempt to understand the other person, to understand how the person feels and thinks and sees the world. It's getting a sense of their perspective. The issue is not to agree, disagree, or make judgements but to make a genuine effort to understand how the person briefing you sees the opportunity or issue. Look at it from their point of view – and then add your own perspective as a communications consultant. At the start of a meeting use similar – or 'matching' – language and body language to assist in building rapport. Show you are interested in the subject so that the person briefing you feels more inclined to engage and communicate back.

Practise. Take every opportunity to practise and improve your listening skills. A colleague of mine listens to Radio 4 documentaries and then recalls key points afterwards and includes these in her blog posts.

Practical active listening techniques

Checking understanding using feedback One of the ways to check your understanding of what has been said is to use feedback. In your own words, repeat back to the speaker what you understood her/him to have said.
This will:

- Check your understanding of what's being said.
- Help eliminate any unintended messages that the speaker didn't mean.
- Achieve real clarity on complex issues.
- Demonstrate your interest in what's being said.
- Demonstrate that you really understand.
- Let the speaker think about what's being said.

For example, you may hear:

'It's a sensitive situation because of the potential financial impact on the business.'

You could check understanding by responding:

'So you're saying that there may be a knock-on effect on profitability?'

Re-statement reflects a genuine attempt to understand the other person's point of view and helps to identify any issues that arise.

Summarizing This is more than re-statement or reflection; it is drawing together the main themes and key points from what you have heard. This facility can often be essential when the briefer has given a rather rambling and incoherent brief. Summarizing what you have heard will help to check back the facts and assumptions.

Summarizing can also:

- Indicate that you have understood what has been said.
- Move the conversation on.
- Make an effective break point or end to the meeting.
- Establish a starting point for a subsequent meeting.

Ten rules for great listening:

1 Stop talking.
2 Put the person who is briefing you at ease.
3 Show that you want to listen – look and act interested.
4 Remove any distractions.
5 Empathize with the person.
6 Be patient, especially with people who have a communication style different from yours.
7 Ask great questions and explore the issue fully before making any judgements or offering counsel.
8 Avoid argument and any implied criticism.
9 Take breaks in discussions if they are long or complex – give yourself a concentration breather.
10 Stop talking!

Questioning

The ability to ask great questions is, in my opinion, one of the most crucial skills anyone working in communications should master. Great questioning helps you get the information you need: to prepare a sound PR proposal, to understand the opinions, thoughts and feelings of a stakeholder, to write a focused report, to assess a situation, to get to the heart of the matter. The right questions achieve clarity, promote reflection, enhance creativity and help work out solutions. As you get more senior and are responsible for coaching and mentoring others, great questions are a key way to help people reflect and learn. Whatever the context, great questions show you are listening and paying attention to your subject. It's not simply a question of the right questions either; it's also the way you ask them – so pay attention to your tone of voice and body language too.

Using the right questioning style:

1 *Open questions* help the other person define the opportunity or problem and to explore it. They provide factual information and the other person's thoughts and possibly feelings behind it. Open questions can also generate thinking and reflection and ensure that focus is kept on the issue. Well-timed open questions can change how someone looks at an issue too and can help identify actions to take. Open questions are always a good place to start a discussion or a briefing as they do exactly that – open up the dialogue. Open questions most often start with, 'What,' 'How,' 'When' and 'Where' or 'Tell me about...' Obviously if you are dealing with a communications/PR issue you need specific questions pertinent to this discipline.

Examples of good open questions asked by consultants:

- What's the opportunity/problem?
- What do you hope for?
- What's your role in this issue?
- What have you tried so far? What worked? What didn't?
- Have you experienced anything like this before? (If so, what did you do?)
- What does the business need?
- What is important about that?
- What is holding you back?
- What if you do nothing?
- What's the cost?
- How much control do you have in this situation?
- What options do you have?
- What support do you need to achieve success?
- What can you do yourselves to make progress?
- What do you need us to do for you?
- What's preventing you from...?
- If you could change one thing, what would it be?
- How will you know you have been successful?
- What does success look like?
- Imagine a point in the future where your opportunity is fully realized/your issue is resolved... how did you get there?
- What would you like to ask us?

Journalists use open questions frequently when interviewing subjects for features and news pieces:

Did you…? Are you…? What's…? How many…? Where…?

Depending on the situation, be careful when asking open questions that begin with 'why'. A 'why' question makes people feel defensive, accountable to justify their actions. You do need to ask 'why' questions – to clarify causation especially when working out what has happened if an incident has taken place – just be careful of the phrasing so it doesn't look sound like any blame is being apportioned and that it doesn't look like finger pointing.

2 *Closed questions* can be used to check facts, or as a summary. Use them sparingly as they tend to result in simple 'yes' or 'no' answers. 'Have you completed this…?' 'What I am hearing is… am I right?'

3 *Clarifying questions* can help you and your subject understand the key points and get to the 'bottom line'. They can uncover the root cause of issues. These are especially useful when conducting research interviews and doing in-depth profiles of case histories. Ask questions about the person's point-of-view, perspectives, beliefs, values and actions. Great provocative questions can prompt light-bulb moments which can shift things positively and quickly. 'When you launched your brand what did you imagine would be the impact on your business?' 'When did you first believe that you were successful?'

4 *Reflecting questions* enable the questioner to clarify what has been said and to get the subject to talk freely and in depth. Reflecting questions call for the questioner to engage in 'active listening'. Using the subject's own words, you encourage further information. Reflecting questions often begin: 'You said that…' 'It sounds as if…' 'From what you have said I get the feeling that…'

5 *Extending questions* are used to invite further explanation and to prompt a further answer: 'Please could you say some more about…' 'How else could you…?'

6 *Comparative questions* are useful where the questioner may need to compare a situation on a 'before' and 'after' basis: 'What difference has that made to the business? 'What has it been like since…?'

7 *Hypothetical questions* may allow the subject to explore ideas and issues in a non-threatening theoretical environment: 'Imagine the launch has been a huge success – in five years' time what will have changed?' 'If you were faced with the same situation again would you do things differently?'

8 *Rephrasing or paraphrasing* may be used when the questioner is not clear what the subject thinks, feels or means and allows you to play back what has been said: 'Are you saying that…?' 'Let me see if I understand the problem completely…'

9 *Linking questions* are useful for picking up clues but depend on active listening. The question is formed by picking up an earlier response from the subject: 'Earlier you said that... so how would you feel if...?'

10 *Leading questions* (a sub-section of closed questions) should generally be avoided. A leading question is asked in order to lead another to a predetermined answer or conclusion. This sort of question comes across as dishonest and manipulative. You can recognize leading questions because they are statements that can often be answered 'yes' or 'no'. That said, journalists may use leading questions in interviews: 'You're a Conservative, aren't you?' 'How did you react? Were you furious?' 'How much money went missing – was it more than 10 million pounds?'

11 *Assumptive questions* (which can be annoying but, if phrased well, can get into interesting areas) are also used extensively by journalists: 'Were you educated in a private or state school?' 'How many redundancies will there be?' 'Are you married or single?' (The answer may be neither...) 'When did you last beat your wife?'

12 *Direct, suggestive or loaded questions* which are manipulative but are often used again by journalists to provoke a response and add tension into proceedings: 'Scientists have proven that cigarette-smoking causes cancer so why should manufacturers be allowed to continue to promote them at all?' 'What sort of person would disagree with campaigns to control birth rates?' 'Gandhi said non-violent protest was the only way – don't you agree?'

Note-taking

When taking a verbal brief you should take notes. Note-taking shows you're attentive, helps you keep a record and provides a basis for confirmation of what is agreed (and evidence in a dispute!). Taking no notes may make others think that you are not very competent or analytical or are not taking the issue seriously. And you have no record of what took place or was agreed between you.

These days, in the interest of efficiency, many people type notes straight on to a pad, a laptop or a smartphone. But this can weaken rapport-building as it not only breaks up eye contact so seriously, it also feels like the relationship is between you and the machine not you and the other person. The newest digital technologies (eg smartpens, which allow you to write notes and also make audio recordings on the conversation) can really help here. You can take a few written notes the traditional way and still pay attention to your client. Also by taking written notes and then typing them up, you have to go over points again and the simple repetition helps reflection and analysis. So review as you type and highlight action points and decisions. And also make a note on what is for information only.

Body language as a key part of communications

Non-verbal communication works alongside our spoken words in order to convey meaning more clearly. Often body language shows the emotional side of our relationships with others – it's something that is usually automatic and subconscious. Body language includes eye contact, body movements and gestures (legs, arms, hands, head and body), posture, muscle tension, skin colouring (eg blushing), even people's breathing rates. Tone and pitch of voice and speed of talking all add meaning to the words that are being used.

The often-quoted research findings from Albert Mehrabian (1972) revealed that non-verbal language makes up 55 per cent of how we communicate in face-to-face interactions. He concluded that we communicate as much as 38 per cent of our message through our voice (tone, pitch and so on), and only around 7 per cent through the words we actually say.

Understanding and recognizing the signs and signals that make up this 55 per cent enable you to communicate more effectively with others. Watch out for times when people – when you – send mixed messages; we 'say' one thing verbally yet our body language gives us away and suggests something different. Importantly non-verbal language affects how we act and react to others, and how they react to us. Positive body language is crucial in showing empathy and building rapport with others. This is at its most obvious when presenting ourselves, when coaching a chief executive to make a speech or appear in a video or a preparing a client to undertake a media interview.

It is also important to recognize that body language does vary between individuals (and we all have idiosyncrasies), and between different cultures and nationalities. With more of us working internationally this is an important aspect to get right.

Body language signs and signals may have a different underlying cause from the ones you suspect. This is often true when people have different past experiences, and particularly where there are significant cultural differences. Check your interpretation of someone's body language by getting to know the person better and by asking some of those questions listed earlier.

To help practise and further develop your skill in picking up body language, engage in people-watching and develop your observational skills – these will help you to pick up signals when you are interacting with others in a business context. Observe people on the train, on the bus, in restaurants. Turn the sound down on TV and video – you can usually pick up the plot from the body language alone. Notice how people act with and react to each other. When you watch others, have a go at guessing what is being said and assess what is going on between them. You might not be able to check whether you were right but it will sharpen your eye.

A word of caution – while it is entirely ethical and appropriate to learn use good and authentic presentation skills techniques, never attempt to manipulate others by deliberately and consciously overusing particular body language patterns. Not only is this unethical it also actively works against you. You will simply come across as shallow and untrustworthy.

Body language essentials

We watch and listen to people to assess their thoughts and feelings even if they are not saying anything. Some important signals we all respond to – consciously, but more often subconsciously – are:

- Eye contact – people who are looking at you are likely to be listening. Confident people make lots of eye contact, and often have a 'smiling' face. Conversely people who look away from you when you talk to them come across as nervous and shifty. (If they have Asperger's Syndrome, that's another matter!) It is fairly clear that a blank stare can mean boredom, a raised eyebrow disbelief or frustration and wide-open eyes indicate surprise. There are some situations where eye contact can be difficult to get and maintain – when sitting side-by-side for example. I have had this experience on three memorable occasions: when producing video and sitting next to an editor so neither of us was able to look at the other as we were both concentrating on the monitors; when sitting beside a client at the European Commission in Brussels and not being able to look at her easily, made more difficult because we were using headsets for translation purposes; and when sitting beside a client on a plane. All occasions when eye contact has been hard to maintain. So just look for opportunities to make sure you do factor in a lot of eye contact before you go into 'eyeless' mode!

- Posture – this can be interpreted in many different ways. Sitting back may be a sign of disinterest or of being relaxed. At an informal meeting sitting on the edge of the seat may be an indication of fear or tension. People who look confident stand tall with shoulders back.

- Head movements – the obvious ones are the nod or shake of agreement or disagreement. Most people will unconsciously nod or shake their heads and this provides you with a lot of information.

- Body movements plus gestures with hands and arms – confident people make purposeful and deliberate movements. Less confident people often fidget and when they move may be erratic and jerky. Simply sitting down can give clues; sitting forwards may indicate someone who is listening intently, whereas someone leaning backwards of slouching is more likely to be feeling bored and disengaged. Wringing of hands often indicates tension and nervousness. Finger tapping can be a habit or an indication of frustration.

- Facial expressions – our faces give us away – not many people can keep a real 'poker face'. Consider the smile; a laughing smile can indicate genuine happiness or humour while a forced smile shows just the opposite. A smile breaks the ice and builds connections. All human beings in all cultures are programmed to respond to smiles. At a meeting, facial expressions such as smiling, frowning, questioning are often unconscious and can reveal information about what the person is thinking. A stroke of the chin is likely to indicate thoughtfulness.

- Speech patterns – confident people speak comparatively slowly and clearly and their tone of voice is moderate to low. Conversely more nervous people speak far too quickly and their vocal tone may be higher. This is often a function of shallow breathing, which again, gives away lower confidence levels.

- Overall body direction – usually in meetings everyone sits facing the chairperson. If someone turns their body away they may be unhappy with what is happening. And changing direction completely or possibly pushing their chair back may show a great degree of dissatisfaction/disengagement.

Body language clues that often reveal what's going on with the listener:

- Smiling, open and positive gestures, standing or sitting close, lots of eye contact, nodding, tilting head = empathy and rapport.

- Sitting with crossed leg towards you = defensiveness, distrust.

- Sitting with crossed leg away from you = willingness to trust.

- Rigid or tense body posture, staring eyes, clenched fists, clasped hands, tightly folded arms, foot tapping, finger pointing = anger, aggression, irritation, nervousness.

- Downcast eyes, hand over mouth, frequently touching face, shifting weight from one leg to another, fidgeting = nervousness.

- Picking fluff from clothes, pulling at ears, stifled yawning, gazing around the room = boredom.

Body language in difficult meetings

Think of a time when you were in a difficult meeting – perhaps where you are negotiating deadlines, fees, contracts. If we want to retain and build relationships with colleagues, clients, journalists, suppliers it's right to aim for a win–win outcome. If that is what is going on, both you and the other person will exhibit confident and assertive body language. You will both be open and receptive to hearing what the other has to say, so that you can reach a conclusion everyone is content with. Things change if people become defensive. Firstly listening suffers as people's inner dialogue becomes louder. Personal objectives harden so the other's point of view isn't heard. Signs that might indicate that a person may be feeling defensive include:

- minimal facial expressions, blankness or a frown;
- hand/arm gestures which are restricted and close to the body;
- body is physically turned away from you;
- arms are crossed in front of body;
- eyes maintain little contact, or are downcast.

By picking up these signs, you can change what you say or how you say it to help the other person become more at ease, and more receptive to what you are saying. Equally, if you yourself are feeling somewhat defensive going into a negotiating situation, you can pay attention to your own body language to ensure that the messages you are conveying show you to be open and receptive to what is being discussed.

Recognizing fibs

You can't do it when you are working remotely and digitally but you can do it much more easily face-to-face. It is hugely important to be able to recognize if someone is being straight with you, whether it's a client, a colleague or a journalist. As with all non-verbal language, while everyone's personal body language is slightly different, classic body language give-aways include:

- little or no eye contact – and then rapid eye movements, with pupils constricted;
- hands and fingers in front of the mouth when speaking;
- the body being physically turned away from you;
- unusual/unnatural body gestures;
- an increase in breathing rate;
- skin colour changes (particularly flushing on the face, neck and chest);
- the voice tightens, there's a change in pitch, and you might get hesitations, stammering and throat clearing.

Don't jump to an immediate conclusion if you see these signs. Instead probe further, ask more questions and explore the issue further. In this way you'll more accurately assess whether you have the truth or not.

Recognizing disengagement in body language

As a rather inexperienced and anxious young consultant I remember my early business meetings and presentations – if I was presenting to very senior clients (who I must admit I was often terrified of) it sometimes felt like they weren't really paying attention. (I know now that a lot of it was down to me – although I nearly trained as an actor and wasn't shy, I had no experience of working in the business context and felt out of my depth.) There were times when I wanted to lead the meeting and get to an agreement on a course of action or a campaign idea. I wanted to get people on board with the ideas. Trouble is I was so nervous about ME I forgot to observe them and so didn't perhaps recognize what was going on. And I didn't have the skills or experience to modify my behaviour.

When you present in a business (in fact in any) context you want high levels of engagement. It just doesn't happen – you have to work at it. Look out for these body language clues that tell you people aren't with you... yet:

- heads are down;
- eyes are glazed, or gazing at something else, or even closed (although with rare individuals, this is because they are concentrating on your words...);
- hands may be fiddling with pens (and doodling... or writing shopping lists);
- people may be yawning, sitting slumped or worst of all asleep;
- NB: using pads and phones in meetings and presentations is now common – who knows whether this means people are entirely engaged and tweeting about you or simply checking out friends on Facebook? Keep calm and carry on!

When you pick up that someone is disengaged, you can do something to re-engage the person, such as asking them a direct question. We'll look at this a little later in presentation skills.

Reflecting time

What do you do when you are asked a really good question? Do you ponder for a few moments before answering? You might simply blurt something out without taking time to think about the answer, or you could take a moment to reflect before answering. By taking some time to reflect on your response, you are indicating to the questioner that they've asked you a good question and it is important enough for you to take some time to consider your answer. I also think people I see doing this have a fair degree of gravitas – and people take them seriously.

In an interview or when negotiating, showing that you are thinking about your response is a positive thing. Some typical signs and signals that a person is reflecting on their answer include:

- eyes look away, returning to engage contact when answering;
- finger stroking on chin;
- hand resting on the cheek;
- head tilted with eyes upwards.

Body language and culture

TABLE 11.3 Body language

Space zones (NB: these are Western values!)	**Close intimate** – 0–15 cm – lovers, children and *very* close friends and relatives **Intimate** – 15–45 cm – no strangers here please! **Personal** – 46 cm–1.2 m – office party, social occasions, first meetings **Social** – 1.2–3.6 m – in shops, on the street, on trains (some chance on the London Underground!) **Public** – 12 m – talking to an audience, front row
First impressions	Clothes, hair, face, body, eyes, mouth then • Catching the eye across a room • Approach, shake hands, introduce • In personal zone • Smiling, listening, nodding • Posture relaxation • If feeling comfortable, mirroring occurs

Greeting	Positive recognition signals (ie someone knows you)
	• Smile
	• Head tilt
	• Eyes widen, eyebrow flash (when forehead wrinkles upwards)
	Handshaking – Western
	• Shows there is no weapon in hand
	• Pump up and down once – Northern Europe
	• Pump up and down repeatedly and vigorously – Southern Europe
	• Palm offered downwards implies domination
	• Amplified handshakes, involving more body contact, implies possible domination
	Salaam – Arabic/Islamic
	• Full version – Sweep right arm upwards with hand open and palm facing body
	   – Touch chest above heart
	   – Bring hand up and touch forehead with fingers
	   – Sweep hand up and out beside face

(Continued)

TABLE 11.3 (*Continued*)

	• Abbreviated version
	  – Move forehead forward slightly
	  – Touching it with your fingertips
	Namaste – Indian
	• Both hands held together as if in prayer
	Bowing – Japanese
	• Lower ranking bows first, further and longer

Signs of superiority	Tilting head back (making someone look smaller, 'looking down the nose') Eye contact – either avoidance (looking through someone/someone is not worth noticing) or glaring (forcing other to lower eyes) While listening – half closed eyes and unsmiling Strutting walk Displaying thumbs – eg by clasping jacket with thumbs up Hand behind back – ie I am self-assured and can leave my front unprotected Language clues – 'Sorry?' 'You'll have to speak up'
Signs of confidence	Standing and walking • Erect, straight back, brisk walk • Conversation • Eye contact, infrequent blinking • No hiding mouth or nose with hand, no head scratching • Smokers blowing smoke upwards • Hand steepling
Defensive gestures	Crossed arms and legs (imply self-clasping/comforting)

The crucial first impression

In the world of communications we meet new people all the time – new clients, new media contacts, new suppliers. We spend evenings networking and socializing building our base of contacts. It takes between three and five seconds for someone to evaluate another person on a first meeting. Opinions are formed, whether we like it or not, based on appearance, body language, general demeanour, mannerisms and how someone is dressed. It is often said that you don't get a second chance to make a good first impression. That's why we spend – or should spend! – a lot of time on our CVs, on our websites and our social media profiles. It's why we polish our shoes for interviews and make sure we're well groomed for first dates. With every single new encounter, we are evaluated and another person's impression of us is formed. And those impressions are like concrete – first impressions are virtually impossible to change, making first encounters extremely important. The first meeting sets the tone for the relationship that follows, whether personally or professionally.

Think of a time when you met someone new at work or watched a speaker deliver a presentation. What first impression did he/she make? Did he/she appear confident or not? Was this a person you would like to spend time with or work with or for? Did this person come across as genuine, warm, authentic and convincing? And what made you think that? Did he/she walk confidently into the room, engage you and maintain eye contact or was he/she hesitant, eyes turned downwards? If a handshake was offered was it firm or limp? When you spoke to each other, did he/she look you in the eye or look away? Was his/her face relaxed or tight and tense? Did he/she fidget? Were gestures open and flowing and or closed and tight? All of these elements contributed to a positive – or negative – first impression.

You will make a good or even great first impression by:

- Being on time. If you can't get this right, you're on a back foot from the start. Everyone is busy; respecting other people's diaries is a no-brainer. On one occasion as a supplier I arrived on time to facilitate a day's training for a client I had only spoken to on the phone – I got up at 5 am to get to the client's offices at 8 am for a 9.30 am start. The people attending the session finally arrived at 12. What did this say about them? That they were so busy and so successful… or that they were understaffed and ill-organized?

- Paying attention to your appearance. While you don't need to look like Audrey Hepburn or George Clooney to make a positive first impression, you do need to take care of your appearance. Someone you are meeting for the first time simply does not know you. Your appearance is the first clue the person has to go on. The word is always 'appropriate'. Your appearance needs to say the right things to help create the right first impression. Plan what you will wear – what is appropriate for the meeting or occasion? We are essentially talking about business situations and in the communications sector. A good place to start is by imagining how the person you'll meet will dress. If you are briefing a senior journalist writing for the national news media or picking up a brief from a client in the financial sector you might want to be quite classic and formal. If meeting a not-for-profit or a fashion client with a reputation for edgy communications you might inject a little more colour. Rapport is built when people 'recognize' the person in front of them – it is almost tribal and we tend to get on with people like ourselves.

- If you work in an international or cross-cultural context, appropriate may mean something very different. Research what is appropriate (what is normal and/or traditional) and dress accordingly.

- Looking (and smelling) good. This is about personal grooming. A clean, tidy appearance is always important. Make friends with a good hairdresser or barber. You might not be able to afford designer labels but anyone can make sure their clothes are clean and fresh. Even if you have the clearest skin, neat tidy make-up looks professional and, for younger consultants, makes you look a little older which is, surprisingly, helpful in that it helps you come across as having more experience and gravitas.

- Relaxing. Human beings are instinctive creatures and we pick up unease very quickly. If you are feeling uncomfortable and on edge, this will rub off and can create the wrong impression. And if you are calm and confident, this rubs off too. You'll immediately make the other person feel more at ease. If you're nervous because you are pitching for new business or meeting an important journalist for the first time that's normal – and most people say a little adrenaline makes them perform better on the day.

- Posture. Use your body language to project appropriate confidence and self-assurance. Stand tall and smile – smiling suggests we are approachable and friendly so, even if you are nervous, a warm, confident smile will put you and the other person at ease. (But be genuine about it and don't overdo it or you will come across as smarmy or insincere.) Make eye contact and offer a firm handshake. All of this will help you project confidence and encourage both you and the other person to feel at ease.

- Prepare. Almost everyone gets a little nervous when meeting someone for the first time and this can lead to fidgeting, sweaty foreheads and palms. By being aware of any nervous habits – for example a nervous laugh or leg jiggling – and keep them in check. Preparing before you meet someone for the first time will give you confidence. You could take a look at their website, LinkedIn profile or Twitter feed.

- Be positive. Your attitude shows in everything you do so project a positive attitude, even if you are nervous or know it is likely to be a difficult discussion. Keeping a win–win attitude is the key to coming through and learning from the experience.

- Be polite. It shouldn't need to be said really but good old-fashioned manners work. Being attentive and courteous contribute towards creating that great first impression. But I expect I am not the only person who has experienced going to meet someone for the first time (in my case picking up an interviewee from reception) and found the person using his mobile phone… and continuing to talk while I stood beside him waiting for him to finish his conversation. Bad manners… and he didn't get the job!

More and more of us are working cross-culturally and I have included in Appendix 2 some hints and tips for working with clients, colleagues and associates across the world which I hope you find interesting and useful.

Assertiveness

What is assertiveness?

At some time in our lives we will have to deal with difficult situation at work. Some examples of these situations for public relations professionals could be:

- reacting to challenging clients, colleagues and journalists;
- giving advice that may not be palatable;
- saying 'no' to somebody, then feeling guilty afterwards.

Assertiveness is being able to express your opinions and feelings in a way that also respects the rights of others. It is a way of relating to others with a positive attitude, respecting oneself and others and believing 'I matter and so do you'. Assertiveness isn't about being aggressive or always getting your own way. It is about standing up for yourself constructively.

Asserting yourself means:

- You can say 'yes' when you mean 'yes' and 'no' when you mean 'no'.
- You can communicate clearly to others what you are feeling in a calm way.
- You do not let fear of conflict stop you from speaking.
- You feel good about yourself.
- You feel entitled to be who you are and to express what you feel.

Why is assertiveness important?

If you don't know how to be assertive, you may experience:

- Depression – a sense of feeling helpless with no control over your life.
- Resentment – anger at others for taking advantage of you.
- Frustration – why did I let that happen?
- Temper – if you can't express anger appropriately it can build up to temper outbursts.
- Anxiety – you may avoid certain situations that make you feel uncomfortable and you may therefore miss out on activities, job opportunities, etc.
- Relationship difficulties – it can be difficult in professional relationships when individuals can't tell each other what they want and need or how the other person affects them.
- Stress-related problems – stress can have a negative impact on the body, and assertiveness can be a good way of managing stress.

Where does non-assertive behaviour come from?

Non-assertive behaviour often comes from our experiences of growing up, relationships and life difficulties. When we were growing up we may have been taught that we should always try to please others and put other people's needs before our own. We may have learnt that if someone says or does something that we don't like, we should be quiet and try to avoid that person in the future. Also, if while we were growing up our self-confidence was damaged, for example being teased at school or criticized at home, then as adults we may be more likely to react passively or aggressively in our relationships and at work, rather than assertively.

Relationship difficulties and experience of loss can cause us to feel that we are unable to take control of our own lives. Low self-esteem and feelings of worthlessness may make us feel guilty about taking care of our own needs.

Passive, aggressive, assertive – recognizing behaviours

Although a person may have learnt to react passively or aggressively in life, they can change and learn to become more assertive. Let's look at the differences between passive, aggressive and assertive behaviours:

TABLE 11.4 Differences between passive, aggressive and assertive behaviours

Passive behaviour I lose – you win	Passive behaviour is not expressing your rights, feelings, opinions and needs. You bottle up your own feelings, give in to others, and see yourself as having little to contribute. The aim of passive behaviour is to avoid conflict at all times and to please others. There may be immediate positive effects of being passive (eg reduction of anxiety, avoiding guilt, etc). However, the long-lasting effects may be negative (eg continuing loss of self-esteem, stress and anger) and may cause others to become irritated by you and develop a lack of respect for you.
Aggressive behaviour I win – you lose	Aggression is expressing your own rights, feelings, needs and opinions with no respect for the rights and feelings of others. You express your feelings in a demanding, angry way. You see your own needs as

(*Continued*)

TABLE 11.4 *(Continued)*

	being more important than others'. You see others as having little to contribute. The aim of aggression is to win, while ignoring the feelings of others. Although the short-term effects of aggression may seem rewarding (eg release of tension, sense of power) the long-lasting effects are less beneficial (eg feeling guilty, resentment from people around you) and may cause problems for you and for those around you.
Assertive behaviour **I win – you win**	In contrast to passive and aggressive behaviour, assertiveness is expressing your own rights, feelings, needs and opinions while maintaining respect for other people's rights, feelings, needs and opinions. You are able to express your feelings in a direct, honest and appropriate way. You recognize that you have needs that should be met otherwise you may feel undervalued, rejected, angry or sad. You have basic human rights and it is possible to stand up for your own rights in a way that does not violate other people's rights. You have something to contribute. Assertion is not about winning, but is about being able to walk away feeling that you put across what you wanted to say.

How will people react to me being assertive?

Assertiveness is an attitude towards yourself and others that is helpful and honest. The benefits of assertion are that you are able to ask for what you want:

- directly and openly;
- appropriately, respecting your own opinions and rights and expecting others to do the same;
- confidently.

You do not:

- violate people's rights;
- expect others to magically know what you want;
- feel anxious and avoid difficult situations.

Before you decide to change your behaviour, it is worth taking some time to think about the consequences. In the majority of cases, assertive behaviour will result in a positive response from others. The result is improved self-confidence and mutual respect from others. If you are planning to try assertive behaviour, remember that people around you may be used to you behaving in a certain way and may feel confused when you change your behaviour. One way to manage this is to tell people that you have learnt about assertiveness and you have decided to try to start to act in a more assertive way.

There is a possibility that some people may even react negatively to your change in behaviour. For example, in some relationships loved ones may get angry if you express your true feelings, or an unreasonable manager at work may not respond well. If you feel this will be the case, you need to carefully consider whether you are prepared to deal with these difficulties. If you do not want to take the risk, you may decide that assertiveness may not be the best approach for you in these situations.

The rules of assertion

All people have basic human rights. By protecting your rights and not letting others violate them you are not being selfish but you are maintaining self-respect. As well as being aware of your own rights, if you respect other people's rights you have the basis for assertive communication.

The 10 rules of assertion

I have the right to:

1 Respect myself: who I am and what I do.

2 Recognize my own needs as an individual: separate from what is expected of me in roles such as 'wife', 'husband', 'partner', 'parent', 'son', 'daughter'.

3 Make clear 'I' statements about how I feel and what I think: for example, 'I feel very uncomfortable with your decision.'

4 Allow myself to make mistakes: recognize that it is normal to make mistakes.

5 Change my mind: if I choose.

6 Ask for 'thinking time': for example when people ask you to do something, you have the right to say: 'I would like to think about it and I will let you know my decision.'

7 Allow myself to enjoy my successes: feel pleased about what I have done and share it with others.

8 Ask for what I want: rather than hoping someone will notice what I want.

9 Recognize that I am not responsible for the behaviour of other adults: you are only responsible for your own actions.

10 Respect other people: and their right to be assertive in return.

(Adapted from 'Being Assertive': Workbook 3 *Overcoming Depression: A five areas approach* by Dr C Williams, 2001.)

Assertiveness techniques

Technique 1: assertive body language Body language is a powerful way of communicating to people how we would like to be treated. Sometimes we are unaware of our body language and the impact it has on others. When you are trying to use the following assertiveness techniques, try to also use assertive body language. Adopting assertive body language will help to reinforce the assertive techniques below and help to show the other person that you respect them but you also respect yourself.

Assertive body language includes the following:

- Face the other person, standing or sitting straight.
- Listen carefully to what they say.
- Have a pleasant facial expression.
- Keep your voice calm and pleasant.
- Make sure that your body language supports what you are saying (eg some people make the mistake of nodding their head when they are trying to say 'no').

Technique 2: 'cracked record' technique The cracked record technique is very effective and can work in a variety of situations. This approach is particularly useful in:

- situations where you feel your rights are being ignored;
- coping with clever, articulate people;
- situations where you may lose self-confidence if you give in.

How to use the cracked record technique:

- Work out beforehand what you want to say and rehearse it.
- Repeat your reply, using exactly the same words, over and over again and stick to what you have decided.
- Keep repeating your point, using a calm, pleasant voice.
- Don't be put off by clever arguments or by what the other person says.
- Don't be pulled into an argument or having to explain your decision.

There is nothing that can defeat this tactic, providing you hold your line!

Example 1: being asked to lend money.

Sarah: 'Jane, can you lend me £10?'

Jasmine: 'I can't lend you any money. I've run out.'

Sarah:	'I really need it, I'll pay you back.'
Jasmine:	'I can't lend you any money. I've run out.
Sarah:	'I thought you were my friend.'
Jasmine:	'I am your friend, but I can't lend you any money. I've run out.'

Example 2: returning faulty goods.

Shop assistant:	'Good morning. How can I help you?'
Maya:	'Good morning. These trousers are faulty and I would like a refund.'
Shop assistant:	'Do you want to change them for another pair?'
Maya:	'No thank you. I would like a refund.'
Shop assistant:	'I can give you a credit note, is that OK?'
Maya:	'No thank you. These trousers are faulty and I would like a refund.'

Example 3: an unreasonable demand at work.

Manager:	'Can you get all these reports finished by the end of today?'
Jon:	'I won't be able to finish them all today, but I will finish them tomorrow.'
Manager:	'But I wanted them all done today.'
Jon:	'I won't be able to finish them all today.'
Manager:	'Can't you just work really late tonight until they are all finished?'
Jon:	'I won't be able to finish them all today. But I will finish them tomorrow.'

Technique 3: using 'I' statements   'I' statements help to keep the focus on the problem, rather than accusing or blaming the other person. They also help to express ownership of your thoughts and feelings, rather than attacking the other person. Again, remember try to keep a calm, pleasant voice.

A good technique is to use this sequence of phrases:

'I feel/felt _____ when _____ because ...'

Example 1:

Say:	'I feel upset when you interrupt me because I can't finish what I am saying.'
Instead of:	'You're always interrupting me!'

Example 2:

Say:	'I feel angry when he breaks his promises because I don't feel I can rely on him.'
Instead of:	'He makes me so angry!'

Example 3:

Say:	'I felt disappointed when I heard that you had told Sam about my problem because I spoke to you in confidence.'
Instead of:	'Why are you telling everyone my business?'

Technique 4: saying 'no' to unfair/unreasonable requests/demands   Many people find saying 'no' difficult. Sometimes by avoiding saying 'no' you may be drawn into situations that you don't want to be in. You may not want to say 'no' because you may have fears about how other people may see or react to you. You may feel scared that you will be seen as being unhelpful, selfish, or that you may be rejected by others. Remember, you are not responsible for the reactions of other adults, but you can be responsible for your own actions. Saying 'no' can be important and helpful, both in how you feel about yourself and also how others perceive you.

Try to practise saying 'no' by using the following suggestions:

- Be straightforward and honest so that you can make your point effectively.
- Don't feel you have to say 'sorry' or give elaborate reasons for saying 'no'. It is your right to say 'no' if you don't want to do something.
- If you do not want to agree to the person's original request but still want to help him/her, offer a compromise such as: 'I won't be able to babysit for the whole afternoon but I can babysit for two hours.'
- Acknowledge the person's feelings about your refusal, for example: 'I know that you will be disappointed, but I won't be able to...'
- Remember that it is better in the long run to be honest rather than feel resentment for not being able to say 'no'.

Technique 5: being direct and clear   One of the most common problems in communication is caused by trying to read other people's minds or expecting them to read yours. If you want people to respond to your ideas and needs you have to be able to say what you want clearly and in a way that will make others want to respond.

Example 1: Say: 'Will you please...?' instead of, 'Would you mind...?'

Example 2: Say: 'I won't be able to...' instead of, 'I'm not sure if I can...'

Example 3: Say: 'I've decided not to...' instead of, 'I don't think I can...'

Giving a brief

We have discussed in other chapters the briefing of photographers, designers, copywriters and other suppliers who will be expected to provide a service for you. In a sense this type of briefing is straightforward. Always write a clear brief, outlining your requirements, objectives, timescales, mandatory elements, budgets and so on.

There will though be other occasions when you will be required to brief colleagues, your boss, other senior people, high-profile supporters, your chief executive or even a minister if you work in the public sector. And possibly celebrities and/or their agents before they represent your organization at, say, a fundraising dinner.

This is a different ball-game. You are not commissioning on these occasions – you are providing information to enable these people to do what they need to do – and that may be to pass on this information at a board meeting, to interpret the information as part of a compelling blog, to handle a difficult TV interview or press briefing, or to deliver a heartfelt and affecting after-dinner speech.

It must be your intention to come across as a confident and competent professional who can distil the key information into a clear verbal briefing, supported perhaps by an operational note.

Presentation skills

Presentations skills are important to most professionals and, I would argue, essential for public relations practitioners. You will need to present at internal meetings, at pitches, to existing and potential clients, to staff, and probably to specific audience and stakeholder groups. Developing the confidence to stand in front of your audience, whether of 10 or 1,000 and speak well, with the aim of persuading, educating and inspiring, makes a good communicator a formidable one. The good news is anyone can give a professional presentation – you just need to prepare, practise and then perform.

Many people are nervous when it comes to presenting. A common reaction to having to speak in public is a release of adrenaline and cortisol into our system. It can feel like a quadruple espresso straight into the bloodstream. Speaking in public is genuinely scary for most people, including many who outwardly seem very calm. But in general your audience wants you to succeed.

Confidence comes with thorough preparation. Good preparation and rehearsal will reduce your nerves by 75 per cent and increase the likelihood of avoiding errors to 95 per cent. (Source: Fred Pryor Organization, a significant provider of seminars and open presentation events.)

There are many different aspects of presentations, determined by audience size, needs and objectives; oral (spoken), multimedia (using various media – visuals, audio, etc), PowerPoint presentations, short impromptu presentations, long, planned presentations, educational or training sessions, lectures, and simply giving a talk on a subject to a group on a voluntary basis.

You or your senior people may seek out opportunities to speak at events as part of your public relations plan. Or you may be approached by many organizations asking you to field a speaker. Speaking opportunities enable organizations to develop regular, high-calibre dialogue with key audiences. Speaking opportunities that offer PR spin-off are of particular benefit as they offer extended communications opportunities. Speaking opportunities should be selected against a set of criteria outlined below, before the decision is made about whether the engagement is accepted or rejected and to avoid speaker exhaustion.

Opportunities must therefore:

- Be of benefit to the organization corporately or to the individual as a development experience, ie must provide a positive communications platform and positioning and/or a challenging experience.
- Reach the right target key audiences, eg:
  - customers/clients;
  - opinion-formers;
  - analysts;
  - specialists;
  - business partners;
  - major corporations.
- Enable the organization to fully explain its role and objectives.
- Provide the organization with the opportunity to 'network' and to secure valuable and beneficial contacts.

The following checklist will help get the facts:

Presentation logistics checklist

TABLE 11.5 Presentation logistics checklist

Presentation/Speaker Event Title?
Annual event/ad hoc?
Logistics Date? Time? Place?
Audience – Who is this presentation for? Main description Other information Numbers

(Continued)

TABLE 11.5 (*Continued*)

Content
What does the audience need/want?
Is there a brief for the speaker?

Presentation timings
Start time?
End time?
Venue? (precise details of the room the presentation will take place in – lecture theatre, hotel room, etc)
Does this include questions?
Can the speaker leave after the presentation or is he/she expected to stay?

Other speakers
Who are they?
What is the running order?
Who is speaking immediately before the presenter?
Who is the chair?
Will the presenter be taking part in a Q&A session?

Technical support
What will be available at the venue on the day?
What technical support (personnel) will be available?
What presenter requires in addition
What is presenter bringing?

Presentation
Required beforehand?
For binding into event documentation?

Accommodation
Before the event
After the event
How are accommodation expenses being budgeted for?

Travel
Please give detailed instructions
How are travelling expenses being budgeted for?

Presenter's checklists:

1 Prepare (see checklist opposite)

TABLE 11.6 Preparation checklist

Subject/content
What do you want to achieve with this presentation? (to persuade, convince, excite, sell, reassure?)
What are the three things you want your audience to remember? (ie your three key messages)
Your level of interest, expertise and knowledge
Existing materials
Need for research
Audience
Their knowledge of you/the subject
Their experience
Their needs/wants
Their involvement – interest/apathy/ hostility levels?
Age groups(s)
Sex (if appropriate)
Attention span
Physical comfort
Emotional safety
Disabilities/special needs
Likely acceptance of subject/issues

(*Continued*)

TABLE 11.6 (*Continued*)

Technique/structure
Strong beginning: • A – get attention • B – explain the benefits of listening • C – give your/the organization's credentials • D – outline direction/signpost so people can follow your presentation
Clear main points (those three key messages again)
Strong ending – call to action/ask for the money/the business
Appropriate and attractive style
Achievement of communication
Barriers to communication?
Notes
Visual, sensory, auditory aids
Use of silence
Props, special effects
Techniques to emphasize

2 Practise

TABLE 11.7 Practice checklist

Work with presentation 'buddy'
Video yourself/others

(*Continued*)

TABLE 11.7 (*Continued*)

Read through
Rehearsal 1
Rehearsal 2
Dress rehearsal
Run-through in venue
Refresher presentation skills training/extra coaching?

3 Perform

TABLE 11.8 Performance checklist

Appearance
Groomed
Appropriateness of dress
Warmth of tone
Body language
Voice
Projection
Warmth
Variety of pitch
Variety of pace
Variety of volume

(*Continued*)

TABLE 11.8 (*Continued*)

Performance quality
Energy level – self and others in team presentations?
Confidence
Humour
Audience participation
Enthusiasm
Sincerity
Effectiveness

A few thoughts and ideas to pep up your presentation style:

Is PowerPoint the 'boiled cabbage' of presentations?

There are clear strengths and weaknesses associated with the use of PowerPoint and in fact in many 'creative' organizations PowerPoint is out of favour. It's brilliant as a delivery system for *pictures* and *video* but not words. Bullet points and diagrams (used wisely) have a use in training workshops but *not* in impactful presentations! Winston Churchill, Steve Jobs and Nelson Mandela never used PowerPoint – beware!

TABLE 11.9 Strengths and weaknesses of PowerPoint presentations

PowerPoint Strengths	PowerPoint Weaknesses
Easy – user-friendly and simple format	**Over-used** – it's estimated that approximately 80% of professional presentations are now given using PowerPoint
Quick – you can create or amend in a matter of minutes – you can create a presentation the night before or even moments before you speak	**Boring/predictable** – Audiences, particularly the media-savvy, have seen it all before

(*Continued*)

TABLE 11.9 (*Continued*)

PowerPoint Strengths	PowerPoint Weaknesses
Cheap – unlike slides and other audio/visual materials	**Tempts overwriting** – ease of writing leads to the use of too many slides and too many bullet points on each slide
Universal – most conferences and event organizers plan for PowerPoint and have compatible kit and projection	**Encourages poor planning** – because it can be done relatively quickly presenters leave no time for reflection
Versatile – you can make the presentation as long or as short as you like, with visuals and graphics	**A crutch** – for the unskilled, weak presenter who lacks confidence and can hide behind the slides
	Potentially disabling/de-skilling – for the strong presenter who performs better without slides
	Incorrect use – Print-outs of PowerPoint slides are frequently requested in advance for inclusion in conference programmes and handouts. A full script or notes would be more appropriate and a simpler presentation would have more impact, ie 'form should follow function'
	Encourages over-presenting – it is easy to wheel out the same old presentation time and time again

If you do use PowerPoint:

- Make it visual – pictures/metaphors and video are all great for supporting messages and making them memorable and use pathway graphics to explain systems, processes and organizational structures.
- Keep it short and sweet – how much you might expect a member of the audience to retain? For example, if a presentation is delivered containing 20 slides each containing four bullet points, this results in 80 pieces of information. In reality it is unlikely that a member of the audience will leave remembering more than three or four points. It is important not to over-egg your pudding!
- If you have to put up bullet points, let them build up as you speak, otherwise the audience is tempted to 'read on' and not listen to what you are saying.

- Don't let the technology drive you – presenters can become slaves to technology, so the slides command you rather than the opposite being true.
- Be an orator – the skills of oration as outlined by the great Roman orator Cicero are, in fact, fundamental to successful, effective and memorable presentation. It is worth researching what Cicero says on the subject.
- Consider preferred learning styles (Honey and Mumford, 1986) – these may be considered as a useful way of structuring presentation content and delivery.

TABLE 11.10 Summary of preferred learning styles

Activist	Pragmatist
Who learns by moving, playing, acting, discussing, speaking, doing	Who learns by practical application
Activist presentation techniques	**Pragmatist presentation techniques**
Workshops, exercises, breakout groups	Examples, case studies, double up presentation with a real case
Theorist	**Reflector**
Who learns by absorbing the theoretical and hungers for references and academic support	Who learns by reflecting and pondering on what is said
Theorist presentation techniques	**Reflector presentation techniques**
Background, sources and references	Evidence, research findings

- Consider NLP theory – (see Chapter 6 on understanding audiences; NLP is discussed on p.120) This may also give clues in terms of how to structure a presentation and what stimulus materials to include to appeal to as broad a section of the audience as possible.

TABLE 11.11 Different ways in which to appeal to an audience

Auditory	Make the presentation a delight to the ears – use alliteration and wordplay, include sounds and music if you can so they hear what you say
Kinaesthetic	Get people to move or raise hands, pass round a prop, give them detail so the story you are telling feels right to them

(*Continued*)

TABLE 11.11 (*Continued*)

Visual	Put visuals and pictures into the presentation – use visual language so they see what you mean
Unspecified	Use steps and/or sequences to gain understanding so they have time to think and can discover your message

- Use a preparation checklist – for each and every presentation you do (see page 301). This will help you plan your presentation better and include appropriate and tailored references.

- Be audience/customer-led – first and foremost, every time. Think what it will be like to be a member of the audience on this occasion. Are they tired, bored, excited, disinterested, hostile, apathetic? Wake them up, entertain them, educate them – above all make sure they leave the presentation understanding more about your organization with your key messages firmly planted in their minds.

- Always, always, always avoid jargon – you cannot rely on your audience understanding the shorthand language you use internally. It is vital that you communicate simply and effectively with as many people in the audience as possible. This means avoiding the use of acronyms if possible and being scrupulous about using Crystal Mark /plain English. Even an audience that may understand your jargon will be grateful to you for making it easy for them to digest.

- In the same vein, avoid acronyms – people can't be expected to 'translate' an acronym every time one crops up.

- Think the 'persuasion cycle' – buyers need to be moved through the 'persuasion cycle'. The issue is what stage are they at – and have they already been turned off because of hearsay or actual experience? (In other words are they a hostile audience?):
  - Awareness – simple ignorance of the facts – what is XXXX anyway?
  - Liking/propensity to buy – may be aware but need to be brought on side and persuaded – why should I bother with this/this person?
  - Buying – on side and engaged – I am already involved with XXXX.
  - Recommending – has experienced XXXX, is convinced and will act as an advocate – I have tried it and I would recommend XXXX to anyone and everyone.

- If there is one, try to listen to the speaker immediately before you – it helps achieve a rhythm and may give you the chance to make a bridge with a comment, reflection or indeed quip – or pick up a line from the chair who introduces you – which may give you the opportunity to make a link or gain the audience's approval.

- Dress comfortably – to suit the occasion and to project the right image to this specific audience. On most business occasions, smart is called for but smart-comfortable will help you breathe more easily.

- Leave some questions unanswered – that way you may get some questions at the end of the session. Often over-egged presentations make the audience feel so stuffed with information they can't utter a word and so the session ends on a flat or even negative note. Aim for briefer, punchier presentations.

- 'Fillet' your presentations – by editing down and down and down to the essence. Journalists use the 'collect, select, reject' process when writing a piece. This same process can be applied to the creation of a presentation

- Craft 90-word verbal descriptors (no jargon) for any complex idea you have to explain.

- Watch the pauses – in the delivery of the presentation any more than a two-beat pause may cause the audience to think something is wrong, that you have lost your place or lost it altogether. (Apparently this is based on body – or Circadian – rhythms, heartbeats and so on.)

- Remember to give audiences processing time – to digest important points or to feel the impact of a statement. 'One out of three children in this country lives in a single-parent household...' This is one time when the two-beat pause can be ignored with great effect.

- Are you going to be American or British? – presentation fashion is very different on either side of the Atlantic right now, with Americans forsaking podia and fixed microphones for radio mics, and a walkabout with no lectern at all. If you need more action in your presentations the walkabout will help give some immediate verve and energy BUT make movement purposeful not just an annoying mindless wander.

- Research and build in contemporary/topical/local/specific references *The Observer Magazine* recently had a leading feature of the meaning and influence of *The Simpsons* in modern life. Even if you are presenting to the most intellectual audience on earth, there is room for popular icons, symbols and characters.

Similarly presenters can demonstrate that they have their fingers on the pulse by including a reference to what is happening in the world this month, this week, today, this very morning. Local references to a local audience force them not only to sit up and take notice, but also to receive the messages on a more personal (and therefore more impactful) level. Plus it is very flattering that the speaker has bothered to find out about his/her audience. References for special groups (for example parents, environmentalists, health professionals) also demonstrate that this is a presentation that has been written and is 'exclusively' for them and that you are not delivering the same tired old presentation just one more time.

- 'Tell them what you are going to tell them, tell them and then tell them what you have told them' – or not? The agenda slide has become an opener in PowerPoint presentations – but gives a dull start and can turn some members of your audience off immediately. You need to consider if you really need to do this so boringly. By all means have a beginning, middle and end but try not to be predictable and dull!

- Avoid openers like 'For the next 15/40 minutes I am going to share my vision with you of…' – so it's all just corporate puff then? What is in it for the audience? Have you really engaged them with this sort of opening? Unlikely, so dare to be more genuine and original.

- Open with a bang – try the ABCD opening:
  - Attention – a question, a story, a killer fact.
  - Benefits – of listening – the 'What's in it for me?'
  - Credentials – why the listeners should bother to listen to you; you as expert, as case history, as reporter of the facts?
  - Direction – the agenda – the three things you are going to tell them – your three key messages.

- Involve the audience whenever possible – ask for a show of hands; ask a question and invite a responder to contribute; invite questions. All these are classic techniques for getting the listener to listen more actively and participate more fully.

- Always give examples – audiences can interpret, engage and understand more fully if they are given a picture they can relate to. Either tell a story or, if you have the resources, show a video. Use case histories or even metaphors. Build these examples into presentations (and see next point).

- Use pictures always and whenever possible – pictures bring presentations alive and can explain and illustrate quickly and easily. A picture paints a thousand words and appeals to the visual people in the audience.

- If you are confident and skilled then use jokes and anecdotes – even if you are not a natural comedian, real live examples and case histories told in a bright and lively way are highly effective as anecdotes to warm things up.

- If you are confident and skilled then you might consider the use of 'theatricals' – props, sound effects, video clips, a second presenter. All of these could provide memorable moments to lift the presentation out of the ordinary and into the memorable. But use judiciously and again with the audience in mind.

- Try thinking about your presentation like a piece for TV – audiences are so used to receiving polished messages in every sort of media that if you are able to deliver a crisp, memorable performance, your organization will be seen as an energetic and professional organization.

- If you have to explain your organization, do it consistently and briefly – if using PowerPoint your logo, pictures of the work you do with a narrative are terrific.

- Review any speaker programmes, share out the opportunities and field engaging presenters to represent the organization.

- Use your title judiciously – generally speaking it is perfectly acceptable to use titles but again be led by the audience. An audience of trade unionists may respond with greater equanimity to Paul White that Dr Paul White OBE... then again, if you want to impress...

- Seek feedback – from colleagues, trusted audience members. You might even consider getting your presentation filmed. As part of your continuous professional development feedback on presentations is very useful.

AFTERWORD

I hope this book offers you lots of useful ideas and suggestions to help you become a confident and competent practitioner. I have included the essential ideas that any and all PR practitioners need to consider in their roles. We should see ourselves in context, appreciating the origins and development of PR alongside some of the developing theories that enable us to position ourselves as serious professionals, able to make a positive contribution to society.

To do this we need to think deeply about why and how we do what we do, to develop well-thought-through public relations programmes and campaigns. We need to be able to understand and work with other professionals to ensure coherence and cohesiveness between different disciplines. A thorough understanding of our audiences enables us to enter into a dialogue rather than simply sermonize. Using the right channels to engage with those audiences will increase the likelihood we will achieve the right level of engagement. Creative, innovative thinking allows us to present our ideas in ways that cut through. And knowing how to respond when an issue or a crisis breaks will help us protect our organizations' reputations.

Of course no book can possibly cover every single aspect of such a complex professional field, so if you are a specialist (for example working in financial PR) you may need to look further for more help on specific issues. There are lots of resources available to you, and the Kogan Page series is a great place to start (see series list on page viii). All of the PR in Practice books, from Anne Gregory's *Planning and Managing Public Relations Campaigns*, through to Tom Watson's and Paul Noble's *Evaluating Public Relations*, offer further insight and support as you progress in your career. Free online support material is also offered – a great benefit to busy PR professionals.

Even if you studied public relations and communications as a first degree, the experience of continuing your study once you have started to work in the field is key. Continuous professional development is essential – rapid change is a feature of this business, and practitioners who do not continue to develop risk losing credibility and moreover cannot give clients and colleagues sound advice. This for me is both a reputational and ethical issue; you never want to come across as an amateur; nor do you want to give poor advice. So ongoing study and reflection is a must and I urge you to consider enhancing your professionalism by working towards a professional qualification.

Membership of the CIPR and/or the PRCA is highly beneficial in this regard. As a member and fellow of the CIPR I have always valued the benefits membership brings, from the online continuous professional development scheme and stimulating workshops that keep me on my toes, to networking events that enable sharing of ideas and discussion with other professionals whose experiences I learn so much from.

This is a wonderful career for people who are fascinated by communication, are interested in people and current affairs, who like a challenge and creative problem solving. I wish you well for the future and for a long and successful career in this fast-moving, stimulating world.

APPENDIX 1
Chartered Institute of Public Relations Code of Conduct and Complaints Procedure

This code, updated in November 2013, comprises five sections:

- Introduction – Maintaining professional standards in the public relations profession.
- Section A – The Chartered Institute of Public Relations Code of Conduct, as approved by the Institute's Council.
- Section B – How to complain, if you think a public relations practitioner has breached the Code of Conduct; and what happens when you do.
- Section C – Regulations Governing Complaints Relating to Professional Conduct (the Complaints Procedure, which includes Conciliation, the Professional Standards Panel and Appeals Panel).
- Section D – Advisory Notes to accompany the Code of Conduct: Social Media Guidelines. (These are not included in this Appendix.)

Introduction

Maintaining professional standards in the public relations profession

Reputation has a direct and major impact on the corporate well-being of every organisation, be it a multinational, a charity, a Government Department or a small business.

That is why the professionalism of those people who guard and mould reputation – public relations practitioners – is so important.

The Chartered Institute of Public Relations, as the voice of the PR profession, plays a key role in setting and maintaining standards.

The Chartered Institute of Public Relations Code of Conduct and Complaints Procedure

Members of the CIPR agree to abide by a Code of Professional Conduct.

The Code of Conduct is one means by which the CIPR and its Members fulfil the purpose set out in the Institute's royal charter: 'to promote for the public benefit high levels of skill, knowledge, competence, and standards of practice and professional conduct on the part of public relations practitioners'.

Anyone can make a Complaint to the Institute if they believe a CIPR Member (or others for whom they are directly responsible) may have breached the Code.

It is the Code, and the fact that the Institute can take steps to uphold it, that makes Members accountable for the standard of their professional conduct. This accountability is a valuable asset both to Members and to those who hire or employ them.

If it appears that the Code has been breached, either the CIPR will help the two parties to negotiate a settlement or the Professional Standards Panel will investigate and adjudicate.

We do not receive many Complaints, but – as the detailed Regulations later in this document make clear – we treat them seriously and carefully. For the sake of our Members, as well as the people who have complained, we must be fair, equal and rigorous.

In certain cases the Institute's Council may expel a Member summarily, that is, without going through the Complaints Procedure: for example, if a Member has been convicted of a crime involving dishonesty or of any sufficiently serious crime, or has breached the rules of a regulatory or other authority by which they are bound.

Outcomes

We resolve most Complaints through informal negotiation.

Failing that, a decision will be imposed by the Professional Standards Panel or the Appeals Panel according to the powers delegated to them by the CIPR Council. (The Appeals Panel considers appeals by Members against decisions of the Professional Standards Panel.)

A decision may be to censure the person you complained about, to expel them from the Institute, or to drop the case if it is found not proven. Where the Code of Conduct is found to have been breached, decisions of the Panels are normally made public.

If a CIPR Member is found to have delivered substandard work to you, the Member may be required to return any fees you paid for that work. If the substandard work was part of a larger contract, the refund is limited to the value of that part of the contract. If you want further compensation, you will have to go to law: the CIPR does not impose damages.

For further information

Contact Martin Horrox MCIPR, Regulatory Consultant, at martinh@ cipr.co.uk, on 07974 964639, or by letter to Chartered Institute of Public Relations, 52–53 Russell Square, London WC1B 4HP

Section A

Chartered Institute of Public Relations Code of Conduct Principles

1 Members of the Chartered Institute of Public Relations agree to:

   a) maintain the highest standards of professional endeavour, integrity, confidentiality, financial propriety and personal conduct;

   b) deal honestly and fairly in business with employers, employees, clients, fellow professionals, other professions and the public;

   c) respect, in their dealings with other people, the legal and regulatory frameworks and codes of all countries where they practise;

   d) uphold the reputation of, and do nothing that would bring into disrepute, the public relations profession or the Chartered Institute of Public Relations;

   e) respect and abide by this Code and related Notes of Guidance issued by the Chartered Institute of Public Relations and ensure that others who are accountable to them (e.g. subordinates and sub-contractors) do the same;

   f) encourage professional training and development among members of the profession in order to raise and maintain professional standards generally.

Putting the principles into practice

2 Examples of good public relations practice include:

Integrity and honesty

- Ensuring that clients, employers, employees, colleagues and fellow professionals are fully informed about the nature of representation, what can be delivered and achieved, and what other parties must do in order to enable the desired result.
- Never deliberately concealing the practitioner's role as representative of a client or employer, even if the client or employer remains anonymous: e.g. by promoting a cause in the guise of a disinterested party or member of the public.
- Checking the reliability and accuracy of information before dissemination.
- Supporting the CIPR Principles by bringing to the attention of the CIPR examples of malpractice and unprofessional conduct.

Capacity, capability and competence

- Delivering work competently: that is, in a timely, cost-effective, appropriate and thoughtful manner, according to the actual or implied contract; applying due professional judgement and experience; taking necessary steps to resolve problems; and ensuring that clients and other interested parties are informed, advised and consulted as necessary.
- Being aware of the limitations of professional capacity and capability: without limiting realistic scope for development, being willing to accept or delegate only that work for which practitioners are suitably skilled and experienced and which they have the resources to undertake.
- Where appropriate, collaborating on projects to ensure the necessary skill base.

Transparency and avoiding conflicts of interest

- Disclosing to employers, clients or potential clients any financial interest in a supplier being recommended or engaged.

- Declaring conflicts of interest (or circumstances which may give rise to them) in writing to clients, potential clients and employers as soon as they arise.
- Ensuring that services provided are costed, delivered and accounted for in a manner that conforms to accepted business practice and ethics.

Confidentiality

- Safeguarding confidences, e.g. of present and former clients and employers.
- Never using confidential and 'insider' information to the disadvantage or prejudice of others, e.g. clients and employers, or to self-advantage of any kind.
- Not disclosing confidential information unless specific permission has been granted or if required or covered by law.

Interpreting the Code

3 In the interpretation of this code, the Laws of the Land shall apply. With that proviso, the code will be implemented according to the decision at the time of the Professional Standards Panel.

Maintaining professional standards

CIPR Members are encouraged to

a) raise and maintain their own professional standards by, for example:
- identifying and closing professional skills gaps through the Institute's Continuing Professional Development programme;
- participating in the work of the Institute through the committee structure, special interest and vocational groups, training and networking events;
- evaluating the practice of public relations through use of recognised tools and other quality management and quality assurance systems (e.g. ISO standards);
- constantly striving to improve the quality of business performance;
- sharing information on good practice with Members and, equally, referring perceived examples of poor practice to the Institute.

b) raise the professional standards of other public relations practitioners to the level of CIPR Members by, for example:

- offering work experience to students interested in pursuing a career in public relations;
- encouraging employees and colleagues to join and support the CIPR;
- specifying a preference for CIPR applicants for staff positions advertised.

c) spread awareness of the CIPR's role as guardian of standards for the public relations profession by, for example:

- displaying the CIPR designatory letters on business stationery;
- referring to the CIPR Code of Conduct in every contract.

Section B

How to complain, if you think a public relations practitioner has breached the Code of Conduct; and what happens when you do

Who may make a Complaint?

Anyone, whether an organisation or an individual.

You do not have to have suffered loss or damage in order to complain: you only have to believe that a Member of the Institute may have breached the Code of Conduct.

Sometimes the Chartered Institute of Public Relations itself will initiate a Complaint or take over the role of Complainant, for instance if the Complaint raises a matter of general principle and/or the Complainant has no personal interest in the outcome. And the Institute's Council may take independent action, e.g. if a Member has been convicted of a crime; in such cases the Complaints Procedure does not apply.

Whom can you complain about?

Members of the Chartered Institute of Public Relations and any staff or sub-contractors for whom they are directly responsible, even if those staff or sub-contractors are not CIPR Members in their own right.

Members agree to be bound by the Code of Conduct when they accept Membership. This is why it makes sense to hire CIPR Members when you need public relations support.

You may recognise Members from the letters FCIPR, MCIPR or ACIPR after their name, but you can also ask us to check whether someone was a Member at the time of the events that you want to complain about. Members cannot avoid responsibility for their past conduct by resigning from the Institute.

We cannot deal with Complaints about PR practitioners who have not been Members of the CIPR.

To register a Complaint

Contact Martin Horrox MCIPR, Regulatory Consultant, at martinh@cipr. co.uk, on 07974 964639, or by letter to

Chartered Institute of Public Relations
52–53 Russell Square
London WC1B 4HP

Martin Horrox will advise you (and the Member you complain about) on the various stages of a Complaint. He is your contact point with the CIPR throughout. The Regulatory Consultant is appointed by the CIPR Council to advise enquirers, the parties to a Complaint (i.e. you and the Member you may wish to complain about) and the CIPR itself on the Complaints Procedure. He may also help you and the Member to resolve your differences before the formal Complaints Procedure is set in motion. He is not a member of the Panels that may adjudicate in formal hearings of a Complaint.

Initial checks

We will check that the person you have complained about is actually a Member – or was, at the time of the events you are complaining about. If this is not the case, there is nothing further that we can do.

We will also tell you if we think the Complaint is not covered by the Code of Conduct.

Written details

You will be asked to state your Complaint in writing (we can help you to do this, if necessary). The person you have complained about will be shown this document and asked to provide a written reply (and the same help is available to them).

A negotiated resolution

Most Complaints are resolved through informal negotiation. This is always the first resort, but it depends on the willingness of both sides to take part.

This is a very informal process. Sometimes it can be achieved with help from the CIPR's Regulatory Consultant, even before there have been any formal exchanges of documents; otherwise a panel of Conciliators will be appointed by the Institute, and they have discretion to run the process in whatever way is most likely to produce an agreement. The process is confidential; no records of the discussions are kept, and the result is not published.

Formal hearings

If no agreement is reached through negotiation, the Complaint will be considered by the Professional Standards Panel and possibly, after that, by the Appeals Panel. The power to discipline Members is granted to the CIPR Council by the Institute's Royal Charter and is delegated to the two Panels.

The Panels are formed of senior and experienced people from public relations and other professions. The Appeals Panel considers appeals by Members against decisions of the Professional Standards Panel.

Any discussions that were held as part of negotiations managed by the Regulatory Consultant or Conciliators are ignored by the Panels, and anyone who acted as a CIPR Conciliator is not allowed to take part in subsequent formal hearings.

Both sides in the dispute are expected to attend a hearing by the Professional Standards Panel, where they will have the chance to state their case in person; they are also allowed to name a friend or a legal adviser, who may accompany and/or represent them at a hearing. (At an Appeals Panel hearing, only the Respondent normally attends but has the same right to be accompanied and/or represented.) At the discretion of the Chairman the parties may also be able to submit further information and to call and cross-examine witnesses. The Panels themselves may ask for additional written evidence and call witnesses.

Although formal hearings are subject to detailed Regulations (see Section C below) they are run, above all, on the principle of natural justice: in other words, both sides should receive fair and equal treatment.

Objections about the way in which a Complaint has been handled may be referred at any time to the Arbiter, who is appointed by the CIPR Council.

Confidentiality

Everyone (and specifically you and the person you have complained about) must keep every detail of the Complaint and the Complaints Procedure confidential until the Chairman of a Panel rules otherwise.

If a case goes to a formal hearing, and the decision is against the CIPR Member, a summary of the Complaint and the outcome will normally be made public.

Outcomes

If the Complaint is not resolved by Conciliation, the Professional Standards Panel or the Appeals Panel may decide to

a) advise the Member (the person you have complained about) to improve the way he or she does business;

b) reprimand the Member;

c) require the Member to repay fees received for work that forms the subject of the Complaint;

d) require the Member to pay the Institute's costs of the Complaints Procedure;

e) suspend or expel the Member;

f) drop the case, if they consider that the Complaint is not proven; or take no further action.

If a Member is found to have breached the Code of Conduct, that decision is normally made public (naming names).

Compensation

The CIPR does not award damages. If you have complained that a CIPR Member carried out substandard work for you, the Member may be required to return any fees that you paid for that work. If the substandard work was part of a larger contract, the refund is limited to the value of that part of the contract. If you want more or different compensation, you should use the courts.

Legal action

Occasionally disputes are pursued through the courts or similar agencies (such as the Information Commissioner's Office) and through a Complaint to the CIPR at the same time. We will normally halt the CIPR Complaints Procedure until the legal action is completed.

Legal action, in other words, does not cancel the CIPR Complaints Procedure, whether the action is taken by you (the person who is complaining) or by the CIPR Member (the person who is complained about).

Section C

Regulations Governing the Complaints Procedure

Contents Regulation

1. Definitions

For the purpose of these Regulations the following words and expressions have the following meanings, unless the context requires otherwise:

> *Arbiter* a Member or Fellow of the CIPR appointed by the Council to consider and adjudicate questions arising in respect of the conduct of the Complaints Procedure, including the interpretation or application of these and other relevant Regulations. The Arbiter is not a member of the Professional Standards Panel or the Appeals Panel.

Chairman the Chairman of the Professional Standards Panel or the Appeals Panel, as the case may be, or a member of a Panel nominated by the Arbiter to act as Chairman in accordance with Regulation 8 (Professional Standards Panel and Appeals Panel: membership), paragraph f).

Complaint facts or matters coming to the attention of the Chief Executive indicating that a Member may have become liable to disciplinary action in accordance with Regulation 15 (Disciplinary Powers) of the Institute's Charter Regulations.

Complainant a person who brings a Complaint.

Council the CIPR Council.

Institute/CIPR the Chartered Institute of Public Relations.

Lay Member an appropriately qualified or experienced person from outside the public relations profession, appointed by the Council to take part in hearings and other activities of the Professional Standards Panel and the Appeals Panel.

Member a Member or Fellow of the Institute at the time the matter complained about occurred.

Panel the Professional Standards Panel or the Appeals Panel, as the case may be.

Regulatory Consultant a person appointed by the Council to give impartial advice on the CIPR Complaints Procedure to people who are, or who may become, parties to a Complaint, and to the CIPR. The Regulatory Consultant is not a member of the Professional Standards Panel or the Appeals Panel.

Respondent a Member against whom a Complaint has been lodged.

Note: It is a condition of Membership that Members remain subject to disciplinary proceedings in relation to their professional activities during the period of their membership, even though they may subsequently have ceased to be Members.

Other words and expressions defined in the Charter and Charter Regulations of the Institute shall have the meanings there assigned to them.

The singular includes the plural and vice versa.

2. The Complaints Procedure: general management of business

a) The Complaints Procedure, including Conciliation, proceedings of the Professional Standards Panel and Appeals Panel and the actions of the Regulatory Consultant, is governed by the rules of natural justice. In particular, the procedure will be managed at all times to ensure that the Respondent has a fair and proper opportunity to answer the Complaint.

b) Unless a Panel decides otherwise, all costs and expenses incurred by the Institute in connection with the Complaints Procedure and these Regulations will be borne by the Institute.

c) Failure to comply with these Regulations in any case will not render the procedure void, but the Chairman of a Panel may act as necessary to redress the failure if he or she considers that it may have disadvantaged the Respondent or the Complainant.

d) The Complaints Procedure is not invalidated if a relevant communication is accidentally not sent, or is not received.

e) i) Subject to sub-paragraph e) (ii) of this Regulation, any disagreement about the conduct of the Complaints Procedure, including the interpretation or application of these Regulations, may be referred to the Arbiter at any time by the Complainant, the Respondent, the Chief Executive of the CIPR, the Chairman of the Professional Standards Panel, the Chairman of the Appeals Panel or the Regulatory Consultant.

   ii) Any reference to the Arbiter concerning a hearing by the Professional Standards Panel or the Appeals Panel must be made within five days of the end of the hearing.

   iii) A decision by the Arbiter concerning the conduct of the Professional Standards Panel may be cited as a ground for an appeal by the Respondent to the Appeals Panel [*Regulation 19. (Appeal against a decision of the Professional Standards Panel) refers*]. In all other instances, the Arbiter's decision is final and binding.

   iv) Decisions by the Arbiter shall be reported in writing to the Complainant, the Respondent and (as the case may be) the Chairman of the Professional Standards Panel and/or the Chairman of the Appeals Panel. If reference has been made to the Arbiter after the end of a hearing by the Appeals Panel, the Arbiter shall report his decision to the Council, and the Council shall accept his decision.

f) The Institute will retain all records of the Complaints Procedure (excluding records of Conciliation) for five years from the date of a hearing by the Professional Standards Panel or the Appeals Panel, as the case may be, or until the Council decides otherwise.

g) Any documents served in connection with the Complaints Procedure shall be deemed to have been validly served on the Respondent and/or the Complainant:

   i) if sent by e-mail to an address that is known to have been active and accurate recently; and

   ii) if sent by recorded delivery post to the last address known by the Institute or an address that they specified in writing (including the address of their legal adviser); or

iii) if handed to them in person; or

iv) if served in any way which may be directed by the Chairman of a Panel.

h) The Regulatory Consultant may at his discretion offer such advice and help to the Complainant and the Respondent as he considers necessary to ensure that

i) a potential Complaint may be resolved by informal negotiation before it is referred to the Professional Standards Panel

ii) the Complainant's and the Respondent's cases are presented fully and fairly by the Complainant and the Respondent to the Professional Standards Panel and Appeals Panel, as appropriate.

His advice is offered in good faith and is not binding upon the Panels or (except as stated elsewhere in these Regulations) upon the Complainant and the Respondent.

3. Confidentiality

a) Details of a Complaint and of its progress through the Institute's Complaints Procedure must be treated as confidential by the Complainant, the Respondent, the Arbiter, the Regulatory Consultant and all Conciliators, Assessors and members of the Professional Standards Panel and Appeals Panel without time limit, except that:

i) the Chairman of a Panel may decide at any time that facts (other than details of any Conciliation) may be published if they are of public concern;

ii) when a breach of the Code of Conduct is found to have occurred, decisions of a Panel will normally be published;

iii) information may be passed to third parties, e.g. witnesses, on a strict 'need-to-know' basis and on condition that the third parties are explicitly bound by the requirement of confidentiality.

b) Any breach, or alleged breach, of confidentiality may itself give rise to a further Complaint.

4. Making Complaints

a) Any person (whether a Member of the Institute or not) may bring a Complaint against a Member. So too may the Chief Executive, on behalf of the Institute, if it appears to be in the public interest or if the person raising the Complaint cannot reasonably be expected to pursue it on his or her own account. Members of the Institute have a duty to bring a Complaint against a Member, where it is in the public interest to do so.

b) Complaints may relate to others, who may or may not be Members (e.g. subordinates or subcontractors) for whose work the Member was directly responsible at the time of events that are the subject of the Complaint.

5. The Institute's initial response to Complaints

a) The Institute will maintain a register of all Complaints received and the decisions on them by a Panel.

b) The Regulatory Consultant will

   i) check that the Complaint concerns a Member of the Institute at the time of the events complained about;

   ii) identify the clause(s) in the CIPR Code of Conduct to which the Complaint refers;

   iii) tell the Complainant whether the Council intends to take summary action, in which case the Complaints Procedure will not apply.

c) If the Council does not intend to take summary action, the Regulatory Consultant will

   i) clarify any matters of uncertainty with the Complainant;

   ii) tell the Complainant about the Complaints Procedure, these Regulations and the Institute's disciplinary powers: specifically, Regulation 3 (Confidentiality);

   iii) explain that the Respondent will be notified of the Complaint in order that he or she may exercise the right of reply.

d) If the Complainant wishes to proceed, the Regulatory Consultant will

   i) tell the Respondent about the Complaint, the Complaints Procedure, these Regulations and the Institute's disciplinary powers: specifically, Regulation 3 (Confidentiality);

   ii) attempt to negotiate an informal resolution of the complaint with and between the Respondent and the Complainant, either before or after the exchange of statements set out in paragraph e) of this Regulation;

e) Before or after any attempt by the Regulatory Consultant to negotiate an informal settlement *[paragraph d) of this Regulation refers]* he may

   i) obtain a written statement of the Complaint, provided or approved by the Complainant, send it to the Respondent and invite him or her to submit a written response to it;

   ii) continue to exchange statements between the Complainant and Respondent until either or both of them have no more to add to

their statements or he notifies them that the exchange will end
after one more submission from each of them.

f) If the Regulatory Consultant is unable to negotiate a settlement
between the Complainant and the Respondent, he will ask the
Chairman of the Professional Standards Panel to start the
Conciliation process under Regulation 6 (Duty to conciliate) or, if
either the Complainant or the Respondent does not agree to that, to
initiate a hearing by the Professional Standards Panel.

g) The Complaint should be referred to the Chairman of the
Professional Standards Panel, as in paragraph f) of this Regulation,
no later than eight weeks after the Complaint was received, unless
both the Complainant and the Respondent agree otherwise.

6. Duty to conciliate

a) The first step in resolving a Complaint, if the Complainant and the
Respondent agree to it, is a process of conciliation, mediation or
arbitration ('Conciliation').

b) Conciliation is an informal process managed at the discretion of the
Chairman of the Professional Standards Panel and of any
Conciliators whom the Institute appoints.

c) Conciliation is a confidential process: no records will be kept
afterwards, and no details of it will be forwarded to the Professional
Standards Panel or Appeals Panel or known to the Chairman of the
Professional Standards Panel.

d) The Conciliators may investigate any facts and circumstances of the
Complaint and take whatever legal or other advice they consider
necessary. However, unlike at a formal hearing of a Complaint, they
are not aiming at a complete understanding of the facts surrounding
the Complaint.

e) If a Complaint is not resolved by Conciliation, it will be considered
at a hearing of the Professional Standards Panel.

7. Conciliation: management of business

a) The Chairman of the Professional Standards Panel will, whenever
necessary, appoint three members of the Professional Standards Panel
to act as a panel of conciliators, one of them as Chairman of the
Conciliation panel. The quorum of a Conciliation panel is two,
including one lay member.

Members of the Conciliation panel ('the Conciliators') will receive
copies of the Complaint and the Respondent's response to it.

b) The Conciliation process should start and run as quickly as possible, and will end in any event within three months after the Conciliators were appointed.

c) The Complainant and the Respondent are expected to speak for themselves at Conciliation meetings, but they may be accompanied by any other person they choose, whom the Chairman may allow to address the Conciliators.

d) The Complainant and the Respondent may state their position and any relevant issues in writing at any time.

e) The Conciliators do not have to reveal to the Complainant what they have been told by, or have said to, the Respondent; and vice versa.

f) The Conciliators may adjourn a Conciliation meeting at any stage.

g) Conciliation will come to an end if:

   i) the Complainant withdraws the Complaint, or part of it, in writing;

   ii) the Chairman of the Conciliation panel reports to the Chairman of the Professional Standards Panel – without giving reasons – that Conciliation has not been successful;

   iii) either the Complainant or the Respondent withdraws from the Conciliation process; or

   iv) the Complainant and the Respondent have not reached agreement within three months.

h) Other things being equal, Regulation 8 (Professional Standards Panel and Appeals Panel: membership) paragraphs b) to g) also apply to members of any Conciliation panel.

8. Professional Standards Panel and Appeals Panel: membership

a) The quorum of the Professional Standards Panel is not less than four and of the Appeals Panel not less than three, including at least one lay member in both cases.

b) Hearings by the Professional Standards Panel and the Appeals Panel will generally be conducted by five or more members in each case, including the Chairman and comprising the smallest possible majority of Members and/or Fellows of the Institute (as the case may be) together with a minority of Lay Members.

c) Unless the Council decides otherwise, once a Panel has started to hear a Complaint, its members remain in membership until the hearing has been completed, even if they were due to retire from the Panel in the meantime.

d) A Panel member shall play no part in considering a Complaint if he or she
   i) has had previous dealings with the Respondent or Complainant personally or professionally;
   ii) has prior knowledge of any matters relating to the Complaint;
   iii) has taken part in any previous consideration of the Complaint or any aspect of the Complaint, including Conciliation; or
   iv) has been subject to an objection by a Respondent or Complainant which has been upheld by the Chairman of a Panel, as set out in Regulation 16 (Convening the Professional Standards Panel) paragraph b), and Regulation 20 (Convening the Appeals Panel) paragraph c).

e) The Chairman must be present throughout the hearing of a Complaint. If any other member of a Panel is absent from any part of the hearing, he or she shall take no further part in it. This will not invalidate the hearing, so long as the number of members present throughout the substantive hearing of the Complaint is not reduced below the quorum.

f) If the Chairman of a Panel is unable to carry out any particular duty, that duty may be carried out by any other member of that Panel nominated in writing by the Arbiter.

g) A Panel may instruct a solicitor and/or counsel to represent it at a hearing if it thinks fit.

9. Professional Standards Panel and Appeals Panel: assessors

a) The Chairman of a Panel may appoint one or more Assessors, who may have specialised knowledge or experience that would assist the Panel.

b) No Assessor shall be appointed who has taken part in Conciliation under Regulation 6 (Duty to conciliate).

c) The Regulatory Consultant may attend hearings in the status of an Assessor.

d) Assessors are not members of the Panel and have no vote on decisions.

10. Professional Standards Panel and Appeals Panel: general management of business

a) Hearings will be in private unless the Chairman decides otherwise.

b) The Chairman may decide that more than one Complaint against the same Member, or Complaints against more than one Member, will be handled together.

c) Unless the Chairman decides that an adjournment is necessary from time to time, the Panel will sit from day to day until it has announced a decision on all aspects of the Complaint.

d) A record will be taken of the proceedings and a copy will be supplied to the Respondent or the Complainant if he or she

   i) requests it within three months of the hearing;

   ii) pays the cost of supplying it.

e) The Chairman may determine that it is in the public interest to resolve a Complaint urgently. In this case the Chairman, in consultation with one or more members of the Panel is entitled to act on behalf of the Panel in all matters, and will report his or her actions to the Panel as soon as reasonably practicable.

f) The Chairman may take whatever steps he or she considers necessary at any time to ensure that the case is handled fairly and efficiently. This may include extending or abridging any time limit that has been imposed on the Respondent or the Complainant or that governs the procedures of the Panel.

g) The standard of proof at all times is the balance of probabilities.

h) In any instances not explicitly covered by these Regulations, the Chairman may manage the business of the Panel as he or she sees fit: for example, in approving any application to postpone a hearing which has not begun, or in adjourning a hearing from time to time to seek further information or to give the Respondent or Complainant time to consider a response.

11. Professional Standards Panel and Appeals Panel: evidence

a) The Panels may admit evidence of any sort, whether or not it would be acceptable in a court of law; although they are expected to take reasonable steps to validate any hearsay evidence with direct evidence.

b) The Panels will normally only consider information and evidence that have been submitted in advance. However:

i) in exceptional circumstances, such as where information and evidence were not previously available, the Chairman may allow new information to be submitted at a hearing;

ii) exceptionally and for good reason, the Panels may consider any evidence or information that has not been submitted by a due date, provided that the Respondent is not disadvantaged as a result.

c) The Panels may take into account any facts or matters which were considered by the Institute on previous occasions in relation to the Respondent.

d) The Panels do not have access to any information relating to Conciliation under Regulation 6 (Duty to conciliate. Otherwise, they may direct the Respondent and Complainant to provide additional information as necessary; and the Respondent and Complainant must provide it within a specified time.

e) Correspondence and discussions between the Regulatory Consultant and the Complainant and Respondent are confidential and will not be considered as evidence by the Professional Standards Panel or the Appeals Panel, except for the Complainant's written statement of Complaint and the Respondent's written statement in reply.

12. Professional Standards Panel and Appeals Panel: decisions

a) Decisions of the Panels will be notified to the Respondent and the Complainant in writing.

b) The Professional Standards Panel may determine that

i) a Complaint does not disclose a case for disciplinary action, in which case the Complaint will be dropped; or

ii) a Complaint does disclose a case for disciplinary action, but no further action will be taken. This decision will be made exceptionally and only if the Panel, taking into account all the circumstances of the case, considers that it would be unreasonable or unjust to impose a penalty; or

iii) a Complaint does disclose a case for disciplinary action, and it intends to proceed as in Regulation 13 (Suspension or termination of Membership) or Regulation 14 (Other penalties) or Regulation 15 (Letters of advice).

c) The Appeals Panel may determine an appeal from a decision of the Professional Standards Panel as follows:

   i) it may dismiss the appeal; or

   ii) it may allow the appeal and quash the decision appealed against; or

   iii) it may substitute for the decision appealed against any other decision that the Professional Standards Panel could have made.

d) The final decision in respect of a Complaint will take the form of a report to the Council by the Professional Standards Panel or the Appeal Panel, as the case may be. The report

   i) will record whether the Respondent was present throughout the proceedings and, if not, confirm that the Institute had duly notified the Respondent of his or her rights and obligations as set out in these Regulations;

   ii) if the Respondent has failed to comply with these Regulations or any direction made under these Regulations, may recommend to the Council that one of the measures under Regulation 13 (Suspension or termination of Membership) or Regulation 14 (Other penalties) or Regulation 15 (Letters of advice) should be exercised against the Respondent;

   iii) will state whether the Respondent should pay any costs and, if so, the amount to be paid or the way in which it is to be calculated, and the deadline for payment.

e) The final decision in respect of a Complaint will come into effect on the date when it is reported to the Council by the Professional Standards Panel or the Appeal Panel, as the case may be. Decisions of the Professional Standards Panel shall not be reported to the Council until the period in which the Respondent may register an appeal has elapsed *[Regulation 19. Appeal against a decision of the Professional Standards Panel refers]*

f) Where the Professional Standards Panel or the Appeals Panel decides that the Respondent has breached the Code of Conduct, the decision will normally be made public. The manner of publication will be determined by the Chief Executive in consultation with the Chairman of the Panel.

g) A decision of the Professional Standards Panel or the Appeals Panel may also be published if the Panel decides that a Respondent has not breached the Code of Conduct, but the Respondent asks in writing that the decision be published. In this event the decision will be published in the terms set out by the Professional Standards Panel or the Appeals Panel, as appropriate.

h) If the Respondent breaches an order made under Regulation 13 (Suspension or termination of Membership) or Regulation 14 (Other penalties) or Regulation 15 (Letters of advice) he or she may be subject to a further Complaint.

13. Suspension or termination of Membership

[Regulation 12 (Professional Standards Panel and Appeals Panel: decisions) paragraph b) iii) refers]

a) The Professional Standards Panel or the Appeals Panel may decide to suspend a Member from Membership of the CIPR for up to two years or may terminate his or her Membership.

b) No refund will be made of Membership fees for the remainder of the membership year after the date of suspension or termination.

14. Other penalties

[Regulation 12 (Professional Standards Panel and Appeals Panel: decisions) paragraph b) iii) refers]

The Professional Standards Panel or the Appeals Panel may order that

a) the Respondent be reprimanded or severely reprimanded;

b) by a specified date the Respondent must return to a client all or part of a fee which the client has paid or remit to a client funds which have been retained by the Respondent in or towards payment of a fee;

c) the Respondent pay to the Institute by a specified date a sum to compensate for all or part of the costs arising under this Complaints Procedure.

15. Letters of advice

[Regulation 12 (Professional Standards Panel and Appeals Panel: decisions) paragraph b) iii) refers]

a) The Professional Standards Panel or the Appeals Panel may order the Respondent to obtain and follow advice from specified sources if it considers that the Complaint has arisen because the Respondent's business, or the business in which the Respondent is employed, has been managed inefficiently.

b) Where relevant, the Professional Standards Panel or the Appeals Panel may seek the assistance of the Respondent's employer in implementing the advice.

16. Convening the Professional Standards Panel

a) At least six weeks' notice of the hearing will be given to the Complainant and the Respondent. The convening notice will

i) give the date, time and place for hearing the Complaint;

ii) set out details of the procedure to be followed at the hearing, including the procedures in Regulations 10-11 (Professional Standards Panel and Appeals Panel: general management of business, evidence) and Regulations 17-18 (Professional Standards Panel: management of business, order of business);

iii) be accompanied by a copy of the written submissions supplied by the Respondent and Complainant;

iv) name the members of the Panel who will take part in the hearing.

b) Within five days of the date of the convening notice the Respondent and Complainant may object in writing to any of the members, stating their grounds. If the Chairman considers that the objection is well founded, he or she shall bar the member(s) in question from hearing that Complaint. The Respondent and Complainant have the same right of objection to anyone who is subsequently appointed as an alternate, to be exercised within five days of the date of the notice of appointment, which shall be given to the Complainant and the Respondent.

c) The Respondent and Complainant will be required within two weeks of the date of the convening notice:

i) to confirm in writing that they intend to be present at the hearing, or to give reasons why they should be permitted not to attend;

ii) to state whether they will be accompanied and/or represented at the hearing and to provide the identity, standing and address of any person who will accompany or represent them;

iii) to provide the names, standing and addresses of any witnesses they seek permission to call, and to deliver a signed written statement setting out the substance of each witness's evidence.

d) The Chairman will decide as soon as practicable whether or not

i) to admit any or all of the witnesses proposed by the Respondent and Complainant, and the evidence of such witnesses;

ii) to accept applications from the Respondent and Complainant to be absent from the hearing and (if applicable) to be represented in their absence *[Regulation 17 (Professional Standards Panel: management of business) paragraph b) refers]*.

17. Professional Standards Panel: management of business

a) The Respondent and the Complainant have the right to attend the hearing in person and each may be accompanied and/or represented at the hearing by another person, who may be legally qualified or not.

b) The Respondent and the Complainant will be expected to attend the hearing unless permitted by the Chairman to be absent in accordance with Regulation 16 (Convening the Professional Standards Panel) paragraph d) ii). The Chairman may direct one or both of the Complainant and the Respondent to attend. The hearing will be conducted in the presence of both of them, unless the Chairman decides otherwise from time to time and subject to paragraph c) of this Regulation. The Chairman may request witnesses to attend.

c) The hearing may proceed even if the Respondent fails to attend or fails to make use of the rights of the Respondent under these Regulations in any other way, provided that the Institute has duly notified the Respondent of his or her rights and obligations as set out in these Regulations.

d) Subject to Regulation 16 (Convening the Professional Standards Panel) paragraph d) i), the Complainant and Respondent may call witnesses and question witnesses. The members of the Panel may also question witnesses.

e) If the Respondent or Complainant fails to attend without permission to be absent and without good cause, his or her absence will be regarded by the Panel as evidence against him or her.

f) The Panel will reach a decision in accordance with Regulation 12 (Professional Standards Panel and Appeals Panel: decisions).

g) The Panel will notify the Respondent of the decision in writing and will report it to the Council not less than 20 days after that notification if

   i)   no disagreement concerning the conduct of the Complaints Procedure has been referred to the Arbiter under Regulation 2 (The Complaints Procedure: general management of business) paragraph e); or

   ii) a disagreement concerning the conduct of the Complaints Procedure has been referred to the Arbiter under Regulation 2 (The Complaints Procedure: general management of business) paragraph e) and the Arbiter has upheld the decision of the Professional Standards Panel; and

   ii) no appeal has been received under Regulation 19 (Appeal against a decision of the Professional Standards Panel); or

iii) an appeal has been received but has been ruled invalid under Regulation 19 (Appeal against a decision of the Professional Standards Panel) paragraph d).

18. Professional Standards Panel: order of business

The normal order of business, subject to the discretion of the Chairman, will be:

a) The Chairman will ensure that everyone present is made known, and explain the procedure that the Panel will follow.

b) The Panel will consider the Complaint and any other written submissions before it and call such witnesses as it sees fit.

c) The Complainant will be called to speak and to present any witnesses.

d) The Respondent will be called to respond, to question the Complainant's witnesses and to present any witnesses of his or her own.

e) The Complainant will be invited to question the Respondent's witnesses.

f) The Panel will consider its decision in private, then announce it in the presence of the Respondent. If any finding is against the Respondent, he or she (or his or her representative) will be invited to address the Panel in mitigation.

g) The Panel will consider its final decision in private, then announce it in the presence of both the Complainant and the Respondent.

19. Appeal against a decision of the Professional Standards Panel

a) Within 14 days of the date of notification of a decision by the Professional Standards Panel under Regulation 17 (Professional Standards Panel: management of business) paragraph g) or, if later, of the date of notification of a decision by the Arbiter concerning the conduct of the Professional Standards Panel under Regulation 2 (The Complaints Procedure: general management of business) paragraph e), the Respondent may state in writing to the Institute that he or she wishes to appeal against the decision. Subject to paragraphs b) – d) of this Regulation, the Complaint will be referred to the Appeals Panel and the Complainant will be informed.

b) An appeal is not an opportunity to have the Complaint reconsidered *ab initio*. The Appeals Panel will consider an appeal solely on the grounds that

i) the decision was flawed, or there was some serious irregularity in the procedure by which the Professional Standards Panel reached it; or

ii) new evidence has arisen that materially alters the evidence previously before the Professional Standards Panel.

c) In giving notice of his or her wish to appeal in accordance with paragraph a) of this Regulation, the Respondent must state the precise and detailed grounds on which the appeal is based.

d) The Chairman of the Appeals Panel may rule an appeal invalid if he or she considers that

i) the grounds do not conform to paragraph b) and/or paragraph c) of this Regulation; or

ii) no arguable ground of appeal has been stated; or

iii) the grounds of appeal had already been addressed wholly or substantively by the Arbiter, and the Chairman upholds the Arbiter's decision.

20. *Convening the Appeals Panel*

a) In the event of a valid appeal by a Respondent against a decision of the Professional Standards Panel in accordance with Regulation 19 (Appeal against a decision of the Professional Standards Panel), the Professional Standards Panel will submit to the Appeals Panel

i) a summary of the facts and matters considered by the Professional Standards Panel, a copy of its written decision in relation to them and its response to the grounds of the appeal;

ii) a copy of the initial written submissions made by the Complainant and the Respondent;

iii) any further relevant information or submissions it may have received from the Complainant or Respondent;

iv) the Respondent's statement of appeal and grounds of appeal.

b) At least eight weeks' notice of the hearing of the Appeals Panel will be given to the Respondent, with a copy to the Complainant. The convening notice will

i) give the date, time and place for hearing the appeal;

ii) set out the procedure to be followed at the hearing, including the procedures in Regulations 10–11 (Professional Standards Panel and Appeals Panel: general management of business, evidence) and Regulations 22–23 (Appeals Panel: management of business, order of business);

   iii) be accompanied by a copy of all documents referred to in paragraph a) of this Regulation;

   iv) give a date, time and place for a pre-hearing review, in the event that the Chairman decides that one is necessary;

   v) explain the purpose and management of a pre-hearing review, as set out in Regulation 21 (Appeals Panel: pre-hearing review);

   vi) name the members of the Panel who will take part in the hearing.

c) Within five days of the date of the convening notice the Respondent may object in writing to any of the members, stating the grounds. If the Chairman considers that the objection is well founded, he or she shall bar the member(s) in question from hearing that appeal. The Respondent has the same right of objection to anyone who is subsequently appointed as an alternate, to be exercised within five days of the notice of appointment, which shall be given to the Complainant and the Respondent.

d) The Respondent will be required within four weeks of the date of the convening notice

   i) to state in writing

a) that he or she intends to be present at the hearing, or to give reasons why he or she should be permitted not to attend;

b) the name, standing and address of any person who will accompany and/or represent him or her;

c) whether he or she wishes to seek permission to call any witness(es) in accordance with paragraph e) of this Regulation and, if so, to state the name, standing and address of the witness(es) and to deliver a signed written statement setting out the substance of each witness's evidence;

d) whether he or she accepts the facts as stated in the accompanying documents; and, if not, which facts are denied, and why;

e) whether he or she accepts the authenticity of the accompanying documents; and, if not, which documents are denied, and why;

   ii) to submit any additional documents on which he or she intends to rely.

f) The Respondent may apply to the Chairman to call one or more witnesses, provided that the witness(es) will adduce new evidence which materially alters the evidence submitted previously by the Respondent to the Professional Standards Panel.

g) The Chairman will decide as soon as practicable whether or not

   i) to admit any or all of the witnesses proposed by the Respondent, and the evidence of such witnesses;

   ii) to accept an application from the Respondent to be absent from the hearing and (if applicable) to be represented in his or her absence *[Regulation 22 (Appeals Panel: management of business) paragraph b) refers]*.

h) Any additional documents submitted by the Respondent under paragraph d) of this Regulation will be copied to the Complainant. If the Complainant chooses to submit a response, this must be received within two weeks and will be copied to the Respondent.

i) In the light of new information or evidence provided, the Chairman may at any stage before the hearing decide in consultation with the Panel to allow the appeal without a hearing and to issue a direction to that effect.

   i) The Chairman shall have discretion to make an order that an appeal will be struck out if specified steps are not taken within a period specified in the order, in the event that the Respondent fails to comply with these Regulations or with any direction issued by the Chairman. The Chairman shall not make such an order before giving him or her reasonable opportunity to show cause why such an order should not be made.

21. Appeals Panel: pre-hearing review

a) The Chairman of the Appeals Panel may conduct a pre-hearing review to clarify the issues before the Panel and generally to ensure that the appeal is handled fairly and efficiently.

b) The date of the pre-hearing review will be given in the convening notice for the hearing. The Chairman will give at least two working days' notice if he or she decides that it is after all not necessary *[Regulation 20 (Convening the Appeals Panel) paragraph b) iv) refers]*.

c) The Chairman may direct the Respondent to appear in person at a pre-hearing review.

d) The pre-hearing review may consider, and the Chairman may issue subsequent directions for the purpose of securing the just, expeditious and economical hearing of the appeal relating to the following matters:

   i) whether the hearing should be held in private or in public;

   ii) what matters other than those before the Professional Standards Panel should be considered by the Appeals Panel;

   iii) whether any aspects of the initial Complaint or of the grounds of appeal should be struck out;

   iv) further evidence considered necessary;

   v) attendance of witnesses;

   vi) supplemental witness statements in the event of a direction for further evidence;

   vii) which documents are admitted and whether the authenticity of any documents is challenged;

   viii) which facts are admitted and which remain in dispute;

   ix) the estimated duration of the hearing;

   x) any other relevant matters.

e) The Chairman may adjourn the pre-hearing review from time to time as he or she considers appropriate.

f) The directions made by the Chairman resulting from the pre-hearing review will be issued to the Respondent.

22. Appeals Panel: management of business

a) Subject to Regulation 21 (Appeals Panel: pre-hearing review), the Appeals Panel will consider the Complaint only in respect of the grounds of appeal.

b) The Respondent has the right to attend the hearing in person and may be accompanied and/or represented at the hearing by another person, who may be legally qualified or not.

c) The Respondent will be expected to attend the hearing unless permitted by the Chairman to be absent in accordance with Regulation 20 (Convening the Appeals Panel) paragraph f) ii). The Chairman may request witnesses to attend, who may include the Complainant. The hearing will be conducted in the presence of the Respondent, unless the Chairman decides otherwise from time to time and subject to paragraph d) of this Regulation.

d) The hearing may proceed even if the Respondent fails to attend or fails to make use of the rights of the Respondent under these Regulations in any other way, provided that the Institute has duly notified the Respondent of his or her rights and obligations as set out in these Regulations.

e) If the Respondent fails to attend without permission to be absent and without good cause, his or her absence will be regarded by the Panel as evidence against him or her.

f) The Panel will reach a decision in accordance with Regulation 12 (Professional Standards Panel and Appeals Panel: decisions). The decision will come into force when it has been reported to the CIPR Council.

23. Appeals Panel: order of business

The normal order of business, subject to the discretion of the Chairman, will be:

a) The Chairman will ensure that everyone present is made known, and explain the procedure that the Panel will follow.

b) The Panel will consider the written submissions before it and call such witnesses as it sees fit.

c) The Respondent will be called to present his or her appeal, present any witnesses allowed by the Chairman and to question any witnesses called by the Panel.

d) The Panel will decide in private on its decision, then announce it in the presence of the Respondent. If any finding is against the Respondent, he or she will be invited to address the Panel in mitigation.

e) The Panel will decide in private on its final decision, then announce it in the presence of the Respondent.

APPENDIX 2
Cross-cultural communications

All sorts of organizations now have an international aspect to their work. I have worked with thousands of people of many cultures in my career – colleagues, clients, media professionals – and am continually learning about how to communicate across cultures, what translates and what doesn't. It's important we have a sense of what works and is acceptable in terms of communications and body language.

Every person has a unique take on the world, drawn from upbringing, history and culture, as well as education, thinking patterns and perceptions. We verbalize and construct sentences in completely different ways. We frame communication from a unique set of criteria that no one else could possibly have. So the potential for miscommunication as a result is therefore very high – even higher if there are language barriers. If the language you are speaking to another person is not their first language there is plenty of room for misunderstanding. And all specialist areas have their own impenetrable jargon. It is so easy to use long sentences and complex vocabulary which others have to work hard to understand. A little forethought, using simpler vocabulary, can make it so much easier and more pleasant, quite apart from being well-mannered. Jargon, business-speak and heavily technical language should be avoided, as these can overcomplicate matters and muddy the message. Gestures and interpretations can cause confusion and communication breakdown, as can the use of hard-to-translate, idiomatic expressions like 'you can't take it with you' or ' a chip off the old block'.

Video conferencing, instant e-mail communication, social networking and cloud computing enable us to stay in touch in business. But there is no substitute for traditional face-to-face communication, and a good old-fashioned handshake. When communicating in business, particularly across international borders, it is important to read and use body language.

Being aware of cultural differences is crucial. Here are a few pointers on body language and etiquette that you may find useful for business purposes.

Europe, and Scandinavia and Russia

Because Europe has such a wide range of cultures, acceptable behaviour varies greatly between countries. Southern Europeans generally are thought to be more open and expressive than northern Europeans.

Czech Republic

Czechs and Slovaks do not go in for much physical contact in public. But at formal meetings everyone shakes hands when they arrive and leave.

Denmark

Like many northern Europeans, the Danes are more formal and stand further away when talking to visitors. Handshakes are mostly firm and short and eye contact is a must. If you are greeting a couple, shake hands with the woman first. This sort of traditional politeness is still very important. Turning your back on people is considered bad manners, so if you need to pass people in order to reach your seat, face them and say thank you. Toasting at formal dinners is popular and the correct form is to look around the group or toast one person, take a small sip and then make eye contact again.

Finland

Men, women and children will shake hands formally when introduced. Making and keeping direct eye contact is important in conversation. Standing with your arms folded will be interpreted as arrogance. If you cross your legs, do so at the knees not your ankles. Never eat with your fingers, not even fruit. It is considered bad manners to leave food on a plate, so only take small portions that you know you will be able to finish.

France

The French don't actually kiss on the cheek – they just touch cheeks and give air kisses. And disconcertingly they rarely smile at strangers. Handshakes are quick, single, frequent up-and-down pumps. In general, a man should wait for a woman to offer her hand first. Business cards are often exchanged, but if you hand your card to someone considered superior to you in the pecking order, you may not necessarily get one in return. At business meetings, don't remove your jacket before the most senior person. Although the French gesture often, in work situations body language and behaviour tend to be more restrained.

Germany

Compared with other countries in Europe, Germans are non-tactile. Men give a firm handshake perhaps with just one pump. Women and children will also shake hands, but less forcefully than men. When meeting a group, shake hands with each person, and the same when leaving. Business cards are exchanged as a matter of routine. Germans don't routinely say 'please' and 'thank you'. For them this isn't bad manners but custom.

Italy

Italy is often considered the most tactile nation in Europe. Even business-men who have met only a couple of times will offer a lingering handshake, perhaps clasping the other man's elbow (but this is not considered an appro-priate gesture between men and women). Like many southern Europeans, Italians may stand much closer to you than you may expect. Avoid stepping away – this could be interpreted as being rude or uninterested. Eye contact is usually more than 90 per cent and is warm and friendly.

Portugal

The Portuguese are not very demonstrative, except with close friends, when men might slap each other's backs and women might embrace. As with other Latin countries, firm, warm handshakes are the norm.

Russia

Russians like strong direct eye contact and a good firm handshake. For male friends and colleagues this may be followed by a bear hug, perhaps with quick kisses to alternate cheeks. Passing in front of people with your back to them, for instance at the theatre or in a crowd, is taboo. Russians don't smile at strangers, especially not in public.

Spain

Friendly eye contact is important (although women need to be careful that it doesn't get confused with signalling amorous interest!). Handshakes are warm and friendly, and a man will often pat someone he knows on the back or shoulder. When arriving at a table in a restaurant or at someone's home, men usually make a point of waiting for all the women to sit down before they do so themselves.

Sweden

Being by and large understated and undemonstrative people, Swedes regard loud, extrovert behaviour as shallow. Maintain eye contact when talking. Crossing your arms is not seen as defensive in Sweden – it signifies you are lis-tening. When talking to someone, keep your body straight and facing the per-son, as angling yourself even slightly away may be read as a sign you are not interested. Handshakes are firm and brief, with one or two pumps only. No other form of body contact takes place. Swedes dislike being interrupted when talking and don't like to move on to another subject before it is dealt with fully.

Switzerland

Swiss customs divide into French, German and Italian forms. Swiss-German greetings are short, firm and without any other touching. French and Italian greetings involve embraces and cheek-kissing. The Swiss especially appreciate an upright stance and good posture. In a restaurant, strangers might take seats that happen to be empty at your table.

Middle East/Arab world

Arabs behave in a conservative manner in public (although backstage they are much more expressive and love to laugh). They are dignified people with gentle manners, very sensitive where self-respect is concerned. Be professional at all times when discussing business. You will find Arab women in the workplace but, because of cultural reasons, they tend to conduct themselves inconspicuously. When arranging an appointment, an Arab may casually tell you to come whenever convenient to you – but will expect you to phone before turning up. Businessmen like to get acquainted with some social chit-chat before engaging in business dialogue. Never offend or contradict Islam or the culture. One small point – the thumbs-up sign is considered rude in Muslim countries so avoid even the most casual use.

Standard behaviours

The standard greeting in Islamic and Arab-speaking countries is a full or abbreviated 'salaam'. Arab men do a lot of touching. Handshaking is often prolonged, and men who know one another well may clasp elbows too. The personal zone is smaller than in Europe and the West. Men will stand much closer to other men when holding a conversation. Any movement away during a conversation is considered bad manners.

Men and women stand farther apart than in the West, with no public displays of affection. Visiting men should wait for an Arab woman to offer her hand. A man greeting another man who he does not know well will shake hands, whereas a man greeting a woman who he does not know well will touch his heart with his right palm.

Avoid pointing directly at another person. This is considered rude.

Remove your shoes before entering a house or a mosque (OK to keep on in most offices). The sole of the shoe or foot is the lowest and dirtiest part of the body, and it is an insult to show it to or point it at anyone.

Use only the right hand for eating, and for presenting or receiving gifts. The left hand is used solely for hygiene purposes in any Islamic country. At meal times, Arabs serve plenty of strong, thick, syrupy coffee in small cups. To indicate that you have had enough, tip the cup back and forth with your fingers.

Egypt

Even though Egyptians are used to westerners, you should dress modestly. Men should wear long trousers. Women should wear long skirts or loose-fitting trousers, loose tops with high necklines and sleeves that cover the elbows.

Iran

Handshakes are customary and shaking hands with children indicates respect for their parents. Women should wear a loose ankle-length skirt with a big, baggy, long-sleeved shirt and loose-fitting mid-thigh-length jacket. Make-up and any jewellery, apart from plain rings such as a wedding ring, should be avoided in order not to cause offence and provoke strong reactions. Men should wear full-length trousers, and keep their arms covered.

Jordan

Jordan is relatively westernized, but immodest dress should be avoided. Women should wear at least knee-length skirts and dresses or trousers and cover their shoulders. At any dinner, if you are offered additional food, you should refuse twice, and only accept on the third time of offering. It is polite to leave small portions uneaten. Although Jordan is one of the few Arabic-speaking countries where alcohol is readily available, drinking anything more than modest amounts is frowned upon.

Israel

Hebrew is an expressive language, with much touching and hand-holding between friends. Visiting women should wait for an Israeli man to offer to shake hands. Women should avoid smiling at strangers, who might get the wrong impression. Orthodox Jews do not touch hands casually or shake hands between genders, even when passing business cards.

Saudi Arabia

At gatherings, you might see men greeting dignitaries and elders by kissing the right shoulder front to show their respect. Saudis may host joint business meetings in one room, with the host moving from one group to the next and back again. If your host interrupts a meeting and is gone for 20 minutes without explanation, it is for prayers. Saudis find crossing your legs disrespectful. Don't expect to be introduced to a veiled woman in the company of a Saudi man. Women should keep their legs, shoulders and arms covered at all times, in loose clothing. You may also need to cover your head with a scarf. Smoking in public is not common. Alcohol and pork are illegal. Don't smoke, drink or eat in public during the holy month of Ramadan or you risk being sent to prison, possibly until the fast is over.

Turkey

In addition to the normal handshakes, friends may put their hands over yours, or even embrace you. At an office or formal gathering, shake everyone's hand. A much younger person may kiss your hand and press it to his head as a sign of respect. Smoking and eating on the street are considered impolite. Show particular respect to elders, who are valued there. When talking, don't cross your arms or put your hands in your pockets. 'No' is indicated by raising the head a little, tipping it back and closing the eyes, or opening the eyes wide and raising the eyebrows.

Lebanon

Children are taught not to talk unless addressed by a visitor. A nod means 'yes', while a sharp upward motion of head and raised eyebrows means 'no'. In urban areas the Lebanese are quite tolerant of western ways and dress, but in rural areas people are more traditional. Outside cities and the larger towns, western women should take care to dress modestly.

Far East

China

The western handshake has become the most common form of greeting, especially in business. But a nod or short bow is fine too. Guests are introduced to Chinese people in order of their hosts' seniority. Business cards will probably be exchanged next, and should, ideally, be in your language and in Chinese. Present cards with both hands as this is more respectful. The Chinese are generally non-tactile people, but they stand closer than westerners.

Chinese people do not like to utter the word 'no', and may shake their heads in silence if they don't like what you're saying or asking for. In the cities there is not much eye contact in public. Silence is a virtue, a sign of politeness and contemplation. During conversation, try not to interrupt. Food bowls are held under the chin. Wait for the host to pick up his chopsticks before eating. Refusing food is also considered impolite. Chinese etiquette is to decline gifts two or three times before accepting them even if they are wanted.

Indonesia

Indonesia consists of around 17,500 islands and some 300 ethnic groups, and gestures and ideas of polite behaviour vary greatly. For urban areas a few general points can apply, particularly for business. A handshake plus a slight nod is customary for greeting, congratulating or parting, for both sexes. Aside from this, men do not touch women in public. You should always use people's titles to address them. In West Java, they use a Thai greeting, with the palms together, fingertips towards chin and a nod. Indonesians do not like to show feelings, especially negative ones. They don't like to disappoint people, so they avoid disagreeing in public and smile to hide shock or embarrassment. You should avoid showing excessive gratitude or outbursts of anger. The sole of the shoe is a taboo. The right hand is used far more than the 'unclean' left. Pointing with fingers is very rude and touching people's heads is not advisable. When dining, leave a little food. A clear plate means you want more.

Hong Kong

The conventional handshake is the most common greeting. The Chinese people do not like body contact, though men may hold hands when walking. They may also stand fairly close by western standards. Don't blink too much in meetings as it can be interpreted as lack of interest. At mealtimes, Chinese and western customs will sometimes be mixed. Chopsticks, for example, may be used in conjunction with knives and forks either for different dishes or different courses. Tea may be served during meetings. If the host leaves his tea untouched for a long time, this may be an indication that he considers the meeting to be over.

Japan

Bowing remains the traditional greeting in Japan. The western handshake is also widespread, but with a lighter grip. Limit eye contact – the Japanese and other Asians find too much direct eye contact confrontational, aggressive and rude. The tiniest gestures have meaning for the Japanese, so be careful to limit your own hand and arm gestures. Business card etiquette here is perhaps more important than anywhere else in the world. The Japanese usually present their business cards while holding them in both hands. To the Japanese, visiting cards are not just bits of stiff card with names printed on them, they are part of their owner's identity, and accordingly are treated with great respect.

When you first receive a card, take time to study it, then put it carefully on the table in front of you. When the meeting is finished put it in your wallet, not in a pocket, and especially not in a hip pocket – that means you could sit on it. Those Japanese who frequently travel abroad are aware of the western approach to business cards, but for those with no foreign experience, this is still a sensitive point. Listening attentively and not interrupting are crucial. The Japanese don't like to say no, so be aware that nodding does not necessarily signal agreement. Japanese chopstick etiquette is much like China's; the major difference is that food bowls are held lower. You should pick up dishes on your left side with your right hand and vice versa. A common Japanese toast is 'kanpai' ('drain the cup'). Remove your shoes when entering a home or restaurant.

South Korea

Bowing is the traditional form of greeting, perhaps combined with a handshake if greeting westerners. Women don't shake hands, just nod. Deference to rank and elders is important. The senior offers to shake hands first; the junior bows first. Koreans are taught to avoid eye contact, and a youngster making eye contact with an elder is regarded as a display of defiance. As in Japan, read business cards thoroughly and keep them to hand. Walking directly behind people can be considered impolite so try to avoid it. Koreans avoid saying 'no' by tipping their heads back and sucking air. Laughter is used to cover up all sorts of emotions. It is disrespectful to pour your own drink – the host should do it – or to open gifts at a time they are given.

Malaysia

The Malaysian population is made up of 57 per cent Malays (Muslim), 32 per cent Chinese and 11 per cent Indians. The handshake is used universally. Within the Chinese population, men and women will shake hands with each other, but not with Indians or Malays. Malays greet with a *salaam*, a slightly different form from the Arab version (extend the hands, putting the fingertips together, then place the hands on the chest). Indians greet with the *namaste*. Before entering Malay mosques and homes, you should remove your shoes and leave them with everyone else's. In this part of the world Indians shake their heads to indicate agreement; very confusing for a westerner.

Philippines

There has long been an American presence in the Philippine Islands, so western gestures are familiar. Handshakes are the norm for men, women and children. Quickly raising the eyebrows is another informal greeting. In public, two women may hold hands, but men do not. Filipino taboos include staring, talking loudly, and women smoking in public. At meals, always leave some food on your plate to indicate that the host has served enough. An empty plate indicates that you would like more. Filipinos will point to something not with the hands, which is seen as rude, but with their eyes, or even sometimes with pursed lips.

Thailand

The Thai greeting is called the *wai* – the hands are held together as if in prayer, and the head nodded in a slight bow, very like the Indian *namaste*. The *wai* can be used for greeting, parting, gratitude and apology. The higher the hands, the more respectful the greeting, but the fingertips should not be higher than the face. Remove your shoes when entering someone's home, even though some Thais defer to the West and will let you keep them on. Don't step on the doorsill as Thais believe that a deity lives there. The feet are lowly, so don't point them or show the soles. Patting someone's back or shoulders is offensive. Two men might hold hands when walking, but otherwise there are no public displays of affection. Thais particularly dislike loud, boisterous or aggressive behaviour, so don't talk in a raised voice, and never show anger during negotiations.

Singapore

Singapore's diverse population includes Chinese, Muslims and Indians. Manners and body language tend to show British influences, given that Singapore was once part of the British Empire. The handshake is the standard greeting, perhaps combined with a slight bow for Asians. Women make the first move when shaking hands. The elderly are held in great respect; people usually rise when they enter a room and give up seats for them in public places. Singapore is a very clean and tidy country and there are severe local penalties – typically large fines – for dropping litter, even cigarette ends.

Samoa

Greetings are formal and Samoans tend to go for quite flowery speeches. When visiting a home, wait until a mat has been laid down before entering, then remove your shoes. Sit cross-legged on the mat. Conversation tends to take place only when people are seated. Be more careful not to point your feet at anyone. The Samoan national drink is called kava. It is traditional to spill a few drops before drinking.

Taiwan

The handshake is the usual greeting, though a nod (with eyes cast downwards) is acceptable. Like other Asian countries, the Taiwanese respect business cards, which should be read carefully and kept to hand. The elderly are treated with great deference. Here, 'no' is indicated by holding the hand up at face level, with the palm out and moving it back and forth. Toast by saying 'kan-pei'. Use both hands to give and receive presents.

America

Americans tend to have a very direct communication style. Straight talking is the norm in business and the same will be expected of you. The most notable differences in business culture are between the East Coast and West Coast of the US. The East Coast has generally a more formal approach to business. Business meetings follow an agenda and are treated very seriously. A brief, firm handshake at the beginning and end of a meeting is the norm. Eye contact is high and ensures people recognize you are interested. Business cards are customarily exchanged and Americans like to use first names in business even with people they meet for the first time. Networking is vital in business in the US and you are expected to follow up and use the connections you make; 'name dropping' is usual and not frowned upon.

Meetings rarely finish inconclusively – Americans like to be clear about actions and outcomes. They also value efficiency and professionalism. They respect deadlines and so punctuality and timekeeping are expected. Lateness is considered disrespectful and unprofessional. Many Americans work outside normal business hours and are likely to respond to business e-mails and calls when on holiday – and they may expect you to do the same.

Although Americans value equality, status and hierarchy are important in business. Show the greatest respect for senior people you are conducting business with.

Politeness and courtesy are highly valued in American culture. Always say 'you're welcome' when being thanked by Americans.

Africa

North African countries, those bordering the Mediterranean are Islamic, so much of what applies in the Arab world applies here too.

In the Muslim countries of northern Africa, you may find men holding handshakes so long that they become a handhold. Do not be alarmed – this is common and usual.

For the rest of Africa, soft handshakes are common. In South Africa, handshakes between whites and whites, and blacks and whites differ. While white people shake the hand of another white person in much the same way as in northern Europe, whites and blacks shake hands with an additional flourish. After shaking the full hand, they grasp thumbs and then return to a full handshake.

If you have a title (Dr, Professor, Lady, Sir) use it – academic titles in particular are highly valued and boost your standing immediately.

In many African countries, people eat with their hands and do not use utensils. Again, as in Arab countries, never eat with your left hand.

REFERENCES, SOURCES AND FURTHER READING

Chapter 1

BBC [accessed 13 January 2014] Leveson Inquiry [Online] http://www.levesoninquiry.org.uk/

BBC [accessed 13 January 2014] Q&A: News of the World phone-hacking scandal [Online] http://www.bbc.co.uk/news/uk-11195407

BBC [accessed 13 January 2014] Saville Enquiry [Online] http://www.bbc.co.uk/news/uk-20026910

Edelman [accessed 13 January 2014] 2013 Edelman Trust Barometer [Online] http://trust.edelman.com/

Financial Times [accessed 13 January 2014] Definitions [Online] http://lexicon.ft.com/Term?term=corporate-communication

Grunig, J (2011) Public Relations and Strategic Management: Institutionalizing organization-public relationships in contemporary society, *Central European Journal of Communications*

Institute of Electrical and Electronics Engineers (IEEE) [accessed 13 January 2014] [Online] http://www.ieee.ca/millennium/radio/radio_unsung.html

Notable Names Database [accessed 13 January 2014] [Online] http://www.nndb.com/media/154/000094869/

Towse, R (2010) *A Textbook of Cultural Economics*, Cambridge University Press, Cambridge

Chapter 2

Bernays, EL and Crispin Miller, M (1928) *Propaganda*, Ig Publishing

Bowen, A and Heath, RL (2005) Issues management, systems, and rhetoric: exploring the distinction between ethical and legal guidelines at Enron Shannon, *Journal of Public Affairs*

Carey, J (1989) *Communication as Culture*, Routledge

Center, AH, Jackson, P, Smith, S and Stansberry, FR (1995, 2007) *Public Relations Practices*, Prentice Hall

Cialdini, R ([first published in 1984] this edition 2009) *Influence: The psychology of persuasion*, HarperCollins

Goleman, D (2006) *Emotional Intelligence: Why it can matter more than IQ*, Random House

Grunig, J and Hunt, T (1984) *Managing Public Relations*, Fort Worth

Heath, R (2011) External organizational rhetoric: bridging management and sociopolitical discourse, *Management Communication Quarterly*

Holtzhausen, DR (2013) *Public Relations as Activism: Postmodern approaches to theory and practice*, Routledge

Kahneman, D (2011) *Thinking, Fast and Slow*, Macmillan

Lasswell, H (1948) The Structure and Function of Communication in Society, in *The Communication of Ideas*, ed L Bryson, Institute for Religious and Social Studies, New York

L'Etang, J (2009) Public relations and diplomacy in a globalized world: an issue of public communication, *American Behavioral Scientist*, Sage [Online] http://www.prconversations.com/wp-content/uploads/2009/12/public-relation-and-diplomacy-letaing.pdf

Mendelsohn, H (1973) Some reasons why information campaigns can succeed, *Public Opinion Quarterly*, 37 (1), pp 50–61

Petty, RE and Cacioppo, JT (1986) *Communication and Persuasion*, Springer, New York

Shannon, CE and Weaver, W (1949) *A Mathematical Model of Communication*, University of Illinois Press, Urbana, IL

Shavitt, SE and Brock, TC (1994) *Persuasion: Psychological insights and perspectives*, Allyn & Bacon

Tench, R and Yeomans, L (2006) *Exploring Public Relations*, Prentice Hall

Thaler, R and Sunstein, C (2009) *Nudge: Improving decisions about health, wealth and happiness*, Penguin

Weintraub Austin, E and Pinkleton, BE (2008) *Strategic Public Relations Management: Planning and managing effective communications programs*, 2nd edn, Routledge

Chapter 3

Kolah, A [accessed 30 January 2013] What to Look Out For in a PR Agency Agreement, Revision 6, *The CIPR Conversation* [Online] http://conversation.cipr.co.uk/posts/ardi.kolah/what-to-look-out-for-in-a-pr-agency-agreement/75427

Chapter 4

Chartered Institute of Public Relation (CIPR) [accessed 13 January 2014] *Research, Planning and Measurement Toolkit* [Online] http://www.cipr.co.uk/content/research-planning-and-measurement-toolkit

Gregory, A (2010) *Planning and Managing Public Relations Campaigns: A strategic approach*, Kogan Page, London

Hon, LC and Grunig, JE (1999) *Guidelines for Measuring Relationships in Public Relations*, The Institute for PR [accessed 13 January 2014, online] http://www.instituteforpr.org/topics/measuring-relationships/

International Association for the Measurement and Evaluation of Communication (AMEC), *Barcelona Declaration of Measurement Principles* [accessed 13 January 2014, online] http://amecorg.com/2012/06/barcelona-declaration-of-measurement-principles/

International Association for the Measurement and Evaluation of Communication (AMEC), *Measuring the True Value of Public Relations* [accessed 13 January 2014, online] http://amecorg.com/wp-content/uploads/2012/11/Measuring-the-True-Value-of-Public-Relations-based-on-the-Barcelona-Principles-11-11-12.pdf

Lindenmann, W (2003) *Guidelines for Measuring the Effectiveness of PR Programs and Activities*, The Institute for PR [accessed 13 January 2014, online] http://www. instituteforpr. org/files/uploads/2002_MeasuringPrograms_1.pdf

Macnamara, JR (2008) Research in public relations: a review of the use of evaluation and formative research, *CARMA: Asia Pacific*

Macnamara, JR (2008) 'Top 10' research methods for planning and evaluation, in *How to Measure PR and Corporate Communications*, MASS Communication Group

Rose, C (2010) *How to Win Campaigns*, Earthscan

Watson, T and Noble, P (2007, 2014) *Evaluating Public Relations*, Kogan Page, London

Yoon, Y (2005) A scale for measuring media relations effort, *Public Relations Review*, **31** (3), pp 434–36.

Chapter 5

Adcock, D, Halborg, A and Ross, C (2001) *Marketing: Principles and practice*, [electronic resource] Pearson Education

Borden, NH (1964) The concept of the marketing mix, *Journal of Advertising Research*, **4** (2) pp 2–7

Chartered Institute of Marketing [accessed 13 January 2014] Glossary [Online] http://www.cim.co.uk/Resources/JargonBuster.aspx

Drucker, PF (2009) *Management*, revised edn, HarperCollins

McCarthy, JE (1960) *Basic Marketing: A managerial approach*, Homewood

Kotler, P and Keller, K (2010) *Marketing Management*, Pearson Education

Kotler, PJ and Armstrong, GM (2010) *Principles of Marketing*, Pearson Education

Chapter 6

Erikson, EH (1966) Eight ages of man, *International Journal of Psychiatry*

Grinder, J and Bandler, R (1993) *Trance-formations*, Real People Press

Hallahan, K (2001) Enhancing motivation, ability, and opportunity to process public relations messages, *Public Relations Review*, **26** (4), pp 463–80

Myers, IB and Kirby, LK (1993) *Introduction to Type: A guide to understanding your results on the Myers-Briggs Type* Indicator, Consulting Psychologists Press

Sriramesh, K and Vercic, D (2009) A theoretical framework for global public relations research and practice, *The Global Public Relations Handbook*, 1–24

Chapter 7

BPW Foundation (2011) Gen y women in the workplace: focus group summary report, *Young Careerist* [Online] http://bpwfoundation.org/documents/uploads/YC_SummaryReport_Final.pdf

Brown, R (2012) *Public Relations and the Social Web: How to use social media and Web 2.0 in communications*, Kogan Page

CIPR [accessed 13 January 2014] *Social Media Guidelines* [Online] http://www .slideshare.net/CIPR/cipr-social-media-guidelines-final-2013

Davies, N (2009) *Flat Earth News*, Vintage

Forbes Insights [accessed 13 January 2014, online] http://www.forbes.com/ forbesinsights/#sthash.u9QLQAYc.dpuf

Mair, J ed. (2013) *After Leveson? The future for British journalism*, Abramis Publishing, Suffolk

Ofcom research [accessed 13 January 2014, online] http://stakeholders.ofcom.org. uk/market-data-research/market-data/communications-market-reports/cmr13/ and http://stakeholders.ofcom.org.uk/binaries/research/consumer-experience/ tce-12/Consumer_Experience_Researc1.pdf

Parry, R (2011)*The Ascent of Media from Gilgamesh to Google via Gutenber*, Nicholas Brealey

Waddington, S ed. (2012) *Share This: The social media handbook for PR professionals*, Wiley

Chapter 8

de Bono, E (1969) Information processing and new ideas: lateral and vertical thinking, *The Journal of Creative Behavior*, 3 (3), pp 159–71

Guilford, JP (1959) Three faces of intellect, *American Psychologist*, 14 (8), p 469

Heath, C and Heath, D (2008) *Made To Stick*, Arrow Books

Sapp, DD (1992) The point of creative frustration and the creative process: a new look at an old model, *The Journal of Creative Behavior*, 26 (1), pp 21–28

Wallas, G (1926) *The Art of Thought*, Jonathan Cape

Chapter 9

Crozier, WR (1996) The psychology of colour preferences. Review of progress in coloration and related topics, *Coloration Technology*, 26 (1), pp 63–72, Wiley [Online library] doi: 10.1111/j.1478-4408.1996.tb00111.x

Lester, PM (2012) *Visual communication: Images with messages*, Cengage Learning

McCandless, D (2009) *Information Is Beautiful*, Collins

Chapter 10

Register, M and Larkin, J (2008) *Risk Issues and Crisis Management in Public Relations: A casebook of best practice*, Kogan Page

Rittel, HW and Webber, MM (1973) Dilemmas in a general theory of planning, *Policy Sciences*, 4 (2), pp 155–69

Syme, C (posted 18 June, 2013) How to use social media to manage a crisis, *Social Media Today* [accessed 13 January 2014, online] http://socialmediatoday.com/chrissyme/1540966/how-use-social-media-manage-crisis

Chapter 11

Behr, E (originally published in 1978; this edition published in 1992) *'Anyone Here Been Raped and Speaks English?'*, Penguin

Bell, A (1991) *The Language of News Media*, Blackwell Publishers, Oxford

Bell, A (2000) Dateline, deadline: journalism, language and the reshaping of time and place in the millennial world, *Georgetown University Round Table on Languages and Linguistics*, pp 46–66

Foster, A (2012) *Writing Skills for Public Relations*, Kogan Page, London

Fowler, HW (1994) *A Dictionary of Modern English Usage*, Wordsworth Editions

Galtung, J and Ruge, MH (1965) The structure of foreign news: the presentation of the Congo, Cuba and Cyprus crises in four Norwegian newspapers, *Journal of Peace Research*, 2 (1), pp 64–90

Harcup, T and O'Neill, D (2001) What is news? Galtung and Ruge revisited, *Journalism Studies*, 2 (2), pp 261–80

Honey, P and Mumford, A (1986) *Using Your Learning Styles*, 2nd edn, Peter Honey Publications, Maidenhead

Mehrabian, A (1972) *Nonverbal Communication*, Transaction Publishers

Orwell, G (1946) *Politics and the English Language,* Penguin

Preston, P, (11 June, 2000) *The Observer*

Roman, K and Raphaelson, J (2000) *Writing That Works*, HarperResource

Staab, JF (1990) The role of news factors in news selection: a theoretical reconsideration, *European Journal of Communication*, 5 (4), pp 423–43

The Economist (2009) *Style Guide: The bestselling guide to English usage*, Profile Books, London

Williams C (2001) *Overcoming Depression: A five areas approach*, Hodder Arnold

INDEX

(*italics* indicate a figure or table in the text)

CPSIA information can be obtained at www.ICGtesting.com
Printed in the USA
BVOW06s2042301014

372992BV00012BA/328/P